Health and Safety in Emergency Management and Response

Health and Safety in Emergency Management and Response

Dana L. Stahl

Registered Office
John Wiley & Sons, Inc., 111 River Street, Hoboken, NJ 07030, USA

Editorial Office
111 River Street, Hoboken, NJ 07030, USA

For details of our global editorial offices, customer services, and more information about Wiley products visit us at www.wiley.com.

Wiley also publishes its books in a variety of electronic formats and by print-on-demand. Some content that appears in standard print versions of this book may not be available in other formats.

Library of Congress Cataloging-in-Publication Data

Names: Stahl, Dana L., 1965- author.
Title: Health and safety in emergency management and response / Dana L.
   Stahl.
Description: First edition. | Hoboken, NJ : Wiley, [2021] | Includes
   bibliographical references and index.
Identifiers: LCCN 2020015446 (print) | LCCN 2020015447 (ebook) | ISBN
   9781119560975 (cloth) | ISBN 9781119561064 (adobe pdf) | ISBN
   9781119561101 (epub)
Subjects: LCSH: Emergency management – Safety measures. | First
   responders – Health and hygiene.
Classification: LCC HV551.2 .S726 2020 (print) | LCC HV551.2 (ebook) |
   DDC 363.34/80289 – dc23
LC record available at https://lccn.loc.gov/2020015446
LC ebook record available at https://lccn.loc.gov/2020015447

Cover design by Wiley
Cover image: © Isaac Howard

Set in 9.5/12.5pt STIXTwoText by SPi Global, Chennai, India

10   9   8   7   6   5   4   3   2   1

Contents

Foreword

My first exposure to the field of Emergency Management came when I was working as an Industrial Hygienist at the Port of Seattle. Michael Mandella, Chief of the Port of Seattle Fire Department and later the Airport Emergency Operations Manager, decided that it was important to include an Industrial Hygienist in the Airport Operations Plan, and provided me with my introduction to the Incident Command System and the National Incident Management System.

In 2008, I changed jobs, and began working at the Central Puget Sound Regional Transit Authority, known locally as Sound Transit, first as a Senior Safety Specialist and later as the Manager of Health, Safety and Emergency Management. When I started, Sound Transit was getting ready to begin light rail operations, and the Safety Division had the responsibility of coordinating interagency emergency response exercises in support of the light rail safety certification plan. This involved working closely with emergency responders in the region, including Seattle and South King County fire and police departments, and my former colleagues at the Port of Seattle.

We had many meetings with our colleagues in these departments, and these meetings were peppered with acronyms commonly used in emergency response. Since I was the only person in my department who had taken any incident command system (ICS) training at the time, I was the only one who knew what these acronyms meant and fully participate in these conversations.

My Division leadership was impressed: Somehow I had suddenly become the expert on emergency management at Sound Transit, and my Director decided that I should be given responsibility for the emergency management program that we now realized that we needed.

I later learned there is a term for what had happened. It is called a "Field Promotion."

I, of course, knew that I had a lot to learn about emergency management. I have a master's degree in industrial hygiene, and am a Certified Industrial Hygienist, and knew that I didn't have nearly as much background to fall back on as I took on the challenge of emergency management. Today, students can obtain degrees in Emergency Management, but this type of training was not so readily available in 2008. Fortunately, I had excellent resources to work with, and I am extremely grateful to my former colleagues at the Port of Seattle, Michael Mandella, Kathleen Gleaves, Ron Harmon, and Kristine Ball, as well as Barb Graff, Laurel Nelson, and Grant Tietje from the Seattle Office of Emergency Management for helping me get started on this program and for patiently answering all of my questions.

I am also grateful to my Division leadership, Hamid Qaasim and Peregrin Spielholtz, for giving me the opportunity to take on the emergency management program, and to my colleagues Selena Ngo and Lori Bisping for the work they did in making this initial emergency management program a reality. Lori, I know the program has come a long way since those early days.

As the program evolved, we continued to sponsor exercises for the Link Light Rail System and Sounder Commuter Rail. One lesson learned from these exercises was that we should be prepared to open an Emergency Operations Center (EOC) in the event of a major incident. Our division sponsored training, and identified personnel throughout the agency who would fill positions.

Our designated EOC staff sought additional training. Our Media Relations Director found training for Public Information Officers sponsored through one of his professional organizations, and our Purchasing Department found training for Logistics Chiefs sponsored through professional organizations that they belonged to. They came to me and asked me if they should attend these trainings. Of course I agreed that they should.

Since we were the Safety Division, the position of Safety Officer had to be one of our staff. I looked for equivalent training for the Safety Officer, but I could not find anything similar to the trainings that our media relations departments and purchasing departments were benefiting from.

This book is the resource I wished I had had then.

At that time, I was also on the board of the Pacific Northwest Section of the American Industrial Hygiene Association (PNS-AIHA), and used this opportunity to sponsor training on emergency management at our section conferences. It seemed to me that industrial hygienists and safety professionals had skills that were critically needed in incident response. The only problem was that they didn't realize it. I organized sessions at conferences and brought in speakers, and over time the role and purpose of the Safety Officer became clearer in my mind. I am especially grateful to Matt Bernard, the FEMA Region 10 NIMS Coordinator, for his assistance in these efforts.

In 2015, I began working at the Pacific Northwest OSHA Training Center as an Instructor and Content Manager. Nancy Simcox, the Center Director, supported my efforts to develop the Emergency Safety Officer professional development course, which is now included in the Center's annual course calendar and offered as a contract course at site locations. One of our initial course offerings was at a local naval base, and included a mix of safety and emergency management personnel. One of the safety managers came up to me as the course ended and told me how beneficial it was that the emergency managers had participated. "Now they know what the Safety Officer is supposed to do! They've never understood that before … they would just have us sit in the corner to do our 'safety thing.' Now they know we need to work together."

This reflected my own experience in that my colleagues in the emergency management field did not know about the resources that industrial hygienists and safety professionals could provide. My emergency management colleagues saw me purely as an emergency manager, and if I tried to explain to them that I was also a safety manager and an industrial hygienist, I'd just get that glazed over look that I so often get in any situation when I try to explain what an industrial hygienist is.

This book is a resource for emergency managers as well as safety professionals. I hope it can in some small way help improve emergency management safety culture. Emergency responders face a high level of risk on the job, and this can come at the price of personal safety.

I had a conversation with a long-time friend of mine a few years ago, Battalion Chief Richard Toledo, as he was contemplating retirement from the San Jose Fire Department. What he told me has stuck with me. "When I was young, I was invincible, like we all are. I would get upset if I missed a fire. Now, I realize that on any day that I go into work, I or someone working under me might die. Retirement isn't looking so bad anymore."

My hope is that improvements in safety culture and safety practice can reduce the number of line-of-duty deaths, serious injuries, and illnesses among emergency responders.

This book is a compilation of the knowledge I have gained on the topic of safety in emergency management throughout my career, and expands upon previous work I have done with the professional organizations that I am involved with and the Pacific Northwest OSHA Training Center.

I would like to extend special thanks to all who have helped me get to the point in my career where I could write a book on this topic. This includes my colleagues at the Port of Seattle, Sound Transit, and the Pacific Northwest OSHA Training Center; the Port of Seattle and Seattle Offices of Emergency Management; those I've worked with at the Seattle and South King County Fire and Police Departments as we developed and held exercises for Link and Sounder operations; the committee members I've worked with on the Washington Governor's Industrial Safety and Health Conference Public Employees panel and the my local American Industrial Hygiene Association section; and the colleagues that I participate with in the American Industrial Hygiene Association Incident Preparedness and Response Working Group. I have learned from you all.

Thank you to Scott Yurczyk, Seattle Fire Department Health and Safety Officer, for allowing me to take photographs of firefighter gear and answering my many questions, and to William Pessemier for our conversations on Fire Department safety culture.

I am grateful for those who encouraged and supported my efforts to write this book, including Bob Esposito at Wiley, Matt Bernard, and my colleague at the University of Washington Department of Environmental and Occupational Health Sciences, Dr. Nicole Errett.

I also appreciate the patience and support of my daughter Celia Jeffery and my son Taylor Jeffery throughout this writing process. My son is an aspiring writer, and Taylor, I look forward to seeing your name in print soon.

Acronyms

AAR	After Action Report
ABIH	American Board of Industrial Hygiene
ACGIH	American Conference of Governmental Industrial Hygienists
ACM	Asbestos Containing Material
ADA	Americans with Disabilities Act
ADCI	Association of Diving Contractors, International
AEP	Airport Emergency Plan
AIHA	American Industrial Hygiene Association
ALARA	As Low As Reasonably Achievable
AKOSH	Alaska Occupational Safety and Health
ANSI	American National Standards Institute
AOA	Airport Operations Area
APELL	Awareness and Preparedness for Emergency at the Local Level Programme
APF	Assigned Protection Factor
APR	Air Purifying Respirators
ARECC	Anticipate, Recognize, Evaluate, Control, Confirm
ARFF	Aircraft Rescue Fire Fighting
ASSP	American Society of Safety Professionals
ASTM	American Society for Testing Materials
ATC	Applied Technology Council
ATSDR	Agency for Toxic Substances and Disease Registry
AV-Gas	Aviation gas
BART	Bay Area Rapid Transit
BCPE	Board of Certification in Professional Ergonomics
BCSP	Board of Certified Safety Professionals
BIA	Business Impact Analysis

BJA	Bureau of Justice Assistance
BLS	Bureau of Labor Statistics
BPA	Business Process Analysis
BSEE	Bureau of Safety and Environmental Enforcement
CAMEO	Computer Aided Management of Emergency Operations
CBRNE	Chemical, Biological, Radiological, Nuclear, and Explosive
CBRN	Chemical, Biological, Radiological, Nuclear
CBT	Cognitive Behavioral Therapy
CDC	Centers for Disease Control
CDL	Commercial Driver's License
CERCLA	Comprehensive Environmental Response, Compensation, and Liability Act
CERT	Community Emergency Response Team
CF	Compassion Fatigue
CFR	Code of Federal Regulations
CG	Coast Guard
CHMM	Certified Hazardous Materials Manager
CHP	Certified Health Physicist
CIH	Certified Industrial Hygienist
CISD	Critical Incident Stress Debriefing
CISM	Critical Incident Stress Management
CMC	Certified Marine Chemist
COG	Continuity of Government
COO	Continuity of Operations
COOP	Continuity of Operations Plan
COP	Common Operating Picture
COPS	Community Oriented Policing Services
CPBD	Community Planning and Capacity Building
CPC	Chemical Protective Clothing
CPE	Certified Professional Ergonomist
CPG	Comprehensive Preparedness Guide
CPHP	Centers for Public Health Preparedness
CPR	Cardiopulmonary Resuscitation
CSP	Certified Safety Professional
DART	(OSHA) Days Away/Restricted Transfer (rate)
DHS	Department of Homeland Security
DOE	Department of Energy
DOSH	Washington State Department of Safety and Health
EAP	Emergency Action Plan
EAP	Employee Assistance Program
ECG	Enduring Constitutional Government

EEW	Earthquake Early Warning
EF	Enhanced Fujita
EMDR	Eye Movement Desensitization and Reprocessing
EMPG	Emergency Performance Grant
EMT	Emergency Medical Technician
EOC	Emergency Operations Center
EOD	Explosives Ordinance Disposal
EOP	Emergency Operations Plan
EPA	Environmental Protection Agency
EPCRA	Emergency Planning and Community Right to Know Act
ERG	Emergency Response Guide
ESA	Essential Supporting Activity
ESF	Emergency Support Function
ExPlan	Exercise Plan
FAA	Federal Aviation Administration
FDA	Federal Drug Administration
FDSOA	Fire Department Safety Officers Association
FE	Functional Exercise
FEMA	Federal Emergency Management Administration
FHWA	Federal Highway Administration
FOD	Foreign Object Debris
FRA	Federal Railroad Administration
FTA	Federal Transit Administration
GERD	Gastroesophageal reflux disorder
GIS	Geospatial information system
GIUE	Government-Initiated Unannounced Exercise
HASP	Health and Safety Plan
HAZWOPER	Hazardous Waste Operations and Emergency Response
HBV	Hepatitis B Virus
HCV	Hepatitis C Virus
HEPA	High-Efficiency Particulate Air
HHE	Health Hazard Evaluation
HICS	Hospital Incident Command System
HIV	Human Immunodeficiency Virus
HLPP	Hearing loss prevention program
HSEEP	Homeland Security Exercise and Evaluation Program
HSGP	Homeland Security Grant Program
HSPD	Homeland Security Presidential Directive
IAP	Incident Action Plan
IARC	International Agency for Research on Cancer
ICS	Incident Command System

IDLH	Immediately dangerous to life and health
IHMM	Institute of Hazardous Materials Management
IIPP	Injury and Illness Prevention Plan
IMPT	Incident Management Planning Team
IND	Improvised nuclear device
IOP	Initial operating facility
IRAT	Influenza Risk Assessment Tool
ISEA	International Safety Equipment Association
IT	Information Technology
JFO	Joint Field Office
JHA	Job Hazard Analysis
JIS	Joint Information System
LEED	Leadership in Energy and Environmental Design
LEPC	Local Emergency Planning Committee
MAC	Multi-Agency Coordination
MACC	Multi-Agency Coordination Center
MBO	Management By Objectives
MCI	Mass casualty incident
MEF	Mission Essential Function
MHFA	Mental Health First Aid
MIOSHA	Michigan Occupational Safety and Health Administration
MOU	Memorandum of Understanding
MSD	Musculoskeletal disorder
MSEL	Master Scenario Events List
MUC	Maximum Use Concentrations
MUTCD	Manual of Uniform Traffic Control Devices
NAMI	National Alliance on Mental Illness
NEF	National Essential Functions
NEP	National Exercise Program
NFPA	National Fire Protection Association
NGO	Nongovernmental organization
NIHL	Noise-Induced Hearing Loss
NIMS	National Incident Management System
NIOSH	National Institute of Occupational Safety and Health
NLEOMF	National Law Enforcement Officers Memorial Fund
NOAA	National Oceanic and Atmospheric Administration
NPL	National Priorities List
NRC	Nuclear Regulatory Commission
NRCC	National Response Coordination Center
NRDF	National Disaster Recovery Framework
NRF	National Response Framework

NRR	Noise Reduction Rating
NRT	National Response Team
NTSB	National Transportation Safety Board
NWS	National Weather Service
O&M	Operations and Maintenance
OEL	Occupational exposure limit
OPIM	Other Potentially Infectious Materials
OR-OSHA	Oregon Occupational Safety and Health Division
OSH	Occupational Safety and Health
OSHA	Occupational Safety and Health Administration
OSHRC	Occupational Safety and Health Review Commission
OSWG	Officer Safety and Wellness Group
PACM	Potentially Asbestos-Containing Material
PADS	Physical Agent Data Sheet
PAH	Polycyclic aromatic hydrocarbon
PAPR	Powered Air-Purifying Respirator
PASS	Personal Alert Safety System
PCB	Polychlorinated byphenyl
PDCA	Plan-Do-Check-Act
PE	Professional Engineer
PEL	Permissible Exposure Limit
PFA	Psychological First Aid
PFD	Personal Flotation Device
PHMSA	Pipeline and Hazardous Materials Safety Administration
PIT	Powered Industrial Truck
PLHCP	Physician or Licensed Health Care Professional
PM10	Particulate Materials with aerodynamic diameters of 10 µm or less
PM2.5	Particulate Materials with aerodynamic diameters of 2.5 µm or less
PMEF	Primary Essential Function
PPD	Presidential Policy Directive
PPE	Personal Protective Equipment
PREP	Preparedness for Response Exercise Program
PSAF	Pandemic Severity Assessment Framework
PSM	Process Safety Management
PtD	Prevention through Design
PTEPP	Passenger Train Emergency Preparedness Plan
PTSD	Post-Traumatic Stress Disorder
RDD	Radiological dispersal device
RED	Radiation exposure device

REL	Recommended Exposure Limit
RIR	(OSHA) Recordable Incident Rate
RRCC	Regional Response Coordination Center
RSF	Recovery Support Function
SAMHSA	Substance Abuse and Mental Health Services Administration
SAR	Supplied Air Respirator
SARA	Superfund Amendments and Reauthorization Act
SCBA	Self-contained breathing apparatus
SDO	Standards Developing Organization
SDS	Safety Data Sheet
SERC	State Emergency Response Commission
SimCell	Simulation Cell
SOP	Standard Operating Procedure
SOT	Society of Toxicology
SSHP	Site Safety and Health Plan
SSO	State Safety Oversight
STEL	Short-term exposure limit
STS	Standard Threshold Shift
STSD	Secondary Traumatic Stress Disorder
TERC	Tribal Emergency Response Commission
TLV	Threshold Limit Value
TNF	Tumor Necrosis Factor
TSD	Treatment Storage and Disposal
TSI	Thermal system insulation
TTX	Tabletop Exercise
TWA	Time-weighted average
USCG	US Coast Guard
USGS	United States Geological Survey
VAN	Volcano Activity Notice
VCF	Victim's Compensation Fund
VOCs	Volatile Organic Compounds
VONA	Volcano Observatory Notification for Aviation
WAC	Washington Administrative Code
WBGT	Wet Bulb Globe Thermometer
WCPR	West Coast Post Trauma Retreat
WHO	World Health Organization
WTC	World Trade Center
WUI	Wildland Urban Interface

1

Safety in Emergencies and Disasters

1.1 Introduction

Employers must develop numerous workplace safety plans in order to meet Occupational Safety and Health Administration (OSHA) requirements. One element of an occupational safety and health plan is the Emergency Action Plan, or EAP. This plan describes what employees are expected to do in an emergency. This primarily involves developing and implementing an emergency evacuation plan, including identification of exit pathways, post-evacuation meeting areas, means to make sure everyone got out safely, and a plan to notify emergency responders if someone was not able to exit the facility and needs help to do so. Certain employees may be assigned to assist with critical operations before exiting, but for the most part, the response to the emergency is carried out by incoming emergency responders.

These plans work because we have resources in our local emergency response departments who are trained and capable of rescuing injured personnel and responding to the emergency. People who work in fire departments or in law enforcement enter hazardous locations when everyone else leaves. When emergency responders show up at our homes or workplaces in this capacity, it is generally because something bad has happened. This bad thing that happens may make this event the worst day of our lives. However, to the emergency responders who show up, this is just a typical day of work.

People who become emergency responders must have a higher personal risk tolerance than that required in many other occupations. Work that is performed in an office setting, for example, has an inherently lower risk. For emergency responders, the reward of the job must outweigh the potential risk of injury, or illness, or worse. An element of self-selection exists in these fields: During training, trainees must come face to face with the hazards of the job and learn how they react to facing these hazards. Those who find that they are not up to facing these risks choose to pursue other lines of work.

Health and Safety in Emergency Management and Response, First Edition. Dana L. Stahl.
© 2021 John Wiley & Sons, Inc. Published 2021 by John Wiley & Sons, Inc.

Although emergency response is a hazardous occupation, appropriate training for personnel who are equipped with appropriate tools and equipment, and appropriate Personal Protective Equipment (PPE), can reduce, or at least, minimize responder injuries and illnesses. Training, practice, and experience build capabilities necessary to perform this work safely every day.

In a large-scale or community-wide emergency, local emergency response resources may be insufficient to meet the needs of the response. Personnel from occupations such as construction have skills that can supplement work done by emergency responders. The Incident Management Team might request these personnel and the equipment they are trained to operate as resources. In other situations, especially when members of a community are involved, volunteers will show up at the scene in the absence of a specific request because they feel compelled to help members of their own community.

Certain emergencies, for example, a mass casualty incident in a large facility such as a stadium, a train derailment, or hazardous materials response to a chemical processing plant that is subject to OSHA's Process Safety Management Standard present unique hazards that emergency responders do not face in their ordinary day-to-day work. Personnel who work in a chemical processing plant, for example, have knowledge and information that is critical for incoming emergency responders. Ideally, the plant operators and local emergency managers and emergency responders need to work together to develop plans to integrate response and share information when an incident occurs. Plant operators, for example, have subject matter expertise that is critical to the response. These plant operators need to be prepared to participate when an emergency incident happens, despite the fact that incident response is outside of their core day-to-day responsibilities.

1.2 9/11 Response

The terrorist attacks of 11 September 2001 exceeded all planned capabilities. Until this date, the United States had not faced an event of this magnitude, and indeed, few could have imagined one. More than 2700 people died in the attacks at the World Trade Center (WTC), including more than 300 firefighters and 50 police officers. In the days that followed, jurisdictions across the United States sent firefighters, emergency medical responders, rescue workers, and other personnel to assist in the response. Industrial hygienists from the Federal Occupational Safety and Health Administration (OSHA) and state occupational safety and health agencies across the United States responded to help with air monitoring and respirator fit testing. The Environmental Protection Agency (EPA) sent personnel to collect air samples. Construction workers responded to move debris. Volunteers responded as well, including members of churches and community organizations, and people who were present in the area immediately after the attacks.

All responders were exposed to multiple health and safety hazards. In addition to the safety hazards one might expect when working around unstable rubble, responders witnessed horrific events, including finding dismembered human remains and watching bodies falling from the towers. Responders worked in a dust cloud of pulverized building materials. The composition of the dust that workers were exposed to during this initial response is essentially unknown, as few measurements were taken, and the composition of the dust likely changed as the response progressed. However, we do know that settled dust included pulverized concrete (and silica), gypsum, fiberglass, metals and sheet rock, asbestos, and plastics. Combustion products contained volatile organic compounds (VOCs), soot, metals, acids, and other toxics, and this may represent the composition of the dusts that workers were exposed to.

Although an effort was made to provide respirators and fit test responders, actual respirator use was sporadic. When decontamination systems were set up, they were often not used, allowing workers to track contaminants offsite. Many workers were untrained in the type of work they were performing and on the hazards they faced [1].

Today, many 9/11 responders suffer from chronic health conditions. The James Zadroga 9/11 Health and Compensation Action of 2010 (Zadroga Act) signed into law by President Obama on 2 January 2011, created the World Trade Center (WTC) Health Program and reopened the September 11th Victim Compensation Fund (VCF). This program is administered by the National Institute for Occupational Safety and Health (NIOSH), and provides monitoring and treatment for conditions that have been determined to be related to 9/11.

Groups included in this monitoring program include:

- Members of the Fire Department of New York who participated in at least one day in the rescue and recovery effort;
- New York City responders, including:
  - Outside responders who participated in rescue, recovery, demolition, debris cleanup, or related work
  - Police department personnel from the Police Department of New York or the Port Authority Police of the Port Authority of New York and New Jersey who participated in onsite rescue, recovery, debris cleanup, or related response
  - Employees from the medical examiners' office who handled human remains from the World Trade Center attacks
  - Workers in the Port Authority Trans-Hudson Corporation Tunnel
  - Vehicle maintenance workers who were exposed to debris while retrieving, driving, cleaning, repairing, and maintaining vehicles contaminated by airborne toxins from the site.

- New York City survivors, including persons who lived, worked, or attended school or daycare in the New York City disaster area, or who worked as a cleanup or maintenance worker in the area;
- Pentagon/Shanksville Pennsylvania responders, including fire department and police department employees, recovery and cleanup workers, and volunteers.

As of 2018, more than 85 000 people are enrolled in the World Trade Center Health Program, and more than 1600 were deceased. The program covers specific conditions (which may change as more information is obtained regarding 9/11 exposure and related health effects). Covered conditions include:

- Acute traumatic injury, such as burns, eye injuries, head trauma, and conditions such as fractures and sprains.
- Aerodigestive disorders, or disorders of the respiratory and gastrointestinal systems such as asthma, upper airway hyper-reactivity and gastroesophageal reflux disorder (GERD).
- Cancers, including more than 60 specific common and rare cancers (Table 1.1).
- Mental health conditions, including Post-Traumatic Stress Disorder (PTSD), substance abuse, and anxiety and depressive disorders.
- Musculoskeletal disorders (MSDs), such as carpal tunnel syndrome, low back pain, and others.[1]

1.3 Deepwater Horizon

The Deepwater Horizon oil platform in the Gulf of Mexico, operated by British Petroleum, exploded on 20 April 2010, releasing millions of barrels of oil into the gulf. More than 50,000 workers participated in the response, which included removing oil and tar balls from beaches, skimming and booming oil near shores, burning of surface oil, applying dispersants, and containment and recovery at the release site.

Numerous federal agencies were involved in the response, including OSHA, and OSHA issued an invitation to NIOSH to assist in the effort to identify and address occupational health needs during the response. One of NIOSH's first actions was to develop a roster of workers; this was initiated in response to "lessons learned" from the 9/11 response, and recognition that such a roster is a critical data element in medical surveillance after the response. The roster provided a demographic analysis of personnel who participated in the response who were not primarily employed as emergency responders: Responders came from construction, transportation, and farming, fishing, and forestry. Others worked in real estate, arts,

---

1 http://www.cdc.gov/wtc (accessed 23 August 2018).

Table 1.1 Cancers covered by the World Trade Center Worker's Compensation Fund.

Type of cancer	Tissue	Type
Childhood cancer		Any type of cancer diagnosed in a person less than 20 years of age
Malignant neoplasms	Blood and lymphoid tissue (including, but not limited to, lymphoma, leukemia, and myeloma)	• Diffuse non-Hodgkin lymphoma • Follicular (nodular) non-Hodgkin lymphoma • Hodgkin's disease • Leukemia of unspecified cell type • Lymphoid leukemia • Malignant immunoproliferative diseases • Monocytic leukemia • Multiple myeloma and malignant plasma cell neoplasms • Monocytic leukemia • Multiple myeloma and malignant plasma cell neoplasms • Myeloid leukemia • Other and unspecified lymphoid, hematopoietic, and related tissue • Other and unspecified types of non-Hodgkin lymphoma • Other leukemias of specified cell type • Peripheral and cutaneous T-cell lymphoma
	Digestive system	• Colon • Esophagus • Liver and intrahepatic bile ducts • Other and ill-defined digestive organs • Rectosignoid junction • Rectum • Retroperitoneum and peritoneum • Stomach
	Eye and orbit	• Eye and adnexa
	Female breast	• Breast
	Female reproductive organs	• Ovary

(Continued)

Table 1.1 (Continued)

Type of cancer	Tissue	Type
	Head and neck	• Accessory sinuses • Base of tongue • Floor of mouth • Gum • Hypopharynx • Larynx • Lip • Nasal cavity • Nasopharynx • Other and ill-defined conditions in the lip, oral cavity, and pharynx • Other and unspecified major salivary glands • Other and unspecified part of the mouth • Other and unspecified parts of the tongue • Oropharynx • Palate • Parotid gland • Piriform sinus • Tonsil
	Respiratory system	• Bronchus and lung • Heart, mediastinum, and pleura • Other and ill-defined sites in the respiratory system and intrathoracic organs • Trachea
	Skin (melanoma and non-melanoma)	• Malignant melanoma of skin • Other malignant neoplasms of skin • Scrotum
	Soft tissue	• Other connective and soft tissue • Peripheral nerves and autonomic nervous system
	Thyroid	• Thyroid gland
	Urinary system	• Bladder • Kidney • Other and unspecified urinary organs • Prostate • Renal pelvis • Ureter
Mesothelioma	Mesothelioma	
Rare cancers	Cancers that occur in less than 15 cases per 100 000 per year	

Source: http://www.cdc.gov/wtc (accessed 23 August 2018).

entertainment and recreation, the retail trade, and other occupations wholly unrelated to hazardous materials spill cleanup or emergency response. A little more than 4% of response participants had been unemployed prior to the incident. The roster also collected information on health history, including smoking, level of training, whether they had been fit tested for respirator use in the past, and use of PPE [2, 3].

NIOSH conducted Health Hazard Evaluations (HHEs) of the Deepwater Horizon workers at the request of British Petroleum, prepared technical guidance and communication for the response, which was updated on an ongoing basis, and analyzed injury and illness data.

Many injuries and illnesses recorded on the log are similar to what might be seen at a typical industrial worksite, such as lacerations, smashed thumbs, debris in eyes, slip and fall, back pain, and vehicle injuries. This is not unexpected, although fatigue and work in unfamiliar conditions could have contributed to a higher frequency of these types of injuries. Other frequent injuries/illnesses included chest pain, bee stings and spider bites, and dehydration, which speaks to the level of exertion required by responders and the environment. Illnesses from carbon monoxide exposure were also reported [4].

Illnesses reported between 23 April and 27 July 2010 included:

- 192 cases of heat-related illness, of which 21 were OSHA recordable and 2 were listed as lost time/restricted duty.
- 171 cases, of which 23 were OSHA recordable listed as "multiple symptoms," which included symptoms consistent with heat stress. Only seven had reported exposure to oils or dispersants.
- 122 gastrointestinal cases, including diarrhea, nausea, and/or vomiting. Of these only one case was attributed to chemical exposure (oil).
- 78 cases of dermatologic illness attributed to irritation from sunscreen wipes, heat rash, and skin infections. Four cases were attributed to oil or dispersant exposure.
- 42 cases of "general symptoms," including malaise, fatigue, and nonspecific allergic reactions.
- 28 cardiovascular cases, of which 13 were OSHA recordable and 4 resulted in time loss from work.
- 13 cases that were respiratory in nature, including asthma, shortness of breath, and respiratory infection. None of these cases recorded exposure to oils or dispersants.

Oil or dispersant exposures were mentioned as a contributing factor in 13 cases in total [5].

NIOSH's HHEs identified heat exposure as a major risk factor for all responders. Musculoskeletal risks were identified for responders conducting beach cleanup and those doing boom repair or maintenance. Noise exposure was also a risk for employees conducting boom repair.

Many airborne exposure samples were taken; only rarely did an air sample produce a result that exceeded an applicable occupational exposure limit (OEL). Overexposures were primarily carbon monoxide produced from burning oil. Skin exposure to oil or chemical dispersants was a factor, but with the exception of boom maintenance workers, the use of PPE was judged as effective in minimizing the risk of exposure to these chemicals via skin contact.

Health symptom surveys were distributed, and workers reported headaches, fatigue and exhaustion, skin symptoms, itching eyes, musculoskeletal pain, and feelings of "work pressure." These symptoms were attributed primarily to heat exposures and work stress. However, the report did note that workers involved in conducting in situ burns, or a controlled burning of oil at the location of the spill, had higher frequencies of these symptoms, and US Coast Guard (USCG) and contractors who reported exposures to oils, dispersants, cleaners, or other chemicals reported more headaches than those who did not report having had chemical exposures. Wildlife cleanup workers and beach cleanup workers who reported chemical exposures also reported more symptoms than those who were not exposed, although symptoms related to heat stress and psychosocial stress were also significant.

Overall, the most frequently reported health stressors reported were as follows:

1. Heat and environmental conditions, intensified by the use of PPE;
2. Basic living issues (including physical and mental fatigue) and food arrangements;
3. Job insecurity;
4. Management and communication issues including a lack of clarity about the chain of command for decision-making and who had tasking authority and priority;
5. Frequent changes in rules, procedures, and protocol; and
6. Varying levels of safety knowledge, experience, and training.

Overall, the HHE-identified heat stress, psychosocial factors, and ergonomics as significant stressors. Chemical exposures in this incident were considered to be well controlled, given the number of air samples that indicated exposures below OELs and the use of PPE (although it was noted that PPE was not always used correctly). The HHE also reported high levels of tobacco use among responders. Tobacco use is associated with numerous adverse health conditions, and contributes additive or synergistic effects when combined with chemical exposures received during the response [6].

Despite NIOSH reports that chemical exposures were well controlled, anecdotally, responders have reported significant health effects related to response work.

In particular, health concerns center around exposure to the dispersants that were used, COREXIT 9500 and COREXIT 9527. The size of the oil spill required use of a higher quantity of dispersants than had ever been used for any previous spill, and the toxicity of these products to human health had not been extensively studied. A group of divers who volunteered to collect coral samples near the site of the spill experienced a variety of symptoms, including skin rashes and blisters, migraines, nausea, and dizziness, which persisted for several years following exposure to the spilled oils and dispersants in the gulf. Although protective gear was identified as a control, many divers did not have appropriate equipment and conducted dives wearing only dry suits, which allowed contact of exposed skin to contaminated waters. Others wore wet suits which sustained damage when they came into contact with oil contaminants and the dispersant [7]. No other protective clothing was worn, and divers likely received fairly significant skin exposures to these agents.

NIOSH sponsored toxicology studies of the dispersants following the incident. In animal models, these products produced health outcomes including immunological and sensitization effects as well as dermatological effects [8], acute/transient cardiovascular and peripheral vascular function [9], neurotoxicity [10], and transient breathing difficulty [11]. Perhaps protections provided for responders would have been stronger had these effects been documented prior to the response. As was the case with 9/11, responders were exposed to health hazards that were unknown or not fully characterized at the time.

The National Institutes of Health and the National Institute of Environmental Health Sciences are studying the health of individuals who participated in oil spill response or cleanup following the Deepwater Horizon disaster. The GuLF Study (Gulf Long Term Follow-up Study) is looking at the impact of current and future effects on health among workers who participated in different aspects of the response. The findings of the study will be useful in decision-making in future oil spill responses [12].[2]

1.4 Emergency Responders

"Save a lot, risk a lot. Save a little, risk a little" is a phrase often used by emergency responders. This refers to the idea that if there is a chance that an emergency responder's actions can save a life, they will take great personal risk to do so. However, if a life cannot be saved, there is no need to take such risks, and shortcuts in personal safety are less likely to be taken.

This phrase says a lot about the mentality of those who become emergency responders, such as firefighters and police officers, and the personal qualities that these professionals bring to the job. As a society, we appreciate that people who

---

2 https://Gulfstudy.nih.gov (accessed 25 August 2018).

are willing to take these risks in order to save us if we need saving. We rely on our heroes.

However, heroes are not infallible and they can be injured, even seriously. A 2016 data from the Bureau of Labor Statistics (BLS) shows that fire responders had an annual recordable incident rate (RIR) of 9.5, and police responders 10.2, compared with the national average of 3.2 for all industries. When looking at injuries that were severe enough to prevent at least an immediate return to duty (Days Away/Restricted/Transfer, or DART), the rate for fire responders was 5.9, and police responders 5.5, as compared with 1.7 for all industries.[3] Most health and safety professionals in any other industry, including high-hazard industries, would consider an RIR that is close to three times the national average to be unacceptable.

BLS publishes data on workplace fatalities annually. This is published as "number of fatalities" rather than rates, which makes this statistic more difficult to compare with that of other industries (Table 1.2). For example, in 2016, construction workers had 970 fatalities, which is the highest number of fatalities of any occupation. This is not surprising, as construction work is considered a high-hazard line of work and construction employs a high number of workers.

BLS also publishes employment numbers as the number of employees per industry, and these numbers can be used to calculate a rough estimate of fatality rate per industry. Based on this data, fatality rates for firefighters and police officers are more than three times the national average for all occupations, and the fatality rates for police officers are in a comparable range with that for construction workers (Table 1.3).

Table 1.2 2016 BLS data: fatalities in Public Administration Emergency Response Occupations.

Occupation	Total fatalities	Violence by person or animals	Transportation accidents	Fires/ explosions	Falls, slips, trips	Exposure to harmful substance or environment	Contact with objects and equipment
Firefighter	35	5	19	1	5	—	3
Police officer	109	61	45	—	—	—	—
Emergency medical technicians (EMT)/ paramedics	10	—	6	—	—	—	—

Source: Bureau of Labor Statistics. www.bls.gov (accessed 1 September 2018).

---

3 Bureau of Labor Statistics. www.bls.gov (accessed 1 September 2018).

Table 1.3 BLS data analysis: 2016 fatalities per 100 000 employees.

Occupation	Total fatalities	Employment, May 2016	Fatalities per 100 000 employees
All occupations	5 190	140 400 040	3.4
Construction	970	5 585 420	17.4
Firefighter	35	315 910	11.1
Police officer	109	662 500	16.5
EMT/paramedic	10	244 960	4

Source: Bureau of Labor Statistics. www.bls.gov (accessed 1 September 2018).

Firefighter injuries and illnesses are also tracked by the National Fire Protection Association (NFPA). NFPA reported that there were 69 "line-of-duty" firefighter deaths in 2016, as compared with 35 reported by BLS, and 62 085 injuries. NFPA includes volunteer firefighters in this data (814 850 in 2016), whereas BLS data represents only paid firefighters employed in protective service occupations (315 910 in 2016). This could in part explain the difference in the number of fatalities reported by the two organizations. Also, OSHA's definition of "work related" differs from NFPA's definition of "line of duty". For example, if a firefighter on shift suffered a fatal heart attack while taking a shower or during a rest period, it would be counted as a "line-of-duty death." If medical findings determined that the heart attack was related to a personal medical condition, and work activities did not contribute to this medical condition, this same heart attack would not be counted as a "work-related" fatality under the OSHA definition, and therefore not included in the BLS data. This makes it difficult to directly compare the two sources of data.

The National Law Enforcement Officers Memorial Fund (NLEOMF) tracks line-of-duty fatalities for police officers, and reported 159 law enforcement deaths in 2016, compared with the BLS fatality count of 109. Similar differences between the definitions for "line of duty" and OSHA's definition of "work related" make it difficult to directly compare these two data sets.

The NLEOMF also reports data on work-related injuries, and reported in 2016 that 58 627 law enforcement officers were assaulted, and of these, 16 677 sustained injuries. Knowledge of the source, or cause, of injuries and illnesses is critical to understanding how to prevent them in the future.

NLEOMF reports that 1511 law enforcement fatalities occurred between 2008 and 2017. Cases of these fatalities were:

- Aircraft accident (20)
- Auto crash (364)
- Beaten (16)

- Bicycle accident (1)
- Boating accident (4)
- Bomb-related incident (10)
- Drowned (21)
- Electrocuted (4)
- Fall (19)
- Horse-related accident (2)
- Job-related illness (325)
- Motorcycle crash (63)
- Poisoned (1)
- Shot (514)
- Stabbed (13)
- Strangled (4)
- Struck by train (3)
- Struck by vehicle (126)
- Terrorist attack (1)

Similarly, NFPA provides additional information on circumstances relating to firefighter injuries, illnesses, and fatalities. NFPA reported that in 2016, of the 69 reported line-of-duty firefighter fatalities:

- 39 were volunteer firefighters;
- 19 were career firefighters;
- 8 were employees of federal land management agencies;
- 1 was a contractor with a state land management agency;
- 1 was a member of an industrial fire brigade, and
- 1 was a prison inmate.

Of the 69 on duty fatalities:

- 17 occurred responding to and returning from alarms (including crashes, falls, sudden cardiac death, and drowning in floodwaters);
- 15 occurred while operating at fires;
- 10 occurred at non-fire emergencies, including medical emergencies, vehicle crashes, and a dock collapse;
- 10 occurred at training exercises, including 7 cardiac arrests and 3 from traumatic injuries;
- 6 experienced sudden cardiac death while performing administrative or station duties;
- 4 died in vehicle crashes;
- 2 died by suicide;
- 1 was shot;
- 1 drowned while diving during body recovery;

- 1 was run over by a fire apparatus that was backing into the station as he was guiding it in;
- 1 fell from a ladder at the station;
- 1 was asphyxiated while inspecting fire extinguishers [13].

The 62 085 line of duty firefighter injuries in 2016 included:

- 24 325 injuries occurred during fireground operations;
- 5200 happened while responding to, or returning from, an incident;
- 8480 happened during training activities;
- 12 780 occurred during non-fire emergency incidents, and
- 11 300 happened during other on duty activities.

Musculoskeletal injuries, cuts and bruises, burns, and smoke or gas inhalation accounted for the majority of injuries. In addition to injuries, there were 9275 documented exposures to infectious diseases and 36 475 exposures to hazardous conditions [14].

Fatality and injury data, however, do not paint the entire picture. In addition to on-the-job injuries and fatalities included in reported numbers, police officers have shorter lifespans and a higher number of years of potential life lost than the general population. This is likely due to chronic stress and Post-Traumatic Stress Disorder, which are linked to increased incidence of physiological disease such as cardiovascular disorders. Obesity and related diseases, including diabetes, is also common and likely is related to poor diet and low physical activity. This is not unexpected given levels of on-the-job stress, and time spent in vehicles. Work can include long periods of time spent on vehicle patrol or stakeouts punctuated by spikes in stress levels. Chemical exposures include illegal drugs and products at clandestine drug laboratories, lead exposure from firearms, toxic components in fingerprint powders, and vehicle exhaust and traffic pollutants [15]. Alcohol abuse, substance abuse, and suicide rates are also high, and many police departments have implemented wellness programs to address these and other health issues common to law enforcement personnel [16, 17].

Firefighters have increased mortality and are at increased risk of developing cancer. The International Agency for Research on Cancer (IARC) listed working as a firefighter as a Group 2B carcinogen (possibly carcinogenic to humans) in 2010. IARC concluded in their assessment that there was limited evidence that work as a firefighter contributed to cancer in humans, and inadequate animal data. IARC noted that the increase in use of plastics in modern buildings contributes to greater toxicity of combustion products than that of traditional buildings and forest fires. Many reports also indicated lack of full compliance with use of personal protective equipment; both factors likely contribute to cancer risk [18].

Research on this topic is ongoing. An epidemiology study of cancer in a cohort of 29 993 firefighters found excess cancer mortality and incidence of digestive and respiratory cancers. Notably, this study reported a fairly strong correlation between firefighting and malignant mesothelioma which is known to be caused by exposure to asbestos [19]; it is not unreasonable to expect that firefighters could receive asbestos exposures from building fires. Further analysis of this cohort found a modest increase in risk of lung cancer and leukemia mortality [20]. In 2018, the United States passed legislature requiring the Centers for Disease Control and Prevention to establish a registry of firefighters to track links between workplace exposures and cancer. This registry will help provide additional data to help better understand the link between firefighting exposures and cancer [21].[4]

Interestingly, the firefighter cohort study found lower mortality from nonmalignant respiratory diseases, cerebrovascular disease, nervous system disorders, and alcoholism than the general population. This speaks to the overall health of the firefighter cohort [19].

1.5 Toxicology: How Do We Know What Causes Cancer or Other Health Effects?

Although job-related stress and exposure to environmental hazards contribute to health decline and years of life lost, these numbers are not included in the annual BLS data, nor the data from NFPA or NLEOMF. Evidence points to the fact that on-the-job exposure to chemicals is related to cancer outcomes in firefighters, and also that police officers have exposure to lead and other substances. However, none of the fatalities reported by BLS, NFPA, or NLEOMF attributed "exposure to harmful substances/environment" as a contributing cause of death. Such cause and effect is difficult to prove.

It is hard to say with certainty that exposure to a particular substance, or a particular exposure event, directly led to an incidence of cancer. Carcinogenesis is a complex, multistage process. When tissues and organs in the body operate as they should, cells go through cycles of division and growth as well as programmed death or "apoptosis." This balance is important: cell division and growth must not occur faster than cell death, and complex signaling systems within cells regulate these cycles. When cell growth occurs faster than cell death, tumors form. If cells escape from the original tumor, or "metastasize," they can form tumors in other locations. If tumor cells acquire the ability to encourage the cardiovascular system to provide the tumor a blood supply, or "angiogenesis," the tumor can receive nutrients to encourage even further growth into additional organs and tissues. Unfortunately, this generally does not lead to a positive outcome for the host organism.

---

4 http://www.cdc.gov/niosh/firefighters/health.html (accessed 30 August 2018).

Hanahan and Weinberg described six Hallmarks of Cancer that occur in most, if not all cases in the process in which a normal, healthy cell transforms into a cancer cell (Figure 1.1):

- Self-sufficiency in growth signals: Normal cells receive and respond to growth signals from other cells. Cancer cells do not.
- Insensitivity to anti-growth signals: Normal cells respond to signals that tell them not to divide at specific times. Cancer cells do not respond to these signals and divide anyway.
- Tissue invasion and metastasis: Normal cells are confined to the tissues and organs that they are a part of. Cancer cells can escape these locations and invade other tissues. They can be transported through the bloodstream, where they then invade tissues at some distance from their original location.
- Limitless replication potential: Organisms utilize biological mechanisms that limit cell replication. Cancer cells become resistant to these mechanisms, and evade the controls that limit growth and replication.
- Sustained angiogenesis: Cancer cells send signals to blood vessels that encourage these vessels to grow and provide a blood supply to the tumor.

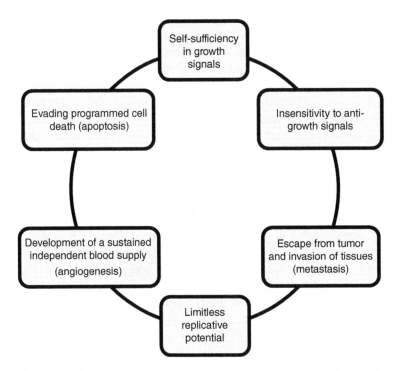

Figure 1.1 Hallmarks of cancer, as described by Hanahan and Weinberg [22].

- Evading apoptosis: Normal cells do not live forever, and are subject to programmed cell death, or apoptosis. Cancer cells develop the ability to evade apoptosis, allowing them to continue to grow and divide long past their usual lifespan.

These capabilities are gained over time, and do not need to be gained in any particular order. A cell that has transformed from a normal cell to a cancer cell has gained all six of these capabilities [22].

Factors such as chemical exposure, diet, inflammation, genetics, and lifestyle can increase or decrease the likelihood of a cell developing any one of these hallmarks or characteristics. Due to the complexity of cancer development, and the fact that humans are exposed to a multitude of chemicals and other environmental factors in their lifetimes, it is challenging to determine with certainty whether or not any particular environmental factor causes cancer.

Controlled studies can be conducted in animals: Animals of the same strain are kept in a controlled environment and dosed with known amounts of a specific chemical through ingestion, inhalation, or skin contact, or other uniform route. At a defined time point, the animals are sacrificed and tumors are counted. As the animals have similar genetics and spend their lives in a controlled environment, the effect of exposure to other potential carcinogens that could interfere with the study are controlled for. If the animals that are dosed with the chemical have more tumors than the controls, the chemical is presumed to have caused this increase in tumors. The results of such studies can tell us whether these chemicals cause cancer in animals.

Animals, however, have a different biology than humans. Proteins and enzymes that are involved in intracellular signaling can be different. Metabolic processes, or toxicokinetics, change the structures of the chemicals that enter the body in order to detoxify them or prepare them for elimination in urine or feces. Sometimes it is a metabolic byproduct of the original chemical that is carcinogenic rather than the original chemical that the organism was exposed to. These metabolic processes vary between species, and a toxic metabolite formed in animals may or may not form in humans. Study of the mechanistic effects of the actions of carcinogens is important, and if sufficient studies exist, this can help shed light on the applicability of animal studies to human health. If the chemical promotes cancer in an animal through a mechanism that is not relevant in human biology, the ability to cause cancer in animals may have limited significance for humans. Mechanistic studies, including studies of metabolism of the chemical and its effects on intracellular signaling, can clarify similarities and differences between humans and animals and can add to the interpretation of significance of the results of animal studies.

It would be unethical to conduct studies in humans the way they are conducted in animals, with controlled environments, defined dosing, and counting of tumors after sacrifice. Information on chemical exposure and carcinogenic outcomes in humans come from epidemiological studies, where incidence of disease is compared between groups that have been exposed to an environmental agent and controls that have not. Epidemiological studies can be retrospective, in which a group of people with a disease, or cohort, is compared with a control group that does not have the disease, and different possible exposures are considered. This is carried out in order to identify whether there was a common exposure in the group that has the disease that the control group was not exposed to. However, past exposures are often based on recall and subject to bias: The disease group may be more likely to overestimate exposures than the control group. Prospective epidemiology studies identify exposure groups and follow them over time in order to determine if there are excess disease outcomes compared with the general population. Exposures are better characterized in prospective studies than in retrospective studies; however, the timeline between exposure and outcome may take many years, or even decades. Results of such studies are not known for years.

Unlike animal studies, epidemiology studies in humans cannot control for exposures to other chemicals or environmental factors that might interfere either positively or negatively with the chemical of interest. For example, smoking and asbestos exposures are known to create a synergistic effect in cancer outcome: The carcinogenic effect of a combined exposure is greater than exposure to either alone [23]. Other exposures can be protective: Dietary substances such as isothyocyanates in Brussels sprouts or other cruciferous vegetables, onions, and garlic can increase the production of anticarcinogenic enzymes and increase resistance to carcinogens [24]. Antioxidant levels, such as Vitamin C in serum have also been associated with a decrease in cancer outcomes [25]. With so many variables, or confounders, epidemiology studies must include large numbers of participants in order to achieve sufficient statistical significance to draw conclusions relating the exposure to outcome. This requires large numbers of participants.

The firefighter cancer registry is an example of a prospective epidemiological study, and it is large enough that results should achieve validity. As with any prospective study of cancer, since cancer develops slowly, it may be many years before we know the outcome.

Current cancer rates in firefighters reflect exposures that happened many years prior, which may or may not reflect the exposures happening today. Use of respiratory protection has improved considerably over time. Pressure-demand self-contained breathing apparatus (SCBA) is commonly used by municipal firefighters today, but these only came into wide spread use in the 1960s and 1970s and were not always used as consistently as they are today. At one time asbestos was used in firefighter's helmets to increase fire resistance of the helmet. These helmets released fibers into the breathing zone. Today, asbestos-free helmets can be selected, reducing this particular exposure. These improvements should reduce cancer outcomes in firefighters.

However, fires are also different now than in the past. While older buildings were primarily built of wood, newer buildings contain more synthetic and petroleum-based materials. This changes the composition of combustion products that firefighters are exposed to, and it is likely that combustion products of modern buildings contain higher levels of carcinogens than those in the past [18]. This may increase cancers in firefighters.

IARC currently lists firefighting as possibly carcinogenic to humans, or a Group 2B carcinogen. IARC classifications are based on strength of scientific evidence of both animal studies and epidemiological studies in humans into the following categories:

Group 1: The agent is carcinogenic to humans. This means that IARC has determined that there is:

- Sufficient evidence that the agent causes cancer in humans;
- In some cases, an agent may be placed in this category when there is less than sufficient evidence that it causes cancer in humans, but sufficient evidence that it causes cancer in animals and there is evidence that it would act through similar mechanisms in humans.

Group 2: This category includes agents in which evidence of cancer in humans is almost sufficient, or agents in which there is no human data, but there is evidence of carcinogenicity in experimental animals. This group is further broken down into:

Group 2A: The agent is probably carcinogenic in humans:

- There is limited evidence that the agent is carcinogenic to humans, but sufficient evidence that it is carcinogenic to animals, or
- If there is inadequate evidence of carcinogenicity, an agent may be placed in this grouping if there is sufficient evidence of carcinogenicity in animals and evidence that the agent would act using similar mechanisms in humans, or
- This grouping also includes agents that demonstrate limited evidence of carcinogenicity in humans but belongs mechanistically to a class of agents that have been classed in Group 1 or Group 2.

Group 2B: The agent is possibly carcinogenic to humans.

- There is limited evidence of carcinogenicity in humans and less than sufficient evidence of carcinogenicity in experimental animals, or

- It may also include agents for which there is inadequate evidence of carcinogenicity in humans but sufficient evidence for carcinogenicity in experimental animals, or
- There is inadequate evidence of carcinogenicity in humans and less than sufficient evidence of carcinogenicity in experimental animals along with supporting evidence from mechanistic or other relevant data that supports placement in this group, or
- An agent may also be placed in his group based solely on strong mechanistic or other relevant data.

The term "probably" in Group 2A indicates a higher likelihood that the agent is a carcinogen than the term "possibly" in Group 2B.

Group 3: The agent is not classifiable as to its carcinogenicity in humans.

- The evidence for carcinogenicity is inadequate in humans and inadequate or limited in experimental animals, or
- The evidence of carcinogenicity is inadequate in humans and sufficient in animals, but there is evidence that the mechanism of carcinogenicity in animals does not operate in humans, or
- The agent does not fall into any other group.

A Group 3 classification is not a determination that the agent is not carcinogenic, nor is it an indicator of safety. It simply means that there is not enough evidence to make a further determination.

Group 4: The agent is probably not carcinogenic to humans.

- There is evidence suggesting lack of carcinogenicity in humans and experimental animals, or
- The data for lack of carcinogenicity is inadequate in humans, but sufficient in animals and there is evidence to support similar mechanisms in animals and humans [26].

The determination that firefighting is a Group 2B carcinogen, possibly carcinogenic to humans, is based on several analyses. First, fire smoke consists of a number of decomposition products that have been determined to be Groups 1, 2A, and 2B carcinogens (Table 1.4), and therefore firefighters are exposed to these compounds in the course of their careers. Several of these compounds are known to interact with biological mechanisms in a manner that could promote cancer. IARC has also determined that shift work is a 2A human carcinogen, for example, and firefighters work extended shifts.

IARC reviewed 42 epidemiological studies of firefighters, and many indicated elevated cancer outcomes. However, there was inconsistency in exposure estimations between the studies, and many studies did not have enough participants to determine outcomes with statistical significance. As a result, the findings of

Table 1.4 IARC groupings of carcinogenic compounds measured at fires considered in IARC's evaluation determining that work as a firefighter is a Group 2B carcinogen.

Chemicals measured at fires	IARC Group
Acetaldehyde	2B
Arsenic	1
Asbestos	1
Benzo[a]anthracene	2B
Benzene	1
Benzo[b]flouranthene	2B
Benzofuran	2B
Benzo[a]pyrene	1
1,3-Butadiene	1
Cadmium	1
Carbon black (total)	2B
Chrysene	2B
Dibenz[a,h]anthracene	2A
Dichlorobenzene	2B (*para*) and 3 (*meta* and *ortho*)
Dichloromethane (methylene chloride)	2B
Ethylbenzene	2B
Formaldehyde	1
Furan	2B
Indeno-[1,2,3-cd]pyrene	2B
Isoprene	2B
Lead compounds, organic	3
Lead compounds, inorganic	2A
Naphthalene	2B
2-Nitrosamisole	2B
Pentachlorophenol	1
Polychlorophenols	2B
Polychlorinated byphenyls (chlorodiphenyl)	2A
Radioactivity-gamma	1
Radioactivity-beta	1
Radioactivity-alpha	1
Silica (crystalline)	1

(Continued)

Table 1.4 (Continued)

Chemicals measured at fires	IARC Group
Silica (amorphous)	3
Styrene	2B
Sulfuric acid	1
2,3,7,8-Tetrachloro dibenzo-para-dioxin	1
Tetrachloroethylene (perchloroethylene)	2A
Toluene diisocyanates	2B
Trichlorothylene	2A
Trichloromethane (chloroform)	2B
Trichlorophenol	2B
Triphenylene	3

Source: From International Agency for Research on Cancer (IARC), World Health Organization [18].

cancer outcomes was not consistent between many of the studies. However, the IARC working group was able to determine that there was evidence that firefighters faced 50% excess risk of testicular cancer, 30% excess risk of prostate cancer, and 20% excess risk of non-Hodgkin lymphoma. No animal studies were available to review (it would be challenging to replicate firefighting in an animal study).

In determining that firefighting deserved a Group 2B classification, IARC determined that there was limited evidence in humans for the carcinogenicity of occupational exposure as a firefighter, and inadequate evidence in experimental animals since there were no studies to review [18].

In conclusion, although there is evidence that firefighters are at greater risk of developing cancer than the general population, there is still a lot we really do not know. Some firefighters develop cancer and others do not. This is also true for survivors of the 9/11 attacks, workers who responded to Deepwater Horizon disaster, and for those who will respond to the next disaster. However, principles of injury and illness prevention can and should still be applied, just as they are for risks that are perhaps more certain to negatively impact health and well-being, such as injuries from vehicle accidents and falls from heights.

1.6 Principles of Injury and Illness Prevention

In 1931, Herbert William Heinrich published his book *Industrial Accident Prevention: A Scientific Approach*. This work described his views on accident causation, which is illustrated by the accident triangle for which he has become very

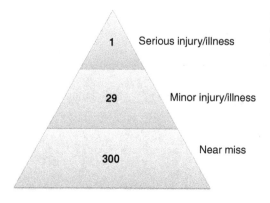

Figure 1.2 Heinrich's theory of accident causation, illustrated by the accident triangle. Source: Heinrich [27].

well known. Heinrich had spent a career in industrial insurance, and over time realized that serious accidents are very rare. He postulated that when a hazard exists in the work environment, 300 times that hazard will cause a "near miss," which is best described as an incident in which no injuries occurred but would have had circumstances been slightly different. He also postulated that 29 times this same hazard would result in a minor injury or illness, and only one time would it result in a serious injury or illness, or fatality (Figure 1.2) [27]. Heinrich did not present the data that he used to support his theory or the relationship of 300 : 29 : 1 illustrated in the Heinrich Triangle. It is likely that these numbers are variable depending on whether the hazard is a high-risk/low-probability event or a low-risk/high-probability event. Regardless, the relationship of many near misses to a few minor injuries to one serious injury is one that is accepted in the field of safety management.

This relationship tells us several things that are important in managing safety programs.

First, when a hazard is present, serious injuries are rare. People who are exposed to hazards can work around the hazard for a long period of time without getting hurt, and this experience can lead to a perception that the hazard is not really something that will lead to an injury. Each exposure to the hazard in which an injury does not happen reinforces this viewpoint. Over time, with repeated reinforcement, the hazard takes on less and less relevance and risk taking becomes more and more accepted. The is term for this is "normalization of deviance," and refers to a pattern in which the risky behavior comes to be accepted as the norm. Normalization of deviance explains why people are willing to take risks such as working without PPE or failing to follow procedures. Then, when the serious injury does happen, which it will, others wonder why the injured party was willing to put themselves at risk.

The perception that a hazard is innocuous is likely even more true when the ill effect is delayed for many years, such as exposure to a carcinogen.

The second thing that Heinrich's accident triangle tells us is that if we are able to identify near misses, and correct them, we can prevent serious injuries and illnesses from occurring. Rather than only looking at fatality accidents, we should be looking at where near misses occur and correcting hazards that have been identified at the bottom of the triangle. This is a basic premise of safety management. Consider how many near misses must have occurred prior to each fatality reported by BLS, NFPA, or the NLEOMF. How many of these fatalities might have been prevented through identifying and correcting these early indicators?

Accidents are only prevented if these near misses are recognized and addressed.

It should be noted that many safety professionals prefer to use the term "incident" rather than "accident" for several reasons. First, "incident" refers to events which result in an injury as well as events which are near misses, whereas "accident" is often thought of as referring to only the events that cause injury. Second, the word "accident" is generally defined as an "unforeseen and unintended event," which implies that the event was not preventable. This concept is counter to the premise that these events can, and should be, prevented. Emergency managers also use the term "incident" to describe an event in which an emergency response is activated, and this could be anything from a vehicle crash to a mass casualty active shooter event to an earthquake. Using the term "incident" for both an employee injury and a major disaster would add to confusion in this book, so with apologies to my colleagues in the safety field, I will use the term "accident" to refer to events that result in employee injuries and illnesses as well as near misses, and the term "incident" to refer to events that require an emergency response.

The idea that an accident is an unintended an unforeseen event is an unfortunate one. In fact, most accidents are entirely preventable if there is a process in place to identify hazards and take corrective measures to prevent them.

Traditionally, a hierarchy of controls is used in prevention of accidents (Figure 1.3).

The first option in the hierarchy of controls is elimination. This is an effective control, because if the hazard is eliminated, it is no longer present and can no longer cause an accident.

The second tier of options on the hierarchy of controls is substitution. The hazard can be substituted with something that is intended to be less hazardous. This is an effective control, although it is possible that the substitute has its own hazards. If a substitute is relatively uncharacterized, as is common with new technology, it is entirely possible that the control could pose greater danger than the original hazard. Therefore, substitution is not as effective of a control as eliminating the hazard.

The third option on the hierarchy of controls is engineering, which generally involves creating a barrier between the hazard and the person who is exposed to the hazard. It is possible to engineer out the hazard by enclosing it, such as

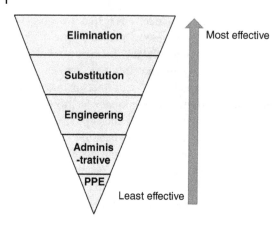

Most effective

Least effective

Figure 1.3 The hierarchy of hazard controls.

installing a guard over a moving part to prevent an employee from getting caught on it, using ventilation to reduce an employee's exposure to a hazardous chemical, or installing a muffler on a vehicle to reduce noise levels. The hazard is still present, but an employee can work around it without inadvertently being exposed to it. This is an effective control when it is feasible.

The fourth option is administrative controls. Administrative controls rely on the employee taking specific actions to prevent exposure to the hazard. Types of administrative controls can include following a procedure, training, or posting warning signs. These controls can generally be implemented quickly and are less costly than engineering controls. However, they rely on human beings to act in a specific manner 100% of the time for the control to work. Human beings, by nature, may be tempted to take short cuts in order to achieve a work goal, or to ignore a safety procedure if they think they cannot achieve their goal in any other way. Since accidents are rare, normalization of deviance can set in and ignoring safety procedures can become commonplace. Humans may also get sick or become distracted, and then may be not able to focus fully on the job at hand. Sometimes they even just make a mistake. Human beings – and this includes all of us – are not infallible. We are all capable of making a human error, even in the presence of a known hazard. Since administrative controls rely on human beings to follow them 100%, and humans are capable of making mistakes, administrative controls are not foolproof. Even the best employee who is fully committed to following safety procedures can inadvertently make such an error. However, if the hazard is such that elimination, substitution, or engineering controls are not options, we have to rely on administrative controls.

Last on the hierarchy is personal protective equipment, or PPE. PPE is the last line of defense against a hazard. Similar to engineering controls, PPE works by creating a barrier between the hazard and the worker but the barrier is physically on the worker's body. There is not a lot of room for failure if the PPE does not work as intended. PPE must be properly selected, so that it is appropriate for the hazard that the worker is exposed to. For example, workers may need to wear chemical protective gloves when working with chemicals, and the glove must be made of a material that cannot react with these chemicals. For example, I once worked in a manufacturing plant when a process change was made to replace a freon product with an alternative that was not an ozone depleter. This product was thought to be safer for the environment, but very little was known about health effects in humans. Almost immediately, the workers in that area reported that they were feeling sick when they used the chemical, and their gloves were dissolving: The old gloves were not resistant to the new chemical. If gloves dissolve, clearly, they are not providing protection. Sometimes the reaction is less visible, and the chemical reaction with the glove may result in pores in the glove that are not obvious rather than fully dissolving it. The workers wearing the gloves think that they are being protected, when in fact, the chemical is leaching inside the glove and getting trapped behind the glove barrier next to the skin. In this case, wearing gloves provides a false sense of security while actually creating a greater hazard.

To illustrate the hierarchy, let us consider a fire hazard that involves sensitive electronic equipment. It is protected by a halon extinguishing system. If the system is activated, the halon will displace oxygen, extinguish the fire, and protect the electronics. However, the sudden displacement of oxygen is quite hazardous for any living creature in the room.

If the electronics are moved, or eliminated, there is no longer a risk of fire and the halon system is not needed. All human beings in the area can rest assured that the oxygen they are breathing will remain at sufficient levels to support life.

However, eliminating electronic systems is not always an option for most businesses. Even if the business elects to pursue cloud computing rather than housing the electronics on site, the hazard is simply transferred to another business or location where the computing storage is housed.

Substitution is next on the hierarchy. Water extinguisher systems do not displace oxygen, and in this respect, are safer for workers. If water is substituted for the halon system, workers will get wet if the system activates. They may get cold, and they may slip on the wet floor as they evacuate. Hazards are still present, but these outcomes are less severe than not breathing.

Water, however, is hazardous to the sensitive electronics, so operations needs preclude selecting this option.

Moving down the hierarchy takes us to engineering controls. The electronics can be placed in fire resistant containers, so that if one does catch on fire, it will not spread. However, this would eliminate air flow, and could cause the equipment to overheat.

Administrative controls are the next option. Rooms with halon extinguishing systems should have signage to warn people of the hazard. Employees who enter these rooms need to be trained on the hazards of halon systems, how to determine when one is about to activate, and what to do if it does activate. In the event that the halon system discharges when someone is in the room, hopefully, they will remember the procedures they have been trained on and follow them.

Last is PPE. A requirement could be made that any employee working in the room wear oxygen-supplying respirators, such as air line respirators or self-contained breathing apparatus (SCBAs). Workers may think this is over kill, especially if they commonly work in this room and have not experienced a halon discharge. Use of respiratory protection devices is cumbersome and uncomfortable, so if the hazard does not seem serious, employees are unlikely to wear them 100% of the time that they work in the room. If respirators are not fitted and worn correctly, they do not provide adequate protection. A more common solution is to place escape-only respirators in rooms with halon systems. Workers must be trained on use of the escape-only respirators. They must remember where they are located. Workers must be able to operate the escape respirator in situations where it is hard to see or breathe. Lastly, escape respirators must be inspected and maintained so that they are functional when the halon system activates and workers inside the room need to escape.

Managing work needs, hazards in the workplace, and selection of options from the hierarchy of controls must be continuously balanced in day-to-day occupational health and safety programs. The same balance occurs in emergency response.

Decisions about routine hazards faced by police officers, firefighters, or nontraditional responders can be based on thorough analysis and input from management and employees, just as it is done in industry. In the early phases of a large incident, especially one that is rapidly changing or is not a routine response, these decisions must be made quickly, without the benefit of a lengthy analysis and often before sufficient resources can be made available. Nevertheless, the same principles of hazard prevention and control apply, and should be used in a well-organized response.

An understanding of hazards that emergency responders face, whether in a routine response by trained emergency responders or a large-scale disaster such as 9/11 or Deepwater Horizon that involves non-traditional responders with various professional backgrounds and volunteers can help with decision-making in the next event.

1.7 Safety Management in Incident Response

The National Incident Management System (NIMS), first adopted by the Federal Emergency Management Administration (FEMA) in 2004 in response to the 9/11 terrorist attacks and updated in 2008 and 2017, provides a template for the management of incidents regardless of scope or size, from a local fire or law enforcement response up to a large-scale incident such as the Deepwater Horizon disaster. It is scalable and flexible, and is designed to address an "All-Hazards" approach to incidents. It provides a Common Operating Picture (COP) and interoperability, to ensure that personnel from different agencies or employers can come together when an incident occurs, and work together efficiently to manage the response. It is intended to be used by all stakeholders including emergency responders and emergency management personnel, nongovernmental organizations (NGOs) such as faith-based and community-based groups, and the private sector as well as elected and appointed officials.

Homeland Security Presidential Directive 5 (HSPD 5) required that all Federal departments and agencies adopt NIMS, and that they make adoption of NIMS as a requirement for providing Federal preparedness assistance through grants, contracts, or other activities. Other organizations adopt NIMS because they recognize the value of participating in a uniform and interoperable system in the event of an emergency incident or planned event.

Industries that are covered by regulations that include emergency response planning requirements, such as those covered by the Occupational Safety and Health (OSHA)'s Process Safety Management Standard, the Federal Railroad Administration (FRA), the Federal Aviation Administration (FAA), and others, are required to work with local emergency responders to jointly plan and prepare to respond to an incident. Local emergency response agencies can, and often do, encourage private entities that are subject to these requirements to adopt NIMS in order to facilitate an effective interemployer response. Other businesses choose to adopt it simply because it makes good business sense.

NIMS covers resource management, command and control, and communications and information management. The Incident Command System (ICS), Emergency Operations Centers (EOCs), Multiagency Coordination Groups (MAC groups), and the Joint Information System (JIS) are components of command and control. ICS is a common organizational approach to incident response, and can be used whether responding to a natural hazard, a technical or "man-made" hazard, or a planned event. ICS uses a common organizational chart for a response, including an Incident Commander, Command Staff, and General Staff. The Command Staff includes the Safety Officer, the Public Information Officer, and a Liaison Officer (Figure 1.4) [28].

NIMS is based on Best Management Practices, and includes characteristics such as Management by Objectives, Manageable Span of Control (or, in other words, not having more people report to a single individual than that person can manage), and Chain of Command or Unity of Command (meaning that each person in the ICS structure only has one boss, and does not receive conflicting direction from multiple individuals). Having the Safety Officer report directly to the Incident Commander as a member of the Command Staff is also based on best practice.

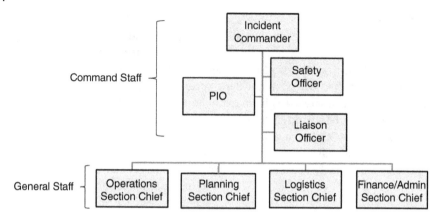

Figure 1.4 The Incident Command System Organization. Source: FEMA [28].

Studies on safety climate have found that management commitment to safety was correlated with organizations that had the strongest safety programs and lowest accident rates. Organizations with the best safety outcomes regard the safety program and safety managers as integral to the organization. Placing the safety function at the executive level reflects this thinking [29].

The position of the safety function within an organization sends a message to employees about the relative importance of safety to the organization. When the safety function reports to the highest level official in the organization, it ensures that safety has direct influence with executive management.

In many workplaces, the safety function may report through a variety of different departments, such as Human Resources, Risk Assessment, Legal, Facilities, Engineering, or even Operations. This can create an inherent conflict of interest, as the safety function supports safety for each of these departments, and may have to counsel employees and management on unsafe work practices, the need for controls that may require a financial investment, or even the need to stop work. If the safety manager, in the course of their job, negatively influences the meeting of department work demands, and the manager of that department is the one writing the safety manager's annual review, the safety manager may be hesitant to proactively enforce safety. This is an inherent conflict of interest.

The Federal Transit Administration (FTA) considered this conflict of interest when they were promulgating requirements for Public Transportation Agency Safety Plans, 49 CFR Part 673: Federal, state, and local agencies also send a message about the importance of safety in the language of the regulations that they write. FTA requires that public transit agencies include on staff a Chief Safety Officer that reports to the agency executive, and also an Accountable Executive. The Chief Safety Officer cannot have duties involving operational, financial, or other responsibilities as that may create a conflict with safety responsibilities [30]. FTA, in creating this requirement, acknowledges the importance of having the safety function reporting to the highest levels of management in reducing accidents and maintaining the safety of both passengers and employees.

Likewise, in placing the Safety Officer in the Command Staff, reporting directly to the Incident Commander, FEMA has demonstrated their view on the importance of the safety function in incident response.

FEMA enhanced the role of safety in incident command in the 2017 refresh of NIMS, and added language on the use of Assistant Safety Officers in complex incidents [28].

Unified Command may be used when multiple agencies or jurisdictions jointly work on a response, and Incident Commanders from each organization come together to jointly manage the incident. When Unified Command is used, there is a single safety officer who is responsible for the safety of all responders regardless of who the safety officer is employed by. The individual fulfilling the role of Safety Officer can change over the course of the incident. In a passenger rail incident, for example, the fire department "owns" the initial stages of the incident until the life safety response is complete, and the safety officer is a member of the fire department with expertise in fire operations. Once the life safety response concludes, law enforcement takes the lead in Unified Command while police conduct an investigation, and the safety officer must have expertise in law enforcement safety. After law enforcement concludes their investigation, the rail agency takes over the response to conduct a rail accident investigation, and the safety officer needs expertise in rail response. However, police, fire, and rail have roles in each stage of the incident regardless of which agency leads that part of the response, and face similar hazards that they each may or may not be familiar with. The rail safety officer must be able to provide information on evolving rail environment hazards to fire and police responders at each phase of the incident, and the fire safety officer may recognize life safety hazards even after the primary fire response has demobilized. Safety representatives from each agency need to work together.

In any multiagency or multiemployer response, whether it is transit related, involves a plant subject to the Process Safety Management rule, or any other operation, there are hazards unique to the operation which may impact the safety of responders. Safety representatives from these companies or operations have unique expertise on these hazards that emergency responders may be less familiar with, and need to coordinate with the Safety Officer to ensure that All Hazards are recognized and addressed. These individuals should be assigned as Assistant Safety Officers who support the Safety Officer in best protecting all responders.

The Safety Officer may also choose to bring in Assistant Safety Officers with unique expertise if it is needed for the response.

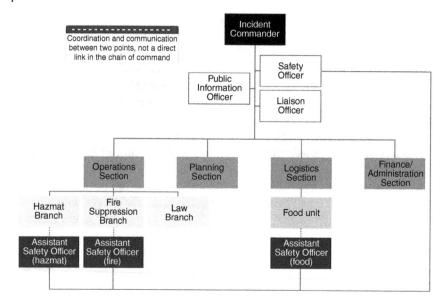

Figure 1.5 Example for use of Assistant Safety Officers in Incident Command. Source: FEMA [28].

Assistant Safety Officers can be assigned to work on scene with individual branches, although they maintain a direct reporting relationship to the Safety Officer (Figure 1.5). Safety personnel with specific expertise may also support the response as assigned technical specialists who support the Safety Officer, Assistant Safety Officer, or others in the ICS.

1.8 Safety Officer Qualifications

Incident Commanders hold responsibility (and liability) for the entirety of the incident response and the health and safety of responders. Incident Commanders rely on their Safety Officer, and those that support the Safety Officer, to guide them and minimize any liability they may incur for hazards that responders face. A knowledgeable and effective Safety Officer is a crucial resource to the Incident Commander as well as all responders (Figure 1.6).

How can an Incident Commander judge the competency of their Safety Officer? The 2017 NIMS refresh requires that jurisdictions qualify, certify, and credential personnel, and has developed a Safety Officer Task Book as a guide. This is a performance-based approach. Evaluation criteria includes competencies in safety management, such as complying with relevant health and safety requirements and

Figure 1.6 Incident Commanders must rely on their Safety Officer to provide knowledgeable support to keep all responders safe and minimize liability. Source: Reproduced with kind permission of Bobbie J. Lange.

recognizing, communicating, and mitigating risk of hazards. Additionally, competencies specific to incident response must be demonstrated, such as being able to follow protocol for communicating with the Documentation Unit and following processes for requesting resources. This position requires strong knowledge of safety management as well as experience and comfort working in the Incident Command System [31].

Many health and safety professionals who work in private industry or local, state, or federal government achieve professional certification, such as Certified Industrial Hygienist (CIH), Certified Safety Professional (CSP), or others (Table 1.5). These certifications are rigorous to obtain, require ongoing continuing education, and include adherence to codes of ethics. Persons with this level of expertise are very valuable to an Incident Commander when they can work effectively within an Incident Command System. In incidents such as planned community events, or spill cleanup, individuals with professional safety experience make great safety officers.

Safety Officers can also be individuals who have an emergency response background, and this is the typical background of a Safety Officer in a fire or law enforcement response. Firefighters, for example, draw on their experience to identify and predict hazards on the fireground that someone with a professional safety background would miss. Law enforcement officers face hazards on a daily basis that many safety professionals have never experienced. When the incident is a fire, or an active shooter, emergency responders are appropriate safety officers.

Incident responders should expect that they will be exposed to traumatic experiences such as seeing, hearing, and smelling people with severe injuries or

Table 1.5 Professional certifications in the health and safety field.

Certification	Expertise	Requirements	Certifying body
Certified Industrial Hygienist (CIH)	Assessing and controlling risk from environmental (chemical, physical, biological), safety, and ergonomic hazards	• Four-year degree with minimum coursework in science-, math-, engineering- or science-based technology • Professional-level industrial hygiene experience • Professional references • Passing score on exam • Continuing education, including ethics	American Board of Industrial Hygiene (ABIH)
Certified Safety Professional (CSP)	Assessing worksites to determine safety risk, hazards, and controls	• Bachelor's degree • Four years of professional safety experience • Passing score on exam • Continuing education	Board of Certified Safety Professionals (BCSP)
Certified Hazardous Materials Manager (CHMM)	Manages or advises others on hazardous materials or situations	• Bachelor's degree • Four years of professional experience in hazardous materials management or related field • References • Passing score on exam • Continuing education	Institute of Hazardous Materials Management (IHMM)

(Continued)

Table 1.5 (Continued)

Certification	Expertise	Requirements	Certifying body
Certified Marine Chemist (CMC)	Determining whether work and entry into confined spaces on marine vessels and in shipyards can be conducted safely	• Bachelor's degree with minimum coursework in chemistry and industrial hygiene • Completion of approved Marine Chemist training curriculum • Completion of a defined trainee program • Three years of experience including laboratory or similar work, and full time employment in marine construction or repair or acceptable marine industrial environment • Flammable cryogenic liquid carrier endorsement • References • Personal thesis • Interview with the Board • Ongoing recertification requirements, including physical and mental evaluation	National Fire Protection Association (NFPA) Marine Chemist Qualification Board
Certified Professional Ergonomist (CPE)	Human factors and ergonomics	• Bachelor's degree meeting ergonomic core competencies • Three year's work experience in ergonomics • Passing score on exam	Board of Certification in Professional Ergonomics (BCPE)

fatalities. Due to their experience, emergency responders are generally much more emotionally prepared to process this type of trauma at an incident scene than safety professionals who spend most of their careers trying to prevent these types of injuries from happening. When I worked in the safety department at our local transit authority, I had to occasionally respond to train accidents. My coworkers provided some good advice: "Try to take your time getting to the scene, so that the blood and guts are cleaned up by the time you get there." This was not hard to do, given traffic in the Seattle area, and the efficiency of our local fire departments.

When I responded to my first accident, I checked in with the transit police officers who had also responded, and asked if this had been a fatality or whether the victim had been transported (the answer to this question would tell me how many phone calls I had to make). "He was transported," I was told, "but he won't make it."

"Did the fire department tell you that?" I asked.

"No," our Seargent said, "but you know when the blood is that orange-y color they aren't going to survive." I was surprised, and a bit horrified, to think of how many similar incidents my law enforcement colleagues had experienced such they knew this. Sure enough, they were right, and the victim died at the hospital.

The experience that professional responders gain over time helps them maintain good judgment and cognitive processing during the event better than someone who is not experienced in processing this level of trauma. Decision-making is less likely to be impacted. However, safety personnel with professional certifications have greater experience and knowledge of safety principles and regulatory requirements than personnel who have not spent careers managing and supporting workplace safety. There are pros and cons to selecting safety officers of either background, but when they work together, they can best contribute to protecting the safety of all responders in an incident. Individuals with either background can fill positions of Safety Officer or Assistant Safety Officer. Each brings different strengths and complementary skills to the position. Given the inherent hazards in emergency response to both career professionals and those nontraditional responders who step up in a crisis, an effective Safety Officer is a critical resource. The ideal Safety Officer is one who is skilled in both incident response and safety management, and is emotionally equipped to work in an austere, changing environment.

1.9 Summary

Emergency responders, including firefighters, law enforcement officers, and emergency medical technicians, face numerous hazards in their work environment. The degree of hazard is reflected in reported injuries and fatalities.

Emergency responders also face long-term health impacts, including cancer. When a large-scale emergency occurs, and personnel resources are insufficient to meet the needs of the response, nontraditional responders step in. These nontraditional responders, such as those that participated in the 9/11 response and Deepwater Horizon disaster response also face long-term health impacts. The environmental hazards that responders are exposed to are often poorly understood, and we are continuing to learn more about the nature and degree of these exposure risks. Regardless, responders must be protected from these known and potential hazards using methods reflected in the traditional hierarchy of hazard controls.

A Safety Officer who serves within an Incident Command System is responsible for the safety of all personnel involved in the response. To be effective, a Safety Officer must be able to function effectively within this management system, make good decisions in a challenging and changing work environment, and have a strong working knowledge of occupational health and safety. This book is intended for Safety Officers who come from both safety and emergency response backgrounds, those who support the Safety Officer as emergency managers, organizational, corporate, and operations safety personnel, Assistant Safety Officers, Technical Specialists, and anyone who works with a Safety Officer in an Incident Command System.

References

1 Crane, M.A., Levy-Carrick, N.C., Crowley, L. et al. (2014). The response to September 11: a disaster case study. *Annals of Global Health* 80: 320–331.

2 NIOSH (2011). *Deepwater Horizon Roster Summary Report*. DHHS (NIOSH) publication no. 2011-175.

3 NIOSH (2011). *Lessons Learned from the Deepwater Horizon Response*.

4 NIOSH (2011). *Deepwater Horizon Incident Response Recordable Injury & Illness Data, April 22, 2010 to July 12, 2010*.

5 NIOSH (2011). *Report of Deepwater Horizon Response/Unified Area Command Illness and Injury Data (April 23–July 27, 2010)*.

6 King, B.S. and Gibbins, J.D. (2011). *Health Hazard Evaluation of Deepwater Horizon Response Workers*. Health hazard evaluation report, HETA 2010-0115 & 2010-0129-3138 (August 2011).

7 Pittman, C. (2013). Divers say they still suffer ailments from 2010 BP oil spill. *Tampa Bay Times* ((26 May 2013)).

8 Anderson, S.E., Franko, J., Lukomska, E.W.A., and Meade, B.J. (2011). Potential immunotoxicological health effects following exposure to COREXIT 9500A

during cleanup of the Deepwater Horizon oil spill. *Journal of Toxicology and Environmental Response Part A* 74 (21): 1419–1430.

9 Krajnak, K., Kan, H., Waugh, S. et al. (2011). Acute effects of COREXIT EC9500A on cardiovascular functions in rats. *Journal of Toxicology and Environmental Response Part A* 74 (21): 1397–1404.

10 Sriram, K., Lin, G.X., Jefferson, A.M. et al. (2011). Neurotoxicity following acute inhalation exposure to the oil dispersant COREXIT EC9500A. *Journal of Toxicology and Environmental Response Part A* 74 (21): 1405–1418.

11 Roberts, J.R., Reynolds, J.S., Thompson, J.A. et al. (2011). Pulmonary effects after acute inhalation of oil dispersant (COREXIT EC9500A) in rats. *Journal of Toxicology and Environmental Response Part A* 74 (21): 1381–1396.

12 Kwok, R.K., Engel, L.S., Miller, A.K. et al. (2017). The GuLF STUDY: a prospective study of persons involved in the Deepwater Horizon oil spill response and clean-up. *Environmental Health Perspectives* 125 (4): 570–578.

13 Fahy, R.F., LeBlanc, P.R., and Molis, J.L. (2017). *Firefighter fatalities in the United States – 2016*. NFPA No. FFD10. National Fire Protection Association https://www.nfpa.org/-/media/Files/News-and-Research/Fire-statistics-and-reports/Emergency-responders/Old-FFF-and-FF-Injuries/2017FFF.ashx (accessed 30 March 2020).

14 Haynes, H.J.G. and Molis, J.L. (2017). *United States firefighter injuries – 2016*. National Fire Protection Association https://www.nfpa.org/-/media/Files/News-and-Research/Fire-statistics-and-reports/Emergency-responders/Old-FFF-and-FF-Injuries/FirefighterInjuries2016.ashx (accessed 13 March 2020).

15 Violanti, J.M., Hartley, T.A., Gu, J.K. et al. (2013). Life expectancy in police officers: a comparison with the US general population. *International Journal of Emergency Mental Health and Human Resilience* 15 (4): 217–228.

16 Kuhns, J.B., Maquire, E.R., and Leach, N.R. (2015). *Health, Safety and Wellness Program Case Studies in Law Enforcement*. Washington, DC: Office of Community Oriented Policing Services.

17 International Association of Chiefs of Police (2017). *Breaking the Silence on Law Enforcement Studies: IACP National Symposium on Law Enforcement Officer Suicide and Mental Health*. Washington, DC: Office of Community Oriented Policing Services.

18 International Agency for Research on Cancer (IARC), World Health Organization (2006). *Monographs on the Evaluation of Carcinogenic Risks to Humans: Volume 98, Painting, Firefighting and Shiftwork*. Lyon, France: IARC.

19 Daniels, R.D., Kubale, T.L., Yiin, J.H. et al. (2014). Mortality and cancer incidence in a pooled cohort of US firefighters from San Francisco, Chicago, and Philadelphia (1950–2009). *Occupational and Environmental Medicine* 71: 388–397.

20 Daniels, R.D., Bertke, S., Dahm, M.M. et al. (2015). Exposure-response relationships for select cancer and non-cancer health outcomes in a cohort of US firefighters from San Francisco. *Chicago and Philadelphia Occupational and Environmental Medicine* 72 (10): 699–706.

21 Firefighter Cancer Registry Act of 2018.

22 Hanahan, D. and Weinberg, R. (2000). The hallmarks of cancer. *Cell* 100: 57–70.

23 Markowitz, S.B., Levin, S.M., Miller, A., and Morabia, A. (2013). Asbestos, asbestosis, smoking, and lung cancer. *New Findings from the North American Insulator Cohort American Journal of Respiratory and Critical Care Medicine* 188 (1): 90–96.

24 Bogaards, J.J.P., Van Ommen, B., Falke, H.E. et al. (1990). Glutathione S-transferase subunit induction patterns of Brussels sprouts, allyl isothiocyanate and goitrin in rat liver and small intestinal mucosa: a new approach for the identification of inducing xenobiotics. *Food and Chemical Toxicology* 28 (2): 81–88.

25 Goyal, A., Terry, M.B., and Siegel, A.B. (2013). Serum antioxidant nutrients, vitamin A, ad mortality in US Adults. *Cancer Epidemiology Biomarkers and Prevention* 22 (12): 2202–2211.

26 International Agency for Research on Cancer, World Health Organization (2006). *Preamble IARC Monographs on the Evaluations of Carcinogenic Risks to Humans.*

27 Heinrich, H.W. (1931). *Industrial Accident Prevention: A Scientific Approach.* McGraw Hill Book Company.

28 FEMA (2017). *The National Incident Management System*, 3e.

29 Zohar, D. (1980). Safety climate in industrial organizations: theoretical and applied implications. *Journal of Applied Psychology* 65 (1): 96–102.

30 Department of Transportation, Federal Transit Administration (2018). 49 CFR Part 673, Public Transportation Agency Safety Plan Preamble. *Federal Register* 83 (139): 34418–34468.

31 FEMA (2017). *National Qualification System (NQS) Position Task Book for the Position of Safety Officer.*

2

Applicability of Safety Regulations in Emergency Response

2.1 The Occupational Safety and Health Act

On 29 December 1970, President Richard M. Nixon signed the Williams-Steiger Occupational Safety and Health (OSH) Act into law. This law established the Occupational Safety and Health Administration (OSHA), the National Institute of Occupational Safety and Health (NIOSH), and the Occupational Safety and Health Review Commission (OSHRC). This period of time saw historic improvements in health and safety protections. Just a few weeks earlier, on 2 December 1970, President Nixon had officially established the Environmental Protection Agency (EPA).

The OSHA administration was established on 28 April 1971 under the Department of Labor. OSHA has the authority to promulgate laws on workplace safety and health and to enforce these laws through the issuance of citations and penalties. Initially, OSHA laws applied only to workers in the private sector. Federal, state, and local employers were not subject to OSHA laws and employees working for public employers were not protected by workplace safety regulations. In 1980, President Jimmy Carter signed Executive Order 12196, which extended OSHA protections to Federal Employees. However, to this day OSHA protections still do not cover state and local employees in the states where OSHA has jurisdiction.

OSHA has established horizontal standards within the Code of Federal Regulations (CFR) in 29 CFR 1910. Horizontal regulations apply to all workplaces, unless covered by a vertical standard. Vertical standards apply to specific industries, such as construction (29 CFR 1926) and Maritime (Shipyards in 29 CFR 1915, Marine Terminals in 29 CFR 1917, Longshoring in 29 CFR 1918, and Gear Certification in 29 CFR 1919). Vertical standards contain requirements unique to an industry; however, depending upon the industry and situation, horizontal standards may also apply.

OSHA offers consultation services to employers in addition to its regulatory role. OSHA consultation services are completely separate from the enforcement

Health and Safety in Emergency Management and Response, First Edition. Dana L. Stahl.
© 2021 John Wiley & Sons, Inc. Published 2021 by John Wiley & Sons, Inc.

branch, and employers who participate in the OSHA consultation program are not issued citations as long as they correct any hazards identified through the consultation process.

The OSH Act also established the National Institute of Occupational Safety and Health (NIOSH) as a research agency focused on the study of worker safety and health. NIOSH is part of the US Centers for Disease Control and Prevention (CDC) and develops Criteria for Recommended Standards, which are intended to provide a basis for OSHA to use in developing workplace safety and health regulations. These documents include a review of available scientific and technical information on hazards and risks, and methods of control. NIOSH also writes Special Hazard Reviews and Occupational Hazard Assessments to complement NIOSH recommendations for standards, conducts Health Hazard Evaluations (HHEs) of new and recurring workplace health hazards, issues hazard alerts, certifies respiratory protection equipment, and manages initiatives such as Prevention through Design (PtD) to reduce occupational injuries, illnesses, and fatalities. NIOSH has provided assistance during large disasters such as 9/11, Hurricane Katrina, and the Deepwater Horizon disaster by providing technical and humanitarian assistance, and manages the World Trade Center Health Program and the Fire Fighter Cancer Registry.

The third agency established under the OSH Act, OSHRC, reviews and issues decisions when employers contest citations and penalties resulting from OSHA inspections.

OSHA's initial workplace standards were adopted in 1971 and 1972, and were based on existing national consensus standards such as those developed by the American National Standards Institute (ANSI), the National Fire Protection Association (NFPA), American Society for Testing and Materials (ASTM), and others.

Additional standards have been adopted since then, and continue to be adopted. OSHA follows a process that starts with publication of a Notice of Proposed Rulemaking, followed by development of the rule, publication of a proposed rule followed by a public comment period, and publication of the Final Rule. This is a lengthy process, and many years can pass between the first Notice of Proposed Rulemaking and publication of the Final Rule. A rule may also be withdrawn at any point during this process. Once a rule is published, industry groups or others can challenge the rule through the judicial process. This can result in modification or even withdrawal of the rule. Most rules that OSHA publishes result in a legal challenge, which OSHA must use resources to defend. As a result, implementation of a new OSHA regulation is fairly rare. NIOSH has published many more Criteria for a Recommended Standard documents than OSHA has published regulations.

Employers and employees can ask for clarification when the requirements of a rule are not clear. OSHA publishes Letters of Interpretation that clarify their expectations on how an employer should comply with the rule.

Many workplace hazards are not specifically covered by an OSHA rule. OSHA can issue citations for such hazards under the General Duty Clause, or Section 5(a)(1) of the OSH Act, which states that

(a) Each Employer
(1) Shall furnish to each of his employees' employment and a place of employment which are free from recognized hazards that are causing or are likely to cause death or serious physical harm to his employees.

The term "recognized hazard" means that an employer knows, or should know, that the hazard exists. If employees, or employees in the same industry or who do similar work, have been harmed by the hazard, for example, and employer should know that the hazard could harm employees. Knowledge of hazard is also presumed if published information acknowledges the hazard. For example, equipment manufacturers provide owner's manuals that include information about how the equipment should and should not be used, as well as general safety information. If employees use the equipment in a manner that is not consistent with the directions in the owner's manual, this would be considered a failure to protect employees from a recognized hazard, even if that specific piece of equipment is not covered by an OSHA standard. Similarly, published consensus standards may serve as documentation that a hazard is recognized.

2.2 State Plan States and Territories

States and Territories can opt to operate their own workplace safety and health programs. These plans must be approved by OSHA. Currently OSHA recognizes 26 state plans in addition to plans operated in Puerto Rico and the Virgin Islands (Figure 2.1, Table 2.1). State plans are monitored by OSHA, and any regulations adopted by state plans must be at least as effective as OSHA's regulations in protecting workers.[1] State plans cover private employers as well as state and local government employers. Federal workers located in state plan states are covered by OSHA rather than the state plan.

Enforcement officers in state plan states are state employees, and employed by the department that manages the state plan rather than by OSHA.

States can choose to adopt Federal OSHA regulations by reference, but enforce them through the state agency, or they can write their own regulations. Five states, Connecticut, Illinois, Maine, New Jersey, and New York, plus the Virgin Islands,

---

1 http://www.osha.gov/dcsp/osp (accessed 3 October 2018).

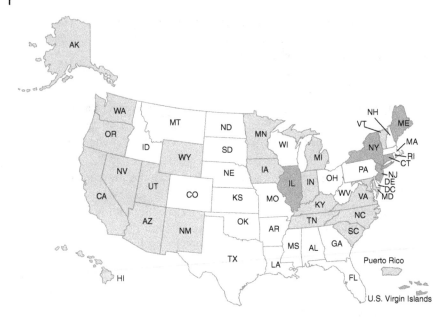

Figure 2.1 28 states and territories operate under approved state plans. Source: http://www.osha.gov/dcsp/osp (accessed 3 October 2018).

have state plans that cover state and local employees only, while private employers continue to be subject to federal OSHA laws and enforcement.

OSHA allows states to promulgate their own rules as long as they are "at least as effective as" the rules set by OSHA. Many states, such as Oregon and Minnesota, incorporate selected OSHA rules by reference but include state-specific requirements. They also write state-specific standards that cover hazards not addressed in by OSHA.

In some states, state law prohibits a straight adoption of Federal CFRs, and in these states, the state health and safety agency must follow the state rulemaking process to enact laws that are "at least as effective as" OSHA regulations. California and Washington have written their own rules, which are codified within their state regulations. When OSHA adopts a new standard, the state must in turn adopt a standard that is at least as effective under state rulemaking requirements.

Often, state plan rules are more protective for workers than Federal OSHA rules, and employers subject to state plan rules must ensure that they are familiar with, and comply with, their state's rules. For example, many state plan states require

Table 2.1 States with approved OSHA state plans.

State	Date of initial approval	Employers Covered
Alaska	10 August 1973	State, local, private
Arizona	5 November 1974	State, local, private
California	1 May 1973	State, local, private
Connecticut	3 November 1978	State and local
Hawaii	4 January 1974	State, local, private
Illinois	1 September 2009	State and local
Indiana	6 March 1974	State, local, private
Iowa	20 July 1973	State, local, private
Kentucky	31 July 1973	State, local, private
Maine	5 August 2015	State and local
Maryland	5 July 1973	State, local, private
Michigan	3 October 1973	State, local, private
Minnesota	8 June 1975	State, local, private
Nevada	4 January 1974	State, local, private
New Jersey	11 January 2001	State and local
New Mexico	10 December 1975	State, local, private
New York	1 June 1984	State and local
North Carolina	1 February 1973	State, local, private
Oregon	28 December 1972	State, local, private
Puerto Rico	30 August 1997	State, local, private
South Carolina	6 December 1972	State, local, private
Tennessee	5 July 1973	State, local, private
Utah	10 January 1973	State, local, private
Vermont	16 October 1973	State, local, private
Virgin Islands	23 July 2003	State and local
Virginia	28 July 1976	State, local, private
Washington	26 January 1973	State, local, private
Wyoming	3 May 1974	State, local, private

Source: http://www.osha.gov/dcsp/osp (accessed 3 October 2018).

employers to establish management/labor safety committees and establish written Injury and Illness Prevention Programs (IIPPs) or Accident Prevention Programs (APPs), which are not required by Federal OSHA.

2.3 Tribes

Tribes in the United States are subject to OSHA law, as specified in 29 CFR 1975.4(b)(3), which states:

> Indians. The Williams-Steiger Act contains no special provisions with respect to different treatment in the case of Indians. It is well settled that under statutes of general application, such as the Williams-Steiger Act, Indians are treated as any other person, unless Congress provided for special treatment. "FPC v Tuscarora Indian Nation" 360 U.S. 99, 115–118 (1960), "Navajo tribe v N.L.R.B." 288 F 2d. 162, 164–165 (D.C. Cir. 1961) cert. den. 366 U.S. 928 (1961). Therefore, provided they otherwise come within this definition of the term "employer" as interpreted in this part, Indians and Indian tribes, whether on or off reservations, and non-Indians on reservations, will be treated as employers subject to the requirements of this Act [1].

OSHA referenced this regulation in an interpretation letter dated 25 March 1993, in response to a question about whether OSHA had jurisdiction over employees working in a reservation clinic. The letter from Roger A Clark, Directorate of Compliance Programs, clarified that OSHA had jurisdictional authority over the worksite and that the employer was required to follow OSHA Standards.

However, the interpretation of OSHA authority with respect to tribal employers has changed with time. An interpretation letter issued on 12 March 1998, in response to a question about OSHA jurisdiction at a tribally operated casino reflected court decisions that had been decided since the 1993 interpretation was issued. John B. Miles, Directorate of Compliance Programs, stated that the OSH Act applied to workplaces located on tribal lands and operated by tribal employers. However, he also wrote:

> The courts have, however, established some limited exceptions to the general applicability of the OSH Act to tribal enterprises. The OSH Act would apply to a tribal enterprise unless its application touched upon purely intramural matters (such as tribal membership, domestic relations and inheritance) or violated a treaty or unless the legislative history of the Federal statute or surrounding circumstances in its enactment indicated

that the statute was not to apply. In light of President Clinton's April 29, 1994 Memorandum, "Government-to-Government Relations With Native American Tribal Governments," we strive to assure that the agency's actions do not interfere in governmental functions which are integral to tribal sovereignty. Since the tribal enterprise in question (a casino) does not appear to involve purely intramural matters, OSHA has the authority to respond to complaints about corresponding working conditions [2].

As sovereign nations, it is understood that tribes have the authority to pass tribal occupational safety and health laws and provide occupational safety and health services through their own agencies and programs. Tribes may adopt Federal OSHA or state plan standards by reference, or they may develop their own workplace safety programs and standards. Relationships to OSHA or state plan agencies with regard to enforcement and the applicability of workplace safety laws may be established through agreements, and for this reason these relationships vary by tribe [3].

2.4 Safety Requirements in Fire Departments

Fire brigades that are established by private companies are subject to OSHA or state plan rules in all states. However, many municipal fire departments are not covered by OSHA rules. Firefighters who work for state and local agencies are not covered by OSHA rules in OSHA states. Fire departments that employ firefighters in state plan states are covered by state plan rules, although volunteer fire departments generally are not. 29 CFR 1975 excludes volunteers from OSHA coverage. Applicability of occupational safety and health rules to volunteers is dependent upon state rules, and this varies by state.

The one exception to this is for OSHA's rule on Hazardous Waste Operations and Emergency Response (HAZWOPER), 29 CFR 1910.120. This rule covers emergency response operations for releases of hazardous substances, in addition to clean up operations of hazardous waste sites. EPA's rule, 40 CFR Part 311, applies the requirements of 29 CFR 1910.120, HAZWOPER, to state and local employees in states that do not have a state plan approved by OSHA. EPA defines employees in this rule as "a compensated or non-compensated worker who is controlled by a State or local government". Therefore, regardless of the state, and regardless of whether they are in a paid or volunteer role, all firefighters who respond to hazardous materials releases must comply with the requirements of OSHA's HAZWOPER Standard. In OSHA States, the enforcement agency is EPA rather than OSHA.

Fire departments in state plan states that violate state plan occupational safety and health standards are subject to citations and fines. Examples of horizontal standards that are applicable to fire departments include Personal Protective Equipment (PPE), respiratory protection, blood-borne pathogens, hazard communication, and exposure to hazardous chemicals. Rules in the vertical standards for construction, such as trenching and shoring, may also apply.

Some states have issued vertical standards for firefighters:

- Washington State Chapter 296-305 Washington Administrative Code (WAC) covers full time, part time, paid firefighters, and unpaid volunteers. This standard includes requirements that are very specific to fire departments, such as sleeping areas, technical rescue, fire suppression, testing of fire service equipment, and sanitation, disinfection, cleaning and storage areas, and rules specific to wildland fire operations. The standard requires that fire departments appoint a Health and Safety Officer. It also points to other rules that have been promulgated by Washington's Department of Safety and Health (DOSH), such as confined space, blood-borne pathogens, respiratory protection and PPE, and hearing conservation, and specifically states that fire departments must comply with these rules.
- Michigan's General Industry Safety and Health Standard, Part 74, Fire Fighting (R 408.17401–R 408.17463) applies to municipal fire services, including full-time, part-time, paid, and volunteer firefighters. This standard specifically adopts several NFPA standards, such as NFPA 1971 (Standard for Protective Ensemble for Structural Firefighting) and NFPA 1982 (Personal Alert Safety System [PASS] for Fire Fighters) as well as Michigan OSHA (MIOSHA) standards on portable ladders, Personal Protective Equipment, automotive service operations, occupational noise exposure, respiratory protection, and medical services, and first aid.

The National Fire Protection Association (NFPA) is accredited as a Standards Developing Organization (SDO) by the American National Standards Institute (ANSI), and has published numerous consensus standards including NFPA 1500, Standard on Fire Department Occupational Safety, Health, and Wellness Programs. NFPA 1500 provides comprehensive minimum requirements for fire department health and safety programs, and incorporates requirements set forth by OSHA such as PPE selection, respiratory protection fit testing, and provision of hearing protection. NFPA 1500 also requires that fire departments establish an Occupational Health, Safety, and Wellness program, establish a safety committee, and appoint a Health and Safety Officer with sufficient resources to administer the program [4].

NFPA 1521, Standard for Fire Department Safety Officer Professional Qualifications, provides additional guidance on the Health and Safety Officer, a position that is responsible for the health, safety, and wellness program within a fire department, as well as for Incident Safety Officers who serve as a Safety Officer in an incident response. The Health and Safety Officer needs to have strong knowledge of health and safety standards, codes and safety management practices applicable to fire departments, and can come from either a safety management or a fire response background so long as other qualifications are met. A fire department should have several qualified Incident Safety Officers who can respond during various shifts, whereas a single Health and Safety Officer could be given overall responsibility for managing the overall program.

Incident Safety Officers come from a fire response background, and must meet additional requirements as a Fire Officer. The programs that the Health and Safety Officer develops support the Incident Safety Officers, and enable them to be most effective in a response [5].

As a consensus standard, NFPA 1500 is not necessarily a requirement. Jurisdictions can choose to adopt NFPA standards by incorporating them into local codes, and if adopted, NFPA 1500 would then be enforced by the local jurisdiction. When NFPA 1500 is not adopted as a local code, unions can negotiate that a fire department follow NFPA standards in labor contracts. If included in the contract, noncompliance with the standard would then be addressed through the grievance process.

When fire departments are subject to inspection by occupational health and safety agencies, elements of 1500 that are not addressed in the state occupational safety and health regulations could be cited under the General Duty Clause or the state equivalent as recognized hazards.

To summarize, the applicability of occupational health and safety in fire departments varies widely. Fire Departments in the United States range from having no requirement to comply with any laws on employee health and safety protection in OSHA states, to having to meet very specific requirements included in vertical standards in state plan states such as Washington and Michigan. Volunteers may or may not be covered by the same laws. Industry standards have been established but, again there is wide variability as to whether or not an individual fire department chooses to adopt or follow them.

2.5 Safety Requirements in Law Enforcement

Law enforcement personnel may work for local police departments, private companies, or Federal Agencies. Police officers in the private sector are always subject to OSHA protections.

Federal law enforcement agencies are covered by 29 CFR 1960, Basic Program Elements for Federal Employees OSHA. In addition to specifying that Federal employees are subject to applicable OSHA regulations and enforcement, 29 CFR 1960 requires that Federal agencies appoint Designated Agency Safety and Health Officials with the rank of Assistant Secretary or equivalent, and provided those in these positions with sufficient qualified staff and budget. The standard also requires training for safety and health specialists, employees with collateral safety and health duties, top management officials and supervisors, employees and representatives, and career development for safety and health specialists. Employees have the right to report unsafe or unhealthful working conditions, and agencies that receive these reports must follow up on them.

Many, if not most, police officers are city or county workers in local police departments. Police departments in OSHA states are not covered by occupational safety and health laws, while those in OSHA state plan states are covered by the individual state health and safety programs. Washington State, which has promulgated a vertical standard for firefighters, has not promulgated a similar vertical standard for police officers, although police work is addressed in other standards. However, several horizontal standards include provisions for law enforcement. For example, Washington's Standard on Occupational Exposure to Bloodborne Pathogens, Chapter 296-823 WAC, includes a section on handling criminal evidence that is contaminated with blood or Other Potentially Infectious Materials (OPIM) in a manner that protects personnel from blood-borne pathogens.

There are no consensus standards equivalent to NFPA 1500 for police departments. However, progress is beginning to be made in the development of industry guidelines for law enforcement.

In 2011, the Office of Community Oriented Policing Services (COPS) and the Bureau of Justice Assistance (BJA) formed the National Officer Safety and Wellness Group (OSWG) to bring attention for the safety and wellness needs of law enforcement officers. The OSWG includes representatives from law enforcement, federal agencies, and research who are working to create tools and resources to enhance safety and wellness among law enforcement agencies. Many of the tools produced to date focus on programs to prevent illnesses such as diabetes and heart disease, and safe driving, as these factor into a majority of line-of-duty fatalities. In addition, the group focuses on promotion of safety values and culture and development of health, safety, and wellness programs.

One publication produced by this group reviewed safety practices in several police departments, including the Fairfax County, Virginia Police Department. Virginia is a state plan state, so law enforcement officers are covered by occupational safety and health laws. This police department developed a safety officer program adapted from NIMS and NFPA 1500. The department established a health and safety officer position who reports to the Captain of Planning and Research, who in turn reports to the Chief of Police. The Fairfax program includes six supplemental (incident) safety officers who are available on-call as needed, although they also have other responsibilities. An important component of the program is that the safety officer is "rank neutral," which allows safety issues to trump rank. The case study noted that this is a unique program within police departments, and the Fairfax County Police Department had not identified similar programs upon which to base their program except for those in fire departments [6]. This program illustrates that best practices outlined in NFPA 1500 and used in fire departments can be extended to law enforcement agencies to improve officer safety and health.

2.6 Additional Federal Safety Regulations

Many Federal agencies adopt worker safety requirements into the regulations that they promulgate for the industries under their authority. These rules can have applicability to responders and recovery workers in events in which one of these agencies has oversight.

The Federal Railroad Administration, for example, includes rules for workplace safety in 49 CFR 214. This regulation covers Personal Protective Equipment (head, foot, and eye protection), fall protection, working over or adjacent to water, and scaffolding for bridge workers, and safety requirements for workers working on tracks and roadway worker protection. Part 227 specifies that OSHA rules apply when the hazard is not addressed by FRA. In addition, FRA has issued a rule on Occupational Noise Exposure for Railroad Operating Employees that is similar to OSHA's Occupational Noise Exposure rule (29 CFR 19010.98), but different enough that following OSHA's rule will not necessarily result in compliance with FRA's rule, and vice versa. In addition, FRA has issued 49 CFR 270.103, which requires that railroads adopt and fully implement a System Safety Program Plan that includes protections for railroad employees and contractors.

FTA's Public Agency Safety Plan rule (49 CFR Part 673) requires that transit operators develop and implement Safety Management Systems, which would incorporate occupational health and safety for transit workers [7]. The Federal Aviation Administration (FAA) also has requirements for Safety Management Systems [8], and the Department of Energy (DOE) has issued worker safety and health requirements for contractor activities at DOE sites in 10 CFR Part 851 which includes references to OSHA construction safety requirements for qualified and competent persons.

2.7 Safety Expectations in the National Preparedness Goal and Supporting Frameworks

Top level commitment to safety is critical to safety outcome in organizations [9]. One way to demonstrate top-level commitment is to include a written commitment to safety that establishes expectations in high-level documentation. The inclusion of worker health and safety, and environmental response as one of the Response Core Capabilities and Critical Tasks within the National Preparedness Goal illustrates the critical importance of worker safety in an incident response [10]. The National Response Framework (NRF) [11] and supporting documents identify critical elements to protect worker safety that include identifying, assessing, and mitigating worker health and safety hazards, as well as disseminating health and safety guidance and resources to response and recovery workers.

The NRF is one of five preparedness mission areas (Prevention, Preparation, Mitigation, Response, and Recovery) that provides strategy and doctrine on how the nation meets the National Preparedness Goal. The response function, as characterized in the NRF, includes actions to save lives, protect property and the environment, stabilize communities, and meet basic human needs following an incident. Response is a period in which work is time-sensitive, and decisions about work and safety must be made in an environment in which both time and other resources may be insufficient. Risk tolerance may be higher than in day-to-day work, thus the philosophy behind "risk a lot, save a lot" in order to meet these response goals. However, a risk balance must still be met, and a risk tolerance that tilts toward meeting incident goals at the expense of responder's health and safety can jeopardize the response. Highly trained response workers are a valuable resource, and if even one resource is lost due to an injury or worse, the lack of this resource will negatively impact the meeting of response goals.

Response is followed by Recovery, or the period after an incident response in which the community recovers and returns to normal (or a "new normal"). Risk tolerance is lower during recovery because resources become more available, and more time can be taken for decision-making. The strategy and doctrine for Recovery is covered in the National Disaster Recovery Framework (NDRF) [12] (Figure 2.2).

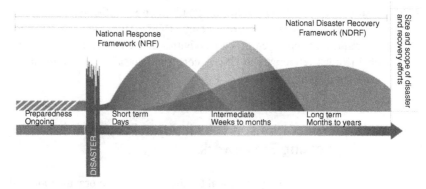

Figure 2.2 Continuum of response and recovery phases. Source: Department of Homeland Security [12].

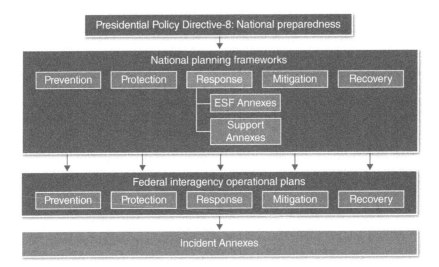

Figure 2.3 Organization of the National Response Framework and Federal Interagency Operational Plans (FIOP). Source: Department of Homeland Security [11].

Coordination of Federal Agencies is outlined in Emergency Support Functions (ESFs) for Response, and Recovery Support Functions (RSFs) for Recovery. Each ESF and RSF assigns Federal Departments and Agencies to the ESF or RSF as Coordinator, Primary Agency or Support Agencies. Support Annexes are similar, and apply to both response and recovery. ESF's, RSF's, and Support Annexes can be activated as necessary in a Federal response (Figure 2.3, Table 2.2).

2.8 OSHA, ESF #8, and the Worker Safety and Health Support Annex

Worker safety is addressed in ESF #8, the Public Health and Medical Services Annex. The Department of Labor is listed as a Support Agency in ESF #8. This ESF covers planning and coordination of Public Health and healthcare delivery. This includes functions such as movement of patients in an emergency, or providing assistance in surge capabilities including those services that augment public health, medical, behavioral, and veterinary functions with health professionals and pharmaceuticals. ESF #8 also disseminates public information on protective actions related to health or environmental threats, such as food and water safety. The Department of Health and Human Services is the ESF #8 Coordinator and Primary Agency. Core capabilities directly supported by this ESF are:

- Public Information and Warning: Public Health and Medical Information;
- Critical Transportation: Patient Movement;

Table 2.2 Emergency Support Functions supporting the National Response Framework and Recovery Support Functions supporting the National Disaster Recovery Framework [11, 12].

Emergency Support Functions	Support Annex	Recovery Support Functions
ESF #1 Transportation Annex	Critical Infrastructure and Key Resources	Community Planning and Capacity Building (CPBD) Recovery Support Function
ESF #2 Communications Annex	Financial Management	Economic Recovery Support Function
ESF #3 Public Works and Engineering Annex	International Coordination	Health and Social Services Recovery Support Function
ESF #4 Firefighting Annex	Private Sector Coordination	Housing Recovery Support Function
ESF #5 Information and Planning Annex	Public Affairs	Infrastructure Systems Recovery Support Function
ESF #6 Mass Care, Emergency Assistance, Temporary Housing and Human Services Annex	Tribal Relations	Natural and Cultural Resources Recovery Support Function
ESF #7 Logistics Annex	Volunteer and Donations Management	
ESF #8 Public Health and Medical Services Annex	Worker Safety and Health	
ESF #9 Search and Rescue Annex		
ESF #10 Oil and Hazardous Materials Response Annex		
ESF #11 Agriculture and Natural Resources Annex		
ESF #12 Energy Annex		
ESF #13 Public Safety and Security Annex		
ESF #14 Cross Sector Business and Infrastructure Annex		
ESF #15 External Affairs Annex		

- Environmental Response/Health and Safety;
- Fatality Management Services;
- Mass Care Services;
- Logistics and Supply Chain Management:
  - Health, Medical and Veterinary Equipment Supplies, and
  - Blood and Tissues;
- Public Health, Healthcare, and Emergency Medical Services:
  - Health Surveillance;
  - Medical Surge;
  - Patient Care;
  - Assessment of Public Health/Medical Needs;
  - Food Safety, Security, and Defense (in coordination with ESF #11);
  - Agriculture Safety and Security (in coordination with ESF #11);
  - Safety and Security of Drugs, Biologics, and Medical Devices;
  - All-Hazard Public Health and Medical Consultation, Technical Assistance, and Support;
  - Vector Control;
  - Public Health Aspects of Potable Water/Wastewater and Solid Waste Disposal;
  - Veterinary Medical Support.

The Department of Labor is assigned as the Support Agency for the Core capability of worker safety and health, and through OSHA supports ESF #8 as the Coordinating Agency for the Worker Safety and Health Support Annex. ESF #8 tasks the Department of Labor with providing personnel and management support, technical assistance, worker exposure assessment, and risk management via the Incident Command System. This includes many industrial hygiene functions, such as conducting exposure monitoring and sampling, analysis of samples, selection of Personal Protective Equipment (PPE), distribution of PPE and training, and conducting respirator fit testing. Department of Labor assistance also includes health monitoring and oversite of the site-specific safety and health plan [13].

Support Annexes, including the Worker Safety and Health Support Annex, support several or all ESFs. The Worker Safety and Health Support Annex assures that health and safety support is provided for both response and recovery workers. The annex describes the coordination mechanisms, policies, and processes for which this support is provided.

OSHA participates in all phases of emergency management, including pre-incident coordination, incident response, recovery, and post-incident follow-up. OSHA provides representatives to support the National Response Coordination Center (NRCC) and the Incident Management Planning Team (IMPT) at the national level, and provides support at the regional or field level by providing staff to coordinate support activities to the Regional Response

Coordination Center (RRCC) and the Joint Field Office (JFO). An Interagency Safety and Health Committee is established at the JFO, and chaired by the OSHA representative.

OSHA also coordinates the Worker Safety and Health Coordination Committee, which is comprised of OSHA representatives and cooperating agencies including the Department of Defense, Department of Energy, Department of Health and Human Services, Department of Homeland Security, and the EPA. This group meets regularly and conducts interagency exercises during the preplanning phase.

During Response and Recovery, OSHA and the Cooperating Agencies provide personnel to support the following activities:

- Worker Safety and Health Needs Assessment: This activity includes identifying and assessing health and safety hazards, and ensuring sources are available to meet resource needs to support worker safety and health. Technical expertise is provided, including industrial hygiene, occupational safety and health, engineering, and occupational medicine.
- Managing, developing and implementing a site-specific Health and Safety Plan (HASP). The HASP outlines basic health and safety requirements for response and recovery workers, and elements are typically integrated into Incident Action Plans (IAPs).
- Safety and Health Assessment, including identification, analysis and mitigation of safety and health hazards. This includes personal exposure monitoring for chemical, biological, and physical stressors. Noise, heat, cold, and ionizing radiation are specifically mentioned.
- Managing, monitoring, and/or providing technical advice and support to an incident PPE program, including selection, use, and decontamination. This includes respiratory protection and fit testing. Procurement of incident PPE is done in coordination with ESF #7 – Logistics Management and Resource Support.
- Data Management, including worker exposure data and accident and injury data such as the OSHA 300 log. OSHA facilitates data sharing among response and recovery organizations to identify trends.
- Training and Coordination: many OSHA regulations include a training component, and workers also are likely exposed to unique hazards in an incident response or recovery operation that they need to be aware of. OSHA coordinates and provides incident-specific training and safety and health communications. OSHA also provides technical assistance in development and distribution of informational materials.
- Medical Surveillance: Many OSHA regulations, such as those covering workers who are exposed to asbestos or lead, include a medical monitoring requirement.

Site-specific exposures may require medical or behavioral health support and follow-up.

OSHA and the cooperating agencies may support additional activities depending upon incident needs.

Notably, the annex specifically states that this support does not replace the responsibilities of employers to provide worker safety and health protections for their employees [14]. An employer's responsibility to protect their own workers does not cease despite the fact that an emergency has occurred. Rather, the Annex provides a safety net by ensuring that resources are available to conduct and support-needed safety functions to protect workers in the event that they are needed.

Employers and emergency managers can use the Worker Safety and Health Support Annex as a guide to planning and resourcing for safety within their own organizations during incident response and recovery.

The fact that OSHA is primarily a regulatory and enforcement agency adds complexity to the role of this agency in supporting a response. For many years OSHA described how the agency planned to fulfill its role in emergency response in their Safety and Health Guide Worker Protection: OSHA's Role During Response to Catastrophic Incidents Guide. This Guide noted that OSHA primarily played a support role during Pre-Planning and Response. Considering that Response is a crisis-management phase, the OSHA plan was to operate primarily in a support role, working cooperatively within the Incident Command System and responding directly to requests from employers and workers. Once the incident response moved to the Recovery phase and ceased operating in a crisis management mode, OSHA planned to continue to operate in a support role. However, at this time, OSHA also would resume an enforcement role, and initiate enforcement actions [15].

This approach was not without controversy. Although OSHA provides expertise and resources, employers may have some reluctance or hesitancy to work closely with a compliance agency. While OSHA communicated that they would not initiate enforcement during response, it remained possible that citations could be issued after the fact once the crisis management phase of the incident was complete. The threat of later enforcement may be an inhibiting factor to full cooperation during a response.

A criticism of this approach was that it failed to protect emergency response and recovery workers, who may be exposed to hazards such as mold, asbestos, and other contaminated materials without adequate protections. Employees who work for employers who do not provide personal protective equipment or training can get sick, which can be exacerbated by unhealthful living conditions during the response phase. OSHA is a small agency, and does not have sufficient funding to establish a response budget. Thus, any response support provided by OSHA must be balanced through a decrease in enforcement activities elsewhere. Lack of OSHA enforcement during response, and limited enforcement during recovery, results in a failure to protect workers. In turn, this allows employers to utilize practices that are ineffective in controlling hazards, or in a worst-case scenario, even abusive to employees [16].

OSHA has since updated their webpage to clarify that OSHA rules remain in effect during the response phase of an incident, and that that OSHA retains the ability to enforce them.[2]

2.9 Safety in State Emergency Management Plans

States and local governments that receive funding through the Homeland Security Grant Program (HSGP) or Emergency Management Performance Grant (EMPG) are required to maintain an Emergency Operations Plan (EOP). These plans must conform with formatting and information outlined in the Comprehensive Preparedness Guide (CPG) 101, version 2. Use of this guide is also encouraged for all organizations and tribal authorities to ensure that plans are developed in a consistent manner in relation to national plans and frameworks. The NIMS and the NRF recognize that incidents start and end at the local level, and when needs exceed local resources, assets from additional layers of government and private industry are incorporated. Therefore, plans need to be vertically integrated to ensure that all response levels have a common operational focus. State and local emergency plans that are modeled after national plans can easily integrate into these plans as an incident expands, later de-escalates, and portions of the response is demobilized.

However, states, tribes, and local jurisdictions and private sector organizations are unique, and government organization at this level does not necessarily reflect the organization of government at the Federal level. Therefore, the CPG recognizes that states, tribes, local government and the private sector need to develop EOPs that reflect their own organizational structures, resources, and capabilities. The EOP structure as presented in the CPG is a guideline, and each organization has leeway in developing their own EOP. As a result, some are structured very similarly to the National Response Framework, while others are more unique.

The CPG presents a traditional functional format as a guideline. This guideline is based on the design and content of the national plans. The format consists of:

- A basic plan, which provides an overview of the jurisdiction's or organizations emergency management system;

---

2 https://www.osha.gov/SLTC/emergencypreparedness/gettingstarted_role.html (accessed 13 December 2019).

- Functional Annexes that are numbered and titled consistently with the National Response Plan ESFs or address responses similar to the ESF's; and
- Hazard, threat or incident-specific annexes such as hurricanes or severe storms, earthquakes, biological incidents, or terror incidents.

Additional Support Annexes, such as Population Protection, Private Sector Coordination, and Worker Safety and Health can be added.

ESFs describe mission critical functions and specific tasks and assignments that must be accomplished to support the response. Support Annexes describe the framework for coordinating and executing common management strategies (such as worker safety) across functional areas.

Smaller communities and organizations may develop simpler plans. Such plans use an agency or department-based format in which tasks and emergency functions are covered in sections written specifically for each agency or department.

A content guide for developing an EOP is included as Appendix C in the CPG, which includes additional information on content that should be included in the Basic Plan and Annexes. This guide includes a list of ESFs numbered consistently with the Federal ESFs, and additional supporting content including:

- Population Protection
- Continuity of Operations
- Warning, or how information is disseminated to the community that a disaster or threat is imminent or has occurred
- Financial Management
- Mutual Aid/Multijurisdictional Coordination
- Private Sector Coordination
- Volunteer and Donations Management
- Worker Safety and Health
- Prevention and Protection Activities [17].

States have addressed worker health and safety in a variety of ways within their written Emergency Operations Plans. For example, Oregon's Comprehensive Emergency Management Plan includes ESFs that reflect those that support the National Response Framework, plus additional ESFs for Military Support, Food and Water, and Business and Industry. Oregon's ESF #8 assigns the Oregon Occupational Safety and Health Division (OR-OSHA) the responsibilities that are identified for OSHA under the Federal Worker Safety and Health Annex [18].

The Michigan Emergency Management Plan has used a nontraditional organization. Emergency Support Functions are grouped differently than the National ESFs, but the listing includes the counterparts in the NRF (Table 2.3). In 2020, Michigan will be moving to the traditional format. OSHA's Worker Safety and Health Annex is listed as a counterpart element in several the Michigan ESFs, including Health and Human Services, Environmental Protection and

Table 2.3 Michigan Emergency Management Plan Emergency Support Functions (ESFs).

Michigan Emergency Support Functions	NRF Counterpart Elements
Direction and Control	• Base Plan • ESF #5 Information and Planning • National Disaster Recovery Framework
Warning and Communications	• ESF #2 Communications • ESF #15 External Affairs • Public Affairs Annex
Information and Planning	• ESF #5 Information and Planning • ESF #15 External Affairs • Public Affairs Annex • National Disaster Recovery Framework
Health and Human Services	• ESF #8 Public Health and Medical Services • ESF #6 Mass Care, Emergency Assistance, Temporary Housing, and Human Services • Worker Safety and Health Support Annex • Biological Incident Annex • Food and Agriculture Incident Annex • Nuclear/Radiological Incident Annex • Mass Evacuation Incident Annex
Environmental Protection	• ESF #10 Oil and Hazardous Materials • ESF #11 Agriculture and Natural Resources • Worker Safety and Health Support Annex • Biological Incident Annex • Food and Agriculture Incident Annex • Nuclear/Radiological Incident Annex
Resource Support	• ESF #6 Mass Care, Emergency Assistance, Temporary Housing, and Human Services • ESF #7 Logistics • ESF #11 Agriculture and Natural Resources
Public Works and Engineering	• ESF #1 Transportation • ESF #2 Communications • ESF #3 Public Works and Engineering • ESF #12 Energy • National Disaster Recovery Framework
Public Safety	• ESF #4 Firefighting • ESF #9 Urban Search and Rescue • ESF #13 Public Safety and Security • Worker Safety and Health Annex • Terrorism Incident Law Enforcement and Investigation Annex • Cyber Incident Annex

Example of an ESF organization that varies from that of the national plans [19]. Michigan will be moving to a traditional NRF plan organization in 2020.

Public Safety. Responsibilities for Michigan OSHA (MIOSHA) are covered the Michigans Public Safety ESF, and direct the MIOSHA Disaster Response Team to provide technical assistance to the ICS Safety Officer during a response. However, MIOSHA representatives do not assume the role of Safety Officer. MIOSHA also retains a compliance authority that includes workplaces affected by a disaster [19].

State Emergency Operations Plans can also establish expectations for the safety of response and recovery workers. Of course, it is presumed that occupational safety and health rules apply to all emergency responders and recovery workers in OSHA state plan states. In OSHA states where the state and local employees who can be expected to make up a bulk of the response are not covered by worker safety and health laws, State and jurisdictional emergency response agencies can establish expectations for worker safety within their written Emergency Operations Plans. Inclusion of worker safety and health expectations in these plans is especially critical for responder safety in OSHA states.

Idaho is a Federal OSHA State. The importance of worker and responder safety is emphasized in several Idaho ESFs. Idaho ESF #5, Firefighting, sets this expectation in its policies section by stating that "Second only to firefighter safety will be the saving of lives and protection of property, in that order." Safety is repeatedly emphasized throughout this ESF, including prioritizing first responder safety in resource allocation. Responder safety is again emphasized in ESF #9, Search and Rescue. The Idaho Worker Safety and Health Annex does not distinguish between employers that are or are not covered by OSHA laws and specifically states that private sector, state and local government employers have responsibility for the safety and health of their employees. As Idaho does not have a state occupational safety and health department to act as a functional counterpart to OSHA in the Federal Worker Safety and Health Annex, the Idaho Office of Emergency Management fills this role and is listed as the Coordinating Agency [20].

Kansas is also a Federal OSHA State that emphasizes worker safety in the state EOP. The Kansas Response Plan assigns the Kansas Department of Labor with the responsibility of conducting public sector worker safety inspections during the incident recovery phase. More importantly, the Kansas Response Plan includes language in the Basic Plan that "protecting life and preserving health and overall safety of the public, responders, and recovery workers" is the first priority in the Planning Assumptions [21]. This clearly establishes an expectation that responder and recovery worker safety is essential to every aspect of the plan.

In contrast, some states do not include any language regarding responder or recovery worker safety in their EOPs. The State of Louisiana Emergency Operations Plan does not include language on response or recovery worker health and safety in the Basic Plan nor in any of the Louisiana Emergency Support Functions. Neither does it reference the Federal Worker Safety and Health Annex or a state equivalent. Since Louisiana is a Federal OSHA State, state and local emergency responders and recovery workers also do not have legal protections for their safety and health on the job [22].

2.10 Liability in Incident Response

On 10 July 2001, four firefighters (Tom Craven, 30; Devin Weaver, 21; Jessica Johnson, 19; and Karen FitzPatrick, 18) died fighting the 30 Mile Wildfire in the North Cascades in Washington State. Their Incident Commander, Ellreese N. Daniels, was charged on 11 counts of gross negligence and lying to investigators. He later entered a plea deal on two of these counts and avoided a trial [23, 24].

Incident commanders and emergency managers have many legal obligations, and may be liable for decisions made and actions taken during a response. Liability may be incurred through:

- Not having an Emergency Operations Plan;
- (Possibly) through not having an adequate Emergency Operations Plan or not maintaining the plan;
- Violation of an internal policy;
- Violation of emergency management law;
- Violation of general application laws, such as OSHA law, personnel law, contract law, or government ethics law.

Incident Commanders also are subject to personal liability, and may be subject to civil lawsuits for personal injury or wrongful death. Failure to follow OSHA laws may be used as evidence of failure to follow a standard of care in a civil lawsuit, and damages may be orders of magnitude higher than the fines that could be imposed by OSHA [25]. Incident Commanders are told during training that they can minimize their liability risks if they listen to their Safety Officer, and a good Incident Commander does just this.

2.11 Multiemployer Worksites

An incident response may consist of responders who work for a single employer, or it may involve responders who work for multiple employers and come together to fill roles within the Incident Command System. In essence, such a response is a multiemployer worksite.

Most workers in the United States are covered by Worker's Compensation which covers an employee's expenses in the event that they are injured on the job. Worker's Compensation is a "no fault" system: Worker's receive coverage regardless of whether they or their employer contributed to the conditions that led to the injury or illness. The "no fault" condition also applies to employer liability: Employees who are covered by Worker's Compensation cannot sue their employer for their injury or illness except in very rare and fairly extreme circumstances, such as when an employer knows the employee will suffer severe health impacts from assigned work but continues to have the employee perform this work anyway. Employees can, however, sue third parties who contributed to the accident, including third-party employers.

In 1990, the Washington State Supreme Court decided a landmark case which has since greatly influenced how OSHA looks at safety responsibilities on multi-employer worksites. Andre Stute worked for a gutter repair contractor which had subcontracted to a general contractor, PMMC. Mr. Stute fell off of a 28-feet-tall roof and sustained serious injuries that prevented him from returning to work in the construction trades. The Washington State Supreme Court held that a general contractor had a specific duty to comply with health and safety requirements, and that this specific duty applied to all workers on the site, including subcontractor's employees [26]. Today, the construction industry accepts as an industry standard that the General Contractor has a duty and responsibility to provide safety oversight for all employees and subcontractors on a worksite.

OSHA Directive CPL 2-00.124 [27] describes OSHA's policy for issuing citations on multiemployer worksites when safety responsibilities are not clarified through contractual documents or Memorandums of Understanding (MOU). Within this Directive OSHA defines categories of employers with respect to the relationship each has to the hazard:

- Creating Employer: an employer that causes a hazardous condition.
- Exposing Employer: an employer whose own employees are exposed to the hazard
- Correcting Employer: an employer who is engaged in a common undertaking on the same worksite as the exposing employer, and has responsibility for correcting the hazard.
- Controlling Employer: an employer who has general supervisor authority over the worksite. This includes the power to control the hazard (by elimination or mitigation) or the power to require others to control the hazard.

An Incident Command structure has a single Safety Officer even when the response involves multiple agencies or employers. The levels of responsibility for employee safety among different employers, as spelled out in OSHA's multiemployer inspection policy, underscores the duty of a Safety Officer to ensure the safety of *all* responders on behalf of his or her Incident Commander, regardless of whether the responders are employed by the same agency as the Safety Officer. Depending upon the incident, the Safety Officer may have less than a full understanding of the hazards faced by employees with job functions that do not match those of his or her primary employer.

For example, in a rail accident, fire responders assume initial command as fire department personnel focus on life safety: Removing passengers from rail cars, providing medical aid and transport, and stabilizing the incident. A support team of rail personnel works to keep rail traffic clear of the scene, and perform other tasks such as operating switches or other controls to facilitate the fire response. The assigned Safety Officer in the ICS chart at this point in the response is a member of the fire department, but is responsible for the safety of rail personnel as well as fire personnel. A good Fire Department Safety Officer should be well versed on the usual hazards faced by fire responders, but is unlikely to fully understand how hazards in a rail environment are managed. The Fire Department Safety Officer also would have limited, if any, experience with the hazards faced by railroad employees. In order to protect both fire and rail responders, and to minimize the liability faced by the Incident Commander, the Safety Officer would need to rely on the expertise of a responding Rail Safety Specialist to fill this knowledge gap. The Rail Safety Specialist can be assigned as an Assistant Safety Officer to formalize this interaction during the response.

A good Safety Officer knows what they do not know, and utilizes available resources to best manage safety for all members participating in a response.

2.12 Summary

Compliance requirements with regard to OSHA or state health and safety regulations varies among states and types of employers. Regardless, the Incident Commander retains responsibility for the safety and health of all responders under his or her command, and can be held liable if responders suffer serious injuries, illness, or fatalities. Even if an Incident Commander is not specifically required to follow OSHA rules or guidelines in consensus standards such as NFPA, failure to follow them can be used as evidence that the Incident Commander did not follow a recognized standard of care in a court of law. A competent Safety Officer who understands these implications is an essential resource to an Incident Commander. In a multiemployer response, the Safety Officer may be less skilled at identifying and addressing hazards faced by all employees, and must rely on the expertise of safety personnel who work for other responding employers to supplement the Safety Officer's own abilities. These personnel can support the Safety Officers if assigned as Assistant Safety Officers, thus formalizing their role in the Incident Command System.

References

1 OSHA (1993). Interpretation letter to Frances Mendenhall. *DDS* (25 March 1993) (1993-03-25-0).

2 OSHA (1998). Interpretation letter to the Honorable Jay Johnson. (12 March 1998) (1998-03-12-1).

3 Office for State, Tribal, Local, and Territorial Support, Centers for Disease Control and Prevention (2017). Selected tribal laws related to occupational safety and health. *Public Health Law* ((20 April 2017)) http://www.cdc.gov/phlp/docs/menu-tribalosh.pdf (accessed 17 March 2020).

4 NFPA (2018). *NFPA 1500 Standard on Fire Department Occupational Safety, Health, and Wellness Program*.

5 NFPA (2015). *NFPA 1521 Standard for Fire Department Safety Officer Professional Qualifications*.

6 Kuhns, J.B., Maquire, E.R., and Leach, N.R. (2015). *Health, Safety, and Wellness Program Case Studies in Law Enforcement*. Washington, DC: Office of Community Oriented Policing Services.

7 Federal Transit Administration, US Department of Transportation (2018). 49 CFR Part 673, public transportation agency safety plan preamble. *Federal Register* 83 (139): 34418–34468.

8 Federal Aviation Administration, US Department of Transportation (2016). *National Policy: Order 8000.369B, Safety Management Systems* (18 March 2016).

9 Zohar, D. (1980). Safety climate in industrial organizations: theoretical and applied implications. *Journal of Applied Psychology* 65 (1): 96–102.

10 Department of Homeland Security (2015). *National Preparedness Goal*, 2e.

11 Department of Homeland Security (2019). *National Response Framework*, 4e.

12 Department of Homeland Security (2016). *National Disaster Recovery Framework*, 2e.

13 Department of Homeland Security (2016). *Emergency March 18, Support Function #8 – Public Health and Medical Services Annex*.

14 Department of Homeland Security (2013). *Worker Safety and Health Support Annex*.

15 Occupational Safety and Health Administration, United States Department of Labor. *Safety and Health Guide. Worker Protection: OSHA's Role During Response to Catastrophic Incidents Guide*. https://www.osha.gov/SLTC/emergencypreparedness/guides/osha_role.html (accessed 22 October 2018).

16 Tracy, K. (2018). *Worker Health and Disaster Center for Progressive Reform From Surviving to Thriving: Equity in Disaster Planning and Recovery Report*.

http://www.progressivereform.org/Surviving/Thriving_workers.cfm (accessed October 2018).

17 Department of Homeland Security (2010). *Developing and Maintaining Emergency Operations Plans.* Comprehensive Preparedness Guide (CPG) 101, Version 2.0.

18 Oregon Office of Emergency Management (2014). *Emergency Support Function #8 – Health and Medical, Oregon Comprehensive Emergency Management Plan (CEMP).*

19 Emergency Management and Homeland Security Division, Michigan State Police (2018). *Michigan Emergency Management Plan (MEMP) September 2018 revision.*

20 Idaho Office of Emergency Management (2017). *Idaho Emergency Operations Plan.*

21 Division of Emergency Management, State of Kansas Adjunct General's Department. (2017). *Kansas Response Plan.*

22 Louisiana Governor's Office of Homeland Security and Emergency Preparedness (2017). *State of Louisiana Emergency Operations Plan.*

23 Bowermaster, D., O'Hagan, M., and Cornwall, W. (2006). Thirty mile crew boss charged in 4 fire deaths. *The Seattle Times* (21 December).

24 Simmons, B. (2008). A plea bargain douses the scandal of the thirtymile fire. *Crosscut* (7 May 2008).

25 Nicholson, W.C. (2006). Chapter 14. Legal issues in emergency management. In: *Fundamentals of Emergency Management by Lindell* (eds. K. Michael, C.S. Prater and R.W. Perry). FEMA free online textbook. https://training.fema.gov/hiedu/aemrc/booksdownload/fem (accessed 31 October 2018).

26 Stute v PMMC (1990). 114 Wn.2d 454, 788 P.2d 545.

27 OSHA Directive CPL 2-00.124 (1999). Multi-Employer Citation Policy.

3

Types of Emergencies and Disasters, and Related Hazards

3.1 The All-Hazards Approach

FEMA has adopted an "All-Hazards" approach to emergency management. This concept is based on the idea that management strategies are consistent regardless of the type of incident that is being responded to. However, goals, objectives, strategies, and tactics will differ depending upon the incident and specific mitigating factors. Likewise, the risks to responders and strategies for keeping them safe will vary depending upon the incident.

Incident types fall into the following three hazard categories (Table 3.1) [1]:

- Natural: Acts of nature or "acts of God";
- Technological: Accidents or failures of systems and structures;
- Human-caused: Intentional acts of humans.

This chapter highlights several types of incidents along with associated hazards to responders.

3.2 Hazardous Materials Release or Spill

A hazardous material is a substance that can negatively impact the health of people, animals, or the environment, and includes biological, chemical, radiological, and physical substances. When used as intended, and when nothing goes wrong, these materials are used safely in the workplace and in our homes. Petroleum products power our vehicles and electrical grids, and are transported through pipelines, rail systems, or over roads. Radiological materials are used in research, for medical treatments, and for providing power. We use chemicals to clean our homes, for maintenance on equipment and systems in our workplaces, and in manufacturing. Much of the time, with appropriate controls, these materials do not negatively impact the health of people or animals, or damage the environment.

Health and Safety in Emergency Management and Response, First Edition. Dana L. Stahl.
© 2021 John Wiley & Sons, Inc. Published 2021 by John Wiley & Sons, Inc.

Table 3.1 Examples of threats and hazards by category.

Natural	Technological	Human-caused
Avalanche	Dam failure	Active shooter incident
Drought	Hazardous materials release	Armed assault
Earthquake	Industrial accident	Biological attack
Epidemic	Levee failure	Chemical attack
Flood	Mine accident	Cyber-attack against infrastructure
Hurricane/typhoon	Pipeline explosion	Explosives attack
Space weather	Radiological release	Improvised nuclear attack
Tornado	Train derailment	Nuclear terrorism attack
Tsunami	Transportation incident	Radiological attack
Volcanic eruption	Urban conflagration	
Winter storm	Utility disruption	

Source: Department of Homeland Security [1].

However, when the unexpected happens, such as a pressure release, a transportation accident, or a spill, these materials can escape their system of intended use and related controls, and are no longer benign (Figure 3.1).

These substances can impact health in a number of ways. Primary exposure routes include inhalation, ingestion, contact with skin or mucous membranes, and injection.

Inhalation is generally considered the pathway of greatest exposure to industrial workers. Gasses, vapors, and airborne particulate matter such as smoke, dust, fumes, or fibers can enter the respiratory system during inhalation. Gasses and vapors are transported to the deep regions of the lungs where they are absorbed into the bloodstream, and transported to other areas of the body.

Particulate materials vary in size, which determines where they settle in the respiratory system (Figure 3.2). Particles with aerodynamic diameters between 25 and 100 μm settle in the nose and mouth, and materials in this size range are referred to as *inspirable*. Depending upon the substance, particles in this range can cause irritation or other effects to tissues in the mouth and nose, but can be expelled from the body through coughing or sneezing. This prevents these materials from remaining in the body for an excessive amount of time.

Particulate materials with aerodynamic diameters between 10 and 25 μm settle in the trachea and bronchi and bronchioles, and are referred to as *thoracic*. Particles in this size range are more problematic than those in the inspirable range. However, the body does have some ability to remove them. Particles that land in this area of the respiratory system are trapped in mucous, and hair cells or cilia in

Figure 3.1 Gas explosion in Seattle's Greenwood neighborhood 9 March 2016. Source: Reproduced with kind permission of Alex Hjelm.

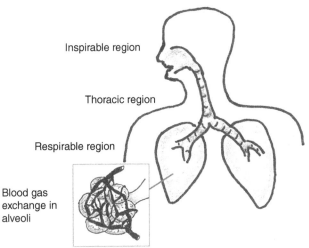

Figure 3.2 Particulate materials are categorized as inspirable, thoracic, and respirable depending upon particle size and the area of the respiratory system where they deposit.

this area of the respiratory track move this mucous up into the upper regions of the respiratory system where it can be expelled through the mouth and nose through coughing and sneezing.

Particulate materials that have aerodynamic diameters 10 μm or less (PM$_{10}$), or the *respirable* fraction, settle into the alveoli, or the deepest regions of the respiratory system. These particles are the most problematic, because the body does not have a mechanism to remove them. The smallest size particles, those under 2.5 μm (PM$_{2.5}$), may be particularly damaging [2]. Metal fumes, vapors, and gasses can permeate the gas exchange regions and enter the blood stream. The circulatory system then transports these substances to other areas of the body leading to systemic health effects.

Materials that cannot be transported out of the respiratory system, such as asbestos or silica, lodge in the alveoli. The body cannot remove these particles, and instead mounts an immune response. Particles become encapsulated and scar tissue forms. Scar tissue interferes with gas exchange in this deep region of the lungs, including the gasses that necessarily must be exchanged: oxygen and carbon dioxide. This leads to long-term respiratory disease.

Respiratory protective equipment that is properly selected, and used, can reduce the amount of particulate materials that enter the respiratory tract. Supplied air respirators, such as self-contained breathing apparatus or SBCAs, are required if the atmosphere is oxygen deficient, if the environment is considered Immediately Dangerous to Life and Health (IDLH) [3], or if the atmosphere is unknown (Figures 3.3 and 3.4).

Air-purifying respirators can be used for exposures below IDLH levels. These respirators contain air-purifying units that filter out contaminants, and are either positive-pressure respirators with the air flow powered by a battery pack, or negative-pressure respirators, where the air moves through the air filtering

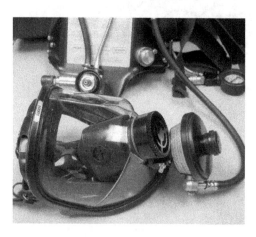

Figure 3.3 Self-contained breathing apparatus (SCBA) mask. Masks must form a tight seal to the face to provide a seal against contaminants.

Figure 3.4 Grade D breathing air is used to provide air to an SCBA.

Figure 3.5 Half-mask negative-pressure air purifying respirator with particulate filters.

Figure 3.6 Full-face negative-pressure air-purifying respirator with prescription spectacle inserts.

devices as the wearer inhales or exhales (Figures 3.5 and 3.6). Air-cleaning devices are selectively chosen to clean the contaminant(s) that is (are) present (Figure 3.7). Organic vapor cartridges are used for organic vapors, but do not protect against particulate materials or gasses. Particulate filter classifications are based on efficiency of filtration (Table 3.2) and resistance to oil (Table 3.3), and are appropriate for exposure to smoke, fume, dust, fibers, aerosols, and mists. Other air-cleaning devices may be specific to a substance such as mercury, or have

Figure 3.7 Air-purifying respirators are fitted with air-purifying devices that are selected for the hazard(s) that workers are exposed to.

Table 3.2 Efficiencies of particulate respirator filters.

Rating	Efficiency
95	95% of airborne particles
99	99% of airborne particles
100	99.97% of airborne particles

Source: 42 CFR 84 [4].

Table 3.3 Oil resistance ratings of particulate respirator filters.

Rating	Oil resistance
N	Not resistant to oil
R	Somewhat oil resistant
P	Strongly oil proof

Source: 42 CFR 84 [4].

applicability against multiple agents likely to be present in a terrorism response (CBRN, or Chemical, Biological, Radiological, Nuclear) (Table 3.4) [5, 6]. It is important to select air-cleaning devices that are appropriate for the environment that a responder is working in. An improperly selected respirator or air-cleaning device will not protect the person wearing it, and may instead provide only a false sense of security. It is also important to change air-cleaning devices on respirators before the capacity is used up. Once the air-cleaning device is "full," it will no longer work to clean the air that the wearer is inspiring, and this also invokes a false sense of security while failing to protect the person wearing the respirator. All respirators and respirator parts must be certified by NIOSH, and this NIOSH certification must be clearly marked.

Table 3.4 Types of air filtration devices.

Contaminant class	Examples of contaminants
Acidic gasses	Hydrogen sulfide, chlorine gas, hydrofluoric acid
Basic gasses	Ammonia
Organic vapors	
Formaldehyde	
Mercury vapors	
Other vapors and gasses	Hydrogen cyanide
All aerosols – high-efficiency filter	Dusts, mists, fumes, droplets, bacteria, viruses, radionuclides
Chemical, Biological, Radiological, Nuclear (CBRN)	

ANSI Z88.7 specifies color coding for respirator cartridges; however, color codes have changed with various updates to this standard. It is important to check the wording on the label to verify the contaminant class of the cartridge used.

Figure 3.8 A filtering facepiece respirator is a half-mask negative-pressure respirator. The entire respirator functions as an air-cleaning device.

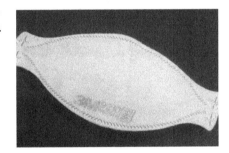

Filtering facepiece respirators are a type of respirator in which the entire surface of the respirator functions as an air-cleaning device (Figures 3.8 and 3.9). Filtering facepiece respirators are certified by NIOSH, and are rated in the same manner as air purifying filters used on other positive or negative-pressure respirators. These look similar to dust masks and surgical masks but in fact, function quite differently. Dust masks can be used for comfort, but do not function as a respirator to protect from respiratory hazards (Figure 3.10). The Federal Drug Administration (FDA) clears surgical masks for use, and surgical masks are intended to prevent the wearer from exposing others to pathogens that may be exhaled by the wearer. A surgical mask does not reduce contaminants in the air inhaled by the wearer, and does not protect the wearer from atmospheric hazards. Surgical masks and filtering facepiece respirators cannot be used interchangeably, unless they are certified

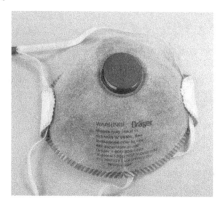

Figure 3.9 Combination organic vapor and particulate N95 respirator with exhalation valve.

Figure 3.10 A dust mask can be worn for comfort, but it is not a respirator and does not provide sufficient protection from respiratory hazards.

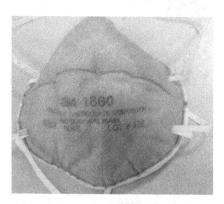

Figure 3.11 Example of an N95 filtering facepiece respirator that has been cleared by FDA as a surgical mask.

for this dual purpose. Certain NIOSH-approved filtering facepiece respirators have also been cleared by FDA as surgical masks and can be used in situations where it is important to protect the wearer from breathing in environmental contaminants while at the same time protecting others from pathogens that the wearer may exhale (Figure 3.11). These devices must be clearly marked as NIOSH-approved respirators and surgical masks [4].

Ingestion of harmful substances is generally unintentional, and typically occurs when food or drink is consumed in areas where these harmful substances are present. Ingestion can also result from hand to mouth activity after touching contaminated surfaces or clothing. It is important to establish designated clean areas where responders can eat and drink, and provide facilities to remove any potential contaminants from hands prior to eating through handwashing.

Hand washing and hand hygiene can reduce exposure via ingestion. The use of hand sanitizers does not: Although hand sanitizers are effective at deactivating pathogens on skin, they do not remove contaminants from the surfaces of the hands. The importance of handwashing facilities cannot be overemphasized.

Inspirable particulate materials that deposit in the mouth during inhalation can also be ingested during swallowing, and contribute to the overall dose.

In most environments, skin serves as a protective barrier to elements in the environment. Certain chemicals, however, such as acrylamide, bromoform, polychlorinated biphenyls (PCBs), and cyanides can be absorbed through the skin, and this pathway can significantly contribute to the dose [7]. Corrosive chemicals, which have a pH of less than 2 or greater than 12.5[1] are very reactive and can destroy tissues that they come into contact with. Prolonged exposure to organic solvents can dissolve protective fatty layers of the skin in a process known as *defatting*. Skin that has been defatted is much less resistant to environmental chemicals, and subsequent exposures after defatting occurs further increases the absorbed dose of the chemical. In addition, chemical contact with eyes or other mucous membranes can add to the received dose.

Gloves and other chemically resistant clothing create a barrier to skin contact as long as chemicals cannot permeate the protective material. It is important to ensure that gloves and protective clothing are chemically resistant to the chemicals to which the person wearing them is exposed. Protective clothing and gloves may or may not show visible evidence of chemical degradation; therefore, it is important to work with experienced personnel who know how to select chemical protection that is appropriate for the chemicals to which responders are exposed. PPE manufacturers can also provide technical information on the chemical resistance of their products.

The use of formal decontamination procedures upon exit from the work zone prevents the spread of chemicals to non-responders, and can also prevent post-work exposures through routes such as ingestion from eating or inadvertent contact with mucous membranes by hands that have touched contaminated work clothing.

Injection can contribute to the dose that a worker receives, and can occur if the worker is cut by a sharp object that is contaminated with a chemical. Needlestick

---

1 http://www.sima.org/news2/2016/10/25/death-by-snow-ice (accessed 16 November 2018).

injuries are an example of an injection exposure that can expose the recipient to biological and chemical hazards. This is a common risk in healthcare and medical response, but can also occur when responding in areas where used needles have been abandoned.

There are several classes of hazardous materials:

- Asphyxiants, which interfere with the body's ability to utilize oxygen
  - Simple asphyxiants displace oxygen in the environment, and decrease the percentage of oxygen in air that is inhaled;
  - Chemical asphyxiants compete with oxygen for binding sites on hemoglobin in red blood cells, so less oxygen is distributed to tissues and organs than is needed;
- Flammable chemicals produce vapors that can be ignited;
- Combustible chemicals can burn and act as fuel when fire is present;
- Corrosive chemicals are strong acids or strong bases that destroy tissues or cause "chemical burns";
- Oxidizers are reactive, and can undergo chemical reactions that result in production of oxygen gas. Excess oxygen can contribute to fires;
- Chemicals can produce toxic health effects:
  - Sensitizers produce greater reactions with each subsequent exposure, similar to allergens;
  - Carcinogens contribute to development of cancer;
  - Mutagens damage DNA;
  - Teratogens damage a developing fetus;
  - Hepatotoxins damage the liver;
  - Nephrotoxins damage the kidneys;
  - Respiratory toxins damage the lungs, alveoli, and bronchial system;
  - Hemotoxins damage red blood cells;
  - Dermal toxins damage the dermal layer of skin;
  - Eye toxins reduce vision or damage structures of the eye;
  - Reproductive toxins damage the reproductive system and damage to germ cells. Mutagens and teratogens are examples of reproductive toxins.

Information on specific hazards of chemical substances can be found on Safety Data Sheets (SDSs) for the chemical that are prepared by the manufacturer of the product. The most recent editions of the NIOSH Pocket Guide to Chemical Hazards and the Pipeline and Hazardous Materials Safety Administration (PHMSA) Emergency Response Guidebook (ERG) are also good resources on chemical hazards.

3.3   Severe Weather

3.3.1   Extreme Heat

Extreme heat emergencies occur when temperatures are much hotter and/or humid than average. Heat levels can impact health of responders in any emergency situation.

The body must maintain a core temperature of 37 °C or 98 °F in order for the brain and internal organs to function properly. In hot conditions, the body responds physiologically to prevent the core from overheating: Blood flow increases in the extremities and the surface of the skin to cool the blood, and sweating increases. It is important to maintain fluid intake in order to facilitate this response and prevent dehydration. Individual physiology, such as sweat rate, metabolic rate, medical conditions or use of medications, and overall health, can reduce the efficiency of these physiological mechanisms and create greater susceptibility to heat-related illness. Use of Personal Protective Equipment, especially impermeable clothing, can interfere with these mechanisms and reduce the body's ability to cool itself.

The respiratory system facilitates thermoregulation. During respiration, warm air is exhaled from the body, carrying heat away, and cooler atmospheric air is inhaled. This cools surface tissues and blood vessels in the nasal passages and other areas of the respiratory system. The use of respirators interferes with this cooling mechanism because inspired air comes from the air inside the facepiece rather than the environment, which is warm compared with the outside air, and does not allow respiratory cooling. "Rebreathing" during respirator use contributes to heat load and increases the risk of developing a heat-related illness.

Expected temperatures can vary by region. Physiologically, people acclimate to the temperatures that they are routinely exposed to. An individual from a milder climate can experience heat-related illness at temperatures that are much lower than those that occur in hotter climates, and may experience heat impacts and heat-related illness at lower temperatures than an individual who is acclimated to higher temperatures. This is something that should be considered during mutual aid responses to long events, in which responders from cooler regions may support a response in a warmer region. It is also a factor in extreme heat emergencies, as responders have not had an opportunity to acclimate to high temperatures.

Heat-related illness includes the following:

- *Heat rash* that appears as red areas on the neck, upper chest, in skin creases, or other areas. The rash may appear as small red clusters, pimples, or small blisters.

- *Heat syncope* (fainting or near fainting) that occurs when there is prolonged pooling of blood in the legs and skin, and is likely to occur from spending long periods of time in static postures in the heat.
- *Heat cramps* are painful muscle cramps that result from electrolyte imbalance and prolonged sweating without adequate fluid and salt intake.
- *Heat exhaustion* occurs when the body needs to pay the price for the work done to cool the body, and when it is beginning to be unable to maintain the effort. Signs and symptoms include the following:
  o Fatigue;
  o Weakness;
  o Blurred vision;
  o Dizziness, headache;
  o Confusion/irritability;
  o High pulse rate;
  o Profuse sweating;
  o Low blood pressure;
  o Insecure gait;
  o Pale appearance;
  o Collapse.
- *Rhabdomyolysis* is associated with heat stress and prolonged physical exertion: This occurs when muscles rapidly break down, rupture, and die, releasing electrolytes and large proteins to the bloodstream that then can cause irregular heart rhythms, seizures, and kidney damage.
- *Heat stroke* is a life-threatening medical emergency, and occurs when the body is no longer able to maintain core body temperatures, which can rapidly rise to 106 °F or higher. Immediate medical treatment must be provided if the following symptoms of heat stroke appear:
  o Hot, dry skin;
  o Shivering;
  o Collapse/loss of consciousness;
  o Sweating is profuse or stops;
  o Seizures;
  o Erratic behavior or euphoria;
  o Red face.

3.3.2 Extreme Cold

Extreme cold occurs when temperatures are much colder than average, and as in extreme heat, the temperatures that define extreme cold vary by region and worker acclimatization. Wind speeds influence the wind chill factor and contribute to health risk from exposure to cold.

In cold conditions, the body redirects blood flow from skin surfaces and the extremities to the core in order to maintain a stable core temperature. Cold-related illness includes the following:

- *Raynaud's Disorder*, or "white finger disease," which occurs when blood vessels in the extremities break down and blood flow in these areas is inhibited. Vibration exposure is also linked to Raynaud's Disorder, and people who are exposed to vibration in cold conditions have increased risk. Damage can be permanent.
- *Chilblains* is a result of permanent damage to capillary beds in skin, and can occur at temperatures as high as 60 °F (coincidentally, depending upon work performed, heat stress symptoms can also occur at 60 °F). Symptoms include redness, itching, blistering, and/or inflammation.
- *Trench Foot* occurs when feet have prolonged exposure to cold, wet conditions (such as working in wet socks and wet shoes), at temperatures below 60 °F. Wet feet lose heat faster than dry feet due to conduction, and when this happens, blood vessels constrict and skin tissue dies due to lack of oxygen and nutrients, and buildup of toxic byproducts. Symptoms include severe pain, tingling, itching, edema, and blisters. Visually it looks very similar to frostbite.
- *Frostbite* occurs when tissues freeze and die. Skin is discolored, and can be white, grayish yellow, reddish violet, or black. Blisters appear, and there is a sensation of burning, numbness, or tingling. Gangrene can set in, which can lead to limb loss.
- *Hypothermia* can be life threatening and occurs when the core temperature falls below 35°C or 95°F. Symptoms include:
  - Shivering;
  - Slow pulse and breathing;
  - Fatigue;
  - Confusion;
  - Disorientation;
  - Loss of coordination;
  - Collapse;
  - Loss of consciousness.

3.3.3 Winter Storms

Snowstorms, blizzards, and winter storms can bring extreme cold as well as freezing rain, snow, ice, and high winds. Travel is risky, and roads may be impassible. Visibility is reduced. Black ice, or a thin layer of ice that is difficult for drivers to see, can cause loss of control of vehicles. High numbers of vehicle accidents then coincide with impeded access for emergency vehicles and response personnel. People can slip and fall in icy conditions, and may fail to detect black ice. Heavy snow accumulation on buildings can cause collapse. In addition, the Snow and Ice Management Association reports that at least 15 people are killed by falling icicles each year.[2]

Power outages can occur, and generators can be used to provide backup power. Generators, however, produce carbon monoxide, and care must be taken to prevent generator exhaust from accumulating in enclosed areas where people may be present. Carbon monoxide levels can also accumulate indoors if outdoor cooking equipment or heaters is used indoors. In the United States, an average of 430 people die from carbon monoxide poisoning each year [8].

Downed power lines are an expected hazard during storms and any power line that is down should be assumed to be a "live" line.

3.3.4 Thunderstorms

The CDC reports that during the years between 2003 and 2012, lightning caused an average of 35 deaths in the United States. About 10% of people struck by lightning die, most often because the lightning strike triggered a heart attack. Lightning can also cause blunt trauma, neurological syndromes, muscle injuries because the electrical charge can cause muscles to spasm and contract violently, eye injuries, skin lesions, and burns.

Responders who must be outside during a lightning storm should:

- Avoid being on tall structures, such as rooftops, scaffolding, utility poles, ladders, trees, and large equipment;
- Not touch anything that can conduct electricity, such as:
  o Metal objects, for example, metal scaffolding or metal equipment;
  o Utility lines;
  o Water, including standing water, water pipes, and plumbing;
- Stay indoors or inside a vehicle if at all possible;
- Stay away from explosive materials.[3]

3.3.5 Hailstorms

Hail forms when updrafts in thunderstorms carry raindrops upward into extremely cold layers of the atmosphere where they freeze into balls of ice. The stronger the updraft, the larger the hailstone can grow.

Hail can damage property and cause injuries to people or animals. Rarely, injuries are fatal. Hail varies in size, from pea size (less than 0.5 inches) to softball size (4.5 inches) (Table 3.5).[4]

---

2 http://www.sima.org/news2/2016/10/25/death-by-snow-ice (accessed 16 November 2018).
3 http://www.cdc.gov/disasters/lightning/index.html (accessed 16 November 2018).
4 http://www.nssl.noaa.gov/education/svrwx101/hail (accessed 16 November 2018).

Table 3.5 National Weather Service guide for determining hail sizes.

Hail size, inches	Description
Less than 0.5	Pea
0.5	Marble/mothball
0.75	Dime/penny
0.88	Nickle
1.00	Quarter
1.25	Half dollar
1.50	Walnut/ping pong
1.75	Golf ball
2.00	Hen egg
2.50	Tennis ball
2.75	Baseball
3.00	Tea cup
4.00	Grapefruit
4.50	Softball

Source: http://www.nssl.noaa.gov/education/svrwx101/hail and http://www.weather.gov/bgm/severedefinitions (accessed 15 November 2018).

3.4 Tropical Storms, Hurricanes, and Windstorms

The term "cyclone" refers to a rotating closed system of winds and thunderstorms that originates over tropical or subtropical waters. Cyclones with sustained wind speeds of 74 mph that originate in the northern hemisphere east of the International Dateline to the Greenwich Meridian are referred to as "hurricanes." Cyclones with the same level of sustained wind speeds are referred to as "typhoons" when they originate in the Pacific north of the equator and west of the International Dateline. Storms with lower sustained wind speeds are referred to as Tropical Storms or Tropical Depressions (Table 3.6).

The National Weather Service issues Watches and Warnings for approaching storms:

- A *Tropical Storm Watch* is issued when tropical storm conditions pose a possible threat to a specified coastal area within 48 hours;
- A *Tropical Storm Warning* is issued when tropical storm conditions are expected in a specified coastal area within 36 hours or less;

Table 3.6 Storm terminology based on sustained windspeeds.

Maximum sustained wind speed, mph	Type of storm
38 or less	Tropical depression
39–73	Tropical storm
74 or higher	Cyclone, hurricane, or typhoon

Source: http://www.weather.gov/mob/tropical_definitions
(accessed 17 November 2018).

- A *Hurricane Watch* is issued when sustained winds of 74 mph or higher are possible within the specified area of the watch. The Watch is issued 48 hours in advance of the onset of tropical storm force winds.
- A *Hurricane Warning* is issued when sustained winds of 74 mph or higher are expected within the specified area of the warning. The Warning is issued 36 hours in advance of the onset of tropical storm force winds.[5]

The primary hazards during a hurricane are damaging winds and flooding. The safest place to be during a hurricane is inside a windowless room in the highest level of a building.

The Saffir–Simpson scale is used to estimate potential property damage. Hurricanes reaching Category 3 or higher have potential for significant loss of life and are considered major hurricanes (Table 3.7). In the western North Pacific, a "super typhoon" refers to cyclones with sustained winds exceeding 150 mph.[6]

Response takes place in the aftermath of the storm, and responders must work in an environment in which transportation and utilities are disrupted (Figure 3.12). Temperature conditions may compound hazards of response, and the use of generators or fuel-powered heating and cooking equipment leads to the risk of carbon monoxide exposure.

Significant storms can do considerable damage to buildings, and it is important to be able to quickly assess whether or not buildings are safe to occupy in the aftermath of the storm. Jurisdictions typically employ building inspectors who are trained to evaluate building safety; however, it is unlikely that any jurisdiction employs enough building inspectors to inspect every damaged building in a timely manner during a disaster. The Applied Technology Council (ATC) has developed a system for rapidly assessing the safety and stability of buildings after windstorms. This system utilizes teams of trained professionals with backgrounds in building design and building inspection, and other disaster workers and

---

5 http://www.weather.gov/bgm/severedefinitions and http://www.weather.gov/mob/tropical_ definitions (accessed 17 November 2018).
6 http://www.nhc.noaa.gov/aboutgloss.shtml (accessed 17 November 2018).

Table 3.7 The Saffir–Simpson hurricane wind scale.

Category	Sustained wind speeds, mph	Types of damage
1	74–95	Some damage: well-constructed frame houses could have damage to roof, shingles, vinyl siding, and gutters. Large branches can snap from trees and shallow rotted trees can topple. Damage to power lines and poles can result in power outages lasting from a few hours to several days
2	96–110	Extensive damage: well-constructed frame homes could sustain major roof and siding damage. Many shallowly rotted trees will snap or be uprooted, and can block numerous roads. Near total power loss is expected and outages could last from several days to weeks
3	111–129	Devastating damage: well-built frame homes may incur major damage or removal of roof decking or gable ends. Many trees will be snapped or uprooted, blocking numerous roads. Electricity and water will be unavailable for several days to weeks after the storm passes
4	130–156	Catastrophic damage: well-built frame houses can sustain severe damage with loss of most of the roof structure and/or some exterior walls. Most trees will be snapped or uprooted and power poles downed. Fallen trees and power poles will isolate residential areas. Power outages will last weeks to possibly months. Most of the area will be uninhabitable for weeks or months
5	157 or higher	Catastrophic damage: a high percentage of framed homes will be destroyed, with total roof failure and wall collapse. Fallen trees and power poles will isolate residential areas. Power outages will last for weeks to possibly months. Most of the area will be uninhabitable for weeks or months

Source: http://www.nhc.noaa.gov/aboutsshws.php (accessed 17 November 2018).

technical staff with backgrounds in building construction to perform an initial rapid evaluation of buildings. A rapid assessment of a single building should take between 10 and 30 minutes to complete, and when done, the building is placarded as Inspected, Restricted Use, or Unsafe (Table 3.8). Any building that receives a Restricted Use placard later receives a detailed inspection by a building official or building design professional. After the detailed inspection, the placard may be changed to Inspected or Unsafe, or it may remain as Restricted Use. Any

Figure 3.12 Vehicle impacted by flooding water and downed branches during Hurricane Harvey (2017). Source: Reproduced with kind permission of Allison Melton.

Table 3.8 Applied Technology Council (ATC) building safety evaluation posting categories.

Posting category	Placard color	Description
Inspected	Green	No apparent hazard found, although repairs may be necessary
Restricted use	Yellow	Safety is questionable, or hazardous conditions exist (or are believed to exist) and this requires restrictions on use or occupancy of the structure. Further evaluation may result in the posting being changed to "inspected" or "unsafe"
Unsafe	Red	Extreme hazard or unsafe situation present. Significant risk of further damage or collapse. Unsafe for occupancy or entry, except as authorized by the local building department

Source: Applied Technology Council [9].

building that is placarded as Restricted Use after the detailed inspection receives an engineering evaluation. The engineering evaluation can take a day or more, and includes a detailed review of construction documents, damage data, and structural calculations. An Unsafe placard does not indicate that the building must be demolished: merely indicates that it is unsafe for occupancy until repairs are made.

Jurisdictions can contact ATC to request training on inspection procedures for individuals who may need to assist in the response by conducting rapid assessments of buildings (www.atcouncil.org).

Building inspectors and rapid response teams are subject to storm-related hazards, such as downed power lines, falling trees or branches, debris, and unstable surfaces (Figure 3.13). Additional hazards include spilled chemicals or damaged gas lines, distressed animals, and people who may be upset or combative if they disagree with the placard assigned to the building [9].

Figure 3.13 Debris from Hurricane
Harvey (2017). Source: Reproduced with
kind permission of Allison Melton.

3.5 Tornados

A tornado is a column of air that contains updrafts that rotate around a vertical access. This column extends from a type of storm called a supercell (usually a thunderstorm but not always) to the ground. The air column rotates violently with great force, and can cause considerable damage to anything in its path.

Tornado ratings are based on wind speed. However, the wind speed of a tornado cannot be estimated directly, and therefore estimates are based on the degree of damage that the tornado caused. Tornado ratings are based on the Enhanced Fujita Scale (EF) (Table 3.9). The original Fujita Scale was introduced by Dr. T. Theodore Fujita in 1971, and estimated tornado strength based on structural damage to buildings and damage to trees. A drawback to this method was that it failed to estimate strength of tornados that occurred over plains, where fewer buildings and trees are present. In 2007, the National Weather Service adopted the Enhanced

Table 3.9 Enhanced Fujita Scale tornado ratings [10].

Category	Description	Fujita Scale (F) (1971–2007) 3 second gust miles per hour	Enhanced Fujita Scale (EF) (2007 to present) 3 second gust miles per hour
0	Gale	45–78	65–85
1	Weak	79–117	86–110
2	Strong	118–161	111–135
3	Severe	162–209	136–165
4	Devastating	210–261	166–200
5	Incredible	262–317	>200

Source: Adopted from the National Weather Service, https://www.weather.gov/oun/efscale (accessed 2 March 2020).

Fujita Scale, which considers a wider range of damage indicators in determining estimates of wind speed [10].

The National Weather Service announces Tornado Watches and Tornado Warnings in locations where tornados may occur. The purpose of these announcements is to provide people in the area with enough information to allow them to take appropriate protective measures such as moving to a place of safety in an interior room on the lowest floor of a sturdy building. Cars, vehicles, and mobile homes are not considered safe locations during a tornado. If personnel are in cars when a Tornado Warning is issued, they should be directed to drive to a place of safety. If that is not possible, personnel should get out of the vehicle and lie down in a low location such as a ditch. When a tornado strikes, it can destroy buildings, uproot trees, and hurl even large objects with deadly force.

- A *Tornado Watch* is issued by the National Oceanic and Atmospheric Administration (NOAA) Storm Prediction Center in Norman, Oklahoma, when weather conditions are favorable for tornados. The watch area is typically large, and may cover multiple counties or even states.
- A *Tornado Warning* is issued by a local forecast office when a tornado has been sighted or identified on weather radar. A Tornado Warning means that a tornado is imminent and that people need to move to a safe location.[7]

There may be significant devastation after the tornado. Responders can expect to face hazards from damaged buildings and infrastructure, as well as environmental hazards such as unstable walking surfaces, downed power lines, chemical spills, stressed animals, and distressed people.

3.6 Floods

Flooding occurs when water overflows onto land that is normally dry. This can happen when heavy rains overfill rivers, streams, or reservoirs, when dams or levees break, when snow melts too fast, or from ocean waves on shore.

A flash flood is a flood that results in a rapid rise of water in a short period of time. This can occur with little or no warning, and with considerable power and speed. Flash floods are the most dangerous types of floods.

Flood types include the following:

- *River floods*, which occur when water levels rise over the top of river banks;
- *Coastal floods*, or inundation of land areas along the coast;
- *Storm surge*, or an abnormal rise in water in coastal areas above the regular astronomical tide. If occurring at high tide, this can result in storm tides reaching up

---

7 http://www.weather.gov/safety/tornado (accessed 29 November 2018).

to 20 feet or more. Storm surge may result from a hurricane or other significant storm;
- Inland floods occur after heavy rains or dam or levee breaks, and can flood canyons or urban streets that are typically dry.[8]

The National Weather Service issues warnings and alerts on floods:

- *Flood Advisory*: A specific weather event has been forecast and nuisance level flooding may occur. Caution should be exercised to prevent situations that may threaten life and/or property.
- *Flood Watch*: Conditions are favorable for a hazardous weather event to occur. Conditions are favorable for flooding; this does not mean flooding will occur, but it is possible.
- *Flood Warning*: A hazardous weather event is imminent or already happening. Flooding is imminent or occurring.
- *Flash Flood Warning*: A flash flood is imminent or occurring. If a flash flood warning is issued, it is imperative to move to high ground.[9]

People who are caught in floodwaters are at risk of injury from fast moving water, drowning, or injury from objects moving in the water. If in shallow waters, and walking is possible, unseen hazards under the water can cause injury. Downed power lines can cause electrical hazards. Cold-related illness is also a risk (Figure 3.14).

Floods contribute to building damage, and building integrity following a flood should be inspected using a process similar to the inspections conducted for weather damage (Figure 3.15). In addition to weather damage, floods damage buildings by degrading materials that are susceptible to water inundation and/or

Figure 3.14 Volunteers used boats to rescue residents after Hurricane Harvey (2017). Source: Reproduced with kind permission of Allison Melton.

---

8 http://www.nssl.noaa.gov/education/svrwx101/floods (accessed 30 November 2018).
9 http://www.weather.gov/safety/flood-watch-warning (accessed 30 November 2018).

Figure 3.15 Flooding following Hurricane Harvey (2017). Source: Reproduced with kind permission of Allison Melton.

contamination from biological or chemical sources, and by adding hydrostatic forces to structures greater than they were designed to withstand. Coastal floods can be particularly damaging, as most structures are not built to withstand the repeated lateral loads that are created by tidal action [9].

Once flood waters recede, contamination may remain and wet building materials can be a source of fungal growth. Moist organic materials are a primary habitat for mold. Any damp, organic materials provides an environment suitable for environmental molds to colonize. These molds are ubiquitous in the environment; however, large colonies are problematic (Figures 3.16 and 3.17).

People who are allergic to mold can develop hay-fever-like symptoms such as sneezing, runny nose, red eyes, or skin rashes. Allergic sensitization can develop over time, so individuals who have not had a reaction to mold in the past could

Figure 3.16 Large area of fungal growth on walls. Wet building materials provide excellent growth media for mold. Source: Reproduced with kind permission of Martin Rose.

Figure 3.17 Black mold (*Stachybotris spp.*). Source: Reproduced with kind permission of Martin Rose.

still be susceptible. Severe health effects include asthma attacks and hypersensitivity pneumonitis, which resembles pneumonia. Molds can cause irritation even in nonallergic individuals, and people who are immune compromised can develop opportunistic infections when exposed to mold.

Mycotoxins are toxic metabolites produced by molds, and can create exposures through inhalation of toxins in the environment, ingestion of mycotoxins in food supplies, injection, and skin exposure. For example, Aflatoxin B1 is a potent carcinogen produced by *Aspergillus* species of mold, and is found in contaminated grains, peanuts, and other food sources.

Aside from the health effects that it causes, mold essentially digests building materials as it grows and can significantly impact the structure of building materials. Any visible mold should be removed.

Hard, impermeable materials such as plastics or metals can be cleaned with water and a mild detergent.

Semi-permeable materials, such as linoleum or vinyl, can be cleaned as well. However, these materials also trap moisture that supports mold growth in the subsurfaces and underflooring where it is not as readily visible, and these materials may need to be removed to determine whether or not mold is present.

Permeable materials, such as ceiling styles and cellulose insulation with visible mold growth should be removed and disposed of.

Biocides may be considered if the building material cannot be removed. However, biocides are primarily used as a preventative measure to inhibit initiation of mold growth rather than to kill existing growth, and are less useful once mold has become established. Even dead, or nonviable, molds can cause allergenic and irritant effects. Industrial hygienists with training and experience in mold evaluation and remediation should be called in to assess the extent of mold contamination and potential for impact on human health before considering use of biocides.

Damp materials should be dried as quickly as possible to prevent mold growth. For many years it was recommended that drying occur within 48 hours, and many agencies still consider drying within this 48-hour time frame to be optimal.

However, research has shown that it can take a week or two before materials become colonized with mold, so the window for drying may be a bit longer.

Workers who participate in remediation activities must take care to prevent skin contact and inhalation of mold. If contamination consists of less than 100 square feet, disposable N-95 respirators, gloves, eye protection, and disposable coverings such as Tyvek should be worn. If mold growth is greater than 100 square feet, an elastomeric respirator with P-100 filters should be used instead of an N-95, as well as full body coveralls with head and foot coverings [11–13].

3.7 Landslides

A landslide is a downslope movement of rock or soil, or both. Landslides can be caused when soil is saturated with water from excessive precipitation or snowmelt, from seismic activity from earthquakes, debris flow from volcanos, forest fires, or other mechanisms. Destabilization of soils as a result of clear cutting or burns can make areas more susceptible to landslides. Human activities and development also increase landslide risk through changes in drainage patterns, destabilization of slopes, and removal of stabilizing vegetation.

Landslides fall into the following categories:

- *Falls (rockfall)* is a detachment of soil or rock, or both, from a steep slope along a steep surface. Falling material descends by falling, bouncing, or rolling. The volume can vary from individual rocks or clumps of soil, to blocks thousands of cubic centimeters in size. Velocity of fall varies depending upon slope steepness, but free falling rocks, soils, or boulders can fall extremely rapidly. This type of fall can cause substantial damage to roads and railroads, and can kill people in the path of the fall.
- *Topple* is the forward rotation out of a slope of a mass of soil or rock around a point or axis below the center of gravity of the displaced mass. Toppling may be driven by gravity exerted by the weight of material upslope. This type of movement can occur in columnar jointed volcanic terrain and on steep banks along rivers and streams. Movement of material can be extremely slow to extremely rapid. When failure is sudden and/or the velocity is rapid, this type of movement can be extremely destructive.
- *Slides* are downslope movements of a soil or rock mass that occurs on surfaces of rupture or on relatively thin zones of intense shear strain. Movement does not initially occur simultaneously over the area of rupture. Movement can be very slow (less than 1 foot every five years) to very rapid. Rapid movements can be

extremely damaging to structures and roads. Large slides can dam rivers, causing flooding.

- *Spreads* occur when a cohesive soil or rock mass subsides over a lower layer of softer underlying material, and may occur when the lower, softer layers experience liquefaction or flow. Lateral spreads occur on gentle slopes or flat terrain, when the stronger upper layer of rock or soil experiences extension and moves over the underlying softer, weaker layer. Movement may be slow to rapid, with rapid movements following triggering events such as earthquakes. Lateral spreads can cause extensive property damage to buildings, roads, and railroads.
- *Flows* are a form of rapid mass movement where loose soil, rock, and possibly organic matter combine with water to form a slurry that flows downslope. They may be referred to as "mudslides." Dry flows that occur in cohesionless sand may be referred to as "sand flows." Movement can be extremely rapid, up to 35 miles per hour, depending on material and slope angle. Debris flow can have a rapid onset, high speed of movement, and may move large boulders or other similarly sized debris, causing substantial damage. Flows can move houses or rapidly fill structures with sediment and organic matter. Deposits can impact water systems [14].

Although work is being done to develop a landslide event magnitude system [15], there is currently no widely adopted system in use to compare size, magnitude, or degree of damage occurring from landslide events.

Responders in landslide events can be exposed to a variety of hazards. For example, hazards identified in the 2014 SR 530 Landslide in Oso, Washington, included:

- Voids and unstable surfaces;
- Potential land movements and falling rocks in slide area;
- Unknown chemical contaminants from residential areas, businesses, and agricultural operations;
- Biological contaminants;
- Compromised pipes and fuel vessels;
- Exposure to sharp objects, debris, and loose nails;
- Vehicle accidents and pedestrian accidents;
- Heavy equipment;
- Hazards from use of boats;
- Water hazards;
- Hypothermia;
- Dehydration;
- Fatigue [16].

3.8 Earthquakes

The Earth is not stable. Earthquakes occur as tectonic plates move and released stored energy, releasing that energy as waves that cause ground motion to occur. Motion can range from unnoticeable to severe.

Earthquakes most commonly occur at the boundaries of tectonic plates as these plates move horizontally past each other. Much of this motion is slow and steady, and is referred to as "creep." As creep occurs, certain segments may become stuck in place, or locked, along a fault line. These locked segments store large amounts of energy; Release of this energy causes "slip-strike" earthquakes. The point of rupture where seismic vibrations are produced is called the "earthquake focus," and the geographic point directly above the earthquake focus is called the "earthquake epicenter." Ground motion can be felt at some distance from the epicenter, and the amount of motion depends upon the size and magnitude of the earthquake as well as the surrounding geology and its susceptibility to movement. There are many active fault lines along the West Coast of the United States, Alaska, and Hawaii, and other fault lines that are less active along the East Coast and interior of the United States. Although earthquakes occur less frequently in the eastern part of the United States, the geology of the East Coast does not absorb energy as well as that of the West Coast, and East Coast earthquakes can cause damage over greater distances.

Midplate earthquakes occur in the interiors of tectonic plates rather than at plate boundaries. These types of earthquakes occur far less frequently than those that occur at plate boundaries, and are less well understood [17].

In some areas of the world, one tectonic plate may move underneath another tectonic plate in addition to the horizontal movement that occurs along plate boundaries. These types of faults are called "megathrust" faults or "subduction zones" and can produce the largest earthquakes in the world. In the United States, subduction zone earthquakes can occur along the Cascadian Subduction Zone, which runs from Northern California, Oregon, and Washington to British Columbia, and the Aleutian Trench in Alaska [18, 19].

Ground shaking from earthquakes can cause significant damage to structures and property, both internally and externally (Figure 3.18). People may be injured by falling objects when shaking occurs, or from secondary hazards that result from the earthquake. Following an earthquake, precautions should be taken for aftershocks that can take place after the main shock.

The amount of damage is related to the size of the earthquake and the amount of energy released.

Figure 3.18 Damage inside a home as a result of the magnitude 6.0 South Napa earthquake 24 August 2014. Source: Reproduced with kind permission of Gayle Young.

Earthquakes can be characterized by their intensity, the amount of damage caused by the earthquake, the magnitude, or the amount of energy released by the earthquake.

The Modified Mercalli Scale was developed as a measure of earthquake strength prior to the placement of reliable monitoring equipment in earthquake prone locations (Table 3.10) [20]. The Modified Mercalli Scale considers earthquake intensity through observed effects or outcomes. These effects are somewhat subjective, and analysis is subject to confounding factors. For example, an earthquake of similar magnitude will cause greater damage in a heavily populated region than in a remote region, and an earthquake that occurs in a locality that has adopted building codes that result in greater earthquake resiliency will cause less damage than an earthquake of similar magnitude that occurs in a location that has not incorporated seismic safety into the building codes.

Over time, seismographs that were capable of measuring the amplitudes of ground oscillation beneath the instrument were placed at monitoring stations in greater numbers, and Charles Richter proposed a method to quantify local earthquake magnitude based on the log of the maximum amplitude measured on the seismograph. Each number on the Richter Scale represents a 10-fold increase in energy over the previous number on the scale (Table 3.11) [21]. As more monitoring stations and seismographs were installed around the world, Richter's model was expanded to include body wave magnitude and surface wave

Table 3.10 Abbreviated description of the levels of the Modified Mercalli Intensity Scale.

Intensity Level	Description
I	Not felt except by a very few under especially favorable circumstances
II	Felt only by a few persons at rest, especially on upper floors of buildings
III	Felt quite noticeably indoors, especially on upper floors of buildings, but many people do not recognize it as an earthquake. Standing motor cars rocked noticeably
IV	During the day felt indoors by many, outdoors by few. At night some awakened. Dishes, windows, doors disturbed; walls made cracking sound. Sensation like heavy truck striking building. Standing motor cars rocked noticeably
V	Felt by everyone; many awakened. Some dishes, windows, etc. broken; a few instances of cracked plaster, unstable objects overturned. Pendulum clocks may stop
VI	Felt by all; many frightened and run outdoors. Some heavy furniture moved; a few instances of fallen plaster. Damage slight
VII	Damage negligible in buildings of good design and construction; slight to moderate in well-built ordinary structures; considerable in poorly built or badly designed structures; some chimneys broken
VIII	Damage slight in specially designed structures; considerable in ordinary substantial buildings with partial collapse. Damage great in poorly built structures. Fall of chimneys, factory stacks, columns, monuments, walls. Heavy furniture overturned
IX	Damage considerable in specially designed structures; well-designed frame structures thrown out of plumb. Damage great in substantial buildings, with partial collapse. Buildings shifted off foundations
X	Some well-built wooden structures destroyed; most masonry and frame structures destroyed with foundations. Rails bent

Source: The USGS uses ratings adapted from the Modified Mercalli Intensity Scale of 1931, Abridged [20]. https://www.usgs.gov/natural-hazards/earthquake-hazards/science/modified-mercalli-intensity-scale?qt-science_center_objects=0#qt-science_center_objects (accessed 2 March 2020).

magnitude. The Moment Magnitude scale was developed and provides greater accuracy for very large earthquakes [22].

In recent history, there have been five earthquakes of magnitude 9.0 or higher. The largest documented earthquake, the Valdivia Earthquake, had a magnitude

Table 3.11 Charles Richter developed the Richter Scale.

Magnitude	Impacts
0	Smallest shocks recorded
1.5	Smallest shocks that can be felt
3	Perceptible over an area 20 km in radius
4.5	Capable of causing slight damage near the epicenter
6	Destructive over a restricted area
7.5	Lower limit of major earthquakes

This scale reflects magnitude and relative impacts of earthquakes [21].

of 9.5 and occurred in Bio-Bio Chile on 22 May 1960.[10] Each of these large earthquakes occurred in subduction zones, and any subduction zone should be viewed as having the potential of producing an earthquake of 9.0 or higher [23]. Slip strike faults have produced earthquakes of magnitude 8.0, but it is not known if this is a maximum magnitude that represents the upper limit of energy that these faults can release. In all likelihood, slip strike faults are capable of producing earthquakes that exceed magnitudes of 8.0 [24].

One of the greatest hazards secondary to earthquakes is failure of buildings and infrastructure. Such failures are more likely to occur atop soils that are loosely held together, such as fill, or in saturated soils. When an earthquake occurs these types of soils undergo liquefaction: They temporarily lose strength and behave like fluids rather than solid materials. Any structure sitting atop such a soil is damaged accordingly.

People can be injured or killed by flying and falling objects during the shaking. Injuries and illnesses, and fatalities also result from failure of buildings or infrastructure such as roads or bridges. Hazardous components in building materials, such as lead or asbestos, or unaddressed fungal growth, can be shaken loose creating exposures for building occupants. Once shaking stops, hazards include fallen power lines or broken gas or sewer lines. Hazardous material spills, fires, landslides, and flooding are additional secondary hazards. Impacts are compounded because emergency response to secondary hazards is affected due to damaged roads and infrastructure, and to the shear extent of damage. Aftershocks can further exacerbate damage and increase hazards.

Earthquakes can occur at any time. Earthquake Early Warning (EEW) systems have been implemented around the world, in Japan, Mexico, Turkey, Taiwan, and

---

10 https://earthquake.usgs.gov/earthquakes/browse/largest-world.php (accessed 18 December 2018).

Romania [25], and is in early development in the United States in California and the Pacific Northwest. When an earthquake occurs, the rupture produces fast moving, low-energy P waves and slow moving, high-energy S waves. If sufficient seismometers have been networked, the P waves can be detected and triangulated in time to provide a warning before damaging S waves arrive. Such systems can provide a few seconds of warning to locations 20 miles from the epicenter and up to a minute of warning at a distance of 150 miles from the epicenter of a strong earthquake. A "blind zone" exists at the epicenter, where no warning would occur.

Warning systems for hurricanes and tornadoes can provide warnings of a few hours or even a few days in advance of the event. Compared with these types of warning systems, an EEW system that provides just a few seconds of notice may not seem like a lot of time. However, it does allow for actions to be taken that can prevent further damage:

- Bay doors at fire stations can be opened, so that they do not jam during shaking and prevent fire apparatus from leaving the station;
- Moving trains can slow or stop, decreasing the probability of derailment;
- Critical surgical tasks can be paused;
- Sensitive manufacturing equipment can be stopped or paused so that it is not damaged;
- Flow of industrial chemicals can be stopped;
- People can drop, cover, and hold in a safe location.

Rail systems in Japan are connected to Japanese EEW system, and slow automatically when an alert occurs. The Bay Area Rapid Transit (BART) system in California is a test user for the ShakeAlert System in the United States, and like Japan, can slow or stop trains upon activation of an alert [26].

The EEW prevented many injuries and saved infrastructure when the magnitude 9.0 Tohoku Earthquake occurred on 11 March 2011.

Following an earthquake, it is important to inspect buildings and infrastructure for safety and stability. ATC has developed procedures for post-earthquake evaluations, similar to the building inspection procedures that they developed for windstorms. Since a large area may be impacted, the earliest information available is based on reconnaissance or "windshield surveys" conducted within the first hours following the earthquake. Ideally, reconnaissance surveys are conducted by local building officials who know the area well and experienced structural engineers. Information from reconnaissance surveys provides preliminary information to plan Rapid and Detailed inspections.

ATC's Rapid Evaluation Method is designed to be used by individuals with at least five years of experience in general building design, construction, or inspection. This could include building inspectors, volunteer civil or structural engineers, architects, or building contractors. Inspection criteria includes damage

Table 3.12 ATC-20 criteria for post-earthquake inspection placards.

Placard	Color	Criteria
Inspected	Green	A building might have suffered some damage, but does not pose a risk for entry or occupancy
Restricted use	Yellow	A building has suffered damage such that the risk of partial collapse, local falling hazard, or other hazard necessitates some entry or occupancy restrictions
Unsafe	Red	High risk for entry or occupancy, which is usually caused by major damage. It is used when a structure has suffered severe damage to such a degree that it has collapsed, could collapse, or when falling or other hazards exist
		Note: This placard does not indicate that the building needs to be demolished

Source: Adapted from Applied Technology Council [27].

observed at the time of inspection due to the earthquake as well as possible hazards that may result from an aftershock. For this reason, the inspection criteria differs from the criteria used for inspection after windstorms or flooding.

The placard rating system and process is similar to that used for windstorms and starts with a Rapid Inspection. Following the Rapid Inspection, placards are dated and placed at all entrances to the building (Table 3.12). Inspected and Restricted Use placards include a caution statement: "Aftershocks since inspection may increase damage and risk." It is understood that re-inspection may be necessary following an aftershock.

Detailed inspections are conducted on buildings that receive Restricted Use placards during Rapid inspections. Personnel conducting detailed inspections should have experience in structural design as well as insight into the earthquake behavior of buildings. If the need for detailed inspections exceed the available resources with these qualifications, structural engineers, structural plan checkers, and other engineers with structural design expertise can be used. Inspectors should have at least 5–10 years of experience and knowledge of the effects of earthquakes on buildings. Detailed inspection teams then update the building placards as Inspected, Restricted Use, or Unsafe.

Buildings that are placarded as Restricted Use following the detailed inspection may be re-evaluated through an Engineering Evaluation. Engineering Evaluations are the responsibility of the building owner, and must be conducted by structural engineers. Following the Engineering Evaluation, and with approval from the jurisdiction, the placard may be changed to either Inspected or Unsafe. Additional specialties may need to participate in this inspection. For example, asbestos inspectors may need to evaluate whether or not asbestos exposures exceed safe levels, or industrial hygienists may evaluate whether or not a building is safe to occupy following a hazardous materials release.

Building inspectors should expect and be prepared to encounter building owners who may be experiencing and exhibiting a wide range of emotional responses. For example, some residents may not react calmly to being told that they may not enter a building that they own or live in to collect belongings, and some may be experiencing stress reactions as a result of the earthquake. Building inspectors may be the first official responders that these community members see in the aftermath of the earthquake. Building inspectors can help defuse emotional situations if they have factual information that they can provide to these community members about the earthquake and resources that are available. Social services departments should work with inspectors to ensure this information is available to them before they go out into the community [27, 28].

3.9 Volcanic Eruption

Molten rock, crystals, and dissolved gasses below the surface of the earth, or magma, can rise up to the surface of the earth through volcanic vents.

Erupting volcanoes emit lava (cooled magma), small rocks called "tephra," steam, and gasses. Eruptions may occur as molten rock pours from the vent, or shoot violently into the air as dense clouds, tephra, and gas. Ash and tephra may be carried many miles away: The smallest particles may even be carried around the world. Dense clouds of material and acid gasses produce ash fall and acid rain. Avalanches and landslides are produced as lava or pyroclastic flows move downwards from the vent. The largest flows, or lahars, resemble a roiling slurry of wet concrete and can move at speeds exceeding 120 miles per hour (mph) on steep slopes and incorporate anything encountered in this path into the flow. The US Geological Survey (USGS) has developed lahar detection systems which can be deployed when eruptions are imminent, or permanently installed. A permanent lahar detection system is installed Mount Rainier in Washington State. If a Lahar Warning is issued, evacuations plans are initiated.

USGS issues Volcano Alerts for active volcanoes (Table 3.13).[11]

Airborne ash clouds can cause significant damage to aircraft. Sufficient ash can interfere with visibility, and ash can damage engines. On 15 December 1999, a 747 jetliner dropped 2 miles in altitude and sustained substantial damage when all four engines stalled as a result of ash from the Redoubt Volcano erupting in Alaska 150 miles away. Ash clouds can be difficult to distinguish from ordinary clouds visually and on radar [29]; therefore, the USGS lists Aviation Color Codes for aircraft flying in the vicinity of volcanos (Table 3.14).

---

11 https://volcanoes.usgs.gov (accessed 20 December 2018).

Table 3.13 USGS volcanic alert levels.

Alert level term	Description
Normal	Volcano is in typical background, non-eruptive state, or, after a change from a higher level, volcanic activity has ceased and volcano has returned to a noneruptive background state
Advisory	Volcano is exhibiting signs of elevated unrest above known background level, or, after a change from a higher level, volcanic activity has decreased significantly but continues to be closely monitored for possible renewed increase
Watch	Volcano is exhibiting heightened or escalating unrest with increased potential of eruption, timeframe uncertain, or eruption is underway but poses limited hazards
Warning	Hazardous eruption is imminent, underway, or suspected

When a volcanic alert level is changed, a Volcano Activity Notice (VAN) is issued.
Source: https://volcanoes.usgs.gov (accessed 20 December 2018).

Table 3.14 Aviation Color Codes for volcanic eruption.

Color code	Description
Green	Volcano is in typical background, noneruptive state, or, after a change from a higher level, volcanic activity has ceased and volcano has returned to a noneruptive background state
Yellow	Volcano is exhibiting signs of elevated unrest above known background level, or, after a change from a higher level, volcanic activity has decreased significantly but continues to be closely monitored for possible renewed increase
Orange	Volcano is exhibiting heightened or escalating unrest with increased potential of eruption, timeframe uncertain, or, eruption is underway with no or minor volcanic-ash emission (ash plume height specified, if possible)
Red	Eruption is imminent with significant emission of volcanic ash into the atmosphere likely, or eruption is underway or suspected with significant emission of volcanic ash into the atmosphere (ash plume height specified, if possible)

When a volcano color code changes, a Volcano Observatory Notification for Aviation (VONA) is issued.
Source: Neal et al. [29].

Particulate matter produced from volcanic eruptions can be inhaled and is a health hazard. Volcanic ash in the environment can produce airborne silica at levels that exceed occupational exposure limits [30] and inhaled ash particles produce immunological reactions in people similar to those produced by silica and asbestos [31]. It is likely that ash consists of additional materials hazardous to health as well, such as metals, nanoparticles, and radioisotopes [32].

3.10 Tsunami

When an earthquake occurs, standing waves develop in closed water systems such as pools, rivers, reservoirs, ponds, or lakes. These types of waves are called "seiches." A tsunami is a giant wave produced by displacement of water due to a sudden uplift of the sea floor, and differs from a seiche. Sea floor uplifts that create the largest tsunamis, and produce large waves in distant locations, are caused by subduction zone earthquakes. Tsunamis can also be generated by landslides, volcanos, and slip-strike earthquakes. These tsunamis do not travel as far as those produced by subduction zone earthquakes but can have significant local impacts.

Weather systems can generate regional "meteotsunamis," which are similar to tsunamis generated by earthquakes.

Once generated, tsunami waves can travel at speeds up to 500 miles per hour in deep water, and can cross an ocean in less than a day. As the tsunami reaches land, speed decreases. Tsunami waves are generally less than 10 feet high in open water, but can exceed 100 feet in height when the wave strikes close to the source.[12]

Tsunami warning centers issue Tsunami Alerts to facilitate safety messaging and planning, and if necessary, evacuation (Table 3.15). However, tsunamis located at an earthquake epicenter or other source cause damage before warnings can be issued. Warning signs of an imminent tsunami include:

- Potential tsunami-generating events such as earthquakes;
- A sudden rise or fall of the ocean, or
- A loud roar from the ocean.[13]

Responders working in coastal earthquake zones should be aware of the indicators that precede a tsunami and be prepared to respond accordingly.

Tsunami waves can carry away anything in their path, including people on the coast or in boats, buildings, and debris. Buildings and infrastructure can be damaged or destroyed from strong wave forces. Flooding and dangerous currents can last for days.[14]

---

12 www.tsunami.gov (accessed 21 December 2018).
13 http://www.weather.gov/safety/tsunami-alerts (accessed 21 December 2018).
14 www.tsunami.gov (accessed 21 December 2018).

Table 3.15 Tsunami Alerts issued by the National Weather Service.

Alert statement	Situation	Action
Tsunami Warning	Take action – Danger! A tsunami that may cause widespread flooding is expected or occurring. Dangerous coastal flooding and powerful currents are possible and may continue for several hours or days after initial arrival	Follow instructions from local officials. Evacuation is recommended. Move to high ground or inland (away from water)
Tsunami Advisory	Take action – A tsunami with potential for strong currents or waves dangerous to those in or very near the water is expected or occurring. There may be flooding of beach and harbor areas	Stay out of the water and away from beaches and waterways. Follow instructions from local officials
Tsunami Watch	Be prepared – A distant earthquake has occurred. A tsunami is possible	Stay tuned for more information. Be prepared to take action if necessary
Tsunami Information Statement	Relax – An earthquake has occurred, but there is no threat or it was very far away and the threat has not been determined. In most cases, there is no threat of a destructive emergency	

Source: http://www.weather.gov/safety/tsunami-alerts (accessed 21 December 2018).

3.11 Fire

In the United States, fire departments respond to more than a million fires every year. In 2017, public fire departments responded to 1 319 500 fires in 2017. Of these, 499 000 were structure fires and 168 000 were highway vehicle fires. A fire department response in the United States occurs once every 24 seconds. Structure fires occur every 63 seconds, home fires occur every 88 seconds, and highway vehicle fires occur every 51 seconds. In 2017, these fires resulted in 3400 civilian deaths and an estimated $23 billion in property damage [33]. In addition, in 2017, an estimated 58 835 firefighters were injured in the line of duty, there were 7345 documented exposures to infectious disease, and 44 530 exposures to hazardous conditions. Of the reported injuries, 24 495 occurred on the fireground and 4555 occurred while responding to or returning from an incident. Other injuries occurred during training, non-fire emergency incidents, and other on-duty activities. Fireground injuries included:

- Sprain, strain, muscular pain: 48%
- Wound, cut, bleeding, bruise: 15%
- Smoke or gas inhalation: 7%
- Burns and smoke inhalation: 5%
- Thermal stress (frostbite, heat exhaustion): 5%
- Burns (fire or chemical): 4%
- Dislocation/fracture: 2%
- Other respiratory distress: 2%
- Other: 12% [34]

3.11.1 Chemical Exposures in Firefighting

The link between firefighting and cancer has given rise to much research on firefighter exposures to airborne contaminants, routes of exposure, and methods to reduce these exposures. Studies have looked at exposures during firefighting tasks such as *search and rescue* and *fire attack* during which firefighters are actively working in a burning structure. Other studies have looked at exposures to firefighters performing tasks such as *outside ventilation*, in which a firefighter is positioned outside the burning structure, and *overhaul* in which firefighters search the scene once the fire is extinguished to prevent reignition. Firefighters routinely wear SCBAs when inside an actively burning structure (search and rescue and fire attack), as is appropriate for any atmosphere in which immediately dangerous to health (IDLH) conditions or oxygen-deficient atmospheres are presumed to exist. Sampling results have indeed shown that firefighters performing *search and rescue* and *fire attack* are indeed exposed to IDLH atmospheres. Firefighters performing *outside ventilation* may be exposed to hydrogen cyanide above IDLH levels as well, which justifies the use of SCBAs when performing tasks immediately outside of the structure (Figure 3.19). Exposures during *overhaul* are less than IDLH, although occupational exposure limits are exceeded. It is not standard practice in many fire departments to continue to wear SCBAs during *overhaul*; however, given that significant exposures can occur during this task, some level of respiratory protection is warranted. Command and support personnel also receive significant enough exposures that respiratory protection should be considered [35].

Although SCBAs are necessary in IDLH environments, they also create strain, contribute to workload, and decrease the body's ability to cool itself during heat exposure. Several studies have looked at the use of air-purifying respirators (APRs) during overhaul work, and have found that APRs with CBRN cartridges effectively reduce exposures of most airborne contaminants to levels of occupational exposure limits. CBRN cartridges, however, do not efficiently prevent exposure to carbon monoxide and formaldehyde [36–38]. For this reason, if APRs are used,

Figure 3.19 Fires create IDLH-level atmospheres, thus SCBA use is warranted. Source: Reproduced with kind permission of Isaac Howard.

carbon monoxide should be monitored. This can best be accomplished with carbon monoxide monitors that alarm when exposure limits are exceeded. SCBAs should be available in the event that carbon monoxide levels exceed occupational exposure limits.

SCBAs provide effective protection from contaminants via the respiratory route. Dermal exposure to contaminants, including those that can be absorbed through skin, is an additional exposure route that must be controlled [35]. Personal Protective Equipment provides protection by reducing the level of contaminants under firefighting gear, but does not eliminate exposure. (Figures 3.20–3.27) In fact, PPE may even trap contaminants in the microenvironment underneath protective gear [39]. Contaminants that have been detected on firefighter gear include volatile organic hydrocarbons, particulate materials including PM_{10} and $PM_{2.5}$ [40], heavy metals including cadmium, chromium, copper and lead [41], arsenic, barium, mercury, and others [42]. Additional contaminants include those that result from combustion of synthetic building materials such as plasticizers, phthalates [43], and flame retardants [44, 45].

These contaminants are also found in fire stations at higher levels than in homes or other occupational settings [45]. In one study, the highest levels of contaminants were detected in kitchens and truck bays, and detectable levels of contaminants were also found in sleeping quarters, break rooms, and offices [40]. Results are not always consistent: Another study also found high levels of contaminants in truck bays but lower levels in kitchens [46]. These differences could be a result of station layout, cleaning and hygiene practices, ventilation, or other reasons. However, the fact that any significant level of contaminants is detected in living areas of fire stations is concerning.

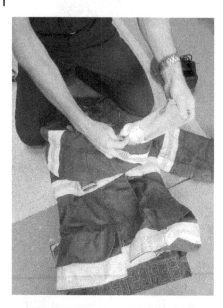

Figure 3.20 Gauntlets on the sleeves of firefighter turnout coats maintain the position of the coat sleeve when the arm is in an extended position. Newer technology such as Lion Manufacturing Red Zone turnout gear has gauntlets with particle blocking properties.

Figure 3.21 The neck of this turnout coat does not have a gauntlet. A particle blocking gauntlet would provide greater protection from contaminants.

Occupational exposure limits for chemical exposures are based on "traditional" work exposures that assume that workers who are exposed to chemicals during work hours also have a recovery period during their off duty hours. Depending on the length of shift worked, workers are assumed to have non-exposure periods of 12–16 hours between shifts. Firefighters, however, live at their stations while

Figure 3.22 The waist of this turnout coat does not have a gauntlet. A particle blocking gauntlet would provide greater protection.

Figure 3.23 This turnout coat uses a Hook and D closure; gaps can allow passage of contaminants under gear.

Figure 3.24 The Velcro fly on this set of turnout pants can create gaps that allow passage of contaminants.

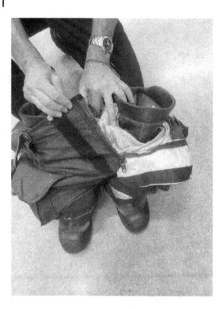

Figure 3.25 Turnout pants with a zipper fly. This closure does not create gaps and provides a better barrier against contaminants.

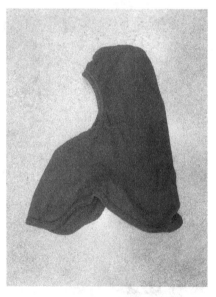

Figure 3.26 Standard firefighter hood worn underneath helmet to protect the neck and head areas.

on duty, and typically work shifts of 24–48 hours. Therefore, firefighters who are exposed to contaminants inside the fire station do not have benefit from the same recovery periods that are assumed from occupational exposure limits.

The finding that contaminants may be present in kitchen areas is particularly concerning. Contaminants in kitchens can be transferred to food items, and

Figure 3.27 Particulate hoods offer greater protection against exposures.

exposure through the ingestion route adds to exposures that are also occurring through inhalation and dermal exposure. A fire station design that locates kitchen areas away from truck bays and showers could reduce tracking of contaminants into the kitchen.

Volatile organic compounds (VOCs) can off-gas from firefighter's Personal Protective Equipment ensembles after use, and can contribute to inhalation exposures if worn or kept in the cab of the fire apparatus cabin when returning from a fire [47]. Protective gear can also absorb fire-retardant compounds, which are expected to readily absorb through skin, especially when skin temperatures are elevated [43]. Clean cab practices, including removal of PPE after a fire and prior and storing it outside the cab during the ride back to the fire station would reduce this exposure (Figures 3.28 and 3.29).

This also suggests that PPE ensembles should be stored away from the living environments at fire stations when not in use.

Field decontamination of PPE can reduce secondary exposures to some compounds and prevent tracking of contaminants back to the station. Several field decontamination methods have been studied: Dry brushing, water only decontamination, and water/soap decontamination. Of these three methods, only water and soap decontamination methods have been shown to significantly reduce contamination [48, 49]. Use of Nomex hoods and wet wiping of exposed skin after exiting the fireground can also reduce contaminants on skin [48].

Traditionally, dirty firefighter gear was viewed as a badge of honor: A firefighter with dirty gear was seen as a good, trustworthy firefighter. However, given

Figure 3.28 Firefighter gear is often kept inside the cab to allow easier access upon arrival at a fire scene. After the fire, gear can off-gas volatile organic compounds, and this creates another exposure source for firefighters.

Figure 3.29 This apparatus contains a compartment for gear storage outside the cab. Storage of gear outside the cab reduces occupant exposures due to off-gassing. A more effective practice would be to bag gear at the scene and decontaminate it before reuse.

current knowledge regarding cancer risks in firefighters, this attitude is changing. Unfortunately, this attitude does not always translate into increased rates of actual decontamination. Decontamination takes additional time, and firefighters may be concerned that having wet gear following decontamination makes it more difficult to do their job, since wet gear may be uncomfortable, reduce mobility, and cause steam burns. Showering after a fire is reportedly a more common practice, although this does not happen 100% of the time [50]. As safety culture evolves, some fire departments have begun to embrace Clean Cab systems, or the concept that anything, including PPE and other equipment, that goes into a fire does not go back into the cab with the firefighters [51].

Use of Nomex hoods can protect against contaminant exposures to skin on the head and neck during firefighting; however, buildup of contaminants on hoods can contribute to secondary exposures. Laundering of hoods reduces levels of polycyclic aromatic hydrocarbons (PAHs) but not fire retardant chemicals. In fact, fire retardant chemicals buildup on fabrics with repeated washings, and appear to cross contaminate materials that were not initially contaminated with these compounds. Flame retardant compounds were also found to increase with subsequent washing. This could indicate that cross contamination occurs in laundry systems or that changes in the fabric occur over time and create conditions that make it more receptive to picking up lipophilic contaminants [52]. More evaluation is needed to identify effective laundering procedures to remove these types of contaminants.

Use of PPE provides protection from exposure, although it is not 100% protection. However, PPE is not always available. Overall, 53% of US fire departments report that they cannot equip every firefighter on shift with an SCBA, and of these, 69% of departments reported that some of their equipment was greater than 10 years old; 13% of departments cannot provide all emergency responders with their own personal protective clothing; and 72% of departments reported that at least some of their personal protective clothing was at least 10 years old [53].

3.11.2 Additional Hazards to Firefighters

Firefighters are exposed to extreme heat conditions, often in temperatures exceeding 200 °F for up to an hour. Although heat protective gear is worn, firefighters are at risk of heat-related illness and dehydration. Methods to combat these risks have been studied. Forearm and leg submersion in cool water during rest breaks [54] and use of cooling garments [55] have been found to mitigate effects of high temperature exposures.

Firefighters are also at risk of Noise-Induced Hearing Loss (NIHL) due to noise exposures. NIHL is considered to be entirely preventable if appropriate hearing protection is worn. Noise sources include sirens and air horns from fire apparatus, use of power tools such as saws or powered hand tools, generators and air compressors, testing SCBA equipment and filling air bottles, and using noisy equipment such as mowers or leaf blowers when doing station work. Noise may be perceived by firefighters as a lower level hazard than others that they face. They also can perceive hearing protective devices to be cumbersome when worn with other required PPE, and are concerned that they may interfere with hearing someone calling out during rescue. For these reasons, firefighters may fail to utilize hearing protection and develop hearing loss [56].

3.11.3 Wildland Fires

1 319 500 fires occurred in 2017 of these, 623 000 occurred outside and at locations identified as "other properties," including the Carr Fire in Northern California. The Carr Fire caused $10 billion in property losses, out of the $23 billion total fire related losses in 2017 [33]. These types of fires include additional hazards including injuries related to working on uneven surfaces, exhaustion and fatigue, and operation of heavy equipment under these conditions. Between 2011 and 2015, grass and forest fires caused an average of 1330 injuries, or 5% of all injuries in firefighters. As a percentage, volunteer firefighters were injured almost twice as often as career firefighters [57].

Wildfires across western North America have increased in number and size over the past three decades. This trend is expected to continue in the future as a result of global warming, the increase in size of the wildland urban interface (WUI), and fuel buildup [58]. The WUI, or the area where houses and wildland vegetation meet is where wildfire is most problematic. Growth in the WUI has occurred rapidly. Between 1990 and 2010 the WUI saw 41% increase in the number of new houses and 33% increase in land area. Human activity in the WUI is often the source of wildfire ignition [59]. The Carr Fire that occurred in northern California in July and August 2017 was particularly damaging: The area had a very wet spring, leading to excess vegetation growth or fuel loading, and was followed by a dry period with half the normal precipitation and record high temperatures. The magnitude of the fire and the high temperatures led to the formation of a tornado-strength fire-generated vortex that was estimated to be equivalent to an EF-3 tornado [60].

The changing dynamics of wildfires along with the increase in occurrence and lengthening of the wildfire season has significance when considering safety of wildland firefighters. A pilot study conducted at the University of Idaho has found that fatigue takes its toll over the season, leading to a reduction in alertness and increase in reaction times as the season progresses. Diet, which consists largely of premade meals, may also play a factor. The pilot study found that firefighters lost muscle mass and gained fat over the course of the study. Air quality is another concern. Although all wildfires produce volatile organic compounds and particulate matter (PM_{10}), wildfires that occur in the WUI can be expected to release larger amounts of combustion products from synthetic materials in buildings than that has been seen in the past [61].

3.12   Transportation Incidents

Responders to transportation incidents face many of the same hazards as those faced by responders to incidents in building. Additional hazards include traffic related hazards, fuel hazards, and hazards from products of combustion of synthetic materials and metals. Mass casualty incidents involving transportation vehicles, such as busses, aircraft, and passenger trains present exposure to biological hazards including blood-borne pathogens. Extrication of injured passengers from tight spaces in busses, aircraft, and railcars is an ergonomics challenge, and responders are susceptible to musculoskeletal injuries in these types of events.

Any transportation incident is considered a possible crime scene until proven otherwise, and preservation of evidence is a consideration during response. Criminal investigators and those conducting the incident investigation are also subject to hazards at the scene.

3.12.1   Aircraft Incidents

The Federal Aviation Administration (FAA) has jurisdiction over air transportation systems, including airlines and airports. Civil aircraft accidents are investigated by the National Transportation Safety Board (NTSB), an independent federal agency which also investigates significant accidents on railroads, highways, and marine and pipeline transportation systems.

Hazards at the scene of an aircraft incident can include:

- Biohazards spread over a large area;
- Hazardous chemicals;
- Combustion products, especially of composite materials;
- Fuel:
  - Jet A used in large aircraft is a combustible liquid;
  - Aviation gas (Av-Gas) used in small aircraft is a flammable liquid;
- Oxygen bottles and tanks;
- Stored energy:
  - Pneumatic systems;
  - Hydraulic systems;
  - Batteries;
- Moving parts in engines or propellers that did not shut off during the incident:
  - Operating engines can suck objects into the engine;
  - Jet blast: air exiting the back of the engine can move at speeds up to 100 miles per hour, with enough force to blow vehicles over;
- Instability of aircraft;
- High heat exposure;

- Penetration hazards;
- Airbags.

Internal spaces in the aircraft can be accessed at designated locations, such as doors and windows. Attempts to create openings in other locations require specialized equipment. Cutting creates risks of severing fuel lines, live electrical lines, pressurized systems, or a ballistic parachute system. Attempts to access personnel through the windshield is ineffective and can delay response to victims. Any potential responder to an aircraft incident should receive training in aircraft response in order to create awareness of unique hazards and build efficiencies into the response.[15]

Certified airports must meet minimum requirements for rescue and firefighting equipment depending upon the type of aircraft and certification level of the airport, including delivery of dry chemical agents and water or foam. Firefighters must receive training and participate in at least one live fire drill every 12 months. Airports are required to coordinate with law enforcement, rescue and firefighter agencies, medical personnel and organizations, and principle tenants of the airport in an Airport Emergency Plan. Class I airports that serve scheduled operations of large aircraft must conduct a full-scale emergency drill once every 36 months [62]. As many parties have roles identified in the Airport Emergency Plan, triennial drills provide an opportunity for these entities to work together, build relationships, and practice working in a multi-agency ICS response.

Fire departments that perform Aircraft Rescue Fire Fighting (ARFF) must comply with NFPA codes for the following:

- NFPA 1981 2007 Edition, Standard on Open Circuit Self-Contained Breathing Apparatus (SCBA) for Emergency Services;
- NFPA 1936 2005 Edition Standard on Portable Rescue Tools;
- NFPA 1971 2007 Edition Standard on Protective Ensembles for Structural Fire Fighting and Proximity Firefighting [63].

Responders to aircraft emergencies at an operating airport must be prepared to encounter hazards on the airfield, including operating aircraft and jet blast from engines, unless all operations have been stopped due to the emergency. Jet blast, or the air that is released from the back of an aircraft engine, has enough force to blow vehicles over.

Proximity firefighting gear is designed to protect firefighters from extreme heat conditions generated by aircraft fires, and is provided for ARFF fire departments. However, many aircraft crashes happen outside airport boundaries, and first responding fire departments from local jurisdictions may not have ARFF training or equipment. In addition, crashes in remote locations create additional hazards

---

15 https://www.faa.gov/aircraft/gen_av/first_responders (accessed 28 December 2018).

for responders, including difficult terrain that can complicate accessing the site and removing victims [64].

3.12.2 Rail Incidents

The Federal Railroad Administration (FRA) has jurisdiction over interstate rail systems. The Federal Transit Administration (FTA) and state transportation departments have jurisdiction over rail systems in which the tracks begin and end in the same state including most local light rail transit systems. As with aircraft incidents, the NTSB investigates significant rail accidents.

Railroads that operate passenger trains or commuter trains under authority of the FRA are required to develop Passenger Train Emergency Preparedness Plans (PTEPP) which must be submitted to, and approved by, the FRA. The railroad is also required to develop relationships and liaison with emergency responders through developing a training program for those responders who could reasonably expect to respond to a train emergency, participating with emergency responders in field exercises, and distributing the PTEPP to emergency responders. Field exercises or simulations must be conducted every two years for commuter railroads that cover less than 150 route miles and less than 200 passenger miles annually. Intercity passenger or commuter railroads, railroads that cover more than 150 route miles, or more than 200 passenger miles every year must conduct field exercises annually [65]. Plans, training, and field exercises should emphasize the rail specific hazards that emergency responders may not be aware of, including:

- The curved surface of the rail is a slip and trip hazard: Rail employees are instructed to always step over a rail and never step on top of the rail. Emergency responders should do the same.
- Extruded rail is maintained under tension during normal operations. If rail tension is released at an accident scene, it can recoil with tremendous force.
- Utility companies contract with railroads to run fiber optic lines, gas lines, or electrical lines along the railroad rights of way. Responders should be prepared to encounter utility lines at depths of 30–45 inches below the railroad ballast.
- Railroad switches, which move trains on intersecting tracks, are operated remotely from dispatch centers that may be located many states away from scene. Switches operate without warning and with enough force to crush medium-sized rocks. Steel-toed boots are not strong enough to withstand this force, and neither are toes and feet.

Hazards related to rescue of passengers from railroad cars are similar to those related to rescue of passengers from aircraft: Passengers may need to be removed from tight spaces, creating ergonomics hazards for responders and risk of musculoskeletal injuries. Pneumatic and electrical lines present stored energy hazards, and fuel from the engine presents a spill or fire hazard. Entry into cars can occur at designated locations only. Rescue equipment is ineffective when used at non-designated locations of the rail car.

One of the greatest hazards when responding to a rail incident is moving trains. Trains are heavy, move at speeds up to 79 miles per hour, and due to the laws of physics they cannot stop quickly. Emergency response vehicles operating with lights and sirens have the right of way on roads; however, this does not change the laws of physics and emergency response vehicles do not have the same right of way at railroad crossings that they do on roadways. Emergency responders cannot expect a train to stop for them at a railroad crossing.

In an incident, emergency responders should assume that a train needs up to 2 miles to stop, and send personnel 2 miles in each direction of an incident scene to flag oncoming trains. This should be done even if they have been told that train traffic has stopped. Coordination between railroad personnel and emergency responders is critical, and Unified Command should be established early in the course of the incident to protect responders by ensuring that timely communication occurs between railroad operations and emergency response agencies [66, 67].

The FRA has established worker safety rules for railroad employees, and emergency responder training should cover those rules that are relevant to emergency responders. In particular, FRA has established procedures for any work that is done on track and within 4 feet of the nearest rail. Emergency responders who "foul the track," or come within 4 feet of the nearest rail without coordinating with, and receiving permission from, the railroad are at high risk of being hit or injured by a moving train [68]. Emergency responder training should also include relevant elements of the railroad's System Safety Program Plan [69].

FTA requires that states establish a State Safety Oversight (SSO) agency to implement FTA requirements for rail transit agencies that are not under the jurisdiction of FRA. SSOs must establish rules meeting FTA requirements for System Safety Program Plans, System Security Plans, review of these plans, hazard management, accident notification and investigation, and corrective action plans [70]. Specific requirements for coordination with emergency responders, emergency responder training, tabletop and field exercises, are determined by the SSO and vary by state.

Many rail transit systems, or light rail systems, operate under electric power rather than by fuel combustion. Electrical power can be supplied through an electrified third rail, or through an overhead catenary system. Responders to a light rail incident must be prepared to encounter electrical hazards as well as other hazards specific to the rail environment, and any responder that comes within 10 feet of the power source must first notify and receive permission from the railroad. In an incident, it is critical to include representatives from Rail Traction Power in Unified Command along with railroad operations and emergency response agencies [71].

3.13 Pandemic

We are exposed to many pathogens in the environment on a daily basis, including viruses, bacteria, molds, and others. Fortunately, we also have immune systems that protect us from these pathogens, as long as our immune systems are functioning as they should. Our immune systems have memories: If we are exposed to a pathogen that we have successfully fought off in the past, we develop antibodies that protect us from future illness caused by that pathogen.

Many viruses circulate the globe, including influenza viruses which cause the "flu," and viruses such as rhinoviruses, adenoviruses, and coronaviruses that cause colds or other illnesses. These viruses mutate quickly, which enable them to infect hosts that have successfully fought off other similar viruses in the past. However, the antibodies that we have developed to protect us to related viruses provide some protection and allow us to fight off mutated versions of the virus.

Viruses are unique to the host species that they infect. However, as mutations occur, the virus can make a jump to infect new species of hosts. This is especially dangerous to the new host, which has not developed antibodies to any part of the novel virus and has a much harder time fighting it off. When novel viruses develop the ability to easily transmit between humans, they can infect many people quickly, spread around the world in a short period of time, and become a pandemic. Past pandemics have resulted in high numbers of fatalities and hospitalizations (Table 3.16).[16]

The World Health Organization (WHO) has developed regulations to protect against, control, and provide a public health response against the spread of disease. Under international regulations, the WHO directorate can declare a Public Health

Table 3.16 Past influenza pandemics.

Year	Name	Subtype	Animal host	Deaths (worldwide)	Deaths (United States)
1889	Russian flu	—	Unknown	—	—
1918–1919	Spanish flu	H1N1	Unknown	50 million	675 000
1957–1958	Asian flu	H2N2	Bird	1.1 million	116 000
1968	Hong Kong flu	H3N2	Bird	1 million	100 000
2009–2010	Swine flu	H1N1	Pig	151 700–575 400	12 469

Source: https://www.cdc.gov/flu/pandemic-resources/basics/past-pandemics.html and https://Info.thelancet.com/pandemic-flu-100 (accessed 31 December 2018).

16 https://www.cdc.gov/flu/pandemic-resources/basics/past-pandemics.html and https://Info.thelancet.com/pandemic-flu-100 (accessed 31 December 2018).

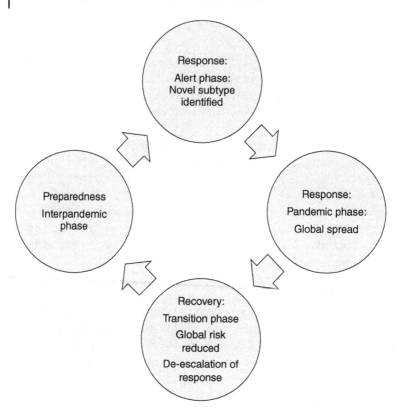

Figure 3.30 World Health Organization pandemic phases [73].

Emergency of International Concern. Member states, including the United States, have signed onto and agreed to follow these international regulations [72].

In support of these regulations, WHO has developed guidance for member countries to follow in the event of an influenza pandemic. The WHO considers that there are four phases to a pandemic (Figure 3.30). The WHO Director-General has the authority to make the declaration of a pandemic. Actions taken during these pandemic phases depend upon risk assessments performed within individual countries. The WHO supports research and information sharing, and maintains strategic stockpiles of antiviral medications and vaccines [73].

In the United States, the Centers for Disease Control and Prevention (CDC) has developed an Influenza Risk Assessment Tool (IRAT) to assess pandemic risk posed by influenza A virus that circulate in animals. The IRAT considers 10 scientific criteria that include categories of "property of the virus," "attributes of the populations," and "ecology and epidemiology of the virus." Influenza experts evaluate novel influenza viruses based on IRAT criteria, and develop a composite score for the virus. Based on the scores, the virus is classified as low, moderate, or high risk. Public health officials will also evaluate emerging virus using the Pandemic Severity Assessment Framework (PSAF) to evaluate clinical severity and transmissibility, or the ability of the virus to spread from person to person. IRAT and PSAF scores then guide decision-making according to the national Pandemic Influenza Plan.

The primary goal of the Plan is to contain, and prevent spread of infection until a vaccine can be developed and distributed. In the 2009–2010 H1N1 pandemic, it took 26 weeks for the first doses of vaccine to become available after the initial decision was made to begin vaccine development, and it was only available in small quantities. Since that time, the United States has worked to develop strategies to decrease the length of time to develop a future novel flu vaccine [74]. Unfortunately, similar infrastructure is not in place for non-influenza pandemic viruses.

A severe pandemic, or one with high IRAT and PSAF scores, causes social and economic disruption in addition to health consequences to individuals. When a large number of people become seriously ill, or stay home from work out of fear of contagion or to care for sick family members, workplaces and government systems are seriously impacted. The CDC, along with state and local public health agencies and governments, can implement control measures such as social distancing, closing schools and events which would attract large crowds, and encourage employers to implement telecommuting and generous leave policies. Recommendations are then be communicated through state and local public health departments, and decisions are then made at the local level based on community needs and risks.

Workplace controls must be implemented to protect employees that come in to work. These include the standard hierarchy of controls: Engineering controls such as ventilation or placement of physical shielding between workers can be used to reduce exposures to airborne pathogens. Administrative controls include education, training, and work practices such as handwashing. Workplace social distancing measures can be implemented, such as having workers come in on rotating shifts and prohibiting in-person meetings. PPE such as eye protection, gloves, and respirators can be used when available [75]. OSHA recognizes several classifications of employees in a pandemic: *Very High Risk Employees,* such as healthcare workers who perform high risk medical procedures on infected persons; *High Risk Employees* such as health care workers, emergency medical responders and mortuary workers who work with persons who may be infected; *Medium Risk Employees* who work with the public (including members of the public who may be infected) such as retail workers; and *Low Risk Employees* who do not interact with the public. When PPE is in short supply, providing it to Very High Risk Employees and High Risk Employees is the priority. Respiratory protection, such as surgical N95 filtering facepiece masks, should be provided to employees who may be exposed to the novel pathogen. When N95 masks are not available, OSHA recommends using half face or full face elastomeric respirators or PAPRs fitted with N, R, or P 95, 99 or 100 filters [84–86].

A severe pandemic has significant impacts on businesses, critical infrastructure, and the supply chain. If 30% of the workforce is absent, for example, businesses cannot perform all the tasks that they can perform when fully staffed. They must identify which core functions are essential and which can be delayed, and need to train and staff accordingly. Many organizations have recognized the importance of Continuity of Operation Planning (COOP) for All Hazards as a result of working on their pandemic flu plans. This is a good business practice, and is required for any operations identified as critical infrastructure:

- Chemical Facilities;
- Commercial Facilities;
- Communications;
- Critical Manufacturing;
- Dams;
- Defense Industrial Base;
- Emergency Services;
- Energy;
- Financial Services;
- Food and Agriculture;
- Government Facilities;
- Healthcare and Public Health;
- Information Technology;
- Nuclear Reactors, Materials, and Waste;
- Transportation Systems;
- Water and Wastewater Systems [76].

3.14 Radiological Incident

Unstable atoms release radiation when they decay to a more stable condition (Table 3.17). Long-term health effects related to radiation exposure include cancer and impacts to fetal development in pregnant women. Short-term exposure to very high levels of radiation, such as exposures that could occur in an emergency, can cause injury to skin as well as Acute Radiation Syndrome: Nausea, vomiting, headache, and diarrhea occurring within minutes to days of the exposure, followed by a stage of serious illness including loss of appetite, fatigue, fever, nausea, vomiting, diarrhea, and possibly seizures and coma.[17]

---

17 https://emergency.cdc.gov/radiation/healtheffects.asp (accessed 14 January 2019).

Table 3.17 Types of radiation.

Type	Source	Protective shielding	Energy
Alpha	Two protons and two neutrons ejected from the nucleus	Paper	Travels a few inches in air; does not penetrate skin
Beta	Electron ejected from the nucleus when a neutron becomes a proton	Plexiglas	Can travel several feet in air and penetrate skin to the germinal layer
Gamma	Photon ejected from the nucleus	Lead	Can travel many feet in air and penetrate many inches in human tissue
X-ray	Photon ejected from an electron shell	Lead	Can travel many feet in air and penetrate many inches in human tissues

Radiological incidents can occur as a result of:

- An incident involving an organization operating under a Nuclear Regulatory Commission (NRC) license or an Agreement State license. Licensees must be prepared to respond and ensure the protection of the public in the event of an incident.
- An incident that is not associated with an NRC licensee, such as a transportation incident. Response agencies would include State, local, and tribal authorities, and federal agencies such as the EPA, Coast Guard (CG), and Department of Energy with support from the NRC.
- Domestic nuclear weapons accidents;
- Terrorism, including use of improvised nuclear devices (INDs), such as:
  o Radiological dispersal devices (RDDs), which release radioactive material into the environment;
  o Radiation exposure devices (REDs), which emit radiation into the environment.
- International incidents that impact or threaten to impact the United States [77, 78].

Responders in a radiological incident are subject to external radiation exposures, or exposure to the alpha or beta particles, or to the gamma rays or X-rays, which are emitted from a radiation source. Internal radiation exposure is more serious, and occurs when radioactive materials enter the body through inhalation, ingestion, dermal exposure, or injection. Absorbed material then emits radiation to internal tissues from inside the body to directly expose internal organs to radioactive energy.

Within the first 15 minutes of an incident, the primary hazard is inhalation of radioactive particulate materials. Protection of personnel focusses on protection from environmental materials through use of self-contained breathing apparatus, or, if not available, respirators with P-100 filters. Body surfaces should be covered as much as possible so that protective coverings can be removed once responders leave the response area and enter a "clean" area. This prevents tracking of contamination into the clean area and reduces subsequent exposures such as ingestion from hand to mouth activities. It is expected that airborne materials will settle after the first 15 minutes of the incident, and PPE can then be downgraded if exposure assessments support it. Protection of personnel should follow the concept of ALARA, which is the principle of maintaining exposures As Low As Reasonably Achievable and using the highest level of protection available [79].

3.15 Terrorism Attack: Chemical or Biological Release

Terrorism includes the unlawful use of force and violence against persons or property to intimidate or coerce a government, the civilian population, or any person in the furtherance of political or social objectives [80]. Terrorism may be inspired or directed by foreign, state-sponsored, terrorist organizations, or by individuals or domestic groups that have extremist ideologies. Significant past terror events include:

- Letter bombs sent by the Unabomber from the 1970s to the 1990s;
- Bombing of the Alfred P. Murrah building in Oklahoma City on 19 April 1995;
- Aum Shinrikyo Sarin release in the Tokyo Underground in 1995;
- 9/11 Terror attacks;
- 2001 Anthrax attacks, in which letters containing anthrax spores were sent to news media offices and Democratic senators;
- Bomb explosions on trains at stations in Madrid, Spain, on 11 March 2004;
- Bomb explosions at the Boston Marathon on 15 April 2013;
- San Bernardino shootings and attempted bombing on 2 December 2015.

Terrorist attacks may be well planned out by trained teams, or cells, as was the case in 9/11. They may be conducted by a small group of individuals who subscribe to an agenda, as in the case with the San Bernardino attacks and the bombing of the Boston Marathon. They may be conducted by single individuals with a personal agenda such as the Unabomber. In planning for a terrorism response, it is assumed that terrorists will attempt to maximize casualties by attacking locations where people congregate. There may be multiple attacks at multiple locations, or secondary attacks at the scene of the first event after emergency responders arrive in order to maximize casualties to emergency responders [81].

Following a terror attack, response workers face a multitude of hazards. Many of these hazards are similar to those faced in response to other emergencies, such as exposures to chemical or biological agents, inhalation hazards, fire hazards, infectious disease exposure, unstable surfaces, buildings and infrastructure, or hazards relating to work around transportation systems including trains and aircraft. However, there are more unknowns when responding to a terrorist incident, and fewer assumptions can be made as to the limits of the hazards faced. Responders entering a terror scene, especially initial responders, should be prepared to encounter a multitude of unknown hazards. In addition, the scene of a terrorist attack is a crime scene, and responders must take care to preserve evidence.

PPE was a limitation in the response to 9/11. The greatest limitation was simply that there was not enough PPE for everyone who responded. However, much of the PPE that was available was not appropriate for the hazards. Ideally, responders would have entered the scene wearing full body protective equipment and self-contained breathing apparatus (SCBAs), but many responders were volunteers and did not have SCBAs. Even professional responders who did have SCBAs found that the quantities of supplied air was insufficient. While air bottles contain sufficient air for a short-term fire response, responders in 9/11 were on scene for hours over many days. Air bottles had to be changed out every 30–60 minutes, and the supply of air to refill used air bottles did not meet demand. Many responders wore air-purifying respirators, without knowing whether the air-purifying filters or canisters were appropriate for the hazard that they were exposed to. This led to a recommendation for the development of new types of PPE that would better protect against universal hazards in future responses [82].

To respond to this need, NIOSH issued standards for certification of CBRN respiratory protection equipment. CBRN respirators have unique characteristics with regard to industrial respirators: In particular, CBRN respirators must have reduced permeability and increased resistance to degradation from the contaminants that may be present in a disaster response.

CBRN canisters provide protection against a minimum of 139 identified CBRN agents which fall into seven families:

- Organic vapors, including sarin
- Acid gasses
- Base gasses
- Hydrides, such as arsine and phosphine
- Nitrogen oxides
- Particulates (including chemical, biological, and radiological particulates)
- Formaldehyde

NIOSH-certified respirators that are not CBRN must only use air-cleaning devices that have been approved for the respirator; a respirator that has been fitted with parts from multiple makes and models of respirators invalidates NIOSH-certification. Respirator manufacturers use unique thread mounts to prevent mixing and matching respirators and air-cleaning devices such as canisters and filters. During the 9/11 response, this led to a resource issue when available cartridges could not be used with responders' respirators. CBRN cartridges and respirators are unique in that they utilize universal thread mounts, and any manufacturer's CBRN cartridges can be used on any manufacturer's CBRN respirator. This is intended to help with resourcing in future responses [83].

3.16 Summary

Preparation for an All-Hazards event must consider potential safety risks from a multitude of different sources and multiple types of emergencies or disasters. Many of these present unique hazards. However, similarities exist in all responses, including exposures to environmental contaminants, environmental conditions such as heat and cold, ergonomics, damaged infrastructure, fatigue, infectious disease, and more. Any individual serving in a safety capacity must have a thorough understanding of hazards related to the types of incidents that responders can encounter, and actions that can be taken to protect responders from these hazards.

References

1 Department of Homeland Security (2018) *Comprehensive Preparedness Guide (CPG) 201: Threat and Hazard Identification and Risk Assessment (THIRA) and Stakeholder Preparedness Review (SPR) Guide*, 3. https://www.fema .gov/media-library-data/1527613746699-fa31d9ade55988da1293192f1b18f4e3/ CPG201Final20180525_508c.pdf (accessed 31 March 2020).
2 Xing, Y.-F., Xu, Y.-H., Shi, M.-H., and Lian, Y.-X. (2016). The impact of PM 2.5 on the human respiratory system. *Journal of Thoracic Disease* 8 (1): E69–E74.
3 National Institute of Occupational Safety and Health (ongoing updates). *Table of IDLH Values*. https://www.cdc.gov/niosh/idlh/intridl4.html (accessed 13 November 2018).
4 42 CFR 84, Respiratory Protective Devices.
5 ANSI/AIHA Z88.7-2010 (and preceding editions). *Color Coding of Air-Purifying Respirator Canisters, Cartridges, and Filters.*
6 29 CFR 1910.1000, Table Z-1, Air Contaminants.
7 40 CFR 261.22, Identification and Listing of Hazardous Waste, Characteristics of Corrosivity.

8 Centers for Disease Control and Prevention (CDC) (2014). QuickStats: Average Annual Number of Deaths and Death Rates from Unintentional, Non-Fire-Related Carbon Monoxide Poisoning by Sex and Age Group – United States, 1999–2010. *MMWR Morbidity and Mortality Weekly Report* 63 (3): 65.

9 Applied Technology Council (2004). *ATC 45 Field Manual: Safety Evaluation of Buildings After Windstorms and Floods*.

10 Edwards, R., LaDue, J.G., Ferree, J.T. et al. (2013). Tornado intensity estimation past, present, and future. *Bulletin of the American Meteorological Society*: 641–653.

11 Environmental Protection Agency (2008). *Mold Remediation in Schools and Commercial Buildings*. EPA 402-K-01-001.

12 New York City Department of Health and Mental Hygiene (2008). *Guidelines on Assessment and Remediation of Fungi in Indoor Environments*.

13 Krause, M., Geer, W., Swenson, L. et al. (2006). Controlled Study of Mold Growth and Cleaning Procedure on Treated and Untreated Wet Gypsum Wallboard in an Indoor Environment. *Journal of Occupational and Environmental Hygiene* 3: 435–441.

14 Highland, L.M. and Borbrowsky, P. (2008). *The Landslide Handbook – A Guide to Understanding Landslides*. US Geological Survey Circular 1325.

15 Tanyas, H., Allstead, K.E., and van Westen, C.J. (2018). An Updated Method for Estimating Landslide-Event Magnitude. *Earth Surfaces Processes and Landforms* 43: 1836–1847.

16 SR530 Slide (2014). Mission #14-0995, Oso, Washington, Incident Action Plans.

17 Kious, W.J. and Tilling, R.I. (1999). *This Dynamic Earth: The Story of Plate Tectonics*. US Geological Survey (online edition, accessed 15 December 2018).

18 Kirby, S., Wang, K., and Dunlop, S. (2002). *The Cascadian Subduction Zone and Related Subduction Systems – Seismic Structure, Intraslab Earthquakes and Processes, and Earthquake Hazards*. US Geological Survey Open-File Report 02-328, Geological Survey of Canada Open File 4350.

19 Ryan, H.F., von Huene, R., Wells, R.E. et al. (2011). History of earthquakes and tsunamis along the eastern Aleutian-Alaska megathrust, with implications for tsunami hazards in the California Continental Borderland. In: *Studies by the U.S. Geological Survey in Alaska*. Professional Paper 1795-A (eds. J.A. Dumoulin and C. Dusel-Bacon). US Geological Survey 31 p.

20 Wood, H.O. and Neumann, F. (1931). Modified Mercalli intensity scale of 1931. *Bulletin of the Seismological Society of America* 21 (4): 277–282.

21 Richter, C.F. (1935). An instrumental earthquake magnitude scale. *Bulletin of the Seismological Society of America* 25 (1): 1–32.

22 Hanks, T. and Kanamori, H. (1979). A moment magnitude scale. *Journal of Geophysical Research* 84 (B5): 2348–2350.

23 McCaffrey, R. (2008). Global frequency of magnitude 9 earthquakes. *Geology* 36 (3): 263–266.

24 Martinez-Garzon, P., Bohnhoff, M., Ben-Zion, Y., and Dresen, G. (2015). Scaling of maximum observed magnitudes with geometrical and stress properties of strike-slip faults. *Geophysical Research Letters* 42: 10230–10238.

25 Allen, R.M., Gasparini, P., Kamigaichi, O., and Bose, M. (2009). The status of earthquake early warning around the world; an introductory overview. *Seismological Research Letters* 80 (5): 682–693.

26 Johnson, L.A., Rabinovici, S., Kang, G.S., and Mahin, S.A. (2016). *California Earthquake Early Warning System Benefit Study*. California Office of Emergency Services.

27 Applied Technology Council (1995). *ATC-20-2 Addendum to the ATC-20 Postearthquake Building Safety Evaluation Procedures*.

28 Applied Technology Council (1989). *ATC-20 Procedures for Postearthquake Safety Evaluation of Buildings*.

29 Neal, C.A., Casadevall, T.J., Miller, T.P. et al. (1997). *Volcanic Ash-Danger to Aircraft in the North Pacific*. US Geological Survey Fact Sheet 030-97.

30 Baxter, P.J., Bonadonna, C., Dupree, R. et al. (1999). Cristabolite in volcanic ash of the Soufriere Hills volcano, Montserrat, British West Indies. *Science* 283: 1142–1145.

31 Damby, D.E., Horwell, C.J., Baxter, P.J. et al. (2018). Volcanic ash activates the NLRP3 inflammasome in murine and human macrophages. *Frontiers in Immunology* 8: 2000.

32 Nanoagri, S.M. (2010). Volcanic ash should not be presumed harmless in long term. *Nature (letters)* 465: 157.

33 Evarts, B. (2018). *Fire Loss in the United States During 2017*. NFPA #FLX10. National Fire Protection Association.

34 Evarts, B. and Molis, J.L. (2018). *United States Firefighter Injuries 2017*. National Fire Protection Association.

35 Fent, K.W., Evans, D.E., Babik, K. et al. (2018). Airborne contaminants during controlled residential fires. *Journal of Occupational and Environmental Hygiene* 15 (5): 399–412.

36 Currie, J., Caseman, D., and Anthony, T.R. (2009). The evaluation of CBRN canisters for use by firefighters during overhaul. *The Annals of Occupational Hygiene* 53 (5): 523–538.

37 Jones, L., Lutz, E.A., Duncan, M., and Burgess, J.L. (2015). Respiratory protection for firefighters-evaluation of CBRN canisters for use during overhaul. *Journal of Occupational and Environmental Hygiene* 12: 314–322.

38 Jones, L., Burgess, J.L., Evans, H., and Lutz, E.A. (2016). Respiratory protection for firefighters – evaluation of CBRN canisters for use during overhaul II: in mask analyte sampling with integrated dynamic breathing machine. *Journal of Occupational and Environmental Hygiene* 13 (3): 177–184.

39 Kirk, K.M. and Logan, M.B. (2015). Firefighting instructors' exposure to polycyclic aromatic hydrocarbons during live fire training scenarios. *Journal of Occupational and Environmental Hygiene* 12: 227–234.

40 Baxter, C.S., Hoffman, J.D., Knipp, M.J. et al. (2014). Exposure of firefighters to particulates and polycyclic aromatic hydrocarbons. *Journal of Occupational and Environmental Hygiene* 11 (7): D85–D91.

41 Gagas, D. (2015). Characterization of contaminants on firefighter's protective equipment: a firefighter's potential exposure to heavy metals during a structure fire. Master's thesis, Eastern Kentucky University.

42 Easter, E., Lander, D., and Huston, T. (2016). Risk assessment of soils identified on firefighter turnout gear. *Journal of Occupational and Environmental Hygiene* 13 (9): 647–657.

43 Alexander, B.M. and Baxter, C.S. (2016). *Flame Retardant Contamination of Firefighter Personal Protective Clothing – A Potential Health Risk for Firefighters.*

44 Alexander, B.M. (2012). Contamination of firefighter personal protective gear. Master's thesis, University of Cincinnati.

45 Shen, B., Whitehead, T.P., McNeel, S. et al. (2015). High levels of polybrominated diphenyl ethers in vacuum cleaner dust from California fire stations. *Environmental Science & Technology* 49: 4988–4994.

46 Sparer, E.H., Prendergast, D.P., Apell, J.N. et al. (2017). Assessment of ambient exposures firefighters encounter while at the fire station. *Journal of Occupational and Environmental Medicine* 59 (10): 1017–1023.

47 Fent, K.W., Evans, D.E., Booher, D. et al. (2015). Volatile organic compounds off-gassing from firefighters' personal protective equipment ensembles after use. *Journal of Occupational and Environmental Hygiene* 12 (6): 404–414.

48 Fent, K.W., Alexander, B., Roberts, J. et al. (2017). Contamination of firefighter personal protective equipment and skin and the effectiveness of decontamination procedures. *Journal of Occupational and Environmental Hygiene* 14 (10): 801–814.

49 Calvillo, A., Haynes, E., Burkle, J. et al. (2019). Pilot study on the efficiency of water-only decontamination for firefighters' turnout gear. *Journal of Occupational and Environmental Hygiene* 16 (3): 199–205. https://doi.org/10.1080/15459624.2018.1554287.

50 Harrison, T.R., Muhamad, J.W., Yang, F. et al. (2018). Firefighter attitudes, norms, beliefs, barriers, and behaviors toward post-fire decontamination processes in an era of increased cancer risk. *Journal of Occupational and Environmental Hygiene* 15 (4): 279–284.

51 Petrillo, Alan M (2018) Two Florida departments implement clean cab concept, *Fire Apparatus & Emergency Equipment* 23 (1). https://www

.fireapparatusmagazine.com/2018/01/27/two-florida-departments-implement-clean-cab-concept/#gref (accessed 31 March 2020).

52 Mayer, A.C., Fent, K.W., Bertke, S. et al. (2019). Firefighter hood contamination: efficiency of laundering to remove PAHs and FRs. *Journal of Occupational and Environmental Hygiene* 16 (2): 129–140. https://doi.org/10.1080/15459624.2018.1540877.

53 National Fire Protection Association (2016). *Fourth Needs Assessment of the US Fire Service*. NFPA USS106.

54 Katica, C.P., Pritchett, R.C., Pritchett, K.L. et al. (2011). Effects of forearm vs. leg submersion in work tolerance time in a hot environment while wearing firefighter protective clothing. *Journal of Occupational and Environmental Hygiene* 8: 473–477.

55 Kim, J.-H., Coca, A., Williams, W.J., and Roberge, R. (2011). Effects of cooling garments on recovery and performance time in individuals performing strenuous work wearing a firefighter ensemble. *Journal of Occupational and Environmental Hygiene* 8 (7): 409–416.

56 Hong, O., Samo, D., Hulea, R., and Eakin, B. (2008). Perception and attitudes of firefighters on noise exposure and hearing loss. *Journal of Occupational and Environmental Hygiene* 5 (3): 210–215.

57 Ahrens, M. (2018). *Brush, Grass, and Forest Fires*. National Fire Protection Association Research.

58 Schoennagel, T., Balch, J.K., Brenkert-Smith, H. et al. (2017). Adapt to more wildfire in western North American forests as climate changes. *Proceedings of the National Academy of Sciences* 114 (18): 4582–4590.

59 Radeloff, V.C., Helmers, D.P., Kramer, H.A. et al. (2018). Rapid growth of the US wildland-urban interface raises wildfire risk. *Proceedings of the National Academy of Sciences* 115 (13): 3314–3319.

60 Lareau, N.P., Nauslar, N.J., and Abatzoglou, J.T. (2018). The Carr fire vortex: a case of pyrotornadogenesis? *Geophysical Research Letters* https://doi.org/10.1029/2018GL080667.

61 Ridler, K. (2018). Study shows health, reaction-time declines in firefighters. *Associated Press News* (2 September 2018).

62 14 CFR Chapter I, Subchapter G, Part 139.

63 Federal Aviation Administration, US Department of Transportation (2008). *AC No.: 150/5210-14B – Advisory Circular Aircraft Rescue Fire Fighting Equipment, Tools and Clothing*.

64 Bane, T.B. (2013). Aircraft firefighting: dangers to responders at general-aviation accidents, firehouse. https://www.firehouse.com/rescue/article/10895018/the-dangers-of-aircraft-firefighting-airplane-emergency-response (accessed 28 December 2018).

65 49 CFR Part 239, Passenger Train Emergency Preparedness.

66 Operation Lifesaver. https://oli.org (accessed 16 March 2020).

67 Central Puget Sound Regional Transit Authority (2012). *Sounder Commuter Rail Emergency Responders Manual*.

68 49 CFR Part 214, Railroad Workplace Safety.

69 49 CFR Part 270, System Safety Program.

70 49 CFR Part 659, Rail Fixed Guideway Systems; State Safety Oversight.

71 Central Puget Sound Regional Transit Authority (2009). *Link Light Rail Emergency Responders Manual*.

72 World Health Organization (2005). *International Health Regulations*, 3e.

73 World Health Organization (2017). *Pandemic Influenza Risk Management: A WHO Guide to Inform and Harmonize National and International Pandemic Preparedness and Response*.

74 United States Department of Health and Human Services (2017). *Pandemic Influenza Plan 2017 Update*.

75 American Industrial Hygiene Association (2006). *The Role of the Industrial Hygienist in a Pandemic*. AIHA Guideline 7-2006

76 The White House (2013). *Presidential Policy Directive 21 – Critical Infrastructure Security and Resilience*.

77 Office of Nuclear Security and Incident Response, US Nuclear Regulatory Commission (2005). *NRC Incident Response Plan, NUREG-0728 Rev. 4*.

78 United State Department of Homeland Security (2016). *Nuclear/Radiological Incident Annex to the Response and Recovery Federal Interagency Operational Plans*.

79 United States Department of Homeland Security (2017). *Radiological Dispersal Device (RDD) Response Guidance Planning for the First 100 Minutes*.

80 28 CFR 0.85 (l), General Functions.

81 Department of Homeland Security (2018). *Planning Considerations: Complex Coordinated Terrorist Attacks*.

82 Jackson, B.A., Peterson, D.J., Bartis, J.T. et al. (2002). *Protecting Emergency Responders Lessons Learned from Terrorist Attacks*. RAND Corporation Science and Technology Policy Institute.

83 Janssen, L., Johnson, A.T., Mansdorf, S.Z. et al. (2018). *CBRN Respiratory Protection Handbook*. DHHS (NIOSH) publication no. 2018-166. US Department of Health and Human Services, Centers for Disease Control and Prevention, National Institute for Occupational Safety and Health.

84 Occupational Safety and Health Administration (OSHA) (2020). *Guidelines on Preparing Workplaces for COVID-19* https://www.osha.gov/Publications/OSHA3990.pdf (accessed 28 March 2020)

85 Occupational Safety and Health Administration (OSHA) (2007). *Guidance on Preparing Workplaces for an Influenza Pandemic* https://www.osha.gov/Publications/OSHA3327pandemic.pdf (accessed 28 April 2020)

86 Occupational Safety and Health Administration (OSHA) (2007). *Pandemic Influenza Preparednessand Response Guidance for Healthcare Workers and Healthcare Employers* https://www.osha.gov/Publications/OSHA_pandemic_health.pdf (accessed 28 April 2020)

4

Regulatory Requirements and Their Applicability in Emergency Response

Many OSHA requirements have applicability in an emergency response. In day-to-day work operations, time is available to identify hazards, choose controls, train employees, and ensure compliance with safety regulations. During a response, the environment is less controlled, and hazards emerge as the situation evolves. Many hazards may have been identified during the planning phase of the emergency management cycle; however, unexpected hazards are also likely to be encountered. Responders, and in particular nontraditional responders, may be assigned tasks outside of their primary job assignment, and in these newly assigned tasks they may encounter hazards that they are not familiar with. Maintaining compliance with OSHA requirements during an emergency response is more challenging than it is during day-to-day work operations, but it is not impossible. Good planning can facilitate success in maintaining compliance during a response.

OSHA standards include horizontal and vertical standards. Horizontal standards apply to all industries, whereas vertical standards apply to specific industries such as construction or maritime operations. States can adopt additional vertical standards, which may have applicability in emergency response. Washington State, for example, has developed a vertical standard for firefighters. Vertical standards also apply to specific operations, such as welding or electrical work, or to specific chemicals, such as asbestos or lead.

Responders in an emergency may fall under horizontal standards, vertical standards, or both.

This chapter provides an overview of OSHA standards that are likely to apply to an All-Hazards response. It does not cover every regulation or every nuance of the regulations, however, and those responsible for ensuring compliance should refer to the specific regulation that covers their operation in their state and industry. Responders in states that operate under their own state plan fall under state regulations, which must be at least as effective as federal OSHA regulations.

Health and Safety in Emergency Management and Response, First Edition. Dana L. Stahl.
© 2021 John Wiley & Sons, Inc. Published 2021 by John Wiley & Sons, Inc.

4.1 Hazard Communication

Hazard Communication is known as the chemical "right to know" standard, and is based on the premise that employees have both the need and the right to know about the hazards of the chemicals they work with. Primarily, in the day-to-day workplace, this applies to chemical products that are purchased from a vendor. The Hazard Communication standard requires that such chemicals be labeled with the product name and hazard warnings, and that a Safety Data Sheet (SDS) be made available to employees for each chemical. Since the United Nations Global Harmonization Standard was adopted in the United States in 2012, SDSs follow a universal format. Employers must maintain an accurate inventory of workplace chemicals, develop a written Hazard Communication program that describes how requirements are met in an individual workplace, and train employees.

Employees may also be exposed to chemicals that do not come in a nicely labeled container, and the Hazard Communication Standards also covers these "nonroutine exposures." These type of exposures might include carbon monoxide exposures from incomplete combustion of engines in vehicles or equipment, byproducts of chemical reactions, and off gassing of chemical contaminants in soils or groundwater [1]. Employees must also know the hazards posed by these types of chemical exposures.

Safety Data Sheets, chemical inventories, and any data relating to routine or nonroutine exposures are considered *exposure records*, and OSHA requires that employers maintain both medical records and exposure records for at least the duration of employment or use plus 30 years. Employees and their representatives have the right to access these records at any point [2].

These rules also apply in an emergency response. If chemical products such as firefighting foam, oil dispersants, or any commercial product are used in a response, the name of the product, manufacturer and any product identification need to be recorded into an inventory of chemicals used in the particular response. Safety Data Sheets must be procured and made available to responders, and responders need to be trained on the hazards of the chemical products that they are working with and how to protect themselves from these hazards. These Safety Data Sheets must be maintained for 30 years. The Safety Officer must work with the Documentation Unit in the Planning Section to make sure that these records are maintained in the incident file.

Exposures to chemicals that do not come in a nicely labeled container are likely to account for a higher degree of exposure in an emergency response than in other work environments. Some exposures may fall under the requirements of OSHA's Hazardous Waste Operations and Emergency Response standard. Others, including combustion products from vehicle exhaust, more clearly fall under Hazard

Communication as a nonroutine exposure. Depending upon the incident, these exposures may take greater effort to fully characterize, and the Safety Officer may need to rely on analysis from a technical specialist.

4.2 Personal Protective Equipment

Use of Personal Protective Equipment (PPE) is considered the method of last resort in controlling hazards, and is to be used when more effective controls, such as engineering or administrative controls, are not feasible. PPE may also be used as an interim measure until more effective controls can be implemented. The nature of emergency response is that it occurs in an environment in which new hazards can emerge rapidly, and for this reason PPE is necessary for most responders.

OSHA requires that an employer conduct a hazard analysis and document it in writing before issuing PPE to employees. The PPE that is selected must be appropriate for the PPE identified in the hazard analysis. For example, the hazard analysis may identify a hazard that could cause a potential head injury, and then select a hard hat meeting ANSI Z-89 standards as an appropriate control. However, hard hats come with different ratings depending upon the hazard that they protect against, including top and/or side impacts, and electrical hazards (Table 4.1). The hazard analysis must identify which specific head hazard exists, and which ratings the selected hard hat must have. A hard hat that is designed to protect against overhead impacts will not protect against lateral impact hazards, and may evoke a false sense of security for the person wearing it if the hard hat is not rated appropriately for the work being performed. A simple approach would be to simply choose the hard hat with the greatest hazard protection such as a Class E, Type II hard hat, which protects against overhead and lateral impacts and provides maximum protection against electrical hazards. However, the increased protection makes the

Table 4.1 ANSI A-89 ratings for hard hats.

Rating	Hazard
Class E	High-voltage electrical hazards up to 20 000 V
Class G	Low-voltage conductors up to 2200 V
Class C	Conductive, do not provide electrical protection
Type I	Impact to the top of the head
Type II	Impact to the top of the head, off center, or from the side of the head
Bump cap	Does not provide protection from electrical or impact hazards, but may prevent bruising to the head from bumping it inside a tight space

hard hat heavier, which can lead to neck fatigue. It is important to select a hard hat from within the appropriate category so that it does not create unnecessary additional hazards or discomfort. This in turn increases the likelihood that it will be worn as needed by the person that it was issued to [3].

Likewise, safety shoes have ratings that indicate which hazards a safety shoe protects against. Safety shoes must meet ANSI or ASTM standards, and are selected to protect against hazards such as impact (I) or compression (C) resistance, protection to the top of the foot or metatarsal (Mt) protection, puncture resistance (PR), electrical hazard resistance (EH), ability to dissipate static (SD) and conductive footware that facilitates transfer of static electricity buildup from the body to the ground (Cd). (ASTM was formerly known as the American Society for Testing Materials and now uses the name ASTM International) [4].

Eye protection meeting ANSI Z87 standards is designed to protect against impact hazards, splash hazards, or light hazards. Vapor-resistant goggles are appropriate for use when chemical vapors are present at levels that can irritate eyes. Face shields can provide impact protection when worn over safety glasses. The use of face shields in the absence of safety glasses or goggles is not permissible [5].

Gloves can be selected to protect against hazards to the hands. These hazards can include:

- Cuts
- Heat
- Cold
- Chemicals
- Mold
- Pathogens, such as bacteria or viruses
- Vibration
- Electrical hazards

Cut-resistant gloves can include work gloves with a polyurethane or nitrile coating to protect against nicks and cuts in the normal course of work. These gloves do not prevent cuts, but can minimize minor nicks and abrasions. Kevlar gloves may be selected when a high degree of cut hazard exists. However, Kevlar cut-resistant gloves significantly decrease dexterity, and can therefore increase risks of developing musculoskeletal injuries in the hands. This tradeoff in risks must be evaluated and considered in making the appropriate selection.

Chemical-resistant gloves may be made of materials such as nitrile, latex, neoprene, butyl rubber, or other materials. Each glove material is resistant to certain chemicals, while other chemicals may chemically react with the glove material and cause it to break down. Breakdown may be visually obvious, as when a glove literally dissolves in the presence of a chemical, or may cause micropermeations that while not visible still allow permeation of the chemical through the glove.

Table 4.2 OSHA 29 CFR 1910.137 ratings for electrical gloves and protective equipment.

Class of equipment	Maximum AC voltage for safe work
00	500
0	1 000
1	7 500
2	17 000
3	28 500
4	36 000

Glove manufacturers can provide data on permeation and the resistance of gloves to different chemical substances.

Disposable gloves made of nitrile or latex are commonly used to protect against biological hazards, such as body fluids or mold-covered surfaces. Latex is an allergen, and for this reason certain individuals may not be able to wear latex gloves. Nitrile is often a better choice than latex.

Working with tools may expose the upper extremities to excessive levels of vibration which can cause permanent damage to tissues, including nerves and capillaries in fingers and hands. Antivibration gloves are made of vibration-dampening materials that can reduce the vibration that reaches hands and fingers [6].

Rubber insulating gloves for electrical protection, as well as rubber insulating sleeves, blankets, covers, matting, and line hose are rated for protection against the incident energy to which an electrical worker may be exposed (Table 4.2) as well as whether or not they are resistant to ozone. Protective equipment must be tested for voltage leaks at least every six months; equipment should not be used if more than six months have passed since the last leak test [7].

State PPE regulations sometimes define additional items as PPE, and these need to be considered in the PPE hazard analysis as well. For example, Oregon includes high-visibility clothing, whole body coverings, and personal flotation devices (PFDs) in their state PPE standard.

PFDs must be Coast Guard approved and worn when working in boats or when working over or in water [8].

The Federal Highway Administration (FHWA) Manual of Uniform Traffic Control Devices (MUTCD) requires that flaggers and workers in traffic control zones wear reflective apparel meeting ANSI/ISEA 107.2004 specifications, and that a person selected by the employer must be responsible for choosing the appropriate classifications for reflective garments. The 2004 ANSI standard identified three classifications of reflective material: Class 1 for use when working near traffic moving at speeds less than 25 miles per hour (mph), Class 2 for use when traffic speeds range from 25 to 50 mph, and Class 3 for use at night or when speeds are greater than 50 mph [9]. The 2015 update of ANSI/ISEA 107-2015 further breaks down these classes into:

- Type "O" Off-Road Class 1
- Type "R" Roadway Class 2
- Type "R" Roadway Class 3
- Type "P" Fire, Police, EMS personnel Class 2
- Type "P" Fire, Police, EMS personnel Class 3 [10]

A label on the high-visibility garment indicates the number of times that the garment can be washed, and provides a place on the label to mark each washing. Once the garment has undergone the maximum number of washings indicated on the label, it is assumed that reflectivity has been reduced to such a level that it no longer meets reflectivity requirements, and the garment can no longer be used as protective apparel.

Once PPE is selected, it must be provided to employees. OSHA rules specify that employers pay for the PPE that employees are required to wear, with limited exceptions. Employers do not need to pay for PPE that is considered "personal in nature," such as safety boots with protective toes that could be worn on or off the job, or prescription safety glasses that could be worn on or off the job. However, if it is unlikely that these items will be worn off the job, PPE is no longer considered "personal in nature" and must be paid for by the employer. Safety shoes with metatarsal protection and prescription eyewear that is designed to be worn with a particular type of respirator are considered PPE that is not "personal in nature."

In an emergency incident, the Safety Officer would need to work with both the Logistics Section and the Finance Section to ensure availability of sufficient quantity of PPE identified in the hazard assessment.

Personnel who are issued PPE must be trained in its use. This training must cover the capabilities and limitations of PPE, and a reminder that PPE is the control of last resort. Training must also include care and maintenance requirements, such as washing instructions for visibility wear and care and storage requirements to prevent degradation of PPE [11].

4.3 Respiratory Protection

Respiratory protection is appropriate when airborne exposures exceed occupational exposure limits. Respirators can be essential equipment in hazardous environments, but they also present many risks. Use of a respirator increases physiological strain when performing work, and OSHA rules require that any worker who must wear a respirator be physically capable of doing so. Respirator use increases the demand on the heart and the lungs. It also increases risk of heat-related illness. Personnel with heart disease, respiratory illness, or other conditions cannot safely use respirators.

An improperly selected respirator, or one that does not fit or function correctly, creates physiological risks without the benefit of protection.

4.3.1   Respirator Selection

OSHA has established legally enforceable exposure limits, or Permissible Exposure Limits. These are listed as a concentration in air, generally in units of parts per million (ppm, or one square centimeter of contaminant per cubic meter of air) or milligrams per cubic meter, averaged over 8 hours of exposure (time-weighted average, or TWA) [12]. State agencies also establish Permissible Exposure Limits (PELs), which are often lower and more protective than those set by OSHA.

The American Conference of Governmental Industrial Hygienists (ACGIH) publishes Threshold Limit Values (TLVs). TLVs are republished each year, and are based on toxicological and epidemiological data. While TLVs are not regulatory limits, they are widely recognized consensus recommendations [13].

OSHA's current PELs were adopted in 1972, and are based on the 1968 TLVs. While the TLVs are updated as more information on health hazards related to specific chemicals becomes available, the PELs are not. OSHA did issue an update to the PELs in 1989 to reflect updated TLVs, but this was challenged in court. In 1992, the 11th Circuit Court of Appeals reversed the update, returning the PELs to the original values adopted in 1972 [14]. Current TLVs reflect an updated understanding of chemical toxicity while the PELs do not. While TLVs are not strictly enforceable, they are considered to be more protective.

NIOSH publishes Recommended Exposure Limits (RELs) expressed as 8-hour TWA air concentrations. RELS are also generally lower and more protective than PELs, and like TLVs, reflect current understanding of chemical health effects [15]. In addition, NIOSH publishes Immediately Dangerous to Life and Health (IDLH) concentrations. IDLH levels indicate an exposure concentration that is likely to cause death or immediate or delayed permanent adverse health effects, or prevent escape from such an environment [16].

When exposure limits are exceeded, employers are required to implement controls to protect employees from the hazard by reducing breathing air concentrations to levels below the exposure limit. Respirators can be used only when this cannot be achieved through suitable engineering or administrative controls. Respirators can also be used while exposures and controls are evaluated, and as an interim measure until more effective controls can be implemented.

Emergency incidents may evolve quickly, and conditions can change before exposure controls can be implemented. Therefore, respirators play a more critical in protecting employees from hazardous atmospheres than would be the case in a controlled work environment.

Appropriate respirators must be selected for the anticipated work exposure. Respirators are selected based on the concentration of air contaminant in relationship to the applicable exposure limit and the Assigned Protection Factor (APF) of the respirator (Table 4.3). Filtering facepiece respirators have the same APF as reusable half-mask air-purifying respirators.

Table 4.3 Respirator Assigned Protection Factors (APF).

Type of respirator	Half mask	Full facepiece	Helmet/hood	Loose fitting facepiece
1. Air-purifying respirator	10	50		
2. Powered Air-Purifying Respirator (PAPR)	50	1 000	25, or 1 000 if the manufacturer has demonstrated performance at this level	25
3. Supplied air respirator (SAR) or airline respirator				
- Demand mode	10	50		
- Continuous flow mode	50	1 000	25, or 1 000 if the manufacturer has demonstrated performance at this level	25
- Pressure-demand or other positive pressure mode	50	1 000		
4. Self-contained breathing apparatus (SCBA)	10	50	50	
- Demand mode		10 000	10 000	
-Pressure-demand or other positive pressure mode (e.g. open/closed circuit)				

Source: 29 CFR 1910.134, Respiratory Protection [17].

The appropriate type of respirator is determined by calculating the Maximum Use Concentration (MUC). The MUC is determined by multiplying the exposure limit by OSHA's assigned protection factor for the type of respirator being considered.

$$MUC = APF \times Exposure\ limit$$

If the MUC exceeds the airborne exposure in which workers are present, this indicates that the respirator is acceptable. If the MUC is less than the exposure, a respirator with a higher APF must be selected.

For example, OSHA has established a PEL of 100 ppm, TWA for xylene. A half-mask, air-purifying respirator has an APF of 10. The MUC is calculated as:

$$MUC = 100\ ppm \times 10 = 1000\ ppm$$

This indicates that that half-mask air-purifying respirators can be worn when airborne xylene concentrations are present between 100 and 1000 ppm. However, this formula is only applicable for exposures under IDLH levels, and NIOSH has assigned an IDLH of 900 ppm for xylene. Therefore, if the exposure is greater than 900 ppm, only respirators suitable for IDLH conditions can be used.

When contaminant levels exceed IDLH levels, OSHA requires that employees wear:

- Full-facepiece SCBA certified by NIOSH for a minimum service live of 30 minutes, or
- A combination full-facepiece pressure-demand Supplied Air Respirator (SAR) with auxiliary self-contained air supply.

Oxygen-deficient atmospheres, or those atmospheres in which oxygen makes up less than 19.5% of total air, are also considered IDLH atmospheres. Atmosphere-supplying respirators with Grade D air supply can be used when oxygen levels are less than 19.5% which is the lower limit allowable limit for percent oxygen at sea level. The percent oxygen for acceptable use of Grade D breathing air varies depending upon elevation (Table 4.4).

When contaminant levels are unknown but IDLH conditions may exist, respiratory protection suitable for IDLH atmospheres must be used until actual exposure concentrations are determined.

When suitable respirators are used to work in IDLH atmospheres, one person must be stationed outside the IDLH environment to monitor conditions, maintain communication with the person inside the IDLH area, and summon rescue in the event that it is needed.

If air-purifying respirators are used, the air-purifying device must be appropriate for the contaminant. The air-purifying cartridges or filters must be replaced before they become full, or have accumulated sufficient air contaminants to the

Table 4.4 Oxygen-deficient environments for which Grade D air atmosphere-supplying respirators may be used.

Altitude, feet	Range, percent oxygen in total air
Less than 3 001	16.0–19.5
3 001–4 000	16.4–19.5
4 001–5 000	17.1–19.5
5 001–6 000	17.8–19.5
6 001–7 000	18.5–19.5
7 001–8 000	19.3–19.5
8 001–14 000	No exemption
14 001	Oxygen-enriched breathing air always required

When oxygen level is less than indicated in this table, oxygen-enriched breathing air must be provided.
Source: 29 CFR 1910.134, Respiratory Protection [17].

extent that they are no longer effective. A person wearing a respirator with filters may notice that it is more difficult to breath once sufficient particulate materials is taken up by the filter, but other types of purifying devices, such as cartridges, do not have warning properties. Change out schedules must be determined, and must be based on factors such as level of contaminant present, the amount of other material in the air (such as water in the form of humidity) that compete for binding space on the cartridge, temperature, breathing rate, and the amount of material in the cartridge.

4.3.2 Medical Qualification for Respirator Wearers

OSHA requires that employees who wear respirators be medically approved before a respirator is issued. Respirator use adds additional strain to the respiratory and cardiovascular systems when performing work, and it is important that individuals who wear respirators can undertake this additional strain without experiencing adverse health impacts. Rebreathing of warm air inside the mask of the respirator impacts thermoregulation mechanisms, and for this reason respirator users can be more susceptible to heat stress. People who are claustrophobic may not able be able to wear respirators. It is important to ensure that employees who wear respirators do not have any personal conditions that create greater risk.

Obtaining medical approval is a fairly simple process. OSHA provides a mandatory medical evaluation questionnaire in Appendix C of the Respiratory Protection Standard. The form consists of two parts: Part A, which lists 15 questions, and Part B, which includes 18 questions. The employee must complete this form confidentially and submit it to a Physician or Other Licensed Healthcare Professional (PLHCP) who also has information on workplace exposure and working conditions. The PLHCP then reviews the questionnaire, and may approve respirator use simply from this review. The PLHCP may contact the employee to review answers to certain questions or request additional testing such as a pulmonary function test before providing medical approval, or the PHLCP may state that the employee is not medically qualified to wear a respirator. Medical approvals must be documented in the form of a written statement provided by the PLHCP to the employer for recordkeeping. The PLHCP cannot include any information that supports this decision, including personally identifiable medical information, as this information is confidential and cannot be provided to the employer. The written statement from the PLHCP simply states that the employee can or cannot wear a respirator under the conditions specified by the employer.

States can add additional criteria for medical approval. For example, the Washington State Respiratory Protection Standard includes additional questions for users of full-facepiece respirators or SCBAs, and a list of discretionary questions that the PLHCP can choose to include [18]. It is important to ensure that state questionnaires are used when applicable, and when state requirements exceed those of OSHA.

Exposures in an emergency response may be such that that respirators are necessary. Responders may not have worn respirators in the past, or they may need to wear a different type of respirator for the response than they do in their day-to-day work. Like all workers, these responders must receive a medical evaluation before being issued a respirator, and sometimes, this may need to happen quickly. If qualified PLHCPs are available to the Incident Management Team, perhaps in coordination with the Medical Unit, they can review questionnaires and issue medical approvals on a real-time basis. Some healthcare providers accept on-line submittals of medical questionnaires, so if electricity and an internet connection are available, such systems can support a response some distance from the clinic. If they are not available, preprinted respirator medical forms can be used. Although some personnel may need additional medical evaluation before receiving approval, many responders will not, and can be medically cleared for respirator use quickly.

Respirator medical approvals need to be maintained throughout the response and after it concludes, and the Safety Officer must work with the Documentation Unit to ensure that this happens.

4.3.3 Respirator Fit Testing

Tight fitting respirators, such as air-purifying half-face and full-face respirators, Powered Air-Purifying Respirators (PAPRs), Supplied Air Respirators (SARs) that utilize a face mask rather than a loose fitting hood, and self-contained breathing apparatus (SCBA)s must form a tight seal to the face in order to function as intended. If the seal is not tight enough, contaminated air leaks through the sides of the respirator and into the breathing zone rather than passing through air-purifying devices. Without a seal, respirators do not provide intended protection, yet they continue to pose hazards to the wearer due to physiological demand.

OSHA requires that fit tests be conducted on employees who are required to wear tight fitting respirators, and has approved both qualitative and quantitative fit test protocols. Quantitative fit testing is required when a fit factor of greater than 100 is required (in practice, this is equivalent to respirators that provide a fit factor higher than 10).

Quantitative fit tests are based on methods that measure concentration of ambient or generated particles inside and outside of the facemask, or by measuring differences in pressure between the inside and the outside of the face mask. A quantitative fit test can be completed in 15–30 minutes per individual. Instrumentation is required to perform these tests, and therefore quantitative fit testing can only be performed if an electrical power source is available.

Qualitative fit test methods utilize a test substance, either isoamyl acetate or "banana oil," saccharine, or bitrex, that can be smelled or tasted by the individual being tested. Irritant smoke may also be used, which causes involuntary coughing. The respirator wearer performs a series of exercises while wearing a respirator with appropriate air filtration devices (organic vapor cartridges for banana oil or N95 filters for saccharine, bitrex, or irritant smoke). If the test substance is detected by the wearer during the test, the respirator does not fit. The respirator wearer passes the fit test for the make, model, and size of the respirator used if the test substance has not been detected by the end of the test. A qualitative fit test can be completed within about 15 minutes per individual, and does not require a power source.

Fit tests must be repeated annually. In a multiemployer response, or one in which mutual aid resources are utilized, a diligent Safety Officer will check that any responders bringing their own respirators have documentation that a fit test has been conducted in the past 12 months. If not, the fit test should be repeated.

4.3.4 Respirator Care and Maintenance

Respirators only work if they are intact and functioning as intended. The shape of the respirator must be maintained in order to form a seal to the face as it did during fit testing. Therefore, respirators must be stored in a manner that prevents the facepiece from becoming distorted. Hard-shelled plastic containers that are large enough to hold the respirator without distorting it should be issued to employees and responders at the same time that they are issued their respirator. The container should be sealable to protect the respirator and air-purifying devices from exposure to airborne contaminants when it is not being worn. Respirators should never be stored in locations where they can be inadvertently crushed by tools, equipment, or other items. They also need to be stored out of direct sunlight and away from heat to maintain integrity of rubber and plastic parts.

Respirators should be taken apart, cleaned in soap and water, disinfected, and inspected after use. Seals, diaphragms, and valves should be inspected, and replaced if they are torn or damaged.

A respirator user must be shown how to conduct positive and negative fit checks each time a respirator is worn in order to verify that it has formed a seal. In addition, a respirator cannot be worn in the presence of facial hair, since the diameter of a single hair is large enough to create leaks that allow respirable size particles to pass through. Respirator users must be clean shaven [17].

4.3.5 Substance Specific Requirements

OSHA has developed specific regulatory standards for certain toxic and hazardous substances (Table 4.5). These standards contain specific requirements for monitoring of airborne exposures, medical monitoring, training, and respiratory protection, and must be followed when employees and responders encounter a covered substance [19].

4.4 Blood-borne Pathogens

Any response that includes a medical aid component carries a risk of exposure to blood or body fluids (Other Potentially Infectious Materials or OPIM) and exposure to blood-borne pathogens. Responders at the scene of a mass casualty incident (MCI) are also at risk from this exposure even if they are not providing direct medical aid.

OSHA's blood-borne pathogens standard was written primarily as a measure to protect workers from the risk of exposure to Human Immunodeficiency Virus (HIV), Hepatitis B Virus (HBV), and later, Hepatitis C Virus (HCV). However, many additional pathogens can be transmitted via the blood-borne route, such as:

- Malaria
- Syphilis
- Babesiosis
- Brucellosis
- Leptospirosis
- Arboviral infections
- Relapsing fever
- Creutzfeldt–Jakob disease
- Human T-lymphotrophic virus Type 1
- Viral hemorrhagic fever (i.e. Ebola) [20]

Table 4.5 Substance-specific OSHA standards.

Chemical substance	Regulatory reference, 29 CFR
Asbestos	1910.1001
Coal tar pitch volatiles	1910.1002
alpha-Napthylamine	1910.1004
Methyl chloromethyl ether	1910.1006
3,'-Dichlorobenzidine (and its salts)	1910.1007
bis-Chloromethyl ether	1910.1008
beta-Napthylamine	1910.1009
Benzidine	1910.1010
4-Aminodiphenyl	1910.1011
Ethyleneimine	1910.1012
beta-Propiolactone	1910.1013
2-Acetylaminofluorene	1910.1014
4-Dimethylaminoazobenzene	1910.1015
N-Nitrosodimethylamine	1910.1016
Vinyl chloride	1910.1017
Lead	1910.1025
Hexavalent chromium	1910.1026
Cadmium	1910.1027
Benzene	1910.1028
Coke oven emissions	1910.1029
Cotton dust	1910.1043
1,2-Dibromo-3-dichloropropane	1910.1044
Acrylonitrile	1910.1045
Ethylene oxide	1910.1047
Formaldehyde	1910.1048
Methylenedianiline	1910.1050
1,3-Butadiene	1910.1051
Methylene chloride	1910.1052

Blood-borne pathogens can be transmitted between hosts when blood-to-blood contact occurs, or when there is OPIM to OPIM contact. This often occurs through needlestick injuries. Other routes of exposure include the mucous membranes, such as a splash to the eyes, or dermal contact when there are cuts or breaks in skin surfaces. Viruses can survive and remain infectious even in dried blood. HBV can remain highly infectious in dried blood for at least one week and probably longer [21]. HCV can remain infectious in dried blood for at least six weeks [22]. For this reason, response workers and recovery workers who arrive at the scene of an incident are also at risk of infection even long after the medical response is complete. Spilled blood or OPIM must be cleaned and sanitized through application of a freshly prepared 10% bleach solution or administration of a disinfectant that has an EPA registration documenting effectiveness against blood-borne pathogens.

Employers are required to provide annual training to workers who are at risk of exposure to blood-borne pathogens and to offer and pay for a series of three Hepatitis B vaccinations given over a period of six months (vaccinations are not currently available for HIV or HCV). Employees can opt out of receiving the Hepatitis B vaccine for any reason, and they are not required to provide their employers with a reason for deciding to decline the vaccine. If the employee declines the vaccine, the employer must have the employee sign a specifically worded statement and maintain this signed declination form as a medical record.

OSHA requires very specific wording on the Hepatitis B Vaccine declination forms, and employers cannot alter this wording:

> I understand that due to my occupational exposure to blood or other potentially infectious materials, I may be at risk of acquiring hepatitis B virus (HBV) infection.
> I have been given the opportunity to be vaccinated with hepatitis B vaccine, at no charge to myself. However, I decline hepatitis B vaccination at this time. I understand that by declining this vaccine, I continue to be at risk of acquiring hepatitis B, a serious disease.
> If in the future I continue to have occupational exposure to blood or other potentially infectious materials and I want to be vaccinated with hepatitis B vaccine, I can receive the vaccination series at no charge to me.

The form must include space for the employee to sign, and a date.

In an emergency response, the Safety Officer will need to work with the Medical Unit and Documentation Units to ensure that vaccines are offered, provided, and that any declination forms are maintained as records. Many responders may have received vaccines through their primary employer, although others may not if they do not work in job environments that put them at risk of blood-borne pathogens exposure. The Safety Officer should never make the assumption that responders outside of his/her organization have received vaccines prior to the response.

OSHA requires medical follow-up with a physician or licensed healthcare professional if an employee receives an exposure to blood or OPIM, such as a needlestick injury or splash to the eye. During the medical follow up, the exposed employee must be offered post exposure prophylaxis with antiretroviral medications. These medications are most effective at preventing development of the disease, or "seroconversion" if they are administered within the first couple of hours after exposure. In an emergency response, a process must be in place to ensure that post exposure medical evaluations and post exposure prophylaxis can happen within 2 hours of the incident.

Documentation that must be provided to the medical evaluator conducting the postexposure evaluation includes the following:

- A description of the employee's duties, as related to the exposure incident;
- Documentation of the route(s) of exposure and circumstances under which the exposure occurred;
- Any of relevant medical records belonging to the exposed employee, such as past Hepatitis B vaccines are immunological testing for blood-borne pathogens;
- The source individuals testing status, if known;
- A copy of the Blood-borne Pathogens Standard.

After the postexposure evaluation is completed, the medical provider must provide a Healthcare Provider's Written Opinion to the employer for recordkeeping. This written opinion must contain only the information that has to be provided to the employer, and may not include any confidential information or personally identifiable health information related to the employee. The Healthcare Provider's Written Opinion must include only:

- Whether the Hepatitis B vaccine was indicated and if it was administered;
- A statement that the employee was informed of the results of the medical evaluation;
- That the employee has been told about any medical conditions that may result from the exposure which require follow-up evaluation or treatment.

When employees are at risk of exposure to blood-borne pathogens, employers are required to develop and implement written Blood-borne Pathogens Exposure Control Plans. In addition to administration of Hepatitis B vaccines, training, and postexposure evaluation, these plans must include:

- An exposure assessment, documenting how and where occupational exposure to blood-borne pathogens can occur;
- Personal Protective Equipment appropriate for these exposures;
- Engineering and administrative controls to protect from exposures;

- Maintenance of a sharps injury log;
- Housekeeping;
- Disposal of contaminated waste.

PPE that protects against splash exposures is critical in a response environment. The exposure assessment considers operations in which splash exposures are possible, and selected PPE must provide coverage of all body parts that could receive such splash exposures.

PPE must be removed and replaced if it becomes contaminated, and employees must thoroughly wash hands with soap and water after PPE is removed. Hand sanitizers may be used as an interim measure when handwashing is not feasible, but the Safety Officer should work with Logistics to ensure that portable handwashing stations are available if fixed facilities for handwashing are not.

PPE does not protect against needlestick injuries. Any discarded needles should be picked up with tongs or pliers, and disposed of in a properly labeled, puncture-resistant sharps container [23].

Blood-borne pathogens exposures are possible when collecting criminal evidence. When evidence that is contaminated with blood or OPIM must be preserved, it should be:

- Allowed to air dry as soon as possible following collection;
- Placed in brown, unbleached heavy paper bags for storage;
- Handled in accordance with requirements of the blood-borne pathogens standard [24].

4.5 Fall Protection

Employees must be protected from falls to a lower level. Under the General Industry standards, protections such as guardrails, travel restraints, positioning systems, or personal fall arrest systems must be utilized when a fall hazard of 4 feet or more exists; under the Construction standard, fall protection is required when fall hazards are 6 feet or more. OSHA standards provide specifications on guardrail design, including a requirement for midrails, toe guards, and a top rail. The top rail must be 42 inches, plus or minus 3 inches, placing it above the center of gravity for most of the population, and must be able to withstand a force of at least 200 pounds from any direction.

OSHA standards also provide specifications for personal fall arrest systems. Such systems must be rated and used for personnel only, and cannot be used to hoist materials or other items. Anchorages for fall arrest systems must be capable of supporting at least 5000 pounds per employee attached: Guardrails, for example, do not meet this support requirement, and it is not acceptable for personnel to tie off to a guardrail [25, 26].

Fall arrest systems must bring the employee to a complete stop before impacting the lower level. A rescue plan must be developed and implemented before an employee performs work using a fall arrest system. Rescue plans ensure that no one is left suspended for a period of time if a fall occurs. Remaining suspended in a harness after a fall can lead to suspension trauma from the pooling of blood in the lower limbs and compression of the femoral arteries by harness straps [27]. Some fall arrest system manufacturers have begun installing foot straps on harness systems. If the worker is conscious after a fall, he or she can pull out the foot straps and use them to support the lower limbs to reduce the risk of suspension trauma. However, these can only be used if the person who fell is alert and is physically able to secure the foot straps. Regardless, it is critical that rescue is completed before serious health risks occur.

Any responder or other worker who is subject to falls to a lower level must receive training.

4.6 Excavations

It may be necessary to create an excavation at some point during an emergency response, and if so, this work must comply with OSHA regulations when the depth of the trench is 5 feet or greater. State requirements may apply when the depth is 4 feet or greater.

Serious injuries can occur to personnel working in trenches. The most serious hazard is risk of a cave-in: A person inside a trench can be suffocated by soil, or they can be crushed by the weight of the soil. A cubic foot of soil weighs 100 pounds. A cave-in of several cubic feet can put enough pressure on a person inside to cause fatal or at least life changing injuries.

A primary goal of excavation safety is to prevent cave-ins. This is done through identifying soils by type (Table 4.6), preventing surcharge conditions, and determining an appropriate protection system such as appropriate sloping, using a trench box, or building a shoring system that meets requirements for the soil type as determined by a Competent Person. The Competent Person is someone who is knowledgeable on regulatory requirements and hazards, and, most importantly, has the authority to take corrective action when necessary. The Competent Person oversees operations, makes decisions based on hazards and regulatory requirements, conducts inspections of the excavation as work occurs, and takes action if conditions occur that change the soil type and required protections. The competent person must also ensure that soil loads and equipment are far enough from the edge of the excavation that they do not contribute to a surcharge that can cause a cave in.

Table 4.6 Soil types as described by OSHA [28].

Type	Description	Unconfined compressive strength, tons per square foot	Notes
Stable rock	Natural solid mineral that remains intact when excavated with vertical sides		If rock contains joints filled with soil, it is Type B or C
			If joints are submerged or seeping water, it is Type C
Type A	Cohesive soil such as clay, silty clay, sandy clay, clay loam or cemented soils	1.5 or greater	Soil cannot be Type A if it is fissured, has been previously disturbed, subject to vibration, or other factors
Type B	Cohesive soil with moderate compressive strength such as silt, silty clay, sandy clay, clay loam, sandy loam, angular gravel, or soils that cannot be classified Type A	Greater than 0.5 but less than 1.5	Granular, little or no clay content, and crumble easily when dry
Type C	Low compressive strength soil such as gravel, sand, loamy sand and submerged unstable soil or rock, or soil from which water is freely seeping	0.5 or less	Rain and weather conditions may require more cohesive soils to be downgraded to Type C

Source: 29 CFR 1926, Subpart P Excavations [28].

A means of egress must be provided for people working inside the excavation, such as stairs or ladders spaced to require 25 feet of lateral travel or less. Fall protection systems or guardrails may be necessary to prevent people from falling into the trench or excavation.

An emergency rescue plan must be in place when people are working inside trenches or excavations. Rescue plans most often involve having a trained technical rescue team on standby to remove personnel in the event of illness, injury, or a cave-in. As crush injuries happen quickly in a cave-in, it is imperative that the standby rescue team be able to implement the rescue plan as soon as possible after the cave-in occurs [28].

4.7 Confined Space

A confined space is one that meets three characteristics:

- Large enough and so configured that a person can enter it and perform work;
- Has limited entrance or egress; and
- Is not designed for continuous human occupancy.

All three characteristics must be present in order for the space to be a confined space.

If the confined space also contains hazards, it must be treated as a permit-required confined space. Such hazards include:

- Hazardous atmospheres, which may be oxygen deficient, explosive, or toxic;
- Engulfment hazards, such as finely grained granular materials or liquids;
- Inwardly converging walls that could trap or asphyxiate;
- Physical hazards; or
- Any other hazard.

Employers must issue a written permit in order for employees to enter permit required confined spaces. The written permit must describe the space to be entered, the purpose for entry, the time period for entry, hazards of the space, and means to control those hazards including air monitoring, ventilation, PPE, and other controls. The permit must also list the names of the individuals entering the space and those providing support roles:

- *Entrant(s)* enter the space to perform work.
- An *Attendant* must remain outside the space to monitor conditions, monitor the entrant, ensure that nonauthorized individuals do not enter the confined space, and summon help in the event that the entrant becomes injured or ill, or cannot self-exit the space. The attendant must never enter the space, or leave the space unless relieved by another attendant. The attendant may not perform any additional duties that interfere with the ability to work as an attendant.
- The *Entry Supervisor* approves the entry by reviewing hazards and controls on the permit, ensuring a rescue plan is in place, ensuring that entrants and attendants are trained and sufficiently qualified, and signs the entry permit to authorize entry. If any unsafe conditions occur during the entry, or if the supervisor is aware that procedures are not being followed, the entry supervisor has a duty to terminate the permit and make sure that all entrants exit the space.

Any person performing any one of these roles must be trained to do so.

Employers must develop written-permit-required confined space programs. Canceled permits must be maintained for one year to facilitate review of the program. Exposure data from air monitoring must be maintained for 30 years.

Confined space entry may need to occur during a response. A responder may need to enter an existing confined space to perform work or make repairs, or may need to enter a space that has formed as a result of emergent conditions and meets the criteria for being a confined space.

The hazards and configuration of a confined space are such that entrants may be overcome and unable to exit the space on their own. Many times, an entrant wears a harness attached to a retractable retrieval line, and if they lose consciousness the attendant can pull them out of the space using the retrieval line. If a fall hazard exists, a separate line may be connected to a fall arrest anchor.

If an entrant cannot be pulled out of a space with a retrieval line, such as in situations where there are turns or bends in the space, or when the line could get caught on obstructions, a technical rescue team may need to be called in to remove the entrant. Technical rescue requires specific skills and training, and rescue drills must be held on an annual basis. Some fire departments provide technical rescue training to a subset of fire fighters, others do not. An employer cannot rely on a fire department to provide confined space rescue unless they have worked with the fire department to preplan rescues, the fire department has the capability of performing technical rescue, and the fire department has agreed to do so. Rescue personnel must be on standby during the confined space entry and ready to respond, so fire departments that provide this service need to bring in supplemental resources in order to meet this requirement. It is common for fire departments to relay the cost of rescue and backfill to the employer performing the confined space entry when they agree to perform this service. The employer may also choose to hire a private rescue service to standby during the entry.

Working at heights, working in trenches, and working in confined spaces all may occur as part of an emergency response, and each type of work requires a rescue plan. An incident in which rescue is required is then an "emergency within the emergency," that must be responded to. The external emergency situation does not negate the need to develop rescue plans and perform as intended when performing this type of work in a response [29].

4.8 Hazardous Waste Operations and Emergency Response (HAZWOPER)

OSHA's Hazardous Waste Operations and Emergency Response (HAZWOPER) regulation applies to employers performing cleanup operations or corrective actions at sites regulated by EPA or state environmental agencies, or local government orders; operations involving hazardous wastes at Treatment, Storage and Disposal (TSD) facilities; or when responding to an uncontrolled chemical release or spill. Work covered under HAZWOPER may be a primary response to a spill, or it can be a secondary response that occurs when spills result from earthquakes, weather, or any other All Hazards response.

A Site Safety and Health Plan (SSHP) must be developed for any work that falls within the scope of this standard. The SSHP must include at a minimum:

- An organizational chart or description of the organizational system;
- A description of work to be performed;
- Site hazard analysis;
- Site control plan;
- Requirements for PPE;
- Training requirements;
- Decontamination procedures for use when leaving the site;
- Environmental and air monitoring;
- Medical surveillance;
- Procedures for handling drums (if applicable);
- An emergency response plan (for an "emergency within the emergency");
- A spill containment program;
- Procedures to meet additional OSHA requirements, such as Confined Space Entry.

The SSHP should be updated and revised as work evolves and more information is learned about site conditions. The SSHP is a separate document from the safety hazard analysis documented on a Form IS 215A (see Chapter 8).

Employers and responders performing work covered under HAZWOPER must be trained, and the level of training needed depends upon the type of work performed (Table 4.7). Workers performing work under HAZWOPER must have completed an 8-hour HAZWOPER refresher course within the past 12 months. State agencies may be more restrictive. Washington State, for example, requires 80 hours of HAZWOPER training if employees must wear atmosphere supplying respirators, rather than 40 as required by OSHA [31]. Employees must also be briefed on the SSHP before beginning work on a site, and receive additional briefings as the SSHP is updated.

The SSHP must include decontamination procedures to prevent workers from tracking contamination outside of the hazard zone. These procedures include specific protocols for orderly removal and drop off of PPE for disposal or cleaning, and washing stations to clean boots, wash hands, or other cleanup as required [30].

4.9 Noise exposures

Exposure to excessive sound levels can damage hearing, and OSHA requires that employers implement a hearing loss prevention program (HLPP) when employees are exposed to sound levels of 85 dBA (deciBels on the A scale) over an 8-hour

Table 4.7 HAZWOPER training requirements.

Type of work performed	Classroom training, hours	Supervised on site field experience, days
General work where chemical exposures may exceed the PEL or require PPE	40	3
Work must occasionally be on site for specific limited tasks such as monitoring, and air contaminant exposures are below the PEL or other published exposure limits	24	1
Workers are regularly on site working in areas that are fully characterized and air contaminant exposures are below PELs or other exposure limits	24	1
Managers or supervisors	40 plus 8 additional hours of specialized training	3

Source: 29 CFR 1910.120, Hazardous Waste Operations and Emergency Response [30].

time-weighted average or higher, or an equivalent noise exposure (Table 4.8). A HLPP includes:

- Training employees on the impacts of noise and hearing;
- Providing hearing protection devices;
- Conducting annual audiograms to detect hearing loss.

Table 4.8 Noise equivalent exposures.

Time of exposure (hours)	Noise equivalent to an 8-hour, 85 dBA exposure requiring a hearing conservation program (dBA)	Noise equivalent to an 8-hour, 90 dBA exposure requiring evaluation and implementation of feasible engineering controls (dBA)
8	85	90
4	90	95
2	95	100
1	100	105
0.5 (30 minutes)	105	110
0.25 (15 minutes)	110	115

Source: 29 CFR 1910.95, Occupational Noise Exposure [32].

Table 4.9 Sound level exposures produced from equipment used at construction sites.

Type of equipment	Sound level, dBA
Backhoe	85
Nail gun	97
Concrete saw	98
Bulldozer	100
Jack hammer	102
Grader/scraper	107
Chain saw	110

Source: Occupational Safety and Health Administration [33].

It is beneficial for employers to take steps to protect their employees hearing. In addition to legal requirements, workers' compensation claims for hearing loss can be very costly.

When employees receive exposures of 90 dBA over an 8-hour time-weighted average, employers are required to evaluate engineering controls, and implement those that are feasible.

Equipment used during a response may generate sufficient noise to meet criteria for operator inclusion in a hearing loss prevention program or engineering controls even when operated for short periods throughout the day (Table 4.9).

OSHA has interpreted that employees who are exposed to 85 dBA for 8 hours, or who receive an equivalent exposure, must be included in an HLPP even if the exposure occurs on only one day per year [34]. Responders who work with noisy equipment can easily reach this exposure threshold. Sound level measurements taken in the hearing zone of the worker or noise dosimetry can verify whether or not these levels of noise exposures are occurring on a response site.

Employees with noise exposures that meet the criteria for inclusion in a hearing loss prevention program must be trained in the hazards of noise exposure and the potential for developing noise induced hearing loss. At least two types of hearing protection must be offered, so that employees have a choice and can opt to wear the type of hearing protection that they prefer. For example, this could include a choice between ear muffs and foam ear plugs.

Hearing protection devices are labeled with a Noise Reduction Rating or NRR. The NRR uses unit of deciBels on the C scale and is determined using EPA criteria. Since OSHA's noise standards are based on the A scale rather than the C scale, an adjusted NRR is determined by subtracting 7 from the labeled NRR. The adjusted NRR must reduce the employee's exposure to a level below an 85 dBA noise equivalent. For example, ear plugs with a labeled NRR of 29 would have an adjusted NRR of 22. For an 8-hour exposure of 92 dBA, this would be a suitable choice because:

$$92 - (NRR - 7) = 92 - (29 - 7) = 70$$

and

$$70 < 85$$

However, field studies have shown that in actual use, the NRR achieved in the laboratory is rarely achieved during field use. For this reason, OSHA recommends (but does not require) derating the adjusted NRR by 50%:

$$92 - \left(\frac{NRR - 7}{2}\right) = 92 - \left(\frac{29 - 7}{2}\right) = 81$$

and

$$81 < 85$$

Annual audiograms must be conducted on employees who are in a hearing conservation program. The first, or baseline, audiogram must be conducted within six months of initial exposure; however, a best practice is to complete the baseline audiogram before any noise exposures occur. Each year the annual audiogram is compared with the baseline audiogram to determine if any hearing loss is occurring. Noise-induced hearing loss first occurs in the high frequencies, so if this type of hearing loss is observed, steps can be taken to improve protections from noise before hearing loss increases and moves to the speech frequencies where it has greater impact on day to day life [32].

Certain chemicals, such as carbon monoxide and solvents such as trichloroethylene, are ototoxic and can cause hearing loss. Exposure to ototoxic chemicals can result in hearing loss seen on audiograms even when noise exposures have been controlled (Table 4.10) [35].

4.10 Sanitation and Temporary Labor Camps

OSHA standards on sanitation and temporary labor camps may apply or serve as guidance during a response. OSHA's standard on sanitation includes requirements for waste disposal, provision of potable water, control of vermin, and restroom facilities. Although the scope of this standard applies to permanent workplaces, criteria for the number of water closets needed per employee can be used in determining how many permanent or portable toilet facilities are needed for responders (Table 4.11). Alternatively, criteria for toilets could be taken from the HAZWOPER

Table 4.10 Ototoxic chemicals capable of causing hearing loss.

Substance class	Chemicals
Pharmaceuticals	• Aminoglycosidic antibiotics (e.g. streptomycin, gentamycin) and some other antibiotics (e.g. tetracyclines) • Loop diuretics (e.g. furosemide, ethacrynic acid) • Certain analgesics and antipyretics (e.g. salicylates, quinine, chloroquinine) • Certain antineoplastic agents (e.g. cisplatin, carboplatin, bleomycin)
Solvents	• Carbon disulfide • *n*-Hexane • Toluene • *p*-Xylene • Ethylbenzene • *n*-Propylbenzene • Styrene and methylstyrene • Trichloroethylene
Asphyxiants	• Carbon monoxide • Hydrogen cyanide and its salts • Tobacco smoke
Nitriles	• 3-Butenenitrile • *cis*-2-Pentenenitrile • Acrylonitrile • *cis*-Crotononitrile • 3,3'-Iminodipropionitrile
Metals and compounds	• Mercury compounds • Germanium dioxide • Organic tin compounds • Lead

Source: Occupational Safety and Health Administration and Centers for Disease Control and Prevention, National Institute for Occupational Safety and Health [35].

Standard (Table 4.12), which considers chemical toilets, recirculating toilets, combustion toilets, and flush toilets to be acceptable if allowed by the local jurisdiction. Showers and change rooms must be provided if work conditions warrant, or if required by another OSHA standard. Separate designated areas must be provided for food consumption as well as preparation and storage [30, 36].

In a prolonged response, responders from outside the area may assist, and will need to be housed. OSHA rules for temporary labor camps provides guidance on housing.

• Sites must be adequately drained;
• Shelters must provide protection against the elements;
• Beds, cots, or bunks and suitable storage areas must be provided:

Table 4.11 Minimum number of water closets specified in
29 CFR 1910.141.

Number of employees	Minimum number of water closets
1–15	1
16–35	2
36–55	3
56–80	4
81–110	5
111–150	6
Over 150	One additional fixture for every 40 employees

Source: 29 CFR 1910.141, Sanitation [36].

Table 4.12 Toilet facilities required under HAZWOPER.

Number of employees	Number of facilities
20 or fewer	One
More than 20, fewer than 200	One toilet seat and one urinal per 40 employees
More than 200	One toilet seat and one urinal per 50 employees

Source: 29 CFR 1910.120, Hazardous Waste Operations and Emergency Response [30].

- o Beds placed no closer than 36 inches, laterally and end to end;
- o Elevated at least 12 inches from the floor;
- o Double-deck bunks must be spaced at least 48 inches laterally and end to end;
- o There must be at least 27 inches of space between the lower and upper bunk;
- o Triple-deck bunks are prohibited.
- Exterior openings must be effectively screened;
- Sanitary facilities must be provided for storing and preparing food;
- Toilet rooms must be located within 200 feet of the door to each sleeping room;
- An adequate supply of toilet paper must be provided;
- One shower head is needed for every 10 people;
- An adequate supply of hot and cold running water must be available;
- Lighting is required in inhabitable rooms and toilet facilities;
- Refuse disposal containers must be provided that are fly tight and rodent tight;
- Measures must be taken to control insects and rodents;
- First aid facilities must be present.

The risk of communicable diseases increases when groups of people are housed in close proximity. OSHA rules require that reports of communicable disease be made promptly to the local public health authority. Likewise, cases of food poisoning or unusual numbers of people suffering from any illness in which fever, diarrhea, sore throat, vomiting, or jaundice is a prominent symptom must also be reported to the local public health authority.

Additional elements of this standard include requirements for sewage, handwashing facilities, and laundry facilities. While the disaster environment may create challenges in meeting the full scope of this standard, at least initially, the Safety Officer should work with logistics and the Incident Management Team to meet these requirements as fully as possible [37].

4.11 Operation of Heavy Equipment

OSHA rules on Powered Industrial Trucks (PITs), or forklift trucks, include detailed criteria on operations and maintenance, as well as operator qualifications. Any employee who is assigned to operate a forklift must have an initial training that covers forklift operations and hazards, as well as specific training on hazards of the worksite. In addition, a qualified evaluator must conduct a skills evaluation of every forklift operator on each type of forklift that the employee will operate. The skills evaluation must be repeated at least every three years, after a forklift accident, and if the employer has any reason to believe that there is a deficiency in skill. OSHA standards also specify that forklifts must be inspected before use, or at least once each shift, that they be maintained, and that they cannot be modified without the manufacturer's approval. Design standards include mandatory rollover guards and seatbelts [38].

OSHA recommends similar training be conducted for aerial lifts operated in the workplace, such as extendable boom platforms, aerial ladders, articulating (jointed) boom platforms, vertical towers, and any combination of these [39]. Many training providers provide such training, although it is not specifically required in the verbiage of the OSHA regulations [40–42]. Similarly, many training providers provide operator training and certification for equipment such as backhoes and bulldozers that is similar to the certification training provided for forklift operators. There is good reason to ensure that operators of such equipment are sufficiently trained despite lack of a requirement for this specific training in the OSHA requirements (although a Commercial Driver's License [CDL] is required if such equipment is operated on public roads). Serious accidents can occur when operating heavy equipment, and the risks are greatly compounded when such equipment is operated in an emergency response (Figure 4.1).

Figure 4.1 OSHA does not specifically require training for heavy equipment operators, but it is a best practice and can prevent accidents. Source: Reproduced with kind permission of Bobbie J. Lange.

In 2018, a Heavy Fire Equipment Operator was fatally injured when the bulldozer he was operating rolled over during the Ferguson Fire in Mariposa County, California. Prior to the rollover, the bulldozer had been flattening a small berm along the outside edge of a trail, and widening it. As this was done during night-time hours and visibility was poor. The bulldozer had slipped off the trail three times prior to the fatal rollover, which should have been an indicator of unsafe conditions. The steep terrain and uneven soil conditions caused the soil to fail and give way under the weight of the equipment. These risks were not recognized by the operator or the Incident Management Team prior to the accident [43]. Had a program been in place requiring training and skills certification for heavy equipment operators (and training for those supervising heavy equipment operators), many of the contributing factors leading up to this incident could have been eliminated.

4.12 General Duty Clause Citations

Emergency responders may face many hazards that are not specifically covered by an OSHA standard. Section 5 of the OSH Act requires that employers provide employment, and a place of employment, that are free from recognized hazards.

OSHA cites hazards that are not covered under a standard as a General Duty Clause citation [44]. A violation of the General Duty Clause can be issued when:

- The employer failed to keep the workplace free of a hazard to which employees of that employer were exposed;
- The hazard was recognized;
- The hazard was causing or was likely to cause death or serious physical harm; and
- There was a feasible and useful method to correct the hazard [45].

The terms "recognized hazard" and "feasible" are broad. A hazard may be recognized if a consensus standard exists, if it is identified by an equipment manufacturer, if a hazard alert has been issued, or if it is generally known within the industry.

The term "feasible" has been subject to many legal interpretations. One perspective is that the term means "economically feasible" as determined by either a cost–benefit analysis or whether the cost would be so high that it would put an employer out of business. Alternatively, the term means "capable of being done" or "achievable" without regards to economic considerations. OSHA believes the latter definition is the one that was intended by the OSH Act [46].

4.13 Heat

OSHA has not promulgated a heat stress standard. However, OSHA can issue citations for overexposure to heat, and references the American Conference of Governmental Industrial Hygienists (ACGIH) Action Levels for heat exposure [47] and NIOSH recommendations in the Technical Manual for compliance officers [48]. The NIOSH Criteria for a Recommended Standard suggests that employers be required to develop programs that protect workers from effects of heat-related illness that include:

- Monitoring environmental heat exposures;
- Medical monitoring, including preplacement medical exams and periodic medical evaluations;
- Surveillance of heat-related sentinel events, or adverse health effects in populations at risk for heat injury or illness;
- Warning signs in locations where dangerous heat levels are present;
- PPE such as water-cooled garments, ice-packet vests, or heat-reflective clothing;
- Worker information and training;

- Engineering and administrative controls; and
- Recordkeeping, including records of environmental surveillance, medical surveillance, and records of heat-related health events and heat-related illnesses [49].

Industrial hygienists most commonly utilize Wet Bulb Globe Thermometers (WBGT) measurements to predict impacts of heat exposure and health, and both ACGIH and NIOSH express exposure limits (TLVs or RELs, respectively) in units of WBGT. A WBGT uses three thermometers to measure temperature:

- Dry bulb, which corresponds to temperatures taken with general purpose thermometers;
- Natural Wet Bulb, which is a dry bulb thermometer covered by a wetted material. The Natural Wet Bulb temperature is influenced by humidity in air as well as wind speed, and its measurements represent sweat evaporation in air.
- Black Globe thermometer, which is a dry bulb with a hollow copper sphere that is painted with a matte black finish. The Globe thermometer is a measure of radiant energy, such as energy that is radiated from surfaces such as machinery, roads, or other surfaces.

A WBGT for outside air is calculated as:

$$\text{WBGT(out)} = 0.7T(\text{nwb}) + 0.2T(\text{g}) + 0.1T(\text{db})$$

where

$T(\text{nwb})$ = natural wet bulb temperature

$T(\text{g})$ = globe temperature

$T(\text{db})$ = dry bulb temperature

For indoor environments, the WBGT is calculated as:

$$\text{WBGT(in)} = 0.7T(\text{nwb}) + 0.3T(\text{g})$$

Action levels and recommended exposure limits are based upon workload, ratio of work/rest within each hour, and clothing worn.

California, Minnesota, and Washington have promulgated state rules to control heat stress hazards.

Minnesota's rule applies to fully clothed, acclimatized workers in indoor environments, and establishes 2-hour time-weighted average Permissible Exposure Limits (Table 4.13). Employees may not be exposed above the listed PELs [50].

California's rule applies to outdoor employment, and requires that a Heat Illness Prevention Plan be either integrated into an employer's Injury and Illness

Table 4.13 Minnesota 2-hour time-weighted average Permissible Heat Exposure Limits.

Work activity	WBGT(in), °F
Heavy work	77
Moderate work	80
Light work	86

Source: Minnesota Administrative Rules 5205.0110 [50].

Prevention Program or written as a separate document. Under this rule, employers must provide access to shade and allow employees to take preventative cool downs in shade when they feel the need to do so. When temperatures exceed 95 °F (dry bulb, not WBGT), employers must implement High Heat procedures. These include:

- Communication to contact a supervisor when necessary;
- Observation of employees for alertness and signs or symptoms of heat-related illness;
- Designating personnel to call for emergency medical services;
- Reminding employees to drink water;
- Pre shift meetings to review high heat procedures.

The written Heat Illness Prevention Plan must include:

- Emergency response procedures in the event an employee has signs or symptoms of heat related illness;
- Acclimatization of new employees, and all employees during a heat wave;
- Employee and supervisor training;
- Procedures for provision of water and access to shade; and
- High-heat procedures [51].

Washington State's rule applies to outdoor heat exposures between 1 May and 30 September when heat levels exceed the state action levels (Table 4.14). Like California, Washington requires that employers develop a written heat exposure safety program and include it in the state required Accident Prevention Program. This program must include:

- Response actions to be taken for signs and symptoms of heat related illness;
- Employee training;
- Supervisor training;
- Supplying drinking water of at least one quart per employee per hour when action levels are exceeded [52].

Table 4.14 Washington State outdoor temperature action levels.

Clothing	Temperature, °F
All other clothing	89
Double-layer woven clothes including coveralls, jackets and sweatshirts	77
Nonbreathing clothes including vapor barrier clothing or PPE such as chemical-resistant suits	52

Note: These temperatures were developed based on Washington State data and are not applicable to other states.
Source: Washington Administrative Code, Chapter 296-62-095 WAC, Outdoor Heat Exposure [52].

Washington's vertical standards for firefighters is more comprehensive, and includes controls for both heat and cold stress. Written programs for fire departments must include:

- Responsibilities for supervisors and incident commanders;
- Signs and symptoms of heat or cold stress;
- Rest-to-work recovery schedules that the incident commander must consider;
- Rehydration schedules, including amount and type of fluids;
- Plans for caloric replacement and electrolyte replacement during longer term emergencies and exercises;
- Medical monitoring during rehabilitation;
- What the incident commander will do if a member shows signs of heat or cold stress even after completing a rest-to-work cycle;
- Medical personnel present in the rehabilitation area.

Employees and supervisors must be trained on all aspects of the written program. Training must also include information on the body's mechanisms for maintaining core temperatures and signs, symptoms, and controls for heat and cold stress.

Rehabilitation areas must be established so that crews can rotate through. Rehabilitation areas must be large enough to accommodate all crew members who may need it, have shade available, have protection from rain as well as cold or wet environments, and must be staffed with a person trained in basic life support. Crew members must be medically cleared for work before leaving the rehabilitation area.

Specific requirements are also included for wildland fires. The regulation specifies that the Incident Commander is responsible for rest, rehabilitation, hydration, and prevention of heat related illness. The standard also restricts individuals who are wearing structural protective clothing from working in high temperatures for more than 1 hour [53].

4.14 Traffic Control

An emergency response may require responders to work along roadways. OSHA references Part IV the Federal Highway Administrations Manual of Uniform Traffic Control Devices (MUTCD) in their criteria for evaluating safety in traffic work zones. Failure to follow worker safety provisions in MUTCD would be criteria for a General Duty Clause Citation [54].

Worker safety considerations include:

- Ensuring that all workers are trained on how to minimize their vulnerability to traffic hazards in the work zone;
- Anyone who places temporary traffic control barriers or uses temporary traffic control techniques must be trained to their level of responsibility;
- Spacing of temporary traffic barriers based on lateral clearance of workers from adjacent traffic, speed of traffic, duration, type of operations, time of day, and volume of traffic;
- Speed reduction through use of speed zone funneling, lane reduction, flaggers or law enforcement. The speed reduction zone should include a buffer space for the protection of workers;
- Planning of the work area to minimize the need to back up heavy vehicles and equipment;
- Assigning a safety professional to conduct a hazard assessment of the worksite, and determining whether engineering or administrative controls, or personal protective equipment is needed;
- The use of high visibility safety apparel and clothing meeting ANSI/ISEA Class 2 or 3 requirements. The only exception to this is for firefighters who are actively engaged in a response that directly exposes them to flame, fire, heat, or hazardous materials if protective gear is retroreflective and meets standards set by an organization such as the National Fire Protection Association [55].

4.15 Ergonomics

Emergency responders are at risk for developing musculoskeletal disorders, such as sprains and strains that injure muscles, tendons, and ligaments, or injuries that impact nerves and nerve function. Ergonomics is the science and practice of modifying work and the work environment to match the physical capabilities and limitations of the human body. When there is a mismatch between the work environment and the capabilities and limitations of the human body, excessive wear and tear on the body leads to injuries. In addition, jobs and tasks that are poorly designed ergonomically result in poorer quality of work and decreased efficiency as the body works against, rather than with, its maximum biomechanical advantage. Unstable environmental conditions and a rapidly changing environment, insufficient resources, and the need to accomplish tasks quickly in order to save lives or meet other priorities can lead responders to take risks that then result in musculoskeletal injuries.

OSHA does not currently have a regulatory standard that requires employers to address ergonomics in the workplace. The standard originally issued in 2000 was rescinded by Congress under Senate Joint Resolution 6, and OSHA is prohibited from issuing a substantially similar rule. OSHA currently develops industry-specific guidelines and other resources to help employers prevent musculoskeletal disorders and, and cites employers for ergonomics hazards under the General Duty Clause. OSHA may choose to issue a Hazard Alert Letter rather than a citation [56].

Washington State also issued an ergonomics rule in 2000, which was repealed by voter initiative in 2003 [57]. Like OSHA and many other state agencies, Washington State Department of Safety and Health issues ergonomics citations under the state equivalent of the General Duty Clause.

California is unique in that it has a specific ergonomics rule that requires employers to develop programs to minimize repetitive motion injuries, and to address ergonomics in general acute care hospitals [58, 59].

In the day-to-day work environment, musculoskeletal injuries account for more than one third of worker's compensation claims [60], and the primary motivation for implementing ergonomics programs comes from cost savings and injury prevention. The same motivation applies in emergency response. The financial cost of injury claims is of course a concern, but even more so is the fact that the disabling nature of back injuries and other soft tissue injuries could quickly deplete the number of responders who are able to perform critical work.

Risk factors for developing musculoskeletal disorders include:

- Forceful exertions, such as pushing or pulling heavy objects;
- Hand position: a "power grip," in which the whole hand wraps around an object, uses less force than a "pinch grip," in which only the fingers are used to grasp an object;
- Repetitive motion, or performing identical motions over and over;
- Awkward postures;
- Static postures, or having to hold the body in an awkward posture without moving;

- Lifting heavy loads;
- Vibration, such as from using vibrating tools or sitting in vibrating vehicles;
- Contact stress that creates pressure points, such as from using tools that are not padded or do not fit the hand;
- Hot temperatures;
- Cold temperatures;
- Stress.

Controls for ergonomic hazards include changing the way in which work is performed in order to minimize risk factors or minimizing the time spent in work with exposure to risk factors.

There are limited options for use of PPE as a control. Those that can be used include:

- Antivibration gloves for using vibrating tools;
- Knee pads to protect against contact stresses to the knees;

Employers may be tempted to issue back belts to employees. Back belts are not PPE, and are unlikely to prevent injury [61]. Wrist braces or other types of splints prescribed by a medical provider can be useful for treating an injury that has occurred, but are not useful as a preventative measure to keep injuries from occurring.

Maintaining good ergonomics can be challenging in a rapidly evolving environment. A Safety Officer with a background in ergonomics can identify hazards as the response evolves, and take corrective measures to minimize injuries. If the Safety Officer is not strong in ergonomics, he or she should identify qualified Assistant Safety Officers or Technical Specialists who can help.

Administrative staff supporting the response are also at risk of injuries from poor ergonomics. Administrative workers may be working long hours in temporary facilities in less than ideal conditions, perhaps at makeshift work stations. Musculoskeletal injuries are one of the highest risks for administrative workers in a response.

4.16 Fatigue

Response and recovery workers may work long hours in less than ideal conditions, wearing PPE, while subject to emotional trauma from the scene of the incident. Travel times may increase as a result of the incident or disaster, or workers may sleep in temporary labor camps or makeshift facilities with other workers under dormitory like conditions. Fatigued increases the risk that workers will suffer injuries or impaired health. Decision-making is also affected: Fatigued workers, particularly those that must make critical decisions, are unlikely to perform at full efficiency and this can negatively impact the response overall.

OSHA does not regulate the number of hours that a worker can work, although other regulatory bodies do place limits on hours worked for safety-sensitive work. For example, the Federal Aviation Administration (FAA) regulates work shift hours for pilots and air traffic controllers, the Federal Railroad Administration (FRA) sets work hour limitations for dispatchers and railroad engineers, and the Federal Motor Carrier Safety Administration limits the number of ours that individual drivers can drive. Guidelines exist for other safety sensitive work, such as nursing and medical care. These positions are not regulated at the federal level, although some states have set limitations on work hours for certain groups.

The National Response Team (NRT) has developed a technical assistance document for managing worker fatigue during disaster operations. This guidance includes recommendations for developing operational and incident specific fatigue management plans, and includes tools to conduct an assessment of fatigue risk factors in an incident.

Fatigue management planning consists of:

• Assessment of past and anticipated future events, and types of work to be performed;
• Identification of risk factors;
• Identification of fatigue management controls;
• Evaluation methods to assess the effectiveness of the program.

Response and recovery workers are subject to a number of fatigue risk factors. Work hours, work rotations, and rest periods are significant risk factors. It is important to allow sufficient off duty time to travel to a place of rest, eat, take care of personal needs, and obtain sufficient sleep. For example, if an off-duty period consists of 8 hours, and an individual must commute for 30 minutes or more to a place of rest before eating and showering, the time left to sleep is less than the recommended 8 hours per night. Over time, a sleep debt will accumulate. If there are insufficient days off during an extended response, sleep debt continues to grow.

If workers are housed at the scene, commute times are reduced but conditions for sleeping may be less than ideal. Mass sleeping arrangements can make it difficult to get good quality sleep. In addition, response and recovery workers may be exposed to emotional stress from the event, and lack of sufficient good quality sleep can interfere with the brain's ability to cope with this stress (Figure 4.2).

Heavy work load, use of PPE, exposures to heat, or other physical or chemical agents also increase fatigue levels.

Figure 4.2 Sleeping quarters Southern California Complex fire, 2007. Source: Reproduced with kind permission of Isaac Howard.

The most effective control to combat fatigue is to allow sufficient time for rest periods, such as a 10-hour minimum off duty period, in a location where good quality sleep can be obtained. Additional control efforts should include:

- Worker education on the health effects of fatigue, signs and symptoms of excessive fatigue, and the plans that are in place to prevent worker fatigue;
- Advance planning to ensure that all responders are prepared prior to the incident, such as ensuring responders have appropriate training and medical clearance in order to begin work upon arrival at the scene and reduce demand on other workers. Also, advance planning should ensure that support services are in place;
- Transportation planning. If transportation routes are impacted by the disaster, travel and commute times increase, cutting into rest periods. In addition, fatigued workers become impaired drivers after working long hours. Planning should consider transportation options;
- Living conditions: Temporary lodging options could include hotels, trailers, or tent cities. Consideration should be given to maximizing privacy, quiet sleep areas, and security as well as providing sanitation and laundry facilities;

- Recuperation: Opportunities should be provided for exercise and recreation to help maintain mental health and combat emotional stress;
- Health Care Services: Support should be provided for workers for medical care, mental health, and stress management [62].

4.17   Food Safety

The Food Unit, within the Logistics Section, is responsible for providing food for responders, although not for evacuees or members of the public affected by the incident. This unit plans menus, orders food, provides cooking facilities, cooks and serves food, maintains food service areas, and manages food security and safety. The Safety Officer supports the effort to maintain food safety [63].

Maintaining food safety is actually a very critical component of incident management. Inadequate washing, handling, and cooking of food before consuming it is a primary cause of foodborne illness, and not many things can derail a response faster than widespread foodborne illness among responders. If plumbing systems are not functioning due to the nature of the incident, the impact is further compounded.

OSHA addresses food safety for emergency responders under HAZWOPER:

> 29 CFR 1910.120(n)(4) Food handling. All food service facilities and operations for employees shall meet the applicable laws, ordinances, and regulations of the jurisdictions in which they are located [30].

Local public health departments have requirements for food storage, including storage temperatures, cooking temperatures, and sanitation. Local requirements should be followed when preparing food for responders. This can be challenging in a disaster environment, especially if water supplies are contaminated or otherwise impacted, and if power systems are down. Generators may need to be brought in, and then the Safety Officer must ensure that generators are used safely. The Safety Officer must in turn ensure that food safety measures are not compromised despite logistical difficulties.

4.18   Summary

The Safety Officer must have a good working knowledge of OSHA laws, as well as state worker safety and health laws, and their applicability to response and recovery workers. A strong background in OSHA law and other applicable standards or guidance allows the Safety Officer to quickly evaluate situations and ensure that these situations are managed in a manner that is consistent with regulatory requirements. This protects the Incident Commander and employers of responders from the risk of citations, and more importantly, liability.

Of course, meeting regulatory specifications is the minimum requirement for ensuring worker safety. Many employers operate for years without receiving citations from OSHA, yet still experience worker injuries. Likewise, simply establishing a goal of meeting OSHA requirements during response or recovery efforts will not eliminate injuries. However, it is certainly a place to start.

References

1 29 CFR 1910.1200, Hazard Communication.
2 29 CFR 1910.1020, Access to Employee Exposure and Medical Records.
3 29 CFR 1910.135, Head Protection.
4 29 CFR 1910.136, Foot Protection.
5 29 CFR 1910.133, Eye and Face Protection.
6 29 CFR 1910.138, Hand Protection.
7 29 CFR 1910.137, Electrical Protective Equipment.
8 Oregon Administrative Rules, OAR 437-002-134, Personal Protective Equipment.
9 Federal Highway Administration (2009). *Manual on Uniform Traffic Control Devices*.
10 ANSI/ISEA 107-2015. *American National Standard for High-Visibility Safety Apparel and Accessories*.
11 29 CFR 1910.132, Personal Protective Equipment General Requirements.
12 29 CFR 1910.1000, Air Contaminants.
13 American Conference of Governmental Industrial Hygienists (published annually). *Threshold Limit Values for Chemical Substances and Physical Agents & Biological Exposure Indices*.
14 AFL-CIO v OSHA, 965 F.2d 962 (11th Cir. 1992).
15 National Institute of Occupational Safety and Health, Centers for Disease Control and Prevention, Department of Health and Human Services (2007). *NIOSH Pocket Guide to Chemical Hazards*. DHHS (NIOSH) publication 2005-149.
16 National Institute of Occupational Safety and Health, Centers for Disease Control and Prevention. *Table of IDLH Values*. https://www.cdc.gov/niosh/idlh/intridl4.html (accessed 4 February 2009).
17 29 CFR 1910.134, Respiratory Protection.
18 Washington Administrative Code, Chapter 296-842 WAC, Respirators.
19 29 CFR 1910 Subpart Z, Toxic and Hazardous Substances.

20 Washington Administrative Code, Chapter 296-823 WAC, Occupational Exposure to Bloodborne Pathogens.

21 Bond, W.M., Favero, M.S., Petersen, N.J. et al. (1981). Survival of hepatitis B virus after drying and storage for one week. *The Lancet* 317 (8219): 550–551.

22 Pantsil, E., Binka, M., Patel, A. et al. (2014). Hepatitis C virus maintains infectivity for weeks after drying on inanimate surfaces at room temperature: implications for risks of transmission. *Journal of Infectious Disease* 209 (8): 1205–1211.

23 29 CFR 1910.1030, Bloodborne Pathogens.

24 Washington State Department of Labor and Industries. Guidance on Handling of Criminal Evidence, Helpful Tool, Chapter 296-823 WAC.

25 29 CFR 1910 Subpart D, Walking-Working Surfaces.

26 29 CFR 1926 Subpart M, Fall Protection.

27 Lee, C. and Porter, K.M. (2007). Suspension trauma. *Emergency Medicine Journal* 24 (4): 237–238.

28 29 CFR 1926, Subpart P, Excavations.

29 29 CFR 1910.146, Permit-Required Confined Spaces.

30 29 CRF 1910.120, Hazardous Waste Operations and Emergency Response.

31 Washington Administrative Code, Chapter 296-843 WAC, Hazardous Waste Operations.

32 29 CFR 1910.95, Occupational Noise Exposure.

33 Occupational Safety and Health Administration (2011). *OSHA Pocket Guide Worker Safety Series Protecting Yourself from Noise in Construction*. OSHA publication 3498-12N 2011.

34 Occupational Safety and Health Administration (2004). Standard interpretation 2004-02-13-1, letter to John O'Green.

35 Occupational Safety and Health Administration and National Institute for Occupational Safety and Health, Centers for Disease Control and Prevention (2018). *Preventing Hearing Loss Caused by Chemical (Ototoxicity) and Noise Exposure*. SHIB 03-08-2018, DHHS (NIOSH) publication no. 2018-124.

36 29 CFR 1910.141, Sanitation.

37 29 CFR 1910.142, Temporary Labor Camps.

38 29 CFR 1910.178, Powered Industrial Trucks.

39 Occupational Safety and Health Administration (2011). OSHA Fact Sheet: aerial lifts. *DSG* (April 2011).

40 29 CFR 1910.67, Vehicle Mounted Elevating and Rotating Work Platform.

41 29 CFR 1910.68, Manlifts.

42 29 CFR 1926.453, Aerial Lifts.

43 CAL FIRE (2018). *Informational Summary Report of Serious or Near Serious CAL FIRE Injuries, Illnesses, and Accidents Green Sheet Bulldozer*

Rollover Fatality (14 July 2018). Ferguson Incident 18-CA-SNF-000745, 18-CA-MMU-014430, California Southern Region.

44 Occupational Safety and Health Act, 29 USC 654.

45 OSHA (2003). Interpretation letter to Mr. Milan Racic (18 December 2003).

46 Occupational Safety and Health Administration (2010). Proposed rule: interpretation of OSHA's provisions for feasible administrative or engineering controls of occupational noise. *Federal Register* 75: 64216–64221.

47 American Conference of Governmental Industrial Hygienists (2017). *Heat Stress and Strain: TLV® Physical Agents*, 7e. Documentation.

48 OSHA Technical Manual (2015). OSHA Instruction TED 01-00-015, Section III, Chapter 4.

49 Jacklitsch, B., Williams, W.J., Musolin, K. et al. (2016). *NIOSH Criteria for a Recommended Standard: Occupational Exposure to Heat and Hot Environments.* DHHS (NIOSH) publication 2016-106. US Department of Health and Human Services, Centers for Disease Control and Prevention, National Institute for Occupational Safety and Health.

50 Minnesota Administrative Rules. 5205.0110 Indoor Ventilation and Temperature in Places of Employment.

51 California Code of Regulations, Chapter 4, Subchapter 7, Group 2, Article 10, 3395 Heat Illness Prevention.

52 Washington Administrative Code, Chapter 296-62-095 WAC, Outdoor Heat Exposure.

53 Washington Administrative Code, Chapter 296-305 WAC, Safety Standards for Fire Fighters.

54 Occupational Safety and Health Administration (2012). *Inspection and Citation Guidance for Roadway and Highway Construction Work Zones.* CPL-02-01-054.

55 Federal Highway Administration, US Department of Transportation (2009). *Manual on Uniform Traffic Control Devices for Streets and Highways*, 2009e.

56 Occupational Safety and Health Administration. Ergonomics. https://www.osha.gov/SLTC/ergonomics/faqs.html (accessed 23 February 2019).

57 Silverstein, M. (2007). Ergonomics and regulatory politics: the Washington state case. *American Journal of Industrial Medicine* 50: 391–401.

58 California Code of Regulations, Chapter 4, Subchapter 7, Group 15, Article 106, 5110 Repetitive Motion Injuries.

59 California Code of Regulations, Chapter 4, Subchapter 7, Group 15, Article 106, 5120 Health Care Worker Back and Musculoskeletal Injury Prevention.

60 Howard, N. and Adams, D. (2018). *Work Related Musculoskeletal Disorders of the Back, Upper Extremity, and Knee in Washington State, 2006-2015: All Washington Industries.* Technical report number 40-19-2018. Safety and Health Assessment and Research for Prevention (SHARP), Washington State Department of Labor and Industries.

61 National Institute for Occupational Safety and Health (NIOSH) (1996). *Back Belts – Do They Prevent Injury?* DHHS (NIOSH) publication number 94-127.

62 NRT Response Committee, US National Response Team, US Environmental Protection Agency (2009). *Volume 1: Guidance for Managing Worker Fatigue During Disaster Operations.* Technical assistance document (30 April 2009).

63 FEMA (2017). *The National Incident Management System*, 3e.

5

Safety Training for a Response

Training is a critical component of every workplace safety program. Workers have both a need and a right to know about the hazards they face on the job, and employers have both a legal and ethical obligation to ensure that their employees receive the training that they need.

Identifying required training, selecting means and methods to provide the training, and ensuring that employees participate in training is also an element of good safety management for employers of professional emergency responders who are expected to face specific types of hazards on the job, such as firefighters. A Fire Department Health and Safety Officer manages the training program just as any safety manager does in any industry. The challenge, in emergency response, is that when the number of first responders is insufficient to meet the needs of the response, personnel from other fields are needed to supplement the work of first responders. This could include employees with skills that can supplement the response, such as those from the construction trades, or volunteers who are willing and able to support their community by helping out. Any nontraditional responder who participates in such a manner will be performing jobs that are new to them, and will require training. It may be tempting to forego this training in order to meet time-sensitive goals and objectives, but that does a disservice to those stepping up to help out and increases liability in the event of a responder's injury or illness.

Determining required training and providing it on a just-in-time basis is challenging, especially in the early phases of a response. This chapter provides an overview of training that could be needed for volunteers or reassigned employees, although specific training needed will be dependent upon the specific nature of the emergency incident and the response.

Health and Safety in Emergency Management and Response, First Edition. Dana L. Stahl.
© 2021 John Wiley & Sons, Inc. Published 2021 by John Wiley & Sons, Inc.

5.1 Respirators

Employers are required to train employees on respirators before they can wear them. Content of this training includes material that applies generally across workplaces, such as training on the content of the respiratory protection standard and regulatory requirements on the use of respirators. Training also must cover information that is specific to the worksite. Training must be repeated annually, or every 12 months, or more often if there are changes in the workplace that impact respirator use. If an employer observes an employee using a respirator incorrectly, or otherwise seems to have failed to retain information covered in training, retraining is also required even if it has been less than 12 months since the last annual training.

An employee who has received training on respirators by a previous employer does not need to be retrained if the training covered the same respirators used by the new employer, and maintenance and storage procedures are similar. However, if different respirators are used, the employee would need to be retrained by the new employer. Likewise, if exposures differ from those they 'have received in past employment, or if maintenance and storage procedures are different, the employee must be trained by the new employer prior to wearing a respirator.

Firefighters most often wear self-contained breathing apparatus (SCBA), but may also utilize airline respirators or negative pressure air purifying respirators. Police officers may need to wear filtering facepiece N95 respirators, if responding to an individual with a potentially infectious disease, or negative pressure air purifying CBRN respirators when responding to a civil disturbance. Their primary employers or departments are required to provide training. If emergency responders provide mutual aid to another department, bring their own equipment, and are exposed to the same types and levels of air contaminants as they would be when working for their primary department, they would not need additional training on respirators before responding as mutual aid.

However, if the response is something other than what is covered under the normal scope of work performed for the primary employer or department, additional training is required. Likewise, if respiratory protection equipment is provided that differs from what is used in the primary or home department, additional training is needed on the new equipment.

Employees or volunteers who are not first responders but serve as nontraditional responders in a response may be subject to exposures that require respiratory protection. These employees and volunteers may or may not wear respirators in their primary job. However, it should be assumed that the exposures that they receive while working the response are not necessarily similar to those that they experience in their primary jobs, and therefore training is needed.

Training topics that must be covered are:

- Why the respirator is required, including an explanation of exposures that the employee will be subjected to, hazards of the exposure, and how the respirator provides protection from these exposures;
- Why a respirator that does not fit properly does not protect from exposures;
- An explanation of storage and maintenance procedures that contribute to maintaining proper fit and function;
- An explanation of the capabilities of the respirator, including how it provides protection from airborne hazards as well as the level of protection that it provides;
- Limitations of the respirator, including types of exposures that the respirator is ineffective against, as well as an explanation of the ways in which respiratory protection can fail if the respirator leaks or is not maintained;
- What to do in an emergency situation, such as when a respirator fails;
- How to inspect the respirator;
- How to put a respirator on and check the seals;
- Procedures for maintenance and storage;
- How to recognize medical signs or symptoms that may interfere with respirator use;
- The general requirements of the OSHA (or State) Respiratory Protection Standard [1].

5.2 PPE

Response and recovery workers need to be provided with PPE such as gloves, eye protection, hard hats, protective footwear, personal flotation devices, or reflective garments for visibility. PPE that is provided is based upon the hazard analysis for the work performed (see Chapter 4), and workers must be given training on the PPE that they are required to wear.

First responders and workers who are reassigned to help with the response may come to the scene with PPE that is provided by their primary employer. Volunteers may come with their own PPE. The Safety Officer should ensure that the PPE that response and recovery workers bring with them matches the PPE identified for the hazard analysis for the assignments that they will be working on.

If the PPE that workers bring to the site is appropriate, exposures do not differ substantially from those that they are exposed to in their day-to-day jobs, and documentation that training has been completed by the primary employer is available, additional training may not be needed. However, the Safety Officer should complete a validation check to ensure that workers are wearing PPE correctly and that they have sufficient knowledge on the use and maintenance of the PPE that they bring in.

If the hazards that employees are exposed to during a response are unique to the incident, employees must be trained on these unique hazards even if prior training is otherwise sufficient. Employees who do not bring PPE with them, those who are assigned different types of PPE than they normally use, those who do not have their own PPE but must wear provided PPE during the response, and volunteers must be provided training that meets all the elements required by OSHA. Employees who bring appropriate PPE but fail to demonstrate sufficient knowledge during the validation check should also attend the full PPE training.

OSHA requires that the following topics be covered during PPE training:

- When PPE must be worn, and why. This could include a review of the PPE Hazard Assessment;
- What PPE must be worn and why, which again could include a review of the PPE Hazard Assessment;
- How to wear and properly adjust the PPE, including the process for putting PPE on and taking it off;
- Limitations of the PPE, including ways in which the PPE can fail to protect from hazards or ways in which PPE can deteriorate;
- How to take care of the PPE, including storage and maintenance;
- The time period in which the PPE can be used before it deteriorates or needs to be disposed of;
- How to dispose of PPE that should no longer be used because it has been damaged or exceeded its useful life. In these situations, the PPE should be disposed of in a manner that would prevent reuse [2].

5.3 Blood-borne Pathogens

Exposure to blood or Other Potentially Infectious Materials (OPIM) is an anticipated hazard for any emergency responder. Emergency responders and medical workers are exposed to blood-borne pathogens in their day-to-day jobs, and in most emergency incidents, the type of exposures will not be substantially different. However, they would need to be trained on any specifics in the incident safety plan's exposure control plan, such as how to obtain needed equipment, who to report an exposure incident to, and how to obtain a post-incident medical evaluation.

Nontraditional responders may or may not have blood or OPIM exposure in their day-to-day jobs. Even if they are covered by their primary employer's blood-borne pathogens exposure control plan, the type of exposures they are likely to be exposed to in an incident response or recovery effort can be very different than the type of exposures that they are familiar with. The Safety Officer should assume that some level of training on blood-borne pathogens is needed.

Training on blood-borne pathogens must be provided by someone who is knowledgeable on the subject as it applies to the workforce being trained. This could include healthcare professionals, such as infection control practitioners, nurse practitioners, registered nurses, occupational health professionals, physician's assistants, and emergency medical technicians. A trainer with a medical background can best relate to personnel in other healthcare fields, and is well versed in the health effects of exposure to blood-borne pathogens. Alternatively, non-healthcare professionals such as industrial hygienists, epidemiologists, or professional trainers who are knowledgeable about the material could conduct the training. Industrial hygienists who can share expertise on exposure routes and controls can be effective trainers.

Training participants must have the ability to ask questions of the instructor as the material is delivered, which could preclude delivery of training via video or electronic methods unless questions can be asked and answered in real time, such as via a hotline during the training session [3].

Training must be provided before employees are exposed to blood or OPIM, and must be repeated annually after that. Training must cover the following:

- A review of a copy of the text of the OSHA (or State) Bloodborne Pathogens Standard;
- An explanation and review of the epidemiology of blood-borne diseases;
- The symptoms and health impacts of exposure to and infection from blood-borne diseases including the Human Immunodeficiency Virus, Hepatitis B and C, and other blood-borne diseases such as syphilis, malaria, or disease caused by animal viruses;
- How blood-borne pathogens are transmitted, including needlesticks, other sharps injuries, mucous membrane exposures, and sexual contact. Although sexual contact is unlikely to be a condition of employment in emergency response, blood-borne pathogens contracted through occupational exposure can be spread to sexual partners and this should also be covered in training;
- A description of the exposure control plan that covers personnel responding to the incident or working during recovery, and how to view a copy of the exposure control plan;
- How to recognize tasks or situations that could involve exposure to blood-borne pathogens;
- Controls, including engineering and work practice controls as well as PPE that are in use to prevent or minimize exposures;

- An explanation on how the Personal Protective Equipment that is provided for use was selected;
- Emergency actions and whom to contact;
- How to report an exposure incident, including whom to report it to;
- The process for obtaining a medical evaluation after an exposure incident has occurred, and the importance of obtaining the medical evaluation timely (such as within 2 hours of the incident);
- What to expect during a postexposure medical evaluation;
- The information that the medical provider must give to the employer after the postexposure medical evaluation is completed, including the fact that medically confidential personal information will not be shared with the employer;
- Signs, labels, and color coding (Figure 5.1);
- Questions and answers [4].

BIOHAZARD

Figure 5.1 Biohazard symbol. Source: 29 CFR 1910.1030, Bloodborne Pathogens [4].

5.4 Noise

Any employee who is exposed to noise above OSHA's action level of 85 dBA 8-hour time-weighted average or dose equivalent, even one day per year, is required to be in a hearing loss prevention program (HLPP). This includes annual audiograms to detect hearing loss, use of hearing protection devices such as ear plugs or ear muffs that are appropriately rated for the noise levels, and annual training.

Many employers utilize an outside service to conduct annual audiograms. This could involve sending employees to an outside clinic, or having a mobile van service with audiometric equipment come out to provide audiograms at the jobsite.

It is a common practice for outside services to provide training just before conducting the audiometric test, and often, this is simply a matter of watching a short 15-minute video inside the van before taking the test. Others may provide hands-on training that goes into greater depth.

OSHA's Occupational Noise Exposure Standard requires that training cover the following:

- The effects of noise on hearing;
- The purpose of hearing protectors;
- Advantages and disadvantages of different types of hearing protectors;
- The differences in attenuation, or level of hearing protection provided, by different types of hearing protectors;

- Instructions on how to select, use, and take care of hearing protectors;
- The purpose of audiometric testing and an explanation of test procedures [5].

If an instructor-led training is used as opposed to a passive method such as watching a video, the instructor can demonstrate use of hearing protection devices and watch students as they insert ear plugs or put on ear muffs. The instructor can work with the students to make adjustments if they put on their hearing protective devices incorrectly. An ear plug must form a seal inside the ear canal, and an ear muff must form a seal on the head around the ear, in order for the device(s) to function as intended. The instructor can see whether or not a seal has been formed, and advise the student on techniques that can be used while putting hearing protection devises on to ensure that a seal is maintained. The instructor can also work with the student to review inspection techniques, such as inspecting the seal of the ear muff to ensure that it has not torn or cracked.

The use of a video or other passive learning method ensures that requirements are met and provides employees with basic information on hearing protection. An instructor-led training with a hands-on review of hearing protection devices provides students with skills that can best protect them from noise-induced hearing loss, and reduces the risk of hearing loss claims.

Early in an incident response, incident priorities and the need for personnel to respond to these priorities may make it difficult to conduct anything more in depth than a short video, and given other needs this would be an appropriate level of training. Later in the response, and in recovery operations, time sensitivity is less critical, and training could be repeated with an instructor that provides hands-on learning.

5.5 Chemical Hazards (General)

OSHA's Hazard Communication Standard requires that employers provide training to employees on the hazards of the chemicals that they work with. Additional training topics required under the Hazard Communication Standard includes following:

- The requirements of OSHA's Hazard Communication Standard;
- What operations include exposure to hazardous chemicals;
- How to access Safety Data Sheets, the list of chemicals used, and the written Hazard Communication program (this could be incorporated into the site safety plan in an incident response);
- How to detect the presence or release of a hazardous chemical, including monitoring equipment, visual appearance, or odor;

- Physical and health hazards of chemicals in the area that employees are working;
- Protections that can be taken to minimize the hazards of these chemicals including work procedures, emergency procedures, and personal protective equipment;
- Additional details of the Hazard Communication program/site safety plan including what labels will be used;
- Information on Safety Data Sheets (SDSs). Specifically, the SDSs for the chemicals that the employees will be working with should be reviewed;
- Information on hazards of chemicals that come from "nonroutine" exposures, such as byproducts of chemicals used or found in the environment [6].

Training must be provided in a language that employees understand. If employees do not understand English, and are given work instructions in a language other than English, training must be provided in the same language that is used to provide work instructions [7].

In a multiagency incident response, responders and other workers come together to work within the Incident Command System. Most employees will have received training on Hazard Communication from their primary employer. These employees do not need to receive comprehensive training in Hazard Communication [8], but they do need to receive training on incident-specific hazards, such as any chemicals brought in to facilitate the response. They also need to be trained on the specifics of how Hazard Communication requirements are addressed within the incident, including how to access SDSs and any relevant information on Hazard Communication within the site safety plan.

5.6 Chemical-Specific Hazards

Chemical-specific standards (see Chapter 4, Table 4.5) each have specific training requirements, and any response or recovery workers who are exposed to chemicals covered by these standards are required to receive chemical-specific training as specified in the relevant standard.

In some situations, potential exposure to these chemicals will be known before responders arrive at the incident, and it may be possible to assign only responders who have received prior training on these chemical hazards to work where these chemical exposures are an issue. In other situations, exposures are unknown. Early in the response exposures may occur before initial evaluations have been completed. Once exposure characterizations have been made, response workers are entitled to training on these hazards.

Other exposures can be anticipated. A building collapse, for example, is likely to release hazardous building materials such as asbestos or lead into the air.

Concrete structures are likely to release silica. Fires that burn hot enough to vaporize paints or colorized plastics can release hexavalent chromium. Workers who routinely respond to such incidents should be trained accordingly.

5.7 Asbestos

Building owners are required to identify Asbestos-Containing Materials (ACM) and Potentially Asbestos-Containing Materials (PACM), and post warning signs where these materials are present. Legible warning signs that are posted on a building that an emergency responder enters are positive confirmation that asbestos is present. However, warning signs may not be apparent because of extensive damage to the building, or possibly because the building owner was not diligent in meeting these requirements. For this reason, emergency responders should always assume that airborne asbestos fibers may be present if there is sufficient damage to a building.

EPA and OSHA regulations cover asbestos training requirements, and states may impose additional requirements as well. Workers who conduct abatement activities are required to attend training courses between 32 and 40 hours in length. Maintenance and custodial workers who conduct activities that could disturb asbestos require Operations and Maintenance (O&M), which covers asbestos regulations and work practices, handling and disposal of ACM, respirator use and protective clothing, and decontamination procedures as well as asbestos awareness. O&M courses generally take between 14 and 16 hours to complete.

Maintenance and custodial staff who are involved in cleaning and minor maintenance activities in which ACM may be accidentally disturbed require 2 hours of awareness training, which covers topics such as:

- Information on asbestos and its health effects;
- The employer's worker protection program;
- Locations of ACM;
- How to recognize ACM that is damaged or deteriorating;
- The O&M program for the building(s) that they work in [9–11].

Emergency responders are not specifically addressed in these work classifications, although exposures to emergency responders are probably at least as high as for those that perform maintenance work that could disturb asbestos. These workers require a minimum of 2 hours of awareness training up to 14 hours of O&M training.

Asbestos regulations remain in effect even during catastrophic events. If a building is in imminent danger of collapse as a result of an emergency, it may need to be demolished without first having had an inspection and subsequent abatement to remove any identified Asbestos-Containing Materials as would be required in a non-emergent demolition. Asbestos exposure should be assumed for anyone working on or near the building. Training for emergency responders should include methods to reduce this presumed exposure through work practices that minimize creating airborne dust, such as wetting down materials to minimize dust levels and using HEPA (High-Efficiency Particulate Air) vacuums rather than sweeping [12].

State environmental agencies and local clean air agencies often include additional training requirements. When applicable, these training requirements must be included.

5.8 Lead

OSHA's lead standard requires that employees receive training on lead before initial assignment to a job where they could be exposed to lead above the action level of 30 mg/m^3, and annually after that. Exposures in an initial emergency response is by nature an unknown, however, it should be presumed that in any incident in which a building is damaged exposures can occur above the action level.

Recovery workers also are at risk of lead exposure. Once operations move to recovery, exposure monitoring can be conducted to determine actual exposures.

Training on lead must include the following:

- The content of OSHA's lead standard.
- The nature of the work operations in which lead exposures may exceed the action level.
- The purpose of respirators and their limitations, including:
  o How respirators are selected;
  o The importance of maintaining a proper fit.
- A description of the medical surveillance program, including:
  o The purpose of the medical surveillance program;
  o Health effects that result from excessive exposure to lead, with particular emphasis on reproductive hazards;
  o Medical removal and medical removal work protections;
  o How chelating agents work to remove lead from the body and the health impacts of using them. Specific instruction must be given that chelating agents only be taken under the direction of a licensed physician.
- Engineering controls that may be used, such as ventilation.
- Work practice controls, such methods to prevent stirring up airborne dust [13].

5.9 Silica

Silica is found in many building materials, such as concrete, brick, cement, drywall, tile, and grout. If building damage occurs, emergency responders and recovery workers are at risk of silica exposures. Exposures above the action level of $25\,\mu g/m^3$ should be presumed in any collapse of a concrete structure until air monitoring can prove otherwise. An initial response may be over before air monitoring results can be obtained, but exposures to recovery workers can be determined and evaluated as work progresses.

Training on silica must cover the following:

- Elements of Hazard Communication, including Safety Data Sheets and labels for any silica-containing products obtained from a manufacturer;
- Health effects of silica, including cancer and effects on the lungs, immune system, and kidneys;
- Tasks that could result in exposure to respirable silica in emergency response or recovery;
- Measures that have been taken to protect employees from exposure to silica, such as engineering controls, work practices, and respirators;
- The contents of OSHA's silica standard;
- Competent persons assigned;
- The purpose of medical surveillance and how it will be performed [14, 15].

5.10 Hexavalent Chromium

Hexavalent chromium is an IARC Group 1 carcinogen and can cause cancers of the lung, sinuses, and nasal passages. It is associated with contact dermatitis, skin ulcers, irritation, and ulceration of the nasal mucosa, and perforation of the nasal septum. Hexavalent chromium exposure is also linked to kidney damage, liver damage, pulmonary congestion and edema, epigastric pain, and erosion and irritation of the teeth.

Construction workers are exposed to hexavalent chromium in building materials containing Portland Cement, such as cement, mortar, stucco, and terrazzo. Welders can be exposed to very high levels of hexavalent chromium, especially when welding or cutting on stainless steel. Hexavalent chromium is found in many paint and colorized products, such as colored plastics. Emergency responders and recovery workers can receive dermal exposures through contact with disturbed material, or respiratory exposures from airborne materials when a building collapses or burns. Recovery workers may be exposed when working with these materials in a similar manner as construction workers [16].

Workers with exposure to hexavalent chromium must receive training that includes the following:

- Elements of the Hazard Communication Standard, including Safety Data Sheets and labels for materials that contain hexavalent chromium;
- OSHA's Hexavalent Chromium Standard;
- The purpose of the medical surveillance program;
- How the medical surveillance program is managed [17].

5.11 Fall Protection

Response and recovery workers must work at heights to perform rescue or carry out other functions or tasks. OSHA Construction Standards apply to construction work where a fall hazard of 6 feet or greater exists, and the General Industry Walking and Working Surfaces Standard applies to all other workers where a fall hazard of 4 feet or greater exists. Response and recovery workers exposed to these fall hazards must receive training before they are exposed to the hazard. OSHA specifies that this training must be delivered by a Qualified Person, which is defined as a person who "by possession of a recognized degree, certificate, or professional standing, or who by extensive knowledge, training, and experience has successfully demonstrated the ability to solve or resolve problems relating to the subject matter, the work, or the project."

Training must be delivered in a manner that is clear and understandable. It must take place before exposure to heights occurs, and needs to be repeated if there is reason to believe that the employee has inadequate knowledge or understanding to perform jobs with fall hazards safely.

Training must cover the following:

- The nature of the fall hazards that workers are likely to be exposed to, and how to recognize these fall hazards;
- Procedures to minimize these hazards;
- Procedures for installing, inspecting, operating, maintaining, and disassembling the personal fall protection systems that are or will be used;
- Correct use of personal fall protection systems as specified in the OSHA standards, such as proper hook up, anchoring, and tie-off techniques;
- Equipment manufacturer's specifications for inspection and storage;
- Other fall protection systems used, such as guardrail systems, safety net systems, warning line systems, safety monitoring systems and employee roles in safety monitoring systems, and/or controlled access zones;
- OSHA fall protection standards.

The construction standard requires that employees be issued a card that shows that they have been trained in fall protection [18, 19].

5.12 Material Handling Equipment

Operators of forklifts or Powered Industrial Trucks (PITs) must receive an initial course on forklifts that includes both classroom and hands-on operational training. Classroom training must include the following:

- Operating instructions, including warnings, hazards, and precautions that need to be taken when operating each type of Powered Industrial Truck that the employee will operate;
- Differences between Powered Industrial Trucks and automobiles;
- Truck controls and instrumentation, including where these are located, what they do, and how they work;
- Engine and motor operation;
- Steering and maneuvering, including the hazards of "backswing";
- Visibility limitations: Powered Industrial Trucks have more blind spots than a car or other vehicle that the operator may be familiar with and a forklift operator may not see pedestrians or other hazards. Loading the forklift decreases visibility further;
- Forks and attachments, including how they work and limitations of their use;
- What is meant by "vehicle capacity" and how to determine the capacity of the Powered Industrial Truck;
- Vehicle stability, including the "stability triangle" on a forklift and how operating outside the stability triangle causes the forklift to tip over;
- Inspection procedures and requirements;
- Maintenance procedures that the operator is required to perform;
- Operating limitations;
- Any additional operating instructions listed in the operator's manual for the vehicle;
- Workplace-related topics:
  o Surface conditions where the vehicle will be operated. Uneven surfaces, cracks, bumps and other disturbances can cause a forklift's load to move outside the stability triangle and increase chances of tip over.
  o Composition of the loads to be moved and the stability of these loads;
  o Load manipulation, stacking, and unstacking;
  o Where pedestrian traffic occurs in areas where the forklift will be operated;
  o Locations of narrow aisles or restricted points;
  o Hazardous locations where the vehicle will be operated, such as locations where flammable vapors or flammable dusts are present;

- Where ramps and slopes are located that could affect the stability of the forklift;
- Closed environments where vehicle exhaust can build up and cause buildup of carbon monoxide: battery-powered forklifts should be used in enclosed areas;
- Other unique or hazardous conditions that could affect the safe operation of the Powered Industrial Truck.

Powered Industrial Truck Operators who have never operated a forklift before, or who have not operated the type of forklift that they will be using for their new assignment, must be given an opportunity to practice operating the equipment. This can be done under the supervision of an instructor and only in locations where they cannot injure others.

Following training, the driving skills of the operator are evaluated. A skills reevaluation must occur every three years. Operators who have completed classroom training and passed a skills evaluation are given a certification of completion and it is common practice for forklift operators to be given wallet cards that show the type of equipment that they are certified for, the date of training, and a signature of the trainer.

OSHA allows portability of training, so if an operator has received classroom training on the same type of truck that they will be operating, they only need training on workplace-specific topics when they move to a new employer or receive a new assignment [20].

An incident response may require resources such as forklifts and forklift operators provided by outside employers. If forklift operators arrive with the same equipment that they use in their day-to-day jobs, and their employer has an established forklift program that meets OSHA requirements, the Safety Officer can request documentation of training from the employer rather than repeating it. Workplace specific training would still need to be provided, since work conditions will differ from that of their primary job. Operating skills need to be evaluated as well, since an unskilled operator, or one who's skills are not a suitable match for the environment, can cause significant damage to property as well as serious injury to themselves, pedestrians or others in the area.

Variability exists in the quality of training across industry. Some employers send employees out to outside locations for training, and many forklift manufacturers and vendors provide training for new operators at their facilities.

Employers may also choose to select an individual from their work organization to send to a train-the trainer course to provide forklift training for their employees. Outside organizations provide "train the trainer" training, and provide the instructor with curriculum, workbooks, training materials, and evaluation criteria and scoring sheets. The train-the-trainer program continues to support instructors by providing updates and refresher training. Since the instructor works with forklift operators day to day, the instructor can provide on-the-job reinforcement of training principles. Some of the safest and most skilled forklift operators have learned their skills in this type of system.

Other employees complete this training requirement by showing employees a video that covers OSHA-required topics.

When a forklift operator shows their operator certification card to a Safety Officer, the Safety Officer may not know if the certification indicates a high-quality training certificate conducted by an in-house trainer supported by a robust train-the-trainer program, or whether the employee simply watched a 20-minute video. This makes the on-site skills evaluation all the more critical.

To be effective, the skills evaluation must be conducted by someone knowledgeable and qualified to identify a high-skilled operator, and who can also identify skill deficiencies that could lead to accidents or injuries at the scene of the response or recovery effort. The skill evaluator must be someone who is trained and experienced in forklift operation.

Equipment such as backhoes, bucket lift trucks, and other worksite material handling equipment are often brought in to assist in response and recovery efforts. As discussed in Chapter 4, OSHA does not mandate training for these types of trucks to the extent that they do for forklifts. However, the potential for property damage or injury to persons is as great as, or even greater, with backhoes and bucket lift trucks than it is for forklifts. Bucket trucks and backhoes can tip over just like forklifts can, and any incident which involves contact between large material handling equipment and a person on the ground is a serious one. Prudent employers implement training programs for operators of this equipment that mirror the programs used for forklift operators. Many equipment vendors provide training, and many forklift train-the-trainer organizations also offer train-the-trainer programs for bucket trucks, backhoes, and other common equipment.

A prudent Safety Officer should ensure that material handling requests specify the equipment needed *and* an operator that can present an operator certification card. Arriving operators should also complete a skills evaluation with a qualified evaluator before given an assignment at the scene.

5.13 Heat Exposure

Training on heat exposure is only required in states that have implemented regulatory standards to control heat in the workplace, or that require employers to develop heat-related illness prevention plans. However, heat exposure is a common hazard in emergency response and recovery work, and response and recovery workers are subject to developing heat-related illness. It is advisable for Safety Officers to ensure measures are taken to reduce instances of heat related illness, including training of workers. Training requirements specified in state regulations can provide guidance in developing training for workers in other states.

Minnesota's rule requires that employees be trained on all physical agent hazards, including heat. This training must cover the following:

- The name(s) of the physical agent;
- Acceptable levels of exposure, and the levels of exposure that are restricted;
- Acute and chronic effects of exposure;
- Symptoms and effects of exposure;
- Appropriate emergency treatment;
- Known proper conditions and exposure;
- Name, phone number, and address, if appropriate, of a manufacturer of any equipment that generates the physical agent such as heat [21, 22].

Washington and California require that employees who are at a reasonably predicted risk of developing heat-related illness and their supervisors receive training. This training must cover the following:

- Environmental factors that contribute to heat-related illness;
- Personal factors that may increase susceptibility to heat-related illness. This includes factors such as age, degree of acclimatization, medical conditions, drinking water consumption, alcohol use, caffeine use, nicotine use, and any personal medications that affect the body's responsible use (This information must be provided for personal use of the employee. Discussion of personal medical conditions or confidential information is not appropriate);
- The importance of removing heat-retaining PPE, such as nonbreathable chemical-resistant clothing, during all breaks;
- The importance of drinking water or other acceptable beverages frequently;
- The importance of acclimatization;
- The different types of heat-related illness, and signs and symptoms of each type;
- First aid procedures for heat-related illness;
- The importance of immediately reporting symptoms of heat-related illness in either themselves or coworkers;
- Procedures that must be followed, including emergency response procedures.

Supervisor training must also cover the following:

- Procedures supervisors must follow as required under the state rule;
- Procedures that a supervisor must follow in an employee shows signs or symptoms of heat-related illness, including emergency response procedures;
- Procedures for transporting an ill employee to a place that can be reached by emergency medical responders;

- How to monitor weather reports and how to respond to hot weather advisories (California) [23, 24].

The State of Alaska requires that employers keep readily available Physical Agent Data Sheets (PADSs) in the workplace, and provide copies to employees upon request. Employers must also provide training on the physical agents covered in PADSs when employees may be exposed to the physical agent. Alaska's Hazard Communication standard requires that PADSs be maintained similarly to SDSs.

PADS prepared by Alaska Occupational Safety and Health (AKOSH) include the following:

- Cold Stress;
- Hand Arm Vibration;
- Heat Stress;
- Ionizing Radiation;
- Lasers;
- Noise;
- Radio Frequency/Microwave Radiation;
- Ultraviolet Radiation [25].

Alaska's Physical Agent Data Sheet for heat stress provides a good overview of the topic, and is a useful resource for those preparing training on this topic even outside of Alaska [26]. Likewise the Cold Stress PADS provides a good overview of cold stress hazards that can be reviewed with employees who are exposed to cold hazards [27].

5.14 HAZWOPER

Employees who perform work covered under the HAZWOPER standard (Hazardous Waste Operations and Emergency Response) are required to receive training. The amount of initial training required in hours is determined by the type of exposure that the employees receive (Table 5.1) [28]. States may require additional training. For example, Washington state requires 80 hours of training for employees who are required to wear SCBAs [29].

Training content should include topics addressed in the HAZWOPER standard, such as types of hazards that can exist during covered work and use of PPE. OSHA provides flexibility on what must be covered during the required 40, 24, or 8 hours of training so that the training can effectively cover the hazards associated with the type of work employees will perform.

Training and supervised on-site-field experience must be provided by a qualified individual. Trainers can be qualified by completing a training program to

Table 5.1 Training required under HAZWOPER.

Type of work/ exposure	Training (hours)	Supervised on-site field experience (days)	Additional training
General site workers with exposure who are regularly on site and/or receive exposures above the PEL	40	3	8-Hour annual refresher
Occasional work and unlikely to be exposed above PELs or other exposure limits	24	1	8-Hour annual refresher
Managers and supervisors of employees performing work covered by HAZWOPER	40	3	8-Hours of additional training on the employer's program 8-Hour annual refresher
Employees who perform emergency response activities, such as spills or releases	Training to a level of competence consisting with assigned duties		

Source: 29 CFR 1910.120, Hazardous Waste Operations and Emergency Response (HAZWOPER) [28].

teach the subjects they are expected to teach, such as a train-the-trainer program, or who have academic credentials to teach the subject matter, including completion of 40 hours of HAZWOPER training and on-site field experience. A number of organizations offer "OSHA-compliant HAZWOPER training". However, OSHA does not actually certify these training programs, and the Safety Officer should be cautious of using a training organization that claims to be "OSHA Certified" [30]. Online HAZWOPER courses are also available. These are advantageous in that HAZWOPER training can be taken at any time without having to locate a classroom offering. However, OSHA considers that a HAZWOPER course must have a hands-on component, and does not feel that solely relying on computer-based training can provide personnel with necessary hands-on skills: Computer-based training can be used for part of a training program, but it must be supplemented with classroom and hands-on training provided by an in-person instructor [31].

Upon completing a HAZWOPER course, students must be provided with a certification that indicates that the instructor has determined that the individual has completed this training successfully. Accepted practice is to provide a paper certification as well as a wallet card that can be carried with the employee. Alternative records, such as a signature on a course attendance sheet, are not acceptable documentation [32].

Once initial training is complete, employees must receive an additional 8 hours of refresher training every year.

Supervisors and managers must receive the same level of training as their employees, plus an additional 8 hours of supervisory training. The 8 hours of supervisory training cannot be counted as an 8-hour refresher training, so an employee that has been previously HAZWOPER certified must receive an additional 16 hours of training in the year in which they become a supervisor [33].

Workers who perform work that requires HAZWOPER certification should provide documentation of HAZWOPER training upon arrival at the scene. If they can provide certification of initial training, but are not current on their refresher training, refresher training must be provided before they begin work. Required training previously covered in this chapter could count towards some of the 8-hour required training. Overlap in training to meet requirements is allowable as long as all training requirements are met [34].

Workers who have certifications for 40- or 24-hour HAZWOPER training and are current on their 8-hour refreshers must also receive site-specific training. Site-specific training must cover at least:

- The names of personnel responsible for the site safety and health plan and alternate contacts;
- Safety, health, and other hazards at the site;
- Use of PPE;
- Work practices in use at the site to minimize exposures;
- How to use equipment and engineering controls safely;
- The medical surveillance program;
- Contents of the site safety plan [28].

5.15   Fatigue

Response and recovery workers are at risk of fatigue. While training on this topic is not required by OSHA, fatigue awareness is important for all personnel within a response or recovery effort.

The Federal Aviation Administration (FAA) requires that air carriers develop Fatigue Risk Management System in order to improve safety performance of employees in the aviation industry. Training programs from the aviation industry can provide guidance for those developing training programs for response and recovery workers, as well as employees in other industries. Topics that should be covered in a fatigue awareness education program include the following:

- Basic information on the causes of fatigue, the importance of sleep, and the effects of circadian rhythms on alertness and performance levels;
- A review of fatigue management protocols and procedures that have been developed, and the responsibilities of management and employees;
- Tools for conducting a personal assessment of fatigue risk;
- How to identify early signs of fatigue in others;
- Procedures to follow when signs of fatigue are identified or suspected in oneself or in others;
- Personal strategies for preventing and managing fatigue risk;
- Procedures for reporting suspected fatigue-related adverse events;
- Any other site-specific fatigue management topics relevant to the work to be performed [35, 36].

The National Response Team also recommends that a training program be implemented as a strategy for mitigating fatigue risk factors, and has developed guidance on topics to be covered in Fatigue Awareness Training:

- Health impacts, signs, and symptoms of fatigue;
- Strategies for preventing fatigue during disaster operations;
- How supervisors can recognize operational fatigue and stress in employees;
- Common fatigue risk factors in disaster operations;
- Information on the employers Employee Assistance program;
- Tips and a checklist on preparing for deployment at a disaster site;
- Information for workers and their families on what to expect during deployments;
- Work zone safety and defensive driving techniques;
- Sleeping strategies for night shift workers;
- Availability of critical incident stress management teams and Employee Assistance Program services;
- Information on any policies and procedures related to work hours and rest periods;
- Job aids to provide clearly defined job tasks and duties;
- Predeployment resources.

In addition, the National Response Team guidance recommends that fatigue-related information be included in site orientations, daily briefings, and safety meetings, and to reinforce reporting of fatigue signs and symptoms [37].

As this is recommended rather than required training, training can be incident specific and tailored toward the needs of response personnel.

5.16   Distracted Driving

Driving accidents are a risk in any incident response. Vehicle accidents are a leading cause of occupational fatalities across the nation, and risk is even greater during response and recovery efforts. Roads that have been damaged or otherwise impacted as a result of the incident create additional hazards. Stress can interfere with attention given to driving (see Chapter 7). Fatigue is another risk factor.

From a risk management standpoint, it is important to include defensive driving in a safety training program. Many defensive driving training programs are available commercially, ranging from short videos available from numerous vendors to comprehensive safe driving programs such as those offered by the National Safety Council. The National Safety Council offers online programs as well as train-the-trainer programs for in person courses.[1]

Information on safe driving should be included in safety messaging and daily briefings as well.

5.17   OSHA 10- and 30-Hour Training

OSHA has established an outreach training program to teach workers about their rights, employer responsibilities, how to file a complaint, and how to recognize, prevent, and abate job-related hazards. Attendance in a class is voluntary. However, many employers have begun to include completion of either 10- or 30-hour OSHA training in published job descriptions. States, local jurisdictions, and unions may enact requirements for employees to complete this training before going on jobsites. Individuals who complete this training are given wallet cards that can be presented to an employer.

The 10- and 30-hour courses are specific to the industries of Construction, General Industry, and Maritime.

These OSHA cards do not relieve employers of their training responsibilities. OSHA standards require a combination of general and site-specific training. An OSHA card indicates that an individual has received an over view of general safety topics and OSHA regulations, but the employer must still provide any required site-specific training.

---

1 http://www.nsc.org/safety-training/defensive-driving (accessed 25 March 2019).

Outreach trainers are authorized to teach 10- and 30-hour outreach courses through regional OSHA Education Centers. Trainers must apply to become a trainer through an OSHA Education Center, and complete an OSHA standards course in for the industry that they will be teaching in as well as a train-the-trainer course. A refresher training course must be completed every four years at an OSHA Education Center. If an OSHA trainer fails to complete their refresher training before their certification date, they must retake the initial train-the-trainer course, and may need to retake the OSHA standards course as well. (Table 5.2).

An applicant who applies to become an outreach trainer must demonstrate that they have experience in managing safety programs and have completed the appropriate Occupational Safety and Health Standards course for their industry. A university degree or professional certification such as a CIH or CSP can be substituted for up to two years of experience. An applicant who is accepted into a trainer course must demonstrate training skills as well as competency on OSHA standards.

Table 5.2 Required courses for OSHA Outreach Trainers by industry offered by OSHA Education Centers [38–40].

Industry program	Required courses
General Industry	OSHA #511 Occupational Safety and Health Standards for General Industry
	OSHA #501 Trainer Course in Occupational Safety and Health Standards for General Industry (within seven years of completing OSHA #511)
	OSHA #503 Update for General Industry Outreach Trainers (every four years)
Construction	OSHA #510 Occupational Safety and Health Standards for the Construction Industry
	OSHA #500 Trainer Course in Occupational Safety and Health Standards for the Construction Industry (within seven years of completing OSHA #510)
	OSHA #502 Update for Construction Industry Outreach Trainers (every four years)
Maritime	OSHA #5410 Occupational Safety and Health Standards for the Maritime Industry
	OSHA #5400 Trainer Course in Occupational Safety and Health Standards for the Maritime Industry (within seven years of completing OSHA #5410)
	OSHA #5402 Maritime Industry Trainer Course Update (every four years)

An authorized outreach trainer must cover specific topics mandated by OSHA in each 10- or 30-hour outreach course (Tables 5.3 and 5.4) [38–41]. Several organizations offer online OSHA 10- and 30-hour courses that are supported by an OSHA Education Center.

Possession of an OSHA outreach card has become valuable, to the point that some entities have created fake, or fraudulent OSHA cards. OSHA takes this issue of fake cards very seriously, and will refer anyone caught falsifying this information for criminal prosecution [42].

5.18 OSHA Disaster Site Worker Outreach Training Program

OSHA has also developed an outreach training program for Disaster Site Workers. The target audience for this outreach training are nontraditional responders who provide skilled support or cleanup services in response to a disaster, such as those who perform utility work, demolition, debris removal, or heavy equipment operators. Like the standards-based 10- and 30-hour training, participation is voluntary, and does not fully meet the training requirements specified in the OSHA standards since the courses do not cover site-specific information. When workers arrive at a scene with a Disaster Site Worker training card, they still must receive required site- or scene-specific training.

The Disaster Site Worker Outreach Course includes a heavy emphasis on the use of respirators. The last part of the class consists of a final exercise to test mastery of skills.

Outreach course students must complete an OSHA 10- or 30-hour course in Construction or General Industry before attending the Disaster Site Worker Course, so it is assumed that they come into the class with a good working knowledge of OSHA standards and requirements.

Requirements for acceptance as a Disaster Site Worker Outreach Trainer include:

- Current OSHA authorization as a Construction or General Industry Outreach Trainer;
- Three years of experience as an Occupational Safety and Health Trainer;
- Either:
  o Completion of a 40-hour Hazardous Waste Operations and Emergency Response (HAZWOPER) course within the past five years;
  o Completion of an 8-hour HAZWOPER refresher within the past 12 months, or
  o Possession of journey level credentials in a building trade union.

Table 5.3 Required topics in OSHA 10-hour courses [38–40].

	General Industry	Construction	Maritime

Mandatory topics	6 Hours of:
	• Introduction to OSHA (1 hour)
	• Walking and working surfaces/fall protection (1 hour)
	• Exit routes, emergency action plans, fire prevention plans, and fire protection (1 hour)
	• Electrical (1 hour)
	• PPE (1hour)
	• Hazard Communication (1 hour)
		6 Hours of:
		• Introduction to OSHA (1 hour)
		• OSHA focus four hazards (4 hours)
		  ○ Falls (1.5 hours)
		  ○ Electrocution (30 minutes)
		  ○ Struck-by (30 minutes)
		  ○ Caught-in or between (30 minutes)
		• PPE and lifesaving equipment (30 minutes)
		• Health hazards in construction (30 minutes)
			For all Maritime courses 3 hours of:
			• Introduction to OSHA (1 hour)
			• Walking and working surfaces (1 hour)
			• PPE (1 hour)
			
			For OSHA course Shipyard Employment 4 hours of:
			• Fall protection/scaffolding (1 hour)
			• Electrical (1 hour)
			• Confined and enclosed spaces (1 hour)
			• Fire protection (1 hour)

Elective topics	2 Hours covering at least 30 minutes of at least 2 of: • Hazardous materials • Materials handling • Machine guarding • Introduction to industrial hygiene • Blood-borne pathogens • Ergonomics • Safety and health program • Fall protection	2 Hours covering at least 30 minutes of at least 2 of: • Cranes, derricks, hoist, elevators and conveyors • Excavations • Materials handling, storage, use and disposal • Scaffolds • Stairways and ladders • Tools hand and power	1 Hour covering one topic for Shipyard Employment 4 Hours covering 30 minutes of at least two topics for Marine Terminals and Longshoring: • Hazard Communication/hazardous materials • Lockout/tagout • Respiratory protection

| Optional | 2 Hours covering at least 30 minutes of:
 • General Industry hazards or policies
 • Expand on mandatory or elective topics | 2 Hours covering at least 30 minutes of:
 • Construction industry hazards or policies
 • Expand on mandatory or elective topics | Additional electives for Marine Terminals and Longshoring:
 • Fall protection
 • Electrical
 • Confined and enclosed spaces
 • Fire protection

 2 Hours for Shipyard Employment and 3 hours for Marine Terminals and Longshoring, 30 minutes each of:
 • Hot work – welding, burning and cutting
 • Material handling
 • Blood-borne pathogens
 • Machine guarding
 • Ergonomics and proper lifting techniques
 • Additional coverage of mandatory or elective topics
 • Any other maritime hazards or policies |

Table 5.4 Required topics in OSHA 30-hour courses [38–40].

	General Industry	Construction	Maritime

Mandatory topics	12 Hours of:
	• Introduction to OSHA (1 hour)
	• Managing safety and health (2 hours)
	• Walking and working surfaces/fall protection (1 hour)
	• Exit routes, emergency action plans, fire prevention plans, and fire protection (2 hours)
	• Electrical (2 hours)
	• PPE (1 hour)
	• Materials handling (2 hours)
	• Hazard Communication (1 hour)
		14 Hours of:
		• Introduction to OSHA (1 hour)
		• Managing safety and health (2 hours)
		• OSHA focus four hazards (6 hours)
		  ○ Falls (1.5 hours)
		  ○ Electrocution (30 minutes)
		  ○ Struck-by (30 minutes)
		  ○ Caught in or between (30 minutes)
		• PPE and lifesaving equipment (2 hours)
		• Health hazards in construction (2 hours)
		• Stairways and ladders (1 hour)
			For all Maritime courses, 7 hours of:
			• Introduction to OSHA (1 hour)
			• Managing safety and health (2 hours)
			• Walking and working surfaces/Fall protection (2 hours)
			• PPE (2 hours)
			
			Shipyard Employment: 8 hours of:
			• Fall protection/scaffolding (2 hours)
			• Electrical (2 hours)
			• Confined and enclosed spaces (2 hours)
			• Fire protection (2 hours)

Elective topics – minimum 30 minutes each	10 Hours covering at least 30 minutes of at least 5 of: • Hazardous materials • Permit required confined spaces • Lockout/tagout • Machine guarding • Welding, cutting and brazing • Introduction to industrial hygiene • Blood-borne pathogens • Ergonomics • Fall protection • Safety and health programs	12 Hours covering at least 30 minutes of at least 6 of: • Concrete and masonry construction • Confined space entry • Cranes, derricks, hoists, elevators and conveyors • Ergonomics • Excavations • Fire protection and prevention • Materials handling, storage, use, and disposal	For shipyard Employment – 2 hours For Marine Terminals and Longshoring 8 hours covering at least two topics At least 30 minutes of: • Hazard Communications/hazardous materials • Lockout/tagout • Respiratory protection

	General Industry	Construction	Maritime
	• Powered Industrial Trucks	• Motor vehicles, mechanized equipment and marine operations; rollover protective structures and overhead protection, and signs, signals and barricades • Powered industrial vehicles • Safety and health programs • Scaffolds • Steel erection • Tools hand and power • Welding and cutting • Foundations of safety leadership (minimum 2.5 hours)	Additional electives for Marine Terminals and Longshoring: • Fall protection • Electrical • Confined and enclosed spaces • Fire protection
Optional	8 Hours • General Industry hazards or policies • Expand on mandatory or elective topics	4 Hours • Construction Industry hazards or policies • Expand on mandatory or elective topics	Shipyard Employment: 13 hours Marine Terminals and Longshoring: 15 hours 30 minutes of: • Hot work – welding burning and cutting • Material handline • Blood-borne pathogens • Machine guarding • Ergonomics and proper lifting techniques • Additional coverage on mandatory or elective topics • Other maritime industry standards or policies

Table 5.5   Topic requirements for OSHA's Disaster Site Worker Outreach Courses.

15 Hour course	7.5 Hour course
<ul><li>Introduction/overview (1.25 hours)</li><li>Incident Command System/Unified Command System (0.75 hour)</li><li>Safety hazards (2.5 hours)</li><li>Health hazards (2.0 hours)</li><li>CBRNE (Chemical, Bological, Radiological, Nuclear, and Explosive) agents (1.0 hour)</li><li>Traumatic incident stress awareness (0.5 hour)</li><li>Respiratory protection (3.5 hours)</li><li>Other PPE (1.25 hours)</li><li>Decontamination (1.5 hours)</li><li>Final exercise (0.75 hour)</li></ul>	<ul><li>Introduction: characteristics of a disaster site and worker responsibilities (1 hour)</li><li>Safety hazards and CBRNE agents (1.0 hour)</li><li>Health hazards and traumatic incident stress awareness (1 hour)</li><li>PPE and respirator activity (2 hours)</li><li>Decontamination (1 hour)</li><li>Incident Command System (1 hour)</li><li>Final exercise (0.5 hour)</li></ul>

Source: OSHA Directorate of Training and Education [43].

Those who are accepted into the training program must complete OSHA #5600 Disaster Site Worker Trainer Course through an OSHA education center. An update course, OSHA #5602 Update for Disaster Site Worker Trainer Course must be completed every four years. Authorized Disaster Site Worker Instructors can then teach either the 7.5- or 15-hour Disaster Site Worker Outreach Course. OSHA requires that specific content be covered in these courses (Table 5.5).

Although OSHA's Directorate of Training and Education allows OSHA 10- and 30-hour courses to be delivered online, the Disaster Site Worker courses must be delivered in a classroom format with a live instructor [43].

The Disaster Site Worker program receives much less participation than the standards outreach programs, in part to the number of prerequisites that must be met to either participate in the outreach courses or become trainers. A number of OSHA education centers have discontinued offering the Disaster Site Worker program, although it continues to be offered through several centers around the country.

5.19   Delivering Training

Meeting training requirements can be a challenge at a disaster site, especially early on in the incident. Therefore, it is advantageous to identify training requirements during the incident planning phase rather than after the incident occurs.

Professional emergency responders are provided with training through their primary employer. If a mutual aid response requires responders to cross state lines, state-specific standards may require additional training. For example, municipal fire fighters in an OSHA state are not covered by OSHA, but if these same firefighters travel to assist in a response in a state plan state, state health and safety rules apply. This could create a need for more expansive training for these firefighters. If mutual aid agreements are implemented, training requirements can be specified in the mutual aid plan.

When the incident is large enough that additional aid is needed from nontraditional responders, the amount of training needed increases. If these workers are identified by state or local emergency planners, much required training can be completed before the incident occurs. When the standards require periodic or annual training on a topic, a balance must be struck between ensuring that arriving workers are fully trained and can begin work immediately, and spending time and resources on annual training that these workers will not need if a disaster does not happen.

Regardless of how much training is completed prior to the incident, site- or scene-specific training must still be completed. Some of this occurs in briefings and safety messaging incorporated into the emergency planning and operations process (see Chapter 8). Some of it will need to be delivered to workers in a more extensive format.

When OSHA standards allow training to be delivered online or in video format, these methods can be used. Watching a video is a passive learning technique, as are many online courses, and retention of material offered through passive learning methods is lower than methods that require participation of the student in the learning process. However, it is an option when both time and instructional resources are limited.

Safety professionals, such as Certified Industrial Hygienists, Certified Safety Professionals or others with safety certifications through the Board of Certified Safety Professionals, or individuals with academic training or experience in occupational safety and health can provide much of the OSHA-required training in a classroom format. If a classroom is not available, safety training can be conducted at a meeting site, in an outdoor meeting area, or even the back of a truck. It does not have to be formal.

If electricity is available, training aids such as PowerPoint presentations or supplemental videos can be used. However, trainers should be prepared to deliver training without these tools if power is not available or is unreliable.

5.20 Learning Styles

Any safety trainer can conduct a training class where they talk through everything that is required to be covered in that training class and in doing so meet requirements for conducting training. A good safety trainer ensures that people who attend the class actually learn the subject. Time is a critical resource even in a nonemergency situation, and it is important to ensure that the time spent in training is actually a good use of an employee's time in that it increases knowledge and awareness of the topics covered. A training class that covers required topics but fails to increase knowledge or change safety behavior is not a good use of the employee's time.

Training programs for adult workers should utilize principles of andragogy, or adult learning theory. Andragogy assumes that adults come into a classroom with a wealth of experience, and that they learn best when they can relate their past experiences to the new topic to be covered. In contrast, pedagogy, or child learning theory, assumes that students who are children come into the classroom with limited life experience, and are in need of an instructor who can help provide them with this experience.

Adults also have a need to know why the topic covered in class is important to them. It is important for an instructor to cover this up front. If the instructor conveys that the only reason workers are in training is to meet regulatory requirements, students are not likely to pay much attention to the topic discussed. However, students are more motivated to learn if the instructor conveys that the class is going to cover topics and tools that will prevent students in class and their coworkers from getting hurt.

Adult learning theory also says that adults need to participate in the learning process. This can be managed by presenting situations and giving students problems to solve, and through class discussions. However, when new or unfamiliar material is presented, students may need some time to process the content before they are comfortable enough with it to move onto problem solving [44].

Individuals process information differently, and it is important to present information in different ways to accommodate everyone in the class. Material that is presented in a format that includes a combination of written words, pictures, and verbal discussion, for example, accommodates multiple learning styles.

5.21 Efficiency

It is expected that time resources for conducting training will be limited in an incident response, and this can pose a challenge in ensuring that training requirements are met. Good planning can increase efficiency of training. For example, a review of hazardous chemicals that will be used on site can be done in conjunction with an annual respiratory protection review to meet requirements under both the Hazard Communication and Respiratory Protection Standard. Linking these topics also helps address the question of "why" response and recovery workers need to sit through this training and explains: "These are the chemicals we are using, here are the health effects, and this is why you need to make sure your respirator works for you."

OSHA accepts hybrid courses when it is appropriate. For example, if an employee needs to complete a 10-hour OSHA outreach class and an 8-hour refresher, it would be possible to create a hybrid class that covered topics required by each as long as it is documented appropriately [34].

5.22 Summary

Numerous training requirements apply to responders and recovery workers, many of whom are going to be working outside of their normal scope of work. Meeting these requirements can be challenging, especially in the early phases of an incident where people resources are insufficient to meet demands. A Safety Officer must prioritize, and determine which training absolutely needs to be completed right away, and which training can be delayed until the ratio of available human resources to incident needs balances out.

As in all areas of incident response, planning is crucial. A training plan that is developed in an organization's or jurisdiction's Emergency Management Plan can identify potential human resources who may supplement primary emergency responders, and associated training needs. Some training of these personal can be completed before an incident occurs. Other training may need to happen after the incident occurs, but before supplemental workers are assigned tasks to support the response or recovery effort. Planning should consider and identify means to ensure that this training happens efficiently and effectively.

Given the number of training requirements, and the time that it takes to meet these training requirements when other pressing immediate needs must be met, it may be tempting for an Incident Management Team to forgo safety training. To do so is a disservice to both response and recovery workers and those they are trying to help. Workers who are not knowledgeable about the hazards they face and how to protect themselves are more likely to be injured, even fatally. When response and recovery workers are injured, they can no longer perform assigned tasks. In a situation where resources are limited and there is little to no back up personnel, the entire operation suffers when worker resources are lost.

References

1 29 CFR 1910.134, Respiratory Protection.

2 29 CFR 1910.132, Personal Protective Equipment General Requirements.

3 OSHA (2008). Interpretation letter to Ms. Mary Ellen Reda (17 January 2008).

4 29 CFR 1910.1030, Bloodborne Pathogens.

5 29 CFR 1910.95, Occupational Noise Exposure.

6 29 CFR 1910.1200, Hazard Communication.

7 OSHA (1988). Interpretation letter to Dr. Richard F. Andree (10 April 1988).

8 OSHA (1988). Interpretation letter to Mr. Blasdel A. Reardon (6 May 1988).

9 29 CFR 1926.1101, Construction Standards, Asbestos.

10 40 CFR Part 763 Subpart E, Appendix C, Asbestos Model Accreditation Plan.

11 29 CFR 1910.1001, Asbestos.

12 Office of Enforcement and Compliance Assistance, US Environmental Protection Agency (2009). *Guidance for Catastrophic Emergency Situations Involving Asbestos.*

13 29 CFR 1910.1025, Lead.

14 29 CFR 1910.1053, Respirable Crystalline Silica.

15 29 CFR 1926.1153, Construction Standards, Respirable Crystalline Silica.

16 National Institute for Occupational Safety and Health, Centers for Disease Control and Prevention, Department of Health and Human Services (2013). *Criteria for a Recommended Standard Occupational Exposure to Hexavalent Chromium.* DHHS(NIOSH) publication no. 2013-128.

17 29 CFR 1910.1026, Chromium (VI).

18 29 CFR 1926 Subpart M, Fall Protection.

19 29 CFR 1910 Subpart D, Walking-Working Surfaces.

20 29 CFR 1910.178, Powered Industrial Trucks.

21 Minnesota Administrative Rules, 5205.0110 Indoor Ventilation and Temperature in Places of Employment.

22 Minnesota Administrative Rules, 5205.0110 Training.

23 Washington Administrative Code, Chapter 296-62-095 WAC, Outdoor Heat Exposure.

24 California Code of Regulations, Chapter 4, Subchapter 7, Group 2, Article 10, 3395, Heat Illness Prevention.

25 Alaska Administrative Code, 8 AAC 61.1110, Additional Hazard Communication Standards.

26 Alaska Department of Labor and Workforce Development Labor Standards and Safety Division Physical Agent Data Sheet (PADS), Heat Stress.

27 Alaska Department of Labor and Workforce Development Labor Standards and Safety Division Physical Agent Data Sheet (PADS), Cold Stress.

28 29 CFR 1910.120, Hazardous Waste Operations and Emergency Response (HAZWOPER).

29 Washington Administrative Code, Chapter 296-843 WAC, Safety Standards for Hazardous Waste.

30 Occupational Safety and Health Administration (2010). Standard interpretation letter 2010-02-16-0, letter to Ms. Paula MacRae.

31 Occupational Safety and Health Administration (2004). Standard interpretation letter 2004-08-16-0, letter to Mr. Ron Grantt.

32 Occupational Safety and Health Administration (1992). Standard interpretation letter 1992-12-30, letter to Hr. Harold E. Durbin.

33 Occupational Safety and Health Administration (1992). Standard interpretation letter 1992-07-27, letter to Mr. Timothy S. Mustard.

34 Occupational Safety and Health Administration (2008). Standard interpretation letter 2008-07-17-0, letter to Ms. Barbara McCabe.

35 14 CFR 117.9, Fatigue Education and Awareness Training Program.

36 US Department of Transportation Federal Aviation Administration (2010). *Fatigue Risk Management Systems for Aviation Safety AC No. 120-103*.

37 National Response Team (2009). *Guidance for Managing Worker Fatigue During Disaster Operations: Technical Assistance Document*, vol. 1.

38 OSHA Directorate of Training and Education (2019). *Outreach Training Program General Industry Procedures*.

39 OSHA Directorate of Training and Education (2019). *Outreach Training Program Construction Industry Procedures*.

40 OSHA Directorate of Training and Education (2019). *Outreach Training Program Maritime Industry Procedures*.

41 OSHA Directorate of Training and Education (2019). *OSHA Outreach Training Requirements*.

42 US Department of Labor (2019). *Response from US Department of Labor Regarding Fake OSHA Cards* (15 February 2019).

43 OSHA Directorate of Training and Education (2019). *Outreach Training Program Disaster Site Worker Procedures*.

44 Merriam, S.B. and Bierema, L.L. (2003). *Adult Learning: Bridging Theory and Practice*. Wiley.

6

Industrial Hygiene and Medical Monitoring

OSHA standards include numerous requirements for evaluating exposures and conducting medical evaluations of employees. Medical evaluations can determine whether an employee has any health conditions that would make it especially dangerous to face certain workplace exposures, or to evaluate whether or not the exposures are contributing to deterioration of health. Adverse health outcomes have been associated with incidents such as 9/11 and Deepwater Horizon, and in careers such as firefighting. OSHA requirements for medical and exposure monitoring provide a starting point for managing health in incident responders.

6.1 Exposure Evaluation and Respirator Selection

As discussed in Chapter 4, the Maximum Use Concentration (MUC) of a respirator is based upon OSHA's Assigned Protection Factor (APF) of the respirator, an acceptable exposure limit such as an OSHA Permissible Exposure Limit (PEL):

$$MUC = APF \times Exposure\ limit$$

The actual exposure must be less than the MUC:

$$MUC > Exposure$$

If exposures are greater than the MUC for a respirator, a different type of respirator with a higher APF must be selected instead.

It is necessary to know the actual airborne concentrations of a chemical or substance in order to know if the MUC has been exceeded or not. Industrial hygienists have many tools to choose from to evaluate these airborne exposure levels, and these methods range from yielding semiqualitative answers to highly accurate quantitative results. The most accurate methods involve collecting air contaminants on sampling media placed at the shoulder in the "breathing zone" of the worker as a known air volume is pulled across the media via a pump worn by

Health and Safety in Emergency Management and Response, First Edition. Dana L. Stahl.
© 2021 John Wiley & Sons, Inc. Published 2021 by John Wiley & Sons, Inc.

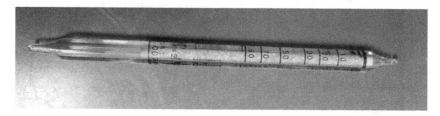

Figure 6.1 Colorimetric tubes can be used to provide a quick semiquantitative measure of an exposure. If a contaminant is present in air, it will produce a color stain in the tube. A specified amount of air is drawn through the tube, and the length of the color stain is equivalent to the concentration of the contaminant in air.

the worker over a work shift. After collection the sampling media is sent to a lab, and depending upon the type of sample, the location of the lab, and the amount of money spent, results can be returned any time within a couple hours to several weeks. Once results are obtained, the degree to which an exposure limit is exceeded is known and respirators can be selected based upon the required MUC.

Quantitative methods provide the most accurate evaluation of airborne exposures, and are invaluable in considering health monitoring and evaluating outcomes after the response is complete. However, decisions may need to be made on respirator use before answers are received, and direct reading methods such as air monitors with electrochemical sensors or colorimetric tubes can be used instead (Figure 6.1). While less accurate than quantitative methods, these methods provide short term answers necessary for decision-making, including the selection of an appropriate respirator.

The highest level of respiratory protection must be worn until exposures are known and respirators can be selected. First responders such as firefighters and Hazmat technicians are equipped with SCBAs and can enter environments before this exposure data is collected. Other supplementary personnel who are not similarly equipped with SCBAs cannot.

It may be possible to rely on exposure data from previous incidents for respirator selection, if the incidents were similar in nature and it is reasonable to conclude that exposures would also be similar. Factors contributing to this decision-making and the logic behind it should be documented when respirator selection is based on past exposures rather than taking measurements of the current exposures [1].

6.2 Respirator Medical Evaluation

Although respirators can provide needed protection against airborne respiratory hazards, they pose an added stress to the body. Air purifying respirators rely on the power of the wearer's lungs to pull air across the air purifying devices and clean the air that passes over them before this air is inhaled. This creates resistance to inhalation. Healthy lungs can easily accommodate this resistance. However, someone who suffers from respiratory impairment or disease may not be able to tolerate this increased breathing resistance. Likewise, those with cardiac conditions may not be able to support the demand from increased breathing effort.

Respirators also decrease the body's ability to thermoregulate and maintain a core body temperature in hot environments. Personnel with medical conditions that also have an effect on thermoregulation are at greater risk of heat-related illness when wearing a respirator.

People who are claustrophobic may have difficulty wearing a respirator, and are at risk of removing their respirator while still in a hazardous atmosphere in response to a claustrophobic episode.

Numerous personal and medical factors must be considered before putting someone in a respirator to ensure that this important piece of protective equipment can be worn safely.

OSHA requires that employees pass a medical clearance prior to wearing a respirator. This process consists of completion of a medical questionnaire which is reviewed by a Physician or Licensed Health Care Provider (PLHCP). The PLHCP reviews the questionnaire, and can provide a medical clearance based on this review. Depending upon how the questions are answered, the PLHCP may contact the employee to clarify answers, or may require that the employee come into the clinic for medical screening, such as a pulmonary function test.

Contents of the questionnaire are specified by OSHA in Appendix C of the Respiratory Protection Standard. State respiratory protection standards may include additional questions; it is important to ensure that the PLHCP utilizes the questionnaire mandated by the state when this is the case. Some clinics offer online portals for employees to submit answers to the questionnaire using a secure internet connection, and approvals can be generated remotely by a PLHCP within minutes of submittal. Utilization of such a program can facilitate medical approval of many (although not all) personnel within a short time period.

The PLHCP must consider exposure and work factors in making the decision as to whether or not to clear the employee for respirator use. The employer must provide the PLHCP with the following information:

- The type and weight of the respirator to be used;
- Duration and frequency of respirator use;
- The expected physical work effort;
- Clothing and additional PPE that will be worn;
- Temperature and humidity levels;
- A copy of the employer's written respiratory protection program;
- A copy of the OSHA or State Respiratory Protection Standard.

The questionnaire must be administered in a confidential manner. No member of the employee's work organization is allowed to look at the answers that the employee submits. If the PLHCP is a member of the employee's work organization, the PLHCP must employ measures to ensure that no other personnel, such as the Safety Officer, Respiratory Program Administrator, Human Resources, Supervisors, or any other employee sees this information.

Once the PLHCPs completes their review, they must provide the employer with a written recommendation. This written recommendation must include the following:

- Whether or not the employee is approved or not approved for the use of the respirator indicated by the employer, for the type of work and work conditions described by the employer;
- Any limitations on respirator use;
- The need for follow-up medical evaluations;
- A statement that the employee was provided a copy of the PLHCP's written recommendation.

The written recommendation cannot include any personally identifiable medical information. If respirator use is not approved, the PLHCP must simply state that respirator use is not approved. No information supporting this statement can be included, and no reference to any medical condition or information can be made.

OSHA requires follow-up medical evaluations of employees who currently wear respirators when:

- An employee reports signs or symptoms that are related to their ability to wear a respirator;
- A PLHCP, a supervisor, or a Respiratory Program Administrator informs the employer that an employee needs to be reevaluated;
- Observations made during annual fit testing or during a program evaluation indicate that additional medical evaluation is needed;
- A change in workplace conditions results in an increase in the physiological burden placed on the employee. This could include physical work effort, protective clothing, or temperature.

Since people age and health conditions can change over time, most PLHCPs include a time frame for a medical reevaluation in the written recommendation. This could range from five years for a young, healthy worker, to one year or less for an older worker with a medical condition.

Medical evaluations, including cost to administer the questionnaire and follow up tests, and the cost of the employee's time, must be covered by the employer [1].

A Safety Officer must ensure that all personnel who must wear respirators in a response or recovery effort are medically qualified to wear a respirator. If personnel respond as a unit, such as a fire department crew, or as a contracted hazmat team, it is likely that team members have received medical clearance through their primary employer for exposures similar to what they will face in the current incident. In this case, the Safety Officer can simply verify that medical clearance has been obtained.

If supplemental workers are needed to assist in the response, either employees who are reassigned from other jobs or volunteers, and these employees need to wear respirators, the Safety Officer needs to ensure that they receive medical clearance before respirators are provided. Even if personnel are medically cleared to wear respirators in their day to day job, the exposures and physical work requirements in the incident likely differ from what was considered during their initial clearance. The type of respirator may be different. Each of these factors triggers the need for additional medical evaluation.

Safety Officers and emergency planners need to consider who can serve as a PLHCP and conduct respirator medical evaluations during an incident, including logistics for ensuring that incoming workers can complete questionnaires confidentially and deliver them to the PLHCP. Online options can expedite review, but only work when electrical power and internet services are available. Hard copies of questionnaires should be prepared and made available in the event that electronic methods are inoperable.

6.3 Blood-borne Pathogens and Hepatitis B Vaccines

OSHA requires that employers offer Hepatitis B vaccines to employees who have potential exposure to blood-borne pathogens. This includes personnel who provide medical response as well as others who may encounter human blood or Other Potentially Infectious Materials (OPIM). This could include exposures to discarded needles in public areas, cleanup after injury accidents, or other situations in which there is potential exposure through contaminated sharps or mucous membrane exposures.

The Hepatitis B vaccine is made up of a Hepatitis B surface antigen that is grown in genetically engineered yeast. It does not contain any active or inactive Hepatitis B Virus, and cannot give someone hepatitis. Administration of the vaccine causes the body to activate an immune response against the surface antigen, and to recognize this response in the event of future exposures to the virus. The vaccine is considered safe for those who do not have allergies or sensitivities to any part of the vaccine, including yeast.

Three vaccines are administered over a period of six months. The second vaccine is given one month after the first, and the third vaccine is given six months after the first. If the series is interrupted, additional vaccines are given but the series is not restarted: A total of three vaccines is sufficient. Booster shots may be recommended in the future, but are not considered necessary at this time.

CDC recommends that high-risk employees such as healthcare workers be given a titer test to check levels of antibodies to the Hepatitis B surface antigen.

Employers are required to offer the vaccine, and titer tests in high-risk occupations, at no cost to the employee. Employees have the right to decline vaccinations by signing a declination form. An employee who declines the vaccine has no obligation to provide a reason for doing so. Employees may decline the vaccine if they have already received the series, perhaps through a previous job, if they have been medically advised not to take the vaccine, or because vaccination is inconsistent with their personal belief systems. The employer is not entitled to ask why the employee is declining the vaccine; the employer's obligation is simply to offer it and allow the employee to decline it if he or she has any reason to do so [2, 3].

Response and recovery workers have potential occupational exposure to blood or OPIM through direct patient care or through work at the incident scene, and the Safety Officer must ensure that these workers have had the opportunity to receive their initial hepatitis B vaccinations before they are subjected to these exposures.

6.4   Medical Evaluations Following Needlestick Injuries and Other Blood-borne Pathogen Exposure Incidents

Personnel who are exposed to blood-borne pathogens through needlestick injuries are at risk of developing disease. Some blood-borne pathogens are highly infectious, whereas others, such as Human Immunodeficiency Virus (HIV) carry relatively low risk of infection.

Risk of testing positive for a virus, or "seroconverting" following a needlestick injury exposure from the following pathogens is:

- Hepatitis B Virus: 37–62%
- Hepatitis C Virus: 1.8%
- HIV: 0.3%

Mucous membrane exposures also carry risk of infection, although the risk is lower than with a needlestick injury. Seroconversion following mucous membrane exposure to HIV is 0.09%. Even viruses in dried blood are capable of causing infection (see Chapter 4).

Risk of seroconversion following an exposure incident can be greatly reduced through administration of anti-retroviral drugs after the incident.

Such postexposure prophylaxis is most effective if these drugs are administered as soon as possible within two hours of the exposure. Any exposure incident should be considered a medical emergency. OSHA requires that exposed employees be provided a confidential medical evaluation following an exposure incident, and that the employer document the circumstances of the event.

If the person whose blood or OPIM contributed to the exposure incident (the "source individual") is known, and if the source individual consents, the source individual's blood should be tested for HIV, Hepatitis B, and Hepatitis C. State and local jurisdictions dictate how testing can be performed when the source individual does not provide consent: In some circumstances consent may not be required, and in others, a court order may be necessary. If the Hepatitis B and C, and HIV status of the source individual is already known, the source does not have to be retested. The results of the source individual's testing are then provided to the exposed employee after the exposed employee is informed of all laws regarding confidentiality and disclosure of the identity and infectivity status of the source individual.

If the exposure incident occurred as a result of a needlestick injury from an abandoned needle, or a sharps injury from an object contaminated with blood, the source individual is not known.

Employees who undergo an exposure incident, such as a needlestick injury, sharps injury, or mucous membrane exposure, must receive postexposure evaluation with a PLHCP as soon as possible. This should happen within 2 hours of the exposure incident. The employer must provide required information to the medical provider conducting the postexposure evaluation:

- A copy of the OSHA or applicable state Bloodborne Pathogens Standard;
- A description of the employee's work duties, as related to the exposure incident;
- Documentation of the exposure incident, including the route of exposure and any other circumstances relevant to the exposure incident;
- Results of the source individual's blood testing, if known;
- All medical records that the employer has on the exposed employee's hepatitis B vaccinations and antibody titer test results.

During the medical evaluation, the medical provider takes a sample of the exposed employee's blood. If consent is given, this blood is tested for Hepatitis B and C, and HIV to provide a baseline infectivity status. If the exposed employee does not give consent for testing, the blood sample is held for 90 days, during which time the exposed employee can request that it be tested at any time.

The healthcare provider also reviews options and provides recommendations for postexposure prophylaxis. Antiretroviral drugs can produce side effects, and the healthcare provider must discuss the risks and benefits of taking these medications in relation to the risk of developing the disease from the exposure incident. If it is decided to begin postexposure prophylaxis, it is started at this time. Also, if the employee has not been given Hepatitis B vaccines, the first vaccine of the series can be administered.

Exposure incidents can be stressful and frightening, and the medical provider provides counseling during the visit. A plan is made for follow-up evaluation and testing. Follow-up blood testing for seroconversion can be discontinued after six months. Follow-up testing for HIV can be discontinued at four months if certain fourth-generation HIV Ag/Ab tests are used, which can detect infections at earlier time points. This testing should be conducted even if the source individual tests negative, as newly infected individuals can transmit virus even before they give a positive test result. Follow-up testing for HIV is less critical if the source individual tests negative using sensitive fourth-generation HIV Ag/Ab tests, although testing for Hepatitis B and C should still be conducted.

The healthcare provider must provide the employer with a Healthcare Provider's Written Opinion within 15 days of the evaluation. This written report cannot contain any confidential information, and can only contain information specified in the OSHA rule:

- Whether or not the hepatitis B vaccine was indicated and whether or not the vaccine was given;
- The healthcare provider's opinion on medical follow-up, including only:
  o That the employee was informed of the results of the evaluation, and
  o That the employee was told of any medical conditions resulting from the exposure incident that require further evaluation or treatment [2–4].

The Safety Officer should make sure protocols are in place to ensure that anyone who experiences a needlestick injury or other exposure incident is treated as promptly as possible by a healthcare provider who is knowledgeable about blood-borne pathogen exposures and current recommendations regarding post exposure prophylaxis. If the incident occurs during nighttime hours, it may be necessary to send the exposed employee to an emergency room rather than to an occupational health clinic with medical providers who have this knowledge. If possible, a knowledgeable provider should be made available who can consult with emergency room personnel over the phone, and to provide a follow-up visit the next day.

6.5 Hearing Tests and Audiograms

OSHA's hearing conservation standard requires that employers evaluate noise exposures. Personal noise exposures are measured with dosimeters: A microphone is placed on the employee's shoulder in the "hearing zone" and the electronics inside the dosimeter calculate an integrated noise exposure for the work shift. At the end of the shift data can be downloaded, and results are shown as a time-weighted average exposure for the duration of noise measurement. Noise measurements can also be taken using a sound level meter, which shows real-time noise levels.

OSHA requires that personnel who receive noise exposures at or above the Action Level of 85 dBA over an 8-hour time-weighted average or equivalent must be enrolled in a hearing loss prevention program that includes annual audiograms. The first, or baseline, audiogram must be performed within six months of exposure, although if the employer utilizes a mobile van service this timeline can be extended to 12 months. Audiograms must be conducted every year thereafter, and results from each annual audiogram are compared with the first baseline exam to detect whether or not any hearing loss has occurred.

A significant marker of hearing loss is a Standard Threshold Shift (STS), defined as an average loss of 10 dB or more at 2000, 3000, and 4000 Hz in either ear. An STS can represent permanent hearing loss, or it may indicate a Temporary Threshold Shift. A Temporary Threshold Shift may show up if the employee has a cold, or if the employee received a high noise exposure prior to participating in the audiogram. A second audiogram can be conducted within 30 days. If the STS is persistent and is again detected on the second audiogram, or if the second audiogram is not conducted, an STS must be recorded on the employer's OSHA 300 log and the audiogram becomes the new baseline for future audiograms. The employer must follow up with the employee, and review use and fit of hearing protection devices.

Medical providers including audiologists, otolaryngologists, or physicians must review audiograms to determine if there is a need for further medical evaluation. Annual audiograms and review are paid for by the employer. If medical pathology or nonoccupational hearing loss is suspected, the employee is informed and can follow up at his or her own discretion and cost [5].

Annual audiograms are required even if an exposure above the action level occurs only one day per year [6].

For many employers, the primary motivation for implementing an effective hearing conservation program is not the threat of an OSHA citation, but to minimize worker's compensation hearing loss claims. Hearing loss claims are expensive, and because hearing loss develops slowly over time, employees may file claims many years after their last date of employment. Employers that seek to minimize this risk are diligent about completing baseline audiograms before employees are exposed to noise on the job, rather than following the allowed timeline of completing the baseline up to 6 or even 12 months after exposure begins. In addition, it is a best practice to complete an audiogram when the employee terminates employment or is no longer exposed to noise from the job.

When working on a multiemployer worksite, employees are covered by worker's compensation through their own employer, and in turn cannot sue their employer for on the job injuries. However, they can sue a third-party employer.

In an incident response, responders may be covered by an emergency funding source rather than worker's compensation. If worker's compensation does apply, responders and recovery workers can litigate for their injuries in a multi-employer response, and the Incident Commander carries this liability. The Safety Officer can protect the Incident Commander from liability through ensuring that baseline and post incident audiograms are conducted, and that records of these audiograms are maintained.

6.6 Lead

When potential lead exposure exists, an employer is required to perform an initial determination to determine whether or not a representative sample of employees is exposed to lead above the action level of 30 µg/m³ over an 8-hour time-weighted average. If initial monitoring shows that there is a possibility that any employee could be exposed above the action level, additional monitoring needs to be performed for each employee who is exposed to lead. When additional monitoring is indicated, it must consist of personal samples collected over at least 7 continuous hours for each representative job classification on each shift. Repeat monitoring must be conducted every six months after that if results indicate exposures above the action level, and every three months if results indicate exposures above the PEL of 50 µg/m³. Additional monitoring must also be conducted when there is a change in work process that could affect exposures. Repeat monitoring can be adjusted when it is demonstrated that engineering and work practice controls have reduced exposures below the action level or PEL.

Respirators are necessary when exposures cannot be reduced below the PEL by other methods, and anyone exposed above the PEL must comply with respirator medical monitoring requirements.

Additionally, specific medical surveillance requirements apply when exposures meet or exceed the action level of 30 µg/m³ over an 8-hour time-weighted average or equivalent exposure. All medical surveillance must be done under the supervision of a licensed physician.

Medical monitoring consists of routine blood tests, medical examinations, and consultations.

Blood tests for blood lead levels and zinc protoporphyrin must be conducted periodically. Zinc protoporphyrin is a compound that is normally present in blood at low levels, but increases if lead is absorbed by the body. Blood lead levels indicate a degree of biological absorption of lead. The frequency for conducting these tests differs slightly between the General Industry and Construction standards,

Table 6.1 Lead medical monitoring requirements in the General Industry and Construction Standards [7, 8].

	General Industry Standard	Construction Standard
Medical monitoring required when:	Exposed above the action level more than 30 days per year	Exposed above the action level on any day
Frequency of blood testing	Every six months	Every two months for the first six months, and every six months after that
Frequency of blood testing when blood lead exceeds 40 µg/dl	Every two months	Every two months
Temporary medical removal	Blood lead ≥60 µg/dl or last three tests ≥50 µg/dl	Blood lead ≥50 µg/dl

and increases when blood lead levels exceed 40 µg/dl. Blood testing may indicate that biological lead levels are so high that it is inadvisable for the employee to continue to be exposed to lead, and must be temporarily removed from the job that creates the lead exposure until blood lead levels return to safer levels (Table 6.1).

Employers must provide initial medical exams and consultations for employees who are assigned to work in an area where lead exposures are above the action level. Additional exams must be provided at least once per year for employees who have had a blood lead level of 40 µg/dl. Additionally, any employee who reports signs or symptoms of lead exposure must be medically evaluated as soon as possible.

Employees may be temporarily medically removed from the job based upon blood lead test results or when it is determined that it is medically inadvisable to be exposed to lead. Any employee who is temporarily removed from the job for medical reasons has job protection benefits, and must be returned to his or her former job status when blood lead levels fall to a level below 40 µg/dl or a physician determines that they are no longer at risk from a medical condition if they return to work. Medical monitoring can be conducted as appropriate while the employee is on medical removal status.

Medical exams conducted under the lead standard must include the following:

- Collection of a detailed work history and medical history, with particular attention to past lead exposures, personal habits, and any history of gastrointestinal, hematologic, renal, cardiovascular, reproductive, and neurological problems;
- A thorough physical exam, with particular attention to:
  - Teeth;
  - Gums;
  - Hematological system (blood);
  - Digestive system/gastrointestinal system;

    o Kidneys and renal system;
    o Cardiovascular system;
    o Reproductive system;
    o Neurological system;
    o Pulmonary system if respirators are used.
- Measurement of blood pressure;
- Blood sample tested for:
    o Blood lead level;
    o Hemoglobin and hematocrit, including red blood cell indices and morphology;
    o Zinc protoporphyrin;
    o Blood urea nitrogen; and
    o Serum creatinine.
- Routine urinalysis with microscopic examination;
- Any other tests or laboratory tests which the examining physician decides are necessary.

Prior to the exam, the employer must provide the examining physician with:

- A copy of the applicable OSHA or state lead standard;
- A description of the employee's duties as related to lead exposure;
- The known or anticipated exposure level to lead and any other toxic substances;
- A description of PPE used;
- Prior blood lead determinations;
- All prior written medical opinions concerning the employee in the employer's possession or control.

Following the exam, the physician must provide the employer with a written medical opinion that includes:

- The physician's opinion as to whether the employee has any detected medical condition that places them at increased risk from exposure to lead;
- Any recommended special protection measures that the employee needs, or any limitations that need to be put into place regarding the employee's lead exposure;
- If the physician determines that the employee cannot wear a negative pressure respirator, a determination on whether they could use a powered air purifying respirator instead;
- The results of blood lead levels.

The physician is obligated to advise the employee of any medical conditions that require further treatment, regardless of whether these conditions are occupational or nonoccupational. The physician cannot divulge any information to the employer regarding any diagnosis or laboratory findings that are unrelated to the employee's workplace lead exposure [7, 8].

6.7   Silica

Emergency responders may be exposed to silica after collapse of concrete structures or following a volcanic eruption (see Chapter 3), as well as other types of incidents. In general industry or construction work, employers are required to assess workplace exposures to silica and determine whether or not exposures exceed the action level of 25 µg/m³ or the PEL of 50 µg/m³. This assessment can be conducted using traditional industrial hygiene monitoring techniques, or through use of objective data from other sources. Similar exposure data is generally not available in an incident response and therefore traditional industrial hygiene monitoring methods will need to be employed in most situations.

Initial monitoring must consist of taking 8-hour TWA breathing zone samples that reflect exposures to employees on each shift, job classification, and work area. Representative sampling should ensure that those employees who are likely to receive the highest exposures are included in the evaluation. If initial monitoring indicates exposures are below the action level, additional monitoring is not needed for these employees. If initial results indicate exposures above the action level but below the PEL, exposure monitoring must be repeated within six months. If exposures are above the PEL, exposure monitoring must be repeated within three months.

Respiratory protection must be provided when exposures exceed the PEL, and the employer must comply with medical monitoring requirements specified in the Respiratory Protection Standard in addition to those required under the applicable silica standard.

Medical surveillance performed by a PLHCP must be made available to any employee exposed to respirable crystalline silica at or above the action level for 30 or more days per year. An initial exam must be offered within 30 days of assignment, unless the employee has received a medical exam in the previous three years that meets the requirements of the respirable crystalline silica standard. Periodic exams must be repeated at least every three years. The initial and periodic medical exams must consist of:

- A medical and work history with emphasis on:
  - Past, present, and anticipated exposure to respirable crystalline silica, dust, and other agents affecting the respiratory system;
  - Any history of respiratory system dysfunction or signs or symptoms of respiratory disease such as shortness of breath, coughing, or wheezing;
  - History of tuberculosis;
  - History of smoking and current smoking status.
- A physical exam with emphasis on the respiratory system;
- A chest X-ray;

- A pulmonary function test;
- Testing for latent tuberculosis infection; and
- Any other tests that the PLHCP decides is appropriate.

Employers must provide the following information to the PLHCP who performs the initial and/or periodic medical exams:

- A copy of the applicable OSHA or state respirable crystalline silica standard (if the employer has not made sure that the PLHCP already has a copy);
- A description of the employee's former, current, and anticipated duties as they relate to the employee's exposure to silica;
- Previous, current, and anticipated exposure levels to silica;
- What PPE is used, or will be used by the employee, including when and how long the PPE will be worn;
- Information from any other employment-related medical examinations that has been previously provided to the employee if the information is under the control of the employer.

Following the exam, the PLHCP must prepare written opinions to both the employee and the employer. The written report to the employee must include:

- A statement indicating the results of the medical exam, and any medical conditions that could put the employee at increased risk from silica exposure. The statement also must include any medical conditions that require further evaluation or treatment.
- Any recommendations for limitations on the use of respirators;
- Any recommendations for limitations on the employee's exposure to silica; and
- If the results of the chest X-ray, a recommendation for follow-up with a specialist.

The PLHCP's written opinion to the employer must contain the following (and only the following):

- The date of the examination;
- A statement that the examination met the requirements of the applicable crystalline silica standard;
- Any recommended limitations on the employee's use of respirators;
- Additional information only if the employee has provided written authorization to provide this information to the employer:
  o Any recommended limitations to the employee's exposure to silica;
  o A statement that the employee should be examined by a specialist if the results of the chest X-ray warrant this recommendation.

If the PLHCP recommends that the employee be seen by a specialist, the employer must ensure that this medical exam is made available within 30 days of receipt of the PLHCP's written opinion. The employer must provide the specialist with the same documents that were sent to the PLHCP, as well as information from the PLHCP regarding the initial or periodic exam that resulted in the referral. Following the exam, the specialist provides a written opinion to the employer [9, 10].

6.8 Asbestos

OSHA has set a PEL of 0.1 fiber per cubic centimeter of air, 8-hour TWA for asbestos, and an excursion limit of 1.0 fiber per cubic centimeter of air averaged over 30 minutes.

Employers are required to perform initial and periodic air monitoring to determine whether or not employees are exposed at these levels. OSHA allows some flexibility in the frequency of periodic air monitoring so long as the periodic monitoring is sufficient to demonstrate reasonable accuracy in determining employee exposures, and as long as sampling takes place at least every six months. During abatement operations, defined as Class I (removal of thermal system insulation or TSI) and Class II (removal of Asbestos-Containing Materials that are not classified as thermal system insulation such as wallboard, floor tile and sheeting, roofing and siding shingles, and construction mastics) operations, each employee performing this work must be monitored daily.

During abatement, regulated areas are established where work is performed, and anyone entering the regulated area must wear a respirator in compliance with OSHA's respiratory protection requirements. For other activities, respirators must be worn when asbestos exposures are above the PEL or excursion limit. Additional protections, such as the use of local exhaust ventilation, must be used as well.

Employers are required to implement medical monitoring whenever employees are, or will be, exposed to airborne asbestos fibers at levels above the PEL or excursion limit, as well as for workers who perform abatement operations (Class I or II work) or perform repair and maintenance tasks that could disturb friable asbestos in Asbestos-Containing Materials (Class III work) more than 30 days per year. Medical exams must be conducted by a physician. Pulmonary function tests may be completed by other medical personnel who have completed satisfactory training courses in spirometry through an academic or professional institution.

Preplacement exams must be provided before employees are exposed to asbestos above the PEL or excursion level. Preplacement exams must include:

- Medical and work history;
- A complete physical exam with emphasis on the respiratory system, cardiovascular system, and the digestive tract;

- Completion of a respiratory disease standardized questionnaire;
- A chest roentgenogram (X-ray);
- Pulmonary function tests; and
- Any additional tests recommended by the physician.

Periodic exams must take place at least annually, and are similar to the pre-placement exam with the exception that chest roentgenograms are not necessarily conducted every year. Chest roentgenograms are scheduled based upon the employee's age and number of years since first exposure to asbestos at a frequency between one and five years.

The employer must provide the following information to the examining physician:

- A copy of the applicable OSHA or state asbestos standard, including appendices;
- A description of the employee's duties as they relate to asbestos exposure;
- The employee's representative exposure level or anticipated exposure level;
- A description of PPE used;
- Information from the employee's previous medical exams that is not available to the physician.

Following the exam, the physician must provide the employer with a signed written opinion. This opinion includes the results of the medical exam, as well as:

- Whether the employee has any detectable medical conditions that places him or her at increased risk from exposure to asbestos;
- Any recommended limitations on the employee or on the use of PPE, specialized clothing, or respirators;
- A statement that the employee has been reformed of the results of the medical exam, and of any medical conditions resulting from asbestos exposure that require further explanation or treatment;
- A statement that the employee has been informed of the increased risk of lung cancer and combined risks of smoking and asbestos exposure.

The physician cannot reveal any specific findings or diagnoses that are unrelated to the occupational exposure of asbestos.

Emergency responders are at risk of asbestos exposure due to fallout from building damage or collapse, or to naturally occurring asbestos in rocks or soil. The Safety Officer should ensure that these exposures are characterized and that anyone who is subject to asbestos exposures receives appropriate medical surveillance [11, 12].

6.9 Hexavalent Chromium

OSHA has established a PEL of $5\,\mu g/m^3$ and an action level of $2.5\,\mu g/m^3$ for hexavalent chromium. Employers must conduct initial air monitoring of employees with potential exposure to hexavalent chromium to determine whether or not the PEL or the action level is exceeded. Periodic monitoring must be conducted at least every six months if initial monitoring indicates exposures above the action level. If initial monitoring shows exposures above the PEL, periodic monitoring must be performed at least every three months. Additional monitoring is needed if there is a change in the work environment that could impact exposures. The hexavalent chromium standard also includes requirements for the use of respirators.

Medical surveillance is required for employees who are exposed above the action level for 30 or more days per year, for those who are experiencing signs and symptoms of adverse health effects associated with hexavalent chromium exposure, and those exposed in emergencies. This includes an initial examination, annual exams, and an exam at the termination of employment.

The medical exam must include:

- A medical and work history, with emphasis on:
  - o Past, present, and future exposure to hexavalent chromium;
  - o Any history of respiratory system dysfunction;
  - o History of asthma, dermatitis, skin ulceration, or nasal septum perforation;
  - o Smoking status and history.
- A physical examination of the skin and respiratory tract; and
- Any other tests recommended by the examining PLHCP.

The employer must provide the examining PLHCP with:

- A description of the affected employee's former, current, and anticipated duties as related to their occupational exposure to hexavalent chromium;
- Past, current, and anticipated hexavalent chromium exposure levels;
- A description of PPE used, including when and for how long the PPE has been used;
- Information from records of employment related medical exams that are in control of the employer.

Following the exam, the PHLCP provides the employer with a written opinion that includes:

- An opinion on whether the employee has any detected medical condition(s) that create increased risk to health from exposure to hexavalent chromium;
- Any recommended limitations on the employee's exposure to hexavalent chromium, or on the use of PPE including respirators;
- A statement that the PLHCP has explained the results of the medical exam to the employee, including medical conditions relating to hexavalent chromium exposure that require further evaluation or treatment, and any special provisions regarding protective clothing or equipment.

The PLHCP cannot include any specific findings or diagnoses that are not related to occupational exposure to hexavalent chromium, nor communicate this information in any other manner.

The employer must provide the employee with a copy of the PLHCP's written opinion within two weeks of receipt [13, 14].

Recovery or response workers who perform tasks such as welding or cutting on stainless steel can be exposed to high levels of airborne hexavalent chromium; exposures can also occur from exposure to paints and skin contact with dusts.

6.10 Benzene

Benzene is a carcinogenic substance found in petroleum products including gasoline, motor fuels, and other fuels. Any incident that results in a petroleum or gasoline spill is likely to create benzene exposures, and OSHA's Benzene Standard applies.

OSHA has established a PEL of 1 part per million (ppm) TWA and a short-term exposure limit (STEL) of 5 ppm over a 15-minute period. Initial air monitoring must be conducted within 30 days of exposure. If initial monitoring shows exposures above the PEL, periodic monitoring must be conducted every six months. If exposures are below the PEL, but above the action level of 0.5 ppm (8-hour TWA), periodic monitoring must be conducted annually. Additional monitoring must be done if workplace exposures change, and after spills or leaks.

Medical surveillance is required for employees who are exposed above the action level for more than 30 days per year, and for employees who are exposed above the PEL for more than 10 days per year.

An initial exam must be conducted unless an exam meeting the requirements of the benzene standard has been conducted within the previous 12 months. The exam must be conducted by a physician, and includes:

- A detailed occupational and medical history, including:
  - Previous work exposures to benzene or other blood toxins;
  - A family history of blood diseases or disorders, including cancers of the blood or blood forming tissues;
  - A history of blood disorders and diseases, including genetic hemoglobin abnormalities, bleeding disorders, or abnormal function of blood elements;
  - A history of kidney or liver dysfunction;
  - Current and previous history of routinely taken medicinal drugs;
  - History of previous exposure to ionizing radiation;
  - Past exposures to blood marrow toxins, including occupational and nonoccupational exposures.

- A complete physical examination;
- Laboratory blood tests that are reviewed by a physician, including:
  - A complete blood count;
  - Leukocyte count;
  - Quantitative thrombocyte (platelets) count;
  - Hematocrit;
  - Hemoglobin;
  - Erythrocyte count;
  - Erythrocyte indices.
- Additional tests as determined by the physician;
- A pulmonary function test and evaluation of the cardiopulmonary system for workers who must wear respirators at least 30 days per year.

Periodic exams must be performed annually. Periodic exams must include:

- A brief history of any new exposure to blood marrow toxins, changes in medicinal drug use, and any physical signs that could be related to a blood disorder;
- Laboratory tests, as done for the initial exam;
- Appropriate additional tests as determined by the physician;
- Pulmonary function tests and cardiopulmonary evaluation every three years for employees who wear respirators at least 30 days per year.

Additional medical exams must be provided if the employee experiences any signs or symptoms that could be associated with exposure to benzene.

When sending an employee to a physician for an exam under the Benzene standard, the employer must provide the physician with:

- A copy of the OSHA or State Benzene standard, including appendices;
- A description of the employee's duties as related to their exposure to benzene;
- The employee's actual or representative exposure level;
- A description of PPE used;
- Information from other employment-related medical examinations.

Following the exam, the physician must provide the employer with a written opinion that includes:

- Occupationally pertinent results of the medical exam and tests;
- Whether the employee has any detected medical conditions that place him or her at greater risk from exposure to benzene;
- Any recommended limitations to the employee's exposure to benzene or use of PPE, including respirators;
- A statement that the employee was informed of the results of the medical exam, and any medical conditions resulting from benzene exposure that require follow-up or treatment.

The written opinion cannot contain any information including records, findings, or diagnosis of conditions that have no bearing on the employee's ability to perform work with benzene exposures.

When exposures occur due to an emergency situation, the exposed employees must provide a urine sample within 72 hours. The urine sample is tested for urinary phenol; if urinary phenol results are less than 75 mg/l of urine, no further testing is required. However, if results are greater than 75 mg/l of urine, the laboratory blood tests included in the initial and periodic exams must be conducted at monthly intervals for three months.

Additional blood tests must be performed if bloodwork done for initial or periodic exams indicate that hemoglobin or hematocrit levels are below normal limits or fall below preexposure norms and cannot be explained by other medical reasons, when thrombocytes fall below normal limits or are 20% below preexposure values, or when leukocyte counts fall below 4000 per mm^3 or if there is an abnormal differential count. If abnormalities persist following repeat bloodwork, the employee is referred to a hematologist or internist for further evaluation, who may determine that additional tests are needed. The employer is responsible for covering the cost of all exams and tests.

Employees who receive referrals to a hematologist or internist as a result of their blood test results cannot work in areas where they are exposed to benzene. They may return to their jobs if the hematologist or internist recommends that they may; within six months the medical provider must make a decision as to whether or not this medical removal must be permanent. Employees who are medically removed from their jobs receive medical removal protection benefits outlined in the standard [15].

6.11 Cadmium

Cadmium is widely used in the manufacturing of rechargeable batteries and solar panels, as a pigment, and as a corrosion inhibitor. Occupational exposure occurs in recycling of nickel cadmium batteries, electronic parts, and plastics as well as in manufacturing, construction, and in nuclear reactors. Emergency responders may be exposed if an emergency incident impacts a facility that utilizes cadmium, nickel cadmium battery fires, or through contamination in soils or waste.

Initial industrial hygiene monitoring is required when there is potential employee exposure to cadmium. Additional personal air samples must be taken periodically as needed to ensure the effectiveness of engineering controls and respiratory protection at least every six months when initial monitoring indicates that the action level of 2.5 µg/m^3 has been exceeded. Employees must be provided with written notifications of monitoring results. If the PEL of 5 µg/m^3 is exceeded, this must be stated in the written notification.

Respirators must be provided for anyone working in areas where the PEL is exceeded, and employees who wear respirators must be medically qualified to wear respirators.

Employees who are exposed to cadmium must take part in a medical surveillance program unless the employer can demonstrate that they are not exposed above the action level for more than 30 days per year. Medical examinations must be performed by a licensed physician who has read, and who understands, OSHA's cadmium standard and appendices.

An initial or preplacement exam must be provided within 30 days of initial assignment. This exam includes:

- A detailed medical and work history with emphasis on:
  o Previous, current, and anticipated future exposure to cadmium;
  o History of renal or kidney dysfunction;
  o History of cardiovascular issues or dysfunction;
  o History of respiratory dysfunction;
  o History of hematopoietic dysfunction or previous issues with blood and blood formation;
  o Reproductive dysfunction;
  o Current use of medication that could be toxic to kidneys;
  o Previous or current smoking habits.
- Urine samples tested for cadmium and beta-2 microglobulin;
- Blood test for cadmium.

Depending upon the results of blood and urine tests, the employer may need to conduct workplace evaluations to determine how to lower exposures, such as through improved hygiene or engineering controls. Additional medical monitoring or repeated blood and urine tests may be needed. If the results from blood and urine biological monitoring are high enough, the employee may need to be medically removed.

Periodic medical surveillance is required for all employees exposed above the action level at least one year following the initial exam and at least every two years after that, unless monitoring results indicate that exams need to be performed more frequently. Periodic medical exams include:

- An updated detailed medical and work history, as is done in the initial exam;
- A complete physical exam with emphasis on blood pressure, the respiratory system, and the urinary system;
- A chest X-ray;
- Pulmonary function tests.

- Urine analysis for:
  - o Cadmium;
  - o Beta-2 microglobulin;
  - o Albumin;
  - o Glucose;
  - o Total and low molecular weight proteins.
- Blood test with analysis for:
  - o Blood cadmium levels;
  - o Blood urea nitrogen;
  - o Complete blood count;
  - o Serum creatinine.
- For males 40 and over, prostate palpation or other diagnostic tests;
- Any additional tests as determined by the examining physician.

In addition, the physician evaluates whether the employee is fit to wear a respirator.

Exams are also required if an employee receives an acute exposure to cadmium during an emergency, and at the termination of employment.

Prior to an exam, the employer must provide the examining physician with:

- A copy of the appropriate OSHA or state cadmium standard;
- A description of the employee's prior, current, and anticipated duties and associated cadmium exposures;
- The employee's previous, current, and anticipated cadmium exposure levels;
- A list of PPE worn or anticipated to be worn by the employee, including respirators, and how long the employee has used this equipment;
- Relevant results of previous biological monitoring and medical exams.

Following the exam, the physician must send a written opinion to the employer that includes:

- The physician's diagnosis for the employee;
- Whether the employee has any detected medical conditions that create greater risk if exposed to cadmium;
- The results of blood, urine, or other tests that assess the employee's absorption of cadmium;
- Recommendations for medical removal or work limitations, if applicable;
- A statement that the physician has clearly and carefully explained the results of the medical exam and test results to the employee; any medical conditions related to cadmium exposure that require further evaluation or treatment, and any limitations needed for the employee's diet or use of medications.

The physician may not reveal any findings or diagnoses unrelated to occupational exposure to cadmium to the employer, either verbally or in the written opinion.

If an employee needs to be medically removed from the job based on the results of an exam or biological monitoring, medical removal protections apply [16, 17].

6.12 Other Substance-Specific Standards

Additional medical monitoring is required when employees are exposed to substances covered by OSHA's Toxic and Hazardous Substances rules (see Table 4.5). These rules contain various requirements for determining airborne exposures and conducting personal industrial hygiene monitoring, respiratory protection, initial and periodic medical exams, and biological monitoring. Rules set requirements for the information that the employer must provide to the medical professional conducting the exam, either a physician or a PLHCP, and the content that must be included in the written opinion that must be provided to the employer.

6.13 First Aid and Emergency Medical Response

OSHA requires that medical aid be available to treat injured employees performing work. Medical aid could be provided by a hospital, clinic, or infirmary at the job site. If medically trained personnel are not readily available, an adequate number of personnel on site must be trained and certified in first aid and cardiopulmonary resuscitation (CPR). First aid supplies, eyewashes, and emergency drenching equipment must be made available as needed [18–20].

6.14 HAZWOPER

OSHA's Hazardous Waste Operations and Emergency Response (HAZWOPER) standard requires medical surveillance for employees performing work covered by the standard and who are exposed to health hazards above an applicable PEL or other appropriate exposure level for 30 or more days per year, those who are required to wear a respirator 30 or more days per year, and for members of hazmat teams.

An initial medical exam must be made prior to assignment to tasks covered by HAZWOPER. Subsequent medical exams must be given every 12 months, although they can occur more or less frequently based on the recommendation of the attending physician. However, exams must be performed at least every two years. Exams must also be provided when employees terminate employment, or when they transfer to jobs where they are not covered by the HAZWOPER standard.

Medical exams must also be provided as soon as possible if the employee develops signs or symptoms related to a possible overexposure of a hazardous substance, and after an emergency if the employee suffers injuries related to an overexposure to a hazardous substance.

Content of medical exams must include:

- A medical and work history (or updated history) with special emphasis on symptoms related to handling of hazardous substances, and:
  o Fitness for duty;
  o Ability to wear required PPE under temperature and other conditions expected at the work site.
- Additional content to be determined by the attending physician.

Additional content of the medical evaluation is based upon the type(s) of chemicals that the employee is exposed to. If any of these chemicals are regulated by OSHA in a substance-specific standard, medical exams and tests required under that standard need to be covered in the HAZWOPER medical exam. Additional guidance is available when determining focus of medical exams under HAZWOPER (Table 6.2).

The employer must provide the following information to the examining physician:

- A description of the employee's duties as they related to hazardous materials exposures;
- Actual or anticipated exposure levels;
- PPE in use or anticipated to be used;
- Information from previous medical examinations of the employee;
- Information required under the applicable OSHA or state respiratory protection standard.

Following the exam, the physician provides the employer with a written opinion that includes:

- Whether the physician detected any medical conditions that would place the employee at increased risk from work under HAZWOPER or from wearing a respirator;
- Any recommended limitations upon the employee's assigned work;
- A statement that the employee has been informed of the results of the medical exam, and of any medical conditions that require further examination or treatment.

Table 6.2 Recommendations for medical exams based on chemical exposures [21].

Aromatic hydrocarbons, including benzene, ethyl benzene, toluene, and xylene	Focus on: • Liver • Kidney • Nervous system • Skin Laboratory tests: • Complete blood count • Platelet count • Kidney function tests • Liver function tests
Asbestos or asbestiform particles	Focus on: • Lungs; • Gastrointestinal system Laboratory tests: • Stool test for occult blood Other screening: • High quality chest X-ray • Pulmonary function tests
Halogenated aliphatic hydrocarbons	Focus on: • Liver • Kidney • Nervous system • Skin Laboratory tests: • Liver function • Kidney function • Carboxyhemoglobin when relevant
Heavy metals	Focus on: • Neurological deficits • Anemia • Gastrointestinal symptoms Laboratory tests: • Metallic content in blood, urine, and tissues • Kidney function tests when relevant • Liver function when relevant Other tests: • Chest X-ray when relevant • Pulmonary function test when relevant
Herbicides	Focus on: • Skin • Nervous system Laboratory tests: • Kidney function • Liver function • Urinalysis

(Continued)

Table 6.2 (Continued)

Organochlorine insecticides	Focus on: • Nervous system Laboratory tests: • Kidney function • Liver function • CBC
Organophosphate and carbamate insecticides	Focus on: • Nervous system Laboratory tests: • Red blood cell count • Cholinesterase levels Other tests: • Delayed neurotoxicity • Other health effects
Polychlorinated biphenyls (PCBs)	Focus on: • Skin • Liver Laboratory tests: • Serum PCB levels • Triglycerides • Cholesterol • Liver function

The physician's written opinion cannot include information on and conditions or diagnoses that are unrelated to occupational exposures. After the employer receives the physician's written opinion, the employer must provide the employee with a copy of it [21, 22].

6.15 Diving

OSHA standards prohibit employers from allowing employees to dive if they have a medical condition or conditions known to the employer that are likely to impact safety or health of a dive team member. OSHA considers medical conditions that may restrict or limit occupational diving or exposure to hyperbaric conditions such as:

- History of seizure disorders, other than early childhood febrile conditions;
- Active malignancies, unless they have been treated and have not recurred within five years;

- Chronic inability to equalize sinus or middle ear pressure;
- Cystic or cavitary disease of the lungs;
- Impaired organ function caused by alcohol or drug use;
- Conditions that required continuous medication to control, including:
  o Antihistamines;
  o Steroids;
  o Barbiturates;
  o Mood altering drugs;
  o Insulin.
- Meniere's disease, an inner ear disorder;
- Blood disorders and diseases that affect red blood cells (hemoglobinopathies) such as sickle cell disease;
- Obstructive or restrictive lung disease;
- Disorders impacting balance (vestibular end order destruction);
- Collapsed lung (pneumothorax);
- Cardiac abnormalities;
- Bone lesions near the joints.

The diving standard includes requirements that personnel be trained in first aid and CPR, that divers be evaluated for signs and symptoms of hyperbaric illness following a dive, and that medical treatment for hyperbaric illness is available, including access to a hyperbaric chamber. OSHA does not require preemployment or periodic medical screening; however, given the risks of diving when restrictive medical conditions are present, such medical surveillance is advisable.

The Association of Diving Contractors International (ADCI) has developed consensus standards for diving and underwater operations, including a consensus standard on conducting medical surveillance for divers. ADCI recommends initial exams evaluating specific criteria before divers are subjected to hyperbaric conditions and periodic exams on an annual basis after that. Additional exams must happen after any diving related injury or illness, and for any non-diving injury or illness that requires any prescription medication, any surgical procedure, or hospitalization. All exams must be conducted by a physician with experience or training to conduct the commercial diver physical examination.

Annual periodic exams should include the same screenings, although initial screenings such as screening for sickle cell disease need not be repeated.

Following the exam, the physician prepares a written report. The physician must determine whether a person's health will be impaired by hyperbaric conditions. The written report should indicate any limitations or restrictions that apply to the employee. Certain conditions identified by ADCI are disqualifying for diving operations [23, 24].

6.16 Ergonomics

OSHA does not currently regulate ergonomics; however, ergonomic injuries can be debilitating and if not treated, can lead to long-term impairment. All employees working in response or recovery efforts are at risk of developing a musculoskeletal disorder (MSD). Administrative support staff may be at increased risk, particularly if resources for performing this work are insufficient and staff are assigned to makeshift workstations. It is a recommended practice for employers to establish a relationship with medical providers who can treat ergonomic injuries early in the course of the disorder. All employees should be trained to recognize early signs and symptoms of MSDs, such as unexplained swelling, discomfort, pain, or stiffness.

Certain symptoms indicate that the employee needs to see a medical provider as soon as possible, including:

- Pain that interferes with sleeping.
- Symptoms of nerve involvement:
  o Numbness;
  o Tingling.

Early treatment and mitigation of ergonomic risk factors can prevent long-term consequences from these disorders [25].

6.17 Payment for Medical Exams

Unless specifically stated otherwise in a regulation, the employer is required to pay for all costs associated with required medical surveillance, including initial exams, periodic exams, tests, and the employee's time to participate in medical surveillance.

In general, if it is required in an OSHA rule, the employer is responsible for the costs. If medical surveillance uncovers a medical issue unrelated to work exposures or employment, the employee is responsible for medical costs related to any follow-up taken in response to this issue.

6.18 Logistics of Conducting Medical Surveillance

Employers of professional emergency responders, such as paid or volunteer firefighters, law enforcement officers, or hazardous materials responders can and should establish medical surveillance programs that include preemployment and periodic medical exams. Periodic exams are generally conducted on an annual basis.

Medical surveillance for hazardous material responders is covered under HAZ-WOPER.

Fire departments that have adopted NFPA 1500 [26] follow requirements to conduct evaluations as outlined in NFPA 1582, Standard on Comprehensive Medical Program for Fire Departments. This program is designed to ensure that firefighters meet physical performance requirements necessary to perform as a firefighter, and includes some additional screening for cancers. Other fire and police departments adopt programs established by their jurisdiction, which may differ from NFPA 1582. Medical surveillance required by OSHA can be incorporated into these existing surveillance programs. Incorporating OSHA requirements can identify workers who are at greater personal risk of exposures to certain chemicals or other agents; if these workers are placed in jobs that do not pose these risks, or are provided greater protections, poor health outcomes can at least be reduced.

The greater challenge in disaster operations is ensuring that medical screening requirements are met for supplemental responders or recovery workers, such as those who are temporarily reassigned to help out in a response, volunteers, or others who participate through other agreements or avenues outside of established agreements. In an ideal situation, adequate medical resources are available to perform initial medical exams of personnel before they are assigned to a task where they could be exposed to hazards that could impair health. Such individuals may have preexisting medical conditions, previous exposures, or family medical histories that would lead an evaluating physician or PLHCP to conclude that they should not perform such work, and can instead be assigned other tasks. This strategy could perhaps reduce some of the poor health outcomes that have been seen in past responses such as 9/11, and others that are still emerging.

Logistics and incident demands can compete with this goal, especially early on in a response when demands exceed the number of resources available and if there is need to put people to work immediately. In this situation, medical surveillance should begin as soon as is practical. Many OSHA regulations allow initial exams to be completed within 30 days of employment or longer, and this timeframe can almost certainly be accomplished.

Some medical exams must be completed before responding personnel can be assigned tasks. Respirator medical exams, for example, must be completed before work requiring respirators is assigned. Fortunately, respirator medical reviews can be accomplished very quickly when the process has been established to do so.

The Incident Command System has an established process for developing a medical plan and including it in the Incident Action Plan. The medical plan is developed by the medical unit leader using ICS Form 206, and approved by the Safety Officer (see Chapter 8, Figure 8.31). Form 206 includes sections to fill in information on medical aid stations, transportation, and nearby hospitals, which is critical information in the event that response personnel suffer from an injury or illness. Medical monitoring should be specified in Section 6 of Form 206 Special Medical Emergency Procedures, and can be written on the form or expanded with attachments. The Safety Officer should ensure that any required medical or exposure monitoring is included in this section. In addition, any follow-up medical monitoring that needs to take place after deactivation of the response needs to be included in the remarks section(s) of ICS 221 Demobilization and Check Out form (see Chapter 8, Figure 8.33). It is important that the Demobilization Unit Leader coordinate with the Medical Unit Leader and Safety Officer to ensure that personnel who are demobilizing are aware of the need for medical follow up.

6.19 Recordkeeping 1910.1020

OSHA rules govern who can access employee medical and exposure records. Exposure records include personal monitoring records to determine exposures, biological monitoring, and Safety Data Sheets, that must be maintained by the employer. Medical records such as medical questionnaires, results of medical examinations, medical opinions, diagnoses, and medical notes are maintained by the physician or PLHCP. Physician or PLHCP-written opinions are provided to the employer and maintained by the employer.

Employees and their authorized representatives have the right to see their own records. Employers must also make records available to OSHA or applicable state program representatives. OSHA can view personally identifiable medical information maintained by the PLHCP only if a written access order has been issued that is approved by the Assistant Secretary upon recommendation of the OSHA medical records officer.

All exposure and medical records must be maintained for 30 years [27].

In an incident response, especially one that involves multiple employers, the Safety Officer must work with the Planning Section to ensure these records are maintained. Exposure records, including industrial hygiene sampling results and Safety Data Sheets, and physician- or PLHCP-written opinions should be maintained with the incident records. Medical records can be maintained by appropriate designated healthcare providers. The location of these records should be documented, and this documentation should be included with incident records for future reference. Any personally identifiable healthcare information should be kept with the medical providers. However, even some of the records that the employer is required to maintain can include information that employees might prefer to maintain private. A medical written opinion that states that an employee cannot wear a respirator, or perhaps cannot be exposed to a certain hazardous chemical, could infer information about the employee's health status that they might not want their employer or coworkers to know about. For these reasons, every effort should be made to maintain these records in as confidential a manner as possible.

6.20 Summary

OSHA requirements include multiple medical monitoring requirements. A diligent safety officer, who can ensure that medical monitoring is completed, can also make sure that employees who are not medically qualified are not assigned work that would put them at risk. OSHA requirements, however, are just a start, and any incident may subject responders to health hazards that while serious, are not covered by OSHA regulations. Medical monitoring may need to be tailored to these exposures, going beyond OSHA requirements.

It can be challenging to complete medical monitoring during an incident, particularly when emergent needs exceed resources. Regardless, medical monitoring should begin as soon as is practical. Emergency planners should ensure that medical monitoring resources that can be utilized are identified in emergency plans.

References

1 29 CFR 1910.134, Respiratory Protection.
2 29 CFR 1910.1030, Bloodborne Pathogens.
3 Centers for Disease Control and Prevention (2001). Updated U.S. Public Health Service Guidelines for the Management of Occupational Exposures to HBV, HCV, and HIV and Recommendations for Postexposure Prophylaxis. *Mortality and Morbidity Weekly Reports* (29 June 2001) 50 (RR11): 1–42.
4 Kuhar, D.T., Henderson, D.K., Struble, K.A. et al. (2013). Updated US Public Health Service guidelines for the management of occupational exposures to human immunodeficiency virus and recommendations for postexposure prophylaxis. *Infection Control and Hospital Epidemiology* 34 (9): 875–892.
5 29 CFR 1910.95, Occupational Noise Exposure.
6 Occupational Safety and Health Administration (2004). Standard interpretation letter 2004-02-13-0 to Dr. Louis Hosek. PhD (13 February 2004).
7 29 CFR 1910.1025, Lead, General Industry.
8 29 CFR 1926.62, Lead, Construction.
9 29 CFR 1910.1053, Respirable Crystalline Silica, General Industry.
10 29 CFR 1926.1153, Respirable Crystalline Silica, Construction.
11 29 CFR 1910.1001, Asbestos, General Industry.
12 29 CFR 1926.1101, Asbestos, Construction.
13 29 CFR 1910.1026, Chromium(VI) General Industry.

14 29 CFR 1926.1126, Chromium(VI) Construction.

15 29 CFR 1910.1028, Benzene.

16 29 CFR 1910.1027, Cadmium, General Industry.

17 29 CFR 1926.1127, Cadmium, Construction.

18 29 CFR 1910.151, Medical Services and First Aid.

19 29 CFR 1926.23, First Aid and Medical Attention.

20 29 CFR 1926.50, Medical Services and First Aid, Construction.

21 NIOSH/OSHA/USCG/EPA (1985). *Occupational Safety and Health Guidance Manual for Hazardous Waste Site Activities.*

22 29 CFR 1910.120, Hazardous Waste Operations and Emergency Response.

23 29 CFR 1910, Subpart T, Commercial Diving Operations.

24 Association of Diving Contractor's International, Inc. (2016). *International Consensus Standards for Commercial Diving and Underwater Operations*, 6.2e.

25 National Institute for Occupational Safety and Health, Centers for Disease Control and Prevention, US Department of Health and Human Services (1997). *Elements of Ergonomics Programs.* DHHS (NIOSH) publication no. 97–117.

26 National Fire Protection Association (2018). *Standard on Fire Department Occupational Safety, Health, and Wellness Program*, NFPA 1500.

27 29 CFR 1910.1020, Access to Exposure and Medical Records.

7

Psychological Hazards Related to Emergency Response

Incident scenes and disaster sites differ from day-to-day workplaces in many ways. In addition to exposure to imminent and emerging hazards, incident response and recovery workers see and experience sights, sounds, and smells on the worksite that most general industry and construction workers might never see in their lifetime.

Professional responders have frequent exposure to death, violence, loss, and tragedy, as well as routine exposure to serious and potentially deadly hazards on a day-to-day basis. They see human suffering up close. These professionals must face the possibility that on any given day that they report to work, they, or someone they work with, could die. They also know that they are exposed to hazards that can cause cancer or other long-term health consequences. Professional responders are good at focusing on the job at hand, perhaps by compartmentalizing the trauma that they see so that they can serve their communities and perform their jobs successfully and professionally, because their communities need them to do this.

In large-scale events, resources may be drawn from the community to assist with the disaster response. This could be because residents of a community feel compelled to help find missing family members and friends: During SR 530 Landslide response in Oso, Washington, emergency managers realized that if these volunteers were not brought into the organized response they would in all likelihood deploy on their own, putting themselves and rescuers at greater risk. It could also be because the need for resources so greatly exceeds those that are available that members of the public are hired to assist in the response, such as the case in the Deepwater Horizon response. These volunteers or newly assigned responders come to the site with various degrees of personal resilience to seeing and smelling bodies, gore, and dismembered body parts, and to hearing anguished cries of injured and possibly dying victims.

Many people can participate in an emergency response without experiencing any negative mental health consequences, and perform quite well. Just as with exposure to carcinogens or other hazards, some people will become ill after the

Health and Safety in Emergency Management and Response, First Edition. Dana L. Stahl.
© 2021 John Wiley & Sons, Inc. Published 2021 by John Wiley & Sons, Inc.

exposure and others will not. Symptoms that do appear may manifest during the response or sometime afterwards. Symptoms occurring after the incident can impact health and quality of life. Symptoms that appear during the response can impact the responder's ability to perform their job and make critical decisions in response to emerging issues. As with other hazards that response and recovery workers face, the Safety Officer must be aware of mental health hazards and symptoms of poor mental health, and have a plan to address them.

7.1 Neurophysiological Response to Fear and Stress

Humans have developed an evolutionary response to fear. In a fearful situation, we respond with a "fight, flight, or freeze" reaction. The same is true of every animal that has developed a brain, and this reaction that has evolved over thousands of years has aided in our survival both as a species and as individuals.

When the source of fear does not require an immediate response, such as when we are at risk from a slow-moving predator, our brains have an opportunity to process this information and make a cognitive decision as to what our next action will be. The cognitive regions of our brains, including the prefrontal cortex and posterior cingulate cortex, activate and process the information that we are receiving. The hippocampus also activates, forming memories of the event. We have time to absorb the information we are receiving and use this same information as we choose how to react. Memories formed in the hippocampus allow us to store this event, and better prepare us for the next time we experience a similar situation.

When the source of fear requires an immediate response, such as when we are in danger from a fast-moving predator, our survival depends on making a reactive response before the cognitive processing regions of our brains can even detect the surrounding stimuli. The midbrain regions activate, and our bodies respond by taking action ("fight"), running ("flight"), or freezing [1]. Since the memory-forming region of the brain, the hippocampus, does not activate, memories of the incident are likely fragmented, or we may have no memory of the event at all. Memories that do form are not well processed by the cognitive regions of the brains, and can be confusing once the danger has passed. Afterwards, we or others may question the actions that we took in response to this immediate threat and ask "What were you thinking?" In fact, we were not thinking. Our brains did not have a chance to think before we had to respond. "Thinking" does not happen when one is in imminent danger.

This understanding is important in emergency and disaster response, when danger in one form or another is ever present and changing. Professional responders undergo training and participate in drills and exercises in part to prepare for hazards they face on the job. Training and experience build muscle memory, and increase the chances that appropriate actions will be taken when an immediate action is required before the cognitive regions of the brain can activate. New emergency responders should work with more experienced responders so that they have an opportunity to build this muscle memory over time, safely, before they must face these dangers alone. However, a large enough disaster or an extremely dangerous situation will present many nonroutine hazards to which emergency responders may be unfamiliar. Nontraditional responders, such as volunteers from the community or employees who have been newly assigned to response activities do not have the same level of training and experience to draw on when in this environment.

Different individuals have differing levels of resilience to stress and fear. Many people do not suffer impacts to their mental health following exposure to fearful or stressful situations. Others go on to develop diagnosable conditions in response to this trauma. Early recognition and treatment can reduce the probability of long-term health consequences.

7.2 Acute Stress Disorder

Individuals exposed to trauma at incident scenes or disaster sites can develop acute stress reactions, or symptoms of Acute Stress Disorder. Symptoms typically begin immediately after the trauma, and last from three days to a month. Individuals experiencing Acute Stress Disorder often reexperience the traumatic event, others may not be able to remember the traumatic event at all. Some people may detach or seem as though they are in a trance. They may show a strong emotional or physiological response when reminded of the trauma. Some people may respond with anger, and may appear irritable or even aggressive. They may begin to display chaotic or impulsive behavior, such as driving recklessly or making irrational decisions.

Some of these symptoms may present even in individuals who do not meet the full criteria for diagnosis for Acute Stress Disorder as defined by the American Psychiatric Association in *Diagnostic and Statistical Manual of Mental Disorders*, 5th edition, DSM-5 [2]. Other psychological disorders, such as mood disorders or panic attacks may be present as well. Physical injuries can contribute to symptom presentation: Symptoms of traumatic brain injury can be similar to those of Acute Stress Disorder, or Acute Stress Disorder may copresent with physical injuries. A person with a traumatic brain injury could also experience symptoms of Acute Stress Disorder as a result of the incident that caused the injury.

7.3 Post-Traumatic Stress Disorder

Post-Traumatic Stress Disorder (PTSD) may be diagnosed if symptoms last more than a month and meet criteria as defined by the American Psychiatric Association in *Diagnostic and Statistical Manual of Mental Disorders*, 5th edition, DSM-5 [2]. Symptoms may cause significant impairment in social functioning, ability to perform work, and in other areas such as relationships. Symptoms may appear soon after the traumatic event(s), or they may be delayed for months or even years.

Individuals experiencing PTSD may reexperience the traumatic event through intrusive memories or flashbacks, which range from brief intrusions into the present to a complete loss of awareness of present surroundings. They may experience recurrent dreams. Others experience disruptions in mood, and symptoms similar to anxiety or depression. They may be quick tempered, and behave aggressively with little or no provocation. Hyperarousal is common, or the feeling that danger is always imminent or just around the corner. Some people detach or dissociate, and may appear vacant and uncommunicative. They may feel numb. They may exhibit self-destructive behavior, such as recklessness, dangerous driving, alcohol or drug use, or even suicide. People with PTSD may startle easily, especially around sounds, sites or smells that serve as reminders of the traumatic event. They may have trouble concentrating and focusing on tasks, and may be forgetful.

In the United States, the lifetime risk of developing PTSD in the general population by the age of 75 is 8.7% [2]. Between 50 and 70% of the US population has been exposed to trauma, and the fact that PTSD actually occurs rarely indicates that other factors influence whether or not someone will develop this disorder after exposure to trauma. People who have experienced previous trauma or had poor psychological adjustment prior to the event, or who had a high perceived life threat are more likely to develop PTSD. Having strong social support is protective; those with low levels of social support are at greater risk.

The risk is much higher in emergency responders such as police, firefighters, and emergency personnel, than in the general public, typically ranging between 17 and 27%. PTSD rates are highest in emergency responders who have worked in large scale disasters: For example, 38% of firefighters who responded to the Oklahoma City bombing in 1995 developing some form of psychopathology.

Social support is a protective factor in preventing PTSD. However, those that provide this social support can also be impacted by the trauma that the emergency responders experience, and are in turn subject to their own mental health distress. For example, wives of firefighters who responded and survived the 9/11 World Trade Center attacks were a primary social support to their husbands. At the same time, they had to take on additional responsibilities in caring for households and children. Many of these firefighter's wives were diagnosed with PTSD related to the 9/11 response that their husbands participated in [3].

PTSD does not just effect mental health. It is also associated with physiological effects. Traumatic stress has a broad effect on brain function and structure, and in particular, the areas associated with memory including the amygdala, hippocampus, and prefrontal cortex. Such changes are seen visually in neuroimaging studies, as well as in studies measuring brain activity and signaling between neurons. Cortisol and norepinephrine regulation, which play a critical role in stress response, is disrupted [4]. Glucocorticoids are normally released by the adrenal glands in response to stress, and communicate to other cells in the body by binding to receptors. In PTSD patients, there are fewer glucocorticoid receptors in red blood cells than in controls, which reduces the physiological response to glucocorticoids [5]. When odors are associated with trauma, neuro-degradation occurs in areas of the brain related to detecting smells [6]. The brains of people who have been diagnosed with PTSD show a hyper-response in the amygdala, the area of the brain that is involved in assessing threats. Other areas of the brain are smaller in PTSD patients. The medial pre-fontal cortex, which processes the extinction of fear, and the hippocampus, which is involved in memory processes and fear conditioning, are smaller in size in patients with PTSD than in non–trauma-exposed controls [7].

7.4 Complex Post Traumatic Stress Disorder

Complex PTSD can develop following exposure to an event, or a series of events that are extremely threatening or horrific, and when escape is difficult or impossible. Such events include torture, slavery, prolonged domestic violence, or repeated childhood sexual or physical abuse. In addition to symptoms characteristic of PTSD, characteristics of Complex PTSD include:

- Problems with affect regulation;
- Beliefs that oneself is diminished, defeated, or worthless, along with feelings of shame, guilt, or failure related to the traumatic event;
- Difficulties in sustaining relationships and feeling close to others [8].

A characteristic of Complex PTSD is that trauma that is experienced is interpersonal and prolonged, and in this sense, Complex PTSD differs from trauma that may be experienced as the result of a natural disaster. Complex PTSDs can develop as a result of childhood trauma, and emergency responders who have a history of such trauma are more likely to be adversely affected by subsequent traumatic events in a disaster [9, 10]. Prevalence of Complex PTSD is not currently well understood, but it is likely that it is more prevalent than PTSD [11].

7.5 Cumulative Traumatic Stress Exposures

The types of trauma that emergency responders are exposed to do not specifically match the types of trauma that lead to Complex PTSD. While certain traumatic events may be extremely threatening or horrific, it is rare that emergency responders would be exposed to these events on a repeated or predictable basis as required for a Complex PTSD diagnosis. It is also less likely that trauma is interpersonal. Still, emergency responders are repeatedly exposed to traumatic events, and this cumulative exposure has an impact just as it does in those who go on to develop Complex PTSD.

The number of traumatic events to which a person is exposed correlates to diagnosis of PTSD, similar to a dose response. People who are exposed to four or more traumatic events in their lifetime have a significantly higher incidence of PTSD, and have higher levels of functional impairment, than those who have been exposed to three or fewer traumatic events [12]. Biological responses, such as neurodegeneration of olfactory senses and desensitization to glucocorticoids also increase with repeated exposures to trauma [5, 6].

Cumulative exposure to traumatic events have been shown to be moderately correlated with rates of PTSD diagnosis in emergency responders. This correlation is not seen with diagnosis of depression or other disorders. PTSD diagnosis correlates most highly with how severely traumatic the event is perceived: Emergency responders who had been diagnosed with PTSD and were asked to score a series of representative events by how severely they perceived the events ("trauma severity") gave these events a much higher score than did emergency responders who were not diagnosed with PTSD.

Types of traumatic events scored by police officers, firefighters, and Emergency Medical Technicians (EMTs) as having a highly perceived severity include:

- Coworker killed or injured intentionally, or killed accidentally;
- Being taken hostage;
- Being shot at;
- Trapped in a life-threatening situation;
- Exposed to risk of AIDS/disease;
- Life threatened by a toxic substance;
- Injured in the line of duty;
- Making a mistake that injures or kills a coworker;
- Seeing someone dying;

- Mutilated body/human remains;
- Making a death notification;
- Sexually assaulted, badly beaten, or severely neglected child;
- Life-threatening man-made disaster [13].

First responders can find it more difficult to seek treatment for mental health symptoms than those in other occupations. First responders are heroes. Being a hero is essentially a part of the job description: A hero's job is to save others, and be strong for the victims that they save. A hero is supposed to be tough. A hero is not supposed to be vulnerable.

In addition, there may be a fear that being seen as weak may result in losing opportunities for promotion or ostracism from peers. As such, first responders may be reluctant to seek treatment when symptoms arise, and untreated PTSD can manifest as extreme irritability or intense anger that cause problems with relationships or in the workplace, substance abuse, or suicide risk. Treatment providers must be able to show sensitivity to first responder culture in order to overcome any resistance and move forward with effective treatment approaches. Mental health practitioners who have previously worked as first responders have an inherent understanding of the culture and can personally relate to the factors that may create resistance to treatment in order to overcome them [7, 10, 14].

When a disaster strikes, all members of the community are impacted. If homes are uninhabitable, large numbers of community members may be displaced to shelters. Hazards related to the disaster, such as chemical exposures from chemical plants, refineries, or environmental contamination create anxiety. Mold growth from flooding, untreated sewage, and possible bacterial contamination of water supplies are another source of fear. After Hurricane Harvey, for example, mental health symptoms of anxiety, depression and PTSD were associated with loss of home, damage to possessions, and perceived exposures to chemicals and toxins. Rates of PTSD after a disaster may be as high as 30–40% of the population, which points to the need to address symptoms and provide treatment as early as possible [15].

In a disaster, first responders and nontraditional responders alike experience trauma related to the response in addition to trauma related to their homes and communities. Some key stressors in a large-scale disaster are damage to home, damage to possessions, difficulty in meeting personal needs, loss of power, and filing claims for damages. These stressors underlie response-related traumatic exposures to loss of life, traumatic injuries, and gore. Risk for PTSD increases for responders who have experienced more than one disaster in their community, such as 9/11 responders who later worked on the Hurricane Sandy response. In particular, nontraditional responders exposed to both disasters were found to be a high-risk group [16].

7.6 Risk Factors for Developing PTSD

Only a fraction of those exposed to emotional trauma go on to develop PTSD.

When trauma is experienced in childhood, this early trauma can increase "fear conditioning," in which the amygdala becomes more efficient at transmitting fearful, traumatic exposure events into behavioral and arousal responses. Individuals who have had traumatic exposures early in life are more vulnerable to developing PTSD after subsequent exposures due to both fear conditioning and failure to develop normal fear learning. There also appears to be a genetic component to fear response. The biochemical and anatomical differences in the brains of PTSD patients and controls may or may not precede the traumatic event: These changes may be a physiological response to trauma, or they may be preexisting factors that increase the likelihood of developing PTSD [17].

Females appear to be at greater risk for developing PTSD than males. This may be because females are more likely to report symptoms, or because females have greater exposures to early childhood traumas and rape traumas. Other risk factors that may predispose for PTSD include:

- Presence of body injury;
- Age when trauma occurred;
- Race (minority status);
- Lower education level;
- Lower income level;
- Being divorced or widowed;
- Unemployment;
- Loss of family members;
- Living far away from parents;
- Family instability;
- Previous trauma;
- General childhood adversity;
- Psychiatric history;
- Being abused as a child;
- Family psychiatric history.

Despite predisposing factors, the risk factors that show the greatest correlation with development of PTSD are those that are in place during or after the trauma, for example:

- Trauma severity;
- Lack of social support;
- Additional life stress [18, 19].

The occupational hazards that responders face may contribute to development of mental health symptoms. Molecular markers of inflammation, which may be present due to exposures to hazard on the job such as heat, exposure to toxic respiratory hazards, fatigue and sleep restriction, physical exhaustion, and physical injury, correlate with PTSD. Inflammatory markers such as C-Reactive Protein, Tumor Necrosis Factor (TNF), and cytokines can cross the blood–brain barrier to directly impact the brain, and it is hypothesized that inflammation can predispose trauma-exposed persons to developing PTSD or other mental health disorders such as depression. It seems likely that chronic physical traumas are related to worsening mental health outcomes [20].

7.7 Compassion Fatigue and Secondary Traumatic Stress

Workers in occupations such as psychotherapy, medical care, and social work are continuously faced with helping people who have experienced traumatic events. Individuals in these helping professions can spend years working with ill or traumatized clients or patients and in empathetically sharing their traumatic experiences. These professionals experience this as *vicarious trauma*, also termed *secondary trauma*. Exposure to vicarious or secondary trauma may develop into Secondary Traumatic Stress Disorder (STSD), with symptoms that are very similar to PTSD.

Workers in helping positions are also at risk of suffering from burnout. This is characterized by the emotionally exhausting nature of working with trauma survivors which requires high interpersonal demands and high emotional investment. Susceptibility to burnout increases when the caregiver has poor social support available, and low sense of personal accomplishment.

Another risk for caregivers is *compassion fatigue* (CF), which results in reducing the caregiver's capacity or interest in bearing the suffering of others. This is a well-characterized phenomenon in counselors and mental health therapists. Caregivers who score high in empathy are well equipped to serve their patients or clients, but a high level of empathy also increases the risk of developing compassion fatigue. On the other hand, high levels of job satisfaction are protective, and can help counteract other risk factors. It is thought that secondary traumatic stress and burnout are interrelated and are components of compassion fatigue [21, 22].

Emergency responders also come into close contact with victims of trauma through their course of work, and experience vicarious trauma and secondary traumatic stress while assisting and helping trauma victims. Emergency responders including emergency medical professionals and paramedics, firefighters, and law enforcement officers are also at risk of developing STSD, burnout, and compassion fatigue. Symptoms may copresent with symptoms of PTSD, although specific indicators of compassion fatigue have been found that are distinct from PTSD. For example, symptoms of burnout, specifically symptoms of emotional exhaustion and depersonalization, are higher during natural disasters than during the normal course of work, and are more likely to result from secondary trauma exposure than from direct exposure [23].

All personnel participating in an emergency or disaster response can be exposed to vicarious trauma. This includes emergency responders working on the front lines of the response. Others who are impacted include personnel working at shelters in close contact with evacuees who have lost loved ones, their homes and possessions, and insurance adjusters evaluating damages. Reporters and media relations personnel report first hand on losses experienced by members within the community. Critical stress management personnel brought in to support both the public and emergency responders are in turn at risk of secondary trauma [24].

A variety of interventions have been evaluated for prevention and management of compassion fatigue, including yoga, structured meditation, music therapy, and other stress reduction techniques. Interventions that appear to be most effective are those that seek to promote resiliency in those who are occupationally exposed to vicarious trauma, which includes programs that educate workers on compassion fatigue, including how to recognize symptoms in themselves and in colleagues, what to do when they identify symptoms, and what tools and resources are available [25]. The culture of the work organization greatly influences the degree to which employees within the work organization experience compassion fatigue, STSD, and burnout: Supportive work organizations are highly protective [26].

7.8 Coping Mechanisms

Several studies have shown a surprising lack of negative mental health outcomes in crime scene investigators and forensic technicians. Although these groups have frequent exposures to severe trauma, symptoms of poor mental health functioning could not be readily measured. It is possible that traumatic exposure is less severe since these groups do not interact on a personal level with trauma victims. However, it is also likely that these groups utilize high levels of internalization and avoidance as a coping mechanism [27, 28].

In other fields, cultural aspects promote social support and protection. Several aspects of first responder culture come together to form a work environment that can help counteract the impacts of trauma exposure. The hazardous nature of work requires that units work together effectively as a team: This team also provides a social support system when trauma occurs. Firefighters and responders deployed to major disasters live together when not actively performing duties. Sharing living quarters and meals facilitates social bonding. Public safety workers as a rule love the work that they do, and have a high level of job satisfaction. This is protective and helps to mitigate other risk factors.

Another element found in emergency response workgroups is the use of "gallows humor," or a dark, blunt, or even disgustingly crude use of humor used to help cope with the high stress nature of this type of work. Humor is physiologically and psychologically therapeutic, and reduces stress, anxiety, and tension. Use of dark, gallows humor is a coping mechanism that helps process events that carry a high emotional charge, and provides an emotionally safe way to create distance from highly stressful situations and discharge tension to help create resilience. However, it does have a downside if it prevents those suffering from traumatic stress disorders from seeking treatment, or if it is used to downplay or minimize other coworker's reactions [10]. Also, it can be very disturbing for members of the public who overhear first responders using gallows humor. Those outside of the emergency response organization may be shocked to hear such behavior from their heroes, and do not understand that such language is merely a coping mechanism. As such, the use of gallows humor can lead to some unfortunate headlines in the media, and employers may wish to prevent such outcomes through the use of alternative stress reduction options.

7.9   The Impact of Preexisting Conditions

The National Alliance on Mental Illness (NAMI) estimates that 20% of US adults experience mental illness in a given year.[1] This can range from minor illness to severe. The prevalence of serious mental illness, including diagnosable illnesses that substantially interfere with life function, is 4.5% (2017 data) [29]. Many patients with severe mental illness end up homeless or in jail; however, many people with mental illness, even serious illness, receive treatment and/or medication, and can function quite well on a day-to-day basis. Due to health privacy protections [30], coworkers and supervisors are likely unaware when a colleague suffers from a mental illness.

Past mental health history can influence an individual's response to current traumas and subsequent outcomes since an individual's psychiatric health history can influence risk for developing PTSD or other trauma disorders [18, 19]. If disaster strikes suddenly, and responders are unable to go home to stock up on personal

---

1 www.nami.org (accessed 31 May 2019).

supplies such as medications used to treat mental health disorders, a previously functional individual may lose some degree of function.

Inability to retrieve medications for physical conditions can also influence coping capability. For example, a hypothyroid patient who is unable to obtain daily thyroid medication can suffer greater emotional extremes and has less than optimal resilience to external traumatic stressors. As discussed in Chapter 6, it is important for the Safety Officer to work with Logistics and the Medical Unit Leader to ensure that a mechanism is in place to obtain needed daily medications for those who need them.

7.10 Stress, Trauma, and Decision-Making

Those in leadership positions, including the Safety Officer and others on the Incident Management Team, must make critical decisions on behalf of others on the response team throughout the response. These decisions are often made under stressful conditions. The Incident Command Post should be set up some distance from the response, in order to give the Incident Management Team a work area to strategize and make decisions with minimal distractions. Field supervisors, such as branch and unit leaders, oversee personnel on the front lines and also need to make critical decisions. Workers on the front lines need to make decisions that impact their own personal risk as well as that of their coworkers.

Stress is known to impact thinking and decision-making. Stress promotes the release of stress hormones inside the body, which then activate areas of the brain involving decisions about acceptable risk and memory. The brain's ability to analyze and adjust risk, and determine an appropriate risk balance, is altered: In calm, nonstressful situations, people tend to favor decisions that carry low risk. Under stress, decision-making favors high-reward outcomes, even if this decision also carries higher risk. High stress increases high-risk/high-reward decision-making, whereas low stress situations favor low-risk/low-reward outcomes. On a personal level, this is seen in the choices people make: Unhealthy eating, smoking, and drug use increase under stress, despite the knowledge that these are risky behaviors.

The fact that our brains are programmed to make riskier decisions under stress is likely an evolutionary trait that has aided survival. The shift from low-risk/low-reward to high-risk/high-reward decision-making has been shown in both humans and animals. Brain alterations under stress alter perceptions of "punishment" as well as reward, and disrupt memory centers. As a result, decisions made under stress may not appear rational to observers or others after the fact, who have the luxury of reviewing these decisions in an environment that favors low risk/low reward [31, 32].

Mechanisms of decision-making, including use of strategy, adjustment from automated response, feedback processing, reward sensitivity, and punishment sensitivity are all altered under stress. Decisions that are made when there is uncertainty regarding the best course of action require an automated response that is balanced with a calculated response. Decisions made under high uncertainty conditions require consideration of relevant factors and potential outcomes of the decision ("feedback"), whereas decisions made in situations where clear rules are in place and uncertainty is low can be somewhat automated. This balance between automatic response and rational adjustments is altered under stress, and interferences with memory can alter feedback mechanisms. This may explain why stress promotes making riskier decisions.

Stress-induced alterations in decision-making can be detrimental in situations that require risk avoidance, such as a making a decision to smoke or use drugs despite the known health effects of doing so.

However, this altered process of decision-making can actually be beneficial in situations which require increased risk taking, such as, for example, deciding to run into a burning building to save a victim. At least, this decision is beneficial for the victim who is saved.

Decision-making is impacted in patients who are diagnosed with depression and anxiety disorders: Such patients show reduced sensitivity to "reward," and tend to avoid making decisions that could result in a high reward. Patients also show altered neural responses when required to make a decision. Since the parts of the brain that are used in decision-making are altered in patients with PTSD, it is expected that these patients would also show altered decision-making [33].

Studies of emergency responders have not shown evidence that a diagnosis of PTSD alters decision making for routine tasks for which the emergency responder is highly trained. However, in acutely stressful nonroutine situations requiring professional judgment, emergency responders with symptoms of PTSD are less able to perform cognitive tasks well, are less able to recall verbal memories, and have a heightened assessment of risk. Exposure to additional traumatic events increases symptoms of acute stress and subsequent reactions: For example, a police officer suffering from symptoms of anxiety would interpret surrounding threats as more dangerous than an officer who is not suffering from similar symptoms would, and have an increased tendency, or bias, to shoot a suspect. Anxiety symptoms also make it difficult to perform verbal reasoning tasks in high stress situations: A paramedic is more likely to make a mistake when calculating a drug dosage or to recall pertinent clinical details during a threatening situation [34].

Altered decision-making in emergency responders with PTSD can impact the way in which they respond to on the job hazards: It has been demonstrated that there is a relationship between PTSD and increased work-related injuries in emergency responders [35]. This is perhaps the result of alterations in risk taking behaviors.

In essence, highly trained emergency response professionals with PTSD can perform routine tasks well. However, decision-making involving nonroutine tasks, changing situations, or particularly threatening events may be impacted, and the decisions made will likely carry a higher level of risk. Mistakes are also more likely to be made, which can endanger the well-being of both responders and those they are trying to help.

Nontraditional responders may be at even greater risk during a disaster. It is to be expected that this group primarily performs tasks for which they are not highly trained, and that they are also less accustomed to the types of environmental stressors that are present. The full impact to this group is less well understood, but the Safety Officer in an incident response involving nontraditional responders should be prepared to address issues of trauma in this group as well as with career responders.

7.11 Substance Abuse

Data from 2017 show that in a single year in the United States, 886 000 individuals (0.33%) used heroin, 11.1 million individuals (4.1%) misused prescription medicines including hydrocodone and oxycodone, and 7.5 million individuals (2.8%) used illicit drugs. In the United States, 14.5 million individuals, or 5.3% of the population suffered from Alcohol Use Disorder, which includes symptoms of withdrawal, tolerance, use in dangerous situations, trouble with the law, and interference with major obligations at work, school, or home. Only 8.4% of those diagnosed with Alcohol Use Disorder sought treatment for it [29].

Alcohol is a part of the culture in emergency responder workgroups. Social drinking can promote social bonding and connections within a team, and many firefighters fall into the category of "moderate" drinkers, defined as up to two drinks per day for men and up to one drink per day for women [36]. In our society, drinking alcohol is widely considered a coping mechanism for stress. Given that alcohol use is prevalent within emergency responder culture, there is an opportunity for abuse. For example, one study found that 16.7% of law enforcement officers demonstrated problematic drinking; other studies have found even higher rates. A study of female firefighters found that nearly 40% reported binge drinking during the previous month, 4.3% reported driving while intoxicated, and 16.5% screened positive for a drinking problem. Problematic alcohol use was related to PTSD, exposure to traumatic incidents and lack of appropriate coping mechanisms when exposed to traumatic incidents, as well as depression and work-related injuries [37, 38].

As with other mental illnesses, individuals with a past history of alcohol or substance abuse disorders may function well in the workplace once the disorder is under control. However, the disorder can only be controlled, not cured. Keeping the disorder under control, and fighting temptations to have another drink or take another pill takes a daily life-long commitment. Fighting this temptation can be even harder when triggering incidents occur, such as exposure to a traumatic event during an emergency response or in a disaster, and especially when there is also a social pressure to join peers for a drink following this traumatic event. There is ample opportunity to "fall off the wagon" when cravings for alcohol or other substances are at their highest.

Given medical privacy protections, coworkers would not know whether or not a team member has or has had issues with alcohol or substance abuse unless this team member chooses to reveal this information. It is entirely possible that a coworker, or a member of an emergency or disaster response team, is someone who is privately fighting this daily battle.

Social bonding and peer support protects against adverse psychological outcomes, and should be encouraged. However, it is best if there are options for alcohol-free social events, or at least to make sure that there are alternatives to drinking alcohol so that those who must avoid it have that option. Incident Management Team members should remind responders of the importance of not pressuring others to drink, and the need to respect those that choose not to.

7.12 First Responder Suicides

Suicide is the most serious adverse mental health outcome. A 2017 White Paper published by the Ruderman Family Foundation demonstrated that firefighters and police officers are more likely to die by suicide than to die in the line of duty. The stigma associated with suicide, particularly in the emergency services, likely results in an under-reporting of suicide deaths, and it is estimated that only 40% of suicide deaths are actually reported as suicides. If this estimate is correct, there are more than twice as many suicides among firefighters and law enforcement officers than line-of-duty fatalities.

Police officers must pass a psychological assessment before entering the law enforcement profession. Considering that police officers must meet a baseline of mental health at the beginning of their careers, it would be expected that police officers would be less likely to commit suicide than the general population, but data does not reflect this hypothesis. The suicides that do occur must reflect the deterioration in mental health that occurs over the course of a law enforcement officer's career.

Considering also that occupational fatality rates in the emergency services are higher than most occupations (see data in Chapter 1), the fact that suicide deaths outnumber line-of-duty deaths to this degree is even more concerning.

Suicide is also highly prevalent among retired emergency services professionals. Risk factors for suicide ideation include "thwarted belongingness," or a belief that one is alone without connections or having lost connections, and "perceived burdensomeness" or a belief that one's continued existence creates a drain on others to the extent that the world would be a better place if they were no longer a part of it. Being a part of a brotherhood, having built in connections, purpose, and a place to belong, is inherent in emergency services work. Risk factors increase when outside factors disrupt or diminish belongingness, such as retirement, or diminish a sense of contribution such as injury, disability, or deteriorating mental health.

Suicide occurs when thoughts of suicide, or suicide ideation, move to carrying out an action. Suicide ideation occurs more frequently than acts of suicide. Transitioning from thinking about suicide to acting on it requires overcoming a natural instinct to survive and avoid pain. A learned capacity to ignore pain, and to avoid violence or death, can lower this threshold. Emergency responders are exposed to pain and the inevitability of death on a daily basis, and are conditioned to face the risk of dying themselves in the course of work on every shift. As a result, avoidance of pain, violence, and death may be less of an inhibiting factor than it is for those who do not experience this level of trauma in their jobs.

The news media rarely reports on first-responder suicides. Line-of-duty deaths garner a lot of media attention: While a police officer dying of a gunshot injury or from a traffic accident makes headlines, suicide deaths are not reported. Internally, the shame and stigma of suicide and mental health disorders can lead to a culture of silence that makes those considering suicide feel all the more alone. First responders who die by suicide may not be buried with honor or memorialized, increasing the stigma of suicide deaths. In a culture in which mental illness is stigmatized, and not discussed, an act of suicide by a peer can trigger the leap from suicide ideation to action in others, leading to "suicide clusters" in police and fire departments [39, 40].

The risk of suicide in nontraditional emergency responders is less well understood. While research on suicide in emergency responders is very limited [41], there is even less for nontraditional responders who come from varying backgrounds and come from occupations that do not provide preemployment psychological screening. The Safety Officer in an incident response must consider this risk in any response that includes nontraditional responders.

Mental illnesses such as depression, PTSD, and substance abuse often precede suicide. Identification of these risk factors, and provision of appropriate treatment, are opportunities to prevent suicides. These indicators are most easily resolved when addressed at their earliest stages and this cannot be done in a culture in which mental health issues are stigmatized. A change in culture is needed, and mental wellness must be institutionalized [42].

7.13 Prevention: Mental Health Wellness

NFPA 1500 includes behavioral health in its standard for Fire Department occupational safety and health programs. The behavioral health component must provide assistance for stress, alcohol and substance abuse, anxiety, depression, traumatic exposure, suicidality, and personal problems that could adversely affect the individual or performance of the department. The behavioral health program must also include:

- Clinical referrals for employees and/or family members when clinically indicated;
- Adoption and adherence to clear written policies regarding alcoholism, substance abuse, and other behavioral conditions that can adversely affect performance or fitness for duty;
- A process for determining fitness for duty if this is in question, as would be followed for a physical injury or disability, or any other factor that would prevent the employee from performing essential functions of the job;
- Confidential handling and retention of records and data in accordance with applicable statutes, regulations, and standards;
- Policies identifying to whom, and under what conditions, such confidential information can be released to for research, program evaluation, and quality assurance;
- Ensuring that individual records maintained by a behavioral health program are not part of the employee's personnel file;
- Access to a program assisting personal resiliency to stress and traumatic exposures;
- Access to a program supporting enhancement of behavioral health and wellness through:
  - o Leadership development;
  - o Organizational group dynamics evaluation;
  - o Training [43].

Large employers, including cities and other jurisdictions, commonly contract to provide Employee Assistance Programs (EAPs). EAPs provide help to employees to work through multiple life challenges, including legal and financial issues, family issues, childcare, and issues including stress, substance abuse disorders, or other mental health issues. Use of an EAP is voluntary and confidential. Employers should ensure that instructions to access the EAP are widely publicized, including phone numbers and website information, and that employees know that anything discussed with the EAP is entirely confidential.

Resiliency, or the capacity to prepare for, recover from, and adapt to stress, adversity, and traumatic critical incidents can be bolstered through training programs. Resiliency training:

- Helps develop good verbal and other cognitive skills;
- Problem-solving skills;
- Ability to plan and anticipate consequences;
- Abstention from maladaptive coping systems;
- Easy temperament;
- Good sociability;
- A sense of social cohesion;
- Recognizing mental and emotional responses of a stressful state;
- Shifting from a stressful state to a more calm and positive state;
- Stress reduction techniques.

Resiliency training can build increased emotional awareness and a feeling of overall well-being. In addition, resiliency results in enhanced problem-solving skills and communication, and increased focus. It builds skills such as thinking rationally under stress, controlling emotions, concentrating effectively, and making effective decisions quickly, all of which improve performance. Learning how to gain control over minds and bodies makes emergency responders better and more effective in their jobs, in addition to feeling better. This sense of performance improvement provides motivation for training participants.

Peer support programs are another element of behavioral health wellness programs. Coworkers are often the first to notice when someone is struggling with personal issues, and are often the most available resources when such issues arise. Peers also understand the stressors that are unique to their profession. Formal peer counseling programs consist of peer support teams who have been provided with formal training in listening and other skills. Peer counselors are not professional therapists, but connecting with one can provide a nonthreatening first step that can be taken before seeking professional assistance. Peer support teams should reach out to department members after they experience personal stressors as well as after critical incidents.

Peer support teams work when they are supported by the department administration, and provided with resources and ongoing training.

Resiliency can also be taught through mentoring programs. In law enforcement, it is common for an experienced officer to work with recruits as they begin police work, and the mentor can help recruits learn to handle some of the unique challenges of the job in a mentally and physically healthy way. Law enforcement employees who are reluctant to seek professional help may feel comfortable talking with a mentor who has experienced similar traumas and can speak to how they dealt with related stress.

Making professional psychological support available is also a component of an effective behavioral health program. This can range from maintaining a psychologist or psychiatrist on staff, to contracting with outside professionals or working with psychologists and psychiatrists at local hospitals or clinics.

To ensure success, departments must place a value on mental health, and through their actions communicate this value to employees [44].

7.14 The Role of Critical Incident Stress Debriefing (CISD)

Jeffrey T. Mitchell pioneered the concept of the Critical Incident Stress Debriefing (CISD) in 1983. Mitchell believed that mandatory participation in a formal debriefing shortly after the incident was critical to prevention of adverse psychological outcomes such as PTSD. This formal process, as proposed by Mitchell, includes:

- The Introductory Phase: The facilitator introduces himself or herself, describes the rules for the session including the need for absolute confidentiality, and encourages participants to make a pact to be silent forever regarding information shared during the debriefing.
- The Fact Phase: The facilitator asks participants to describe facts about themselves, the incidents, and what they did in the incident. Participants are encouraged to share what they heard, saw, and smelled in order to make the incident "come to life again" within the CISD room.
- The Feeling Phase: Once the incident scene has come to "vivid life," the facilitator asks feeling oriented questions such as "How did you feel when this happened?" "How are you feeling now?" and "Have you ever felt anything like that in your life before?" At this point, the facilitator's role is limited to making sure everyone has a chance to share and that no one dominates the discussion as it is expected that people will start talking and little guidance is needed.
- The Symptom Phase: The Facilitator asks questions such as "What unusual things did you experience at the time of the incident?" "What unusual things are you experiencing now?" and "Has your life changed in anyway since the incident?" In this phase, it is expected that participants will freely discuss their own stress response syndromes.
- The Teaching Phase: The Facilitator covers stress response syndromes, and describes that it is normal and natural to experience a variety of signs, symptoms, and emotional reactions related to the incident.

- The Re-Entry Phase: During this phase, the Facilitator seeks to wrap up loose ends, answers outstanding questions, offers reassurances, and works with participants on a plan of action. Personnel are advised on getting additional help should they need it.

Mitchell believed this formal CISD session should last between 3 and 5 hours. He also firmly believed that it should take place within 24–48 hours after the incident. Although he believed CISD would be ineffective if too much time passed, he also believed that emergency response professionals would be too worked up over the incident in the first 24 hours after the incident to participate, and that feelings would only come to the surface after 24 hours [45].

Since 1983, the effectiveness of Mitchell's CISD process and variations of it proposed by others have come under scrutiny. Several published meta-analysis examining the effectiveness of CISD at preventing PTSD have failed to demonstrate positive outcomes, and in fact, several have shown negative outcomes in that PTSD rates were higher than expected among responders who participated in a CISD session.

The studies showing negative outcomes following CISD are particularly concerning, and there are several possibilities as to why CISD participants may have increased adverse outcomes. First, CISD assumes that all persons follow the same trajectory of response following a traumatic event, and that discussing the trauma is therapeutic while denying it is not. However, it is more likely that individual responses vary, and individual timelines of "readiness" for such discussion may not fit neatly into Mitchell's proposed 24–48 hour time period. Some individuals may need to create distance from the event in order to process it, and this distance may actually be an adaptive response rather than a form of denial. Additionally, "reliving" the event through the CISD process can produce secondary or vicarious trauma [46].

It is possible that conducting the debriefing within 24–48 hours of the event may be too soon. Responders may be focused on rebuilding elements of their personal lives during this time, particularly if the incident impacted their communities or homes. Participants may be reluctant to share strong feelings with coworkers, and since the CISD process focusses so strongly on sharing of feelings, participants may not be fully involved in the process. Perhaps most importantly, listening to coworkers who do share their thoughts and feelings exposes participants to vicarious trauma [47].

It is recognized that not every individual exposed to trauma will go on to develop PTSD or other psychological disorders. In fact, most do not. Mandatory inclusion of all personnel involved in a response includes personnel who are not going to develop a disorder as well as those who are at greater risk. The very act of holding a CISD intervention may "medicalize" normal symptoms of distress after a trauma. Thus, normal coping mechanisms may be reinterpreted as pathological [48].

That's not to say that CISD is never beneficial. In a meta-analysis of ambulance personnel, a positive correlation with CISD participation and outcome occurred in a group in which participation in CISD was voluntary rather than mandatory. Those who had lower levels of social support were more likely to state that CISD was beneficial [49]. Allowing participants to self-select into the process appears to be key, and speaks to the need to provide support for those who do not have their own built-in support systems.

Proponents of CISD counter that studies showing negative mental health outcomes among CISD participants are a result of poor study design, or that poor outcomes are due to administration of the process by untrained personnel. In addition, proponents feel that CISD was never intended as a stand-alone treatment for prevention of PTSD. Rather, CISD should be a component of an overall Critical Incident Stress Management (CISM) program that includes:

- Precrisis preparation for both the individual and organization, including the training of managers to support employees and development of a process to follow after the incident;
- Large-scale demobilization procedures for use after mass disasters (including rest and recovery periods in extended disasters);
- Individual acute crisis counseling;
- Brief small group discussions ("defusing") to assist in acute symptom reduction;
- Longer small group discussions (the CISD) to provide closure and/or facilitate the referral process for further support (in practice, this is now recommended to take place within 24–72 hours post incident);
- Family crisis intervention techniques;
- Follow-up procedures and/or referral for psychological assessment or treatment [50].

Occupational health professionals can play a role in the development of an organization's CISM program. This includes coordinating pre-incident education on stress and healthy coping skills, developing a process to provide intervention and support as soon as is practical following an incident, and developing a process to provide individual support such as individual crisis intervention, defusion, or CISD, and providing resources and/or referrals for follow-up psychotherapy when symptoms present, such as:

- Displaying physical symptoms without a definitive diagnosis;
- Voicing fear of returning to work;
- Increased expression of concerns about work safety;
- Increased absences from work;
- Lack of focus on the job;
- Increased number of errors on the job;

- Deteriorating performance;
- Lost sense of humor;
- Withdrawing from peer interactions;
- Initiating conflict with management or authority figures [51].

In practice, CISM interventions are most likely to be effective when they are voluntary and culturally appropriate. Individual sessions with trained mental health professionals should be an option for those who are not comfortable participating in a group setting. Those leading sessions should be competent in the culture of the profession that responders come from, for example, interventions for police officers should be facilitated by trained professionals with a police background or someone who is at least familiar with law enforcement culture, interventions with paramedics should be conducted by someone with a paramedic background or is familiar with the work environment and culture, and so forth [10].

Some CISM systems have begun to utilize "defusion" and "peer support" in place of CISD. Defusion and peer support is certainly less costly to the organization than utilization of a trained facilitator. Involvement of peer diffusers can result in lower rates of employee time loss after critical incidents. However, the process for defusion and peer support is less clearly defined than the process for CISD, and there is a risk that untrained peer supporters who are also untrained in professional boundaries could inadvertently disclose personal information about their coworkers. Such information could have detrimental effects on promotions and career prospects. The fear of exposure of personal information could inhibit participation in a peer support process [52].

7.15 Additional Treatment Options

Cognitive Behavioral Therapy (CBT) with a trained and qualified therapist has been evaluated as a method of treatment for personnel experiencing stress reactions, including symptoms of Acute Stress Disorder. CBT includes:

- Education about common posttraumatic reactions;
- Progressive muscle relaxation training;
- Exposure to the traumatic memory through imagining it;
- Cognitive restructuring of distorted trauma-related beliefs;
- Exposure to situations previously avoided;

Like CISD, the effectiveness of early CBT treatment has mixed results in the literature. Effectiveness is most apparent when CBT is provided from one month after the trauma occurs and onward [47].

Additional techniques used in treatment of PTSD patients includes hypnotherapy and Eye Movement Desensitization and Reprocessing (EMDR). Effectiveness of these treatments is, at least in part, related to the provider's expertise in emergency response culture, whether through personal experience or receptivity to learning about the world that emergency responders work in. Association of the event with a higher level spiritual meaning, which may or may not include organized religion, is beneficial as well. Encouraging participation in a spiritual organization facilitates the building of social supports, which is also a factor in recovery [10].

When symptoms do not resolve, participation in a residential treatment program such as the On-Site Academy program in Massachusetts or the West Coast Post Trauma Retreat (WCPR) program in Marin County, California, is an option. The WCPR program is based on the On-Site Program: A six-day residential program designed by psychologists who are also police officers. The goal of the program is to focus on resiliency, improvement in quality of life, and to reduce symptoms of post-traumatic stress through education, peer support, and clinical work. Participants share their story many times, beginning with an intake phone session prior to arrival, and throughout the six-day program, allowing for gradual desensitization to recalling the trauma. Participants take part in individual and group therapy, peer counseling and support, critical incident debriefing, EMDR, and family or origin work. An educational component includes classes on topics such as alcohol and substance abuse, physiological effects of stress, and goal planning. Participants develop a 90-day action plan to maintain recovery once they return home.

Participants in this program had significantly fewer symptoms of anxious arousal, depression, anger and irritability, dissociation, and defensive avoidance after completion of the program. The length of time between the initial trauma and participation in the program did not impact degree of improvement, so it appears that participation in the program at any time interval following the traumatic event is beneficial [7].

7.16 Psychological First Aid

The concept of providing Psychological First Aid (PFA) to disaster workers was first introduced by Timothy Singer in 1982. Singer recognized that disaster responders underwent an emotional processing that was really no different from that of any other disaster survivor, and that there were times that response workers required some degree of support and intervention [53].

The use of Psychological First Aid (PFA) has begun to replace CISD as a method to support the psychological health of those exposed to trauma in a disaster. Psychological first aid is a supportive intervention that can be delivered by mental health disaster response workers embedded in a response, or by lay persons who have been trained in PFA (such as trained peer response teams).

The National Child Traumatic Stress Network and the National Center for PTSD have developed guidelines for providing PFA for those most at risk for long-term mental health consequences, such as children, medically frail members of the population, those who been injured, those with serious mental illness or physical disabilities, adolescents who are risk takers, and others. Disaster response personnel are included in this list. This guidance describes eight core actions of PFA:

- Contact and Engagement: To initiate contact in a nonintrusive, compassionate, and helpful manner;
- Safety and Comfort: Enhance immediate and ongoing safety, and provide physical and emotional support;
- Stabilization: Calm and orient, emotionally overwhelmed, or disoriented survivors;
- Information Gathering on Current Needs and Concerns: Identify immediate needs and concerns and gather additional information so that Psychological First Aid interventions can be tailored to the needs of the individual;
- Practical Assistance: Offer practical help in addressing immediate needs and concerns;
- Connection with Social Supports: Establish brief or ongoing contacts with primary support systems and other sources of support, including family members, friends, and community resources;
- Information on Coping: Provide information about stress reactions and coping to reduce distress and promote functioning;
- Linkage with Collaborative Services: Link to immediately available services if needed, or to resources that can be utilized at a later time [54].

The World Health Organization (WHO) has also published guidance on PFA for people who have been very recently affected by a crisis event, which includes seven themes:

- Providing practical care and support, which does not intrude;
- Assessing needs and concerns;
- Helping people to address basic needs (for example, food and water, information);
- Listening to people, but not pressuring them to talk;
- Comforting people and helping them to feel calm;
- Helping people connect to information, services, and social supports;
- Protecting people from further harm.

The WHO guidance makes it clear that PFA is NOT professional counseling or therapy. It is also not psychological debriefing: PFA providers are encouraged to listen to people's stories, but not pressurize them to talk about their feelings or reactions to the event. Rather, it is intended to make people feel safe, connected, calm, and hopeful [55].

Additional guidance on PFA has been developed by various universities, state public health agencies, the Red Cross and Red Crescent Societies, and other organizations such as the National Firefighters Association. More than 25 manual and guidance documents were published between 2005 and 2013. Although methodology differs, they contain common elements such as:

- Safety;
- Keeping calm;
- Connectedness;
- Self-efficacy;
- Hope.

To date, research has not been able to demonstrate that PFA effectively reduces outcomes of PTSD or other long-term mental health disorders [56]. In part, this is due to the fact that research that would demonstrate the effectiveness of PFA has not been conducted in a manner that stands up to scientific scrutiny, such as using a defined intervention with a test group, and providing no intervention to a control group [57]. Such studies are difficult to achieve in a disaster setting, and even if they could be done, it would present an ethical dilemma if people presenting traumatic stress symptoms were denied support. In addition, since multiple methodologies exist for the framework in which PFA is provided, and the level of training provided to those who practice PFA, it would be difficult to establish consistent findings.

Despite the lack of scientific proof that PFA is helpful, it continues to be accepted as an effective option that can be used by trained volunteers with people who have experienced a traumatic event. PFA is widely supported by available objective evidence including observations and expert opinions. It is important to remember that PFA is not treatment, and although PFA addresses immediate needs, it is the responsibility of mental health professionals to treat actual mental health problems. However, even licensed professionals may only be able to practice to a level of first aid in the immediate moments of crisis where time and resources are limited [58]. Unlike CISD, there is no evidence that PFA causes harm.

A group at Johns Hopkins has developed a PFA protocol based on core disaster mental health competencies put forth by the Centers for Public Health Preparedness (CPHP) Disaster Mental Health Collaborative Group. This protocol includes:

- Employ active/reflective listening skills;
- Identify medical needs and identify basic human needs such as food, clothing, and shelter;
- Identify social and emotional needs;

- Determine level of functionality, or the ability to care for oneself and others;
- Follow medical advice and safety orders;
- Recognize mild psychological and behavioral distress reactions and distinguish them from potentially incapacitating reactions;
- Provide appropriate stress management, if needed;
- Connect to available resources such as food, shelter, medical, transportation, crisis intervention services; local counseling services; financial resources, and natural support systems such as family, friends, coworkers, and spiritual support.

The Johns Hopkins model (RAPID-PFA) consists of the following core elements:

- *Reflective listening*, including active listening techniques, establishing empathy, and determine important aspects of the survivor's experience;
- *Assessment of needs*: Asking yes–no screening questions to determine if there are indicators that functioning is reduced or maladaptive;
- *Prioritize severe versus mild stress reactions*: Triage to guide an acute intervention plan for more severe physical, psychological, and behavioral reactions. Physical and medical needs are priorities;
- *Intervention*, including stress management, or cognitive or behavioral techniques to reduce acute stress;
- *Disposition*: Determining if the survivor has regained the functional capacity to return to daily living, or if it is necessary to refer transition them to other clinical or social support services.

Johns Hopkins has also developed and tested a training curriculum to teach PFA providers how to utilize the RAPID-PFA model. The learning objectives for the RAPID-PFA course are:

- Participants will increase their understanding of, and the ability to listen actively;
- Assess and prioritize basic human needs;
- Recognize benign, non-incapacitating psychological/behavioral reactions;
- Recognize more severe, potentially incapacitating reactions;
- Mitigate acute distress using selected cognitive behavioral crisis and stress management interventions, as appropriate;
- Recognize when to facilitate access to further mental health support;
- Reduce the risk of adverse outcome associated with intervention;
- Practice self-care.

A test of the 6-hour curriculum determined that it did in fact meet the learning objectives. Participants gained information on the subject material, gained confidence on their own personal resiliency in a disaster situation, and were able to apply PFA [59, 60].

The efficacy of RAPID-PFA was tested with volunteers who were asked to recollect a stressful event. The test group worked with someone who was trained in the RAPID-PFA method, and a control group worked with someone who practiced active listening, but did not offer empathy or apply any other form of RAPID-PFA. Measures of stress in the RAPID-PFA group were significantly lower than their baseline 30 minutes following the end of the session, while in the control group, stress levels were the same as their baseline levels or slightly higher. Although it is not known whether this method can significantly reduce long-term mental health outcomes, the study did demonstrate that it is effective in mitigating short-term stress. In the midst of a disaster response, the ability to either resolve a stress reaction so that a responder can return to work or make a referral to professional care may be the more critical measure [61].

7.17   Mental Health First Aid

Mental Health First Aid (MHFA) is a program that is similar to PFA. While PFA is primarily intended for personnel experiencing a disaster, MHFA addresses a variety of mental health conditions that can occur in the general population in addition to trauma resulting from a disaster. The program was developed by Betty Kitchener in Australia, and has since opened programs internationally. It models first aid training for physical injuries and illnesses, and is intended as a method that a lay person such as a friend or family member can use until professional help can be obtained. Mental illness is common in the general population, and it is very likely that any of us will encounter a friend, family member, or coworker in need of help at some point in our lives [62].

Mental Health First Aid uses the acronym ALGEE to describe the steps of its action plan:

- *Assess* for risk of suicide or harm;
- *Listen* nonjudgmentally;
- *Give* reassurance and information;
- *Encourage* appropriate professional help;
- *Encourage* self-help and other support strategies.

The training curriculum covers risk factors and warning signs for individuals experiencing mental health or addiction crisis as well as noncrisis situations. There is an emphasis on treating the person being helped with respect. The curriculum also provides additional information on mental health disorders, including resources that can provide help:

- Depression and mood disorders;
- Anxiety disorders;
- Trauma;
- Psychosis;
- Substance use disorders.[2]

7.18 Responders in Their Own Community: Missing or Deceased Family Members

Responses start and end locally. Although county, state, and even federal resources can be called in when local resources are depleted, local responders are the first at the scene and stay throughout the response as they are able. As a result, they are impacted by any personal trauma that is incurred as well as the sights, sounds, and smells that are present at any disaster scene.

One of the greatest sources of stress is a missing family member. This can generate a number of feelings including denial, worry, hope, anger, shock, or guilt. Relatives may be certain that the person is alive or certain that he or she is dead or may alternate between these beliefs. They may blame authorities for not having answers, or for not trying hard enough to find the missing person. Some people will want to search for the missing person themselves, even if it is not safe to do so.

In a community response, it is also probable that responders will know someone who has died in the event. Although everyone experiences this differently, acute grief reactions can be very intense and can include strong feelings of grief, guilt, and regret. It may take some time to accept that this person is really dead, and there may be a period of denial or belief that a miracle will take place. This is all part of the grieving process.

When talking to survivors, it is important to remember that the person who is dead is someone very real. Always refer to the person by name: Do not refer to this person as "the deceased" or "the dead person."

Many people find their spiritual beliefs to be of comfort after someone close to them has died, and may want to talk about these spiritual beliefs. In American workplaces, coworkers may practice a variety of different religions, and it is for the most part considered not acceptable to discuss one's own spiritual beliefs in the workplace. Many workers may find it uncomfortable to talk about spiritual beliefs that they do not share. Regardless, it is important to listen supportively

---

2 www.mentalhealthfirstaid.org (accessed 1 July 2019).

in this situation. If the grieving person asks others to join them in prayer, it is acceptable to join them if it is comfortable to do so, or listen silently if it is not. The time immediately following the death of a loved one, especially right after a death notification is received, is not the time to get into an argument over one's own spiritual beliefs [54].

Grief can be profound when a coworker or member of the response team dies. Rather than a single member of the team grieving, the entire team experiences this loss. Workplaces in which an employee has died often experience increased rise in absenteeism and reduction in productivity, which can severely impact a response in an emergency. It is highly advisable that grief counselors be made available in the event that a team member dies [63].

7.19 Stress Management Programs

The Substance Abuse and Mental Health Services Administration (SAMHSA) provides many resources for managing stress and promoting mental health among emergency services and disaster workers, including guidebooks, fact sheets, and training aids.[3]

Emergency services employers can take steps to minimize stress before, during and after an incident.

Certain workplace characteristics are known to reduce stress in workers, such as good communication and clearly defined roles and responsibilities. Utilization of NIMS and ICS concepts provide both. Providing ICS training, practicing it in drills and exercises, and using ICS during activations ensures that these procedures are institutionalized within the organization.

It is also important to maintain and update emergency contact information for each employee, as well as contact information for family members. Plans should also include means for emergency service workers to check in with their families if needed, especially when a local disaster strikes while on shift.

During the response, it is best to partner inexperienced workers with those who have more experience. They should work as buddies, with the more experienced worker ensuring that safety protocols are followed and monitoring for stress. Workers should be rotated through higher stress assignments, and have options to take breaks in respite areas that visually separate workers from the scene and the public. If feasible, flexible schedules can allow workers to balance home and job responsibilities when their homes are also impacted by the disaster. Safety procedures and programs must be followed: Every step taken to ensure work is done safely in a hazardous or ever changing environment creates a sense of security.

---

3 www.samhsa.gov (accessed 1 July 2019).

Workers may be relieved once the incident is over, but also experience a sense of loss and "letdown" which can make it difficult to transition back to normal life. It is important to manage this transition. Some workers will need time off before returning to their regular jobs, or may need to be assigned initially to less demanding jobs. Counseling options should be made available, and training and educational programs can help put their experiences into perspective. Educational workshops should also cover stress management and self-care [64].

Lastly, it is important to celebrate successes in the response. While tragedy may be visible, and lives may have been loss, it is important to remember what was achieved, how many lives were saved, and the good that was done. Management can help promote this sense of accomplishment. Celebrations are important, with alcohol-free options of course.

7.20 Summary

Response and recovery workers are exposed to sights, odors, and sounds of trauma. In addition to the physical hazards encountered in an emergency response or disaster, response, and recovery workers are at risk of developing stress-related disorders such as Acute Traumatic Stress Disorder or PTSD. The majority of responders will not go on to develop a disorder, but individual risk factors such as previous trauma exposure, previous mental illness, or poor social support can create greater risk. Responders who help members of the public may experience secondary or vicarious trauma, which can put them at risk for Secondary Traumatic Stress Disorder. Early efforts to address these traumas through Critical Incident Stress Debriefing have not been shown to reduce adverse psychological outcomes, and may even exacerbate outcomes. Comprehensive Critical Incident Stress Management programs are more holistic, and include elements such as resiliency training before the incident, peer supporters trained in Psychological First Aid, and access to professional support.

References

1 Qi, S., Hassabis, D., Sun, J. et al. (2018). How cognitive and reactive fear circuits optimize escape decisions in humans. *Proceedings of the National Academy of Sciences* 115 (12): 3186–3191.

2 American Psychiatric Association (2013). *Diagnostic and Statistical Manual of Mental Disorders*, 5e. DSM-5.

3 Linkh, D.J. (2005). Fire from a cloudless sky: a qualitative study of loss, trauma and resilience in the families of surviving New York City firefighters in the

wake of the terrorist attacks of September 11th, 2001. Doctor of philosophy dissertation, Columbia University.

4 Bremmer, D.J. (2006). Traumatic stress: effects on the brain. *Dialogues in Clinical Neuroscience* 8 (4): 445–461.

5 Gola, H., Engler, A., Morath, J. et al. (2014). Reduced peripheral expression of the glucocorticoid receptor α isoform in individuals with posttraumatic stress disorder: a cumulative effect of trauma burden. *PLoS One* 9 (1): e86333.

6 Cortese, B., Schumann, A., and Uhde, T. (2017). Accelerated neurodegeneration: effects of cumulative trauma exposure and chronic posttraumatic stress disorder (PTSD) in relatively young combat veterans. *Biological Psychiatry* 81: S233.

7 Cantrell, S.A. (2010). The change in first responders symptoms after participation in a residential recovery program. Doctor of philosophy dissertation, Wright Institute Graduate School of Psychology.

8 World Health Organization (2018). *International Classification of Diseases 11th Revision ICD-11 for Mortality and Morbidity Statistics 6B41 Complex Post Traumatic Stress Disorder.*

9 Agarastos, A., Pittman, J.O.E., Angkaw, A.C. et al. (2014). The cumulative effect of different childhood trauma types on self-reported symptoms of adult male depression and PTSD, substance abuse, and health-related quality of life in a large active-duty military cohort. *Journal of Psychiatric Research* 58: 46–54.

10 Rosemond, K.V. (2017). Posttraumatic stress disorder in public safety workers: cultural aspects and implications for effective treatment. Doctor of philosophy dissertation, Saybrook University.

11 Karatzias, T., Cloitre, M., Maercker, A. et al. (2018). PTSD and complex PTSD: ICD-11 updates on concept and measurement in the UK, USA, Germany and Lithuania. *European Journal of Psychotraumatology* 8: 141803.

12 Karam, E.G., Friedman, M.J., Hill, E.D. et al. (2014). Cumulative traumas and risk thresholds: 12-month PTSD in the World Mental Health (WMH) surveys. *Depression and Anxiety* 31: 130–142.

13 Geronazzo-Alman, L., Eisenberg, R., Shen, S. et al. (2017). Cumulative exposure to work-related traumatic events and current post-traumatic stress disorder in New York City's first responders. *Comprehensive Psychiatry* 74: 134–143.

14 Lewis-Schroeder, N.F., Kieran, K., Murphy, B.L. et al. (2018). Conceptualization, assessment, and treatment of traumatic stress in first responders: a review of critical issues. *Harvard Review of Psychiatry* 26 (4): 216–227.

15 Schwartz, R.M., Tuminello, S., Kerath, S.M. et al. (2018). Preliminary assessment of Hurricane Harvey exposures and mental health impact. *International Journal of Environmental Research and Public Health* 15: 974.

16 Bromet, E.J., Clouston, S., Gonzalez, A. et al. (2017). Hurricane Sandy exposure and the mental health of World Trade Center responders. *Journal of Traumatic Stress* 30: 107–114.

17 Yehuda, R. and LeDoux, J. (2007). Response variation following trauma: a translational neuroscience approach to understanding PTSD. *Neuron* 56 (1): 19–32.

18 Brewin, C.R., Andrews, B., and Valentine, J.D. (2000). Meta-analysis of risk factors for posttraumatic stress disorder in trauma-exposed adults. *Journal of Consulting and Clinical Psychology* 68 (5): 748–766.

19 Sandica, B.A. and Pop, B. (2014). Risk factors for PTSD. *Journal of Trauma & Treatment* S4: e002.

20 Walker, A., McKune, A., Ferguson, S. et al. (2016). Chronic occupational exposures can influence the rate of PTSD and depressive disorders in first responders and military personnel. *Extreme Physiology & Medicine* 5: 8. https://doi.org/10.1186/s13728-016-0049-x.

21 Figley, C.R. (2002). Compassion fatigue: psychotherapists' chronic lack of self care. *Journal of Clinical Psychology/In Session* 58: 1433–1441.

22 Adams, R.E., Boscarino, J.A., and Figley, C.R. (2006). Compassion fatigue and psychological distress among social workers: a validation study. *American Journal of Orthopsychiatry* 76 (1): 103–108.

23 Bissett, J.L. (2002). The relationship between burnout and compassion fatigue in fire fighter-paramedics. Doctor of philosophy dissertation, University of Houston.

24 Stamm, B.H. (2017). A personal-professional experience of losing my home to wildfire: linking personal experience with the professional literature. *Clinical Social Work Journal* 45: 136–145.

25 Cocker, F. and Joss, N. (2016). Compassion fatigue among healthcare, emergency and community service workers: a systematic review. *International Journal of Environmental Research and Public Health* 13: 618.

26 Argentero, P. and Setti, I. (2011). Engagement and vicarious traumatization in rescue workers. *International Archives Occupational and Environmental Health* 84: 67–75.

27 Hyman, O. (2004). Perceived social support and secondary traumatic stress symptoms in emergency responders. *Journal of Traumatic Stress* 17 (2): 149–156.

28 Waugh, J.R. (2017). *Crime Scene Investigators and Traumatic Event-Related Stress: A Quantitative Study*. Sage Publications Ltd.

29 Center for Behavioral Health Statistics and Quality, Substance Abuse and Mental Health Services Administration (SAMHSA), US Department of Health and Human Services (2019). *Behavioral Health Barometer United States*, vol. 5. HHS publication no. SMA-19-BARO-17-US.

30 Health Insurance Portability and Accountability Act of 1996.

31 Arnsten, A., Lee, D., and Pittenger, C. (2017). Risky business: the circuits that impact stress-induced decision making. *Cell* 171: 992–993.

32 Friedman, A., Homma, D., Bloem, B. et al. (2017). Chronic stress alters striosome-circuit dynamics, leading to aberrant decision making. *Cell* 171: 1191–1205.

33 Starcke, K. and Brand, M. (2012). Decision making under stress: a selective review. *Neuroscience and Biobehavioral Reviews* 36 (2012): 1228–1248.

34 Regehr, C. and LeBlanc, V.R. (2017). PTSD, acute stress, performance and decision-making in emergency service workers. *Journal of the American Academy of Psychiatry and the Law* 45: 184–192.

35 Katsavouni, F., Bebetsos, E., Malliou, P., and Beneka, A. (2016). The relationship between burnout, PTSD symptoms, and injuries in firefighters. *Occupational Medicine* 66: 32–37.

36 Carey, M.G., Al-Zaiti, S.S., Dean, G.E. et al. (2011). Sleep problems, depression, substance use, social bonding, and quality of live in professional firefighters. *Journal of Occupational and Environmental Medicine* 53 (8): 928–933.

37 Menard, K.S. and Arter, M.L. (2013). Police officer alcohol use and trauma symptoms: associations with critical incidents, coping, and social stressors. *International Journal of Stress Management* 20 (1): 37–56.

38 Haddock, C.K., Poston, W.S.C., Jahnke, S.A., and Jitnarin, N. (2017). Alcohol use and problem drinking among women firefighters. *Women's Health Issues* 27 (6): 632–638.

39 Heyman, M., Dill, J., and Douglass, R. (2018). *The Ruderman White Paper on Mental Health and Suicide of First Responders*. Ruderman Family Foundation.

40 Gist, R., Taylor, V.H., and Raak, S. (2011). *White Paper, Suicide Surveillance, Prevention, and Intervention Measures for the US Fire Service: Findings and Recommendations for the Suicide and Depression Summit*. National Fallen Firefighters Foundation, Everyone Goes Home Project, Behavioral Health Initiative (FLSI 13).

41 Koopmans, E., Wagner, S., Schmidt, G., and Harder, H. (2017). Emergency response services suicide: a crisis in Canada? *Journal of Loss and Trauma* 22 (7): 527–539.

42 International Association of Chiefs of Police (IACP) (2014). *IACP National Symposium on Law Enforcement Officer Suicide and Mental Health: Breaking the Silence on Law Enforcement Suicides*. Washington, DC: Office of Community Oriented Policing Services.

43 National Fire Protection Association (2018). *NFPA 1500: Standard on Fire Department Occupational Safety, Health, and Wellness Program 2018*.

44 Center for Officer Safety and Wellness, The International Association of Chiefs of Police (2018). *The Signs Within: Suicide Prevention Education and Awareness*. Washington, DC: Office of Community Oriented Policing Services.

45 Mitchell, J.T. (1983). When disaster strikes ... the critical incident stress debriefing process. *JEMS, A Journal of Emergency Medical Services* 8 (1): 36–39.

46 Rose, S.C., Bisson, J., Chrchill, R., and Wessely, S. (2002). Psychological debriefing for preventing post traumatic stress disorder (PTSD) (Review). *Cochrane Database of Systematic Reviews* 2002 (2): 1–49.

47 McNally, R.J., Bryant, R.A., and Ehlers, A. (2003). Does early pshycological intervention promote recovery from posttraumatic stress? *Psychological Science in the Public Interest* 4 (2): 45–79.

48 Mitchell, A.M., Sakraida, T.J., and Kameg, K. (2003). Critical incident stress debriefing: implications for best practice. *Disaster Management and Response* 1 (2): 46–51.

49 Smith, A. and Roberts, K. (2003). Interventions for post-traumatic stress disorder and psychological distress in emergency ambulance personnel: a review of the literature (Prehospital care). *Emergency Medicine Journal* 20 (1) http://dx.doi.org/10.1136/emj.20.1.75.

50 Everly, G.S. Jr., Flannery, R.B. Jr., and Mitchell, J.T. (1999). Critical incident stress management (CISM): a review of the literature. *Aggression and Violent Behavior* 5 (1): 23–40.

51 Lim, J., Childs, J., and Gonsalves, K. (2000). Critical incident stress management. *Workplace Health and Safety Journal (AAOHN)* 48 (10): 487–499.

52 Pack, M.J. (2012). Critical incident stress management: a review of the literature with implications for social work. *International Social Work* 56 (5): 608–627.

53 Singer, T.J. (1982). An introduction to disaster: some considerations of a psychological nature. *Aviation, Space, and Environmental Medicine* 53 (3): 245–250.

54 Brymer, M., Jacobs, A., Layne, C. et al. (2006). *Psychological First Aid: Field Operations Guide*, 2e (July 2006). National Child Traumatic Stress Network and Center for PTSD.

55 World Health Organization, War Trauma Foundation and World Vision International (2011). *Psychological First Aid: Guide for Field Workers*. Geneva: WHO.

56 Shultz, J.M. and Forbes, D. (2014). Psychological first aid: rapid proliferation and the search for evidence. *Disaster Health* 2 (1): 3–12.

57 Dieltjens, T., Moonens, I., Van Praet, K. et al. (2014). A systematic literature search on psychological first aid: lack of evidence to develop guidelines. *PLoS One* 9 (12): e114714.

58 Fox, J.H., Burkle, F.M., Bass, J. et al. (2012). The effectiveness of psychological first aid as a disaster intervention tool: research analysis of peer-reviewed literature from 1990-2010. *Disaster Medicine and Public Health Preparedness* 6: 247–252.

59 Everly, G.S. Jr., Barnett, D.J., and Links, J.M. (2012). The Johns Hopkins model of psychological first aid (RAPID-PFA) curriculum development and content validation. *International Journal of Emergency Mental Health* 14 (2): 95–103.

60 Everly, G.S. Jr., McCabe, O.L., Semon, N.L. et al. (2014). The development of a model of psychological first aid for non-mental health trained public health personnel: the Johns Hopkins RAPID-PFA. *Journal of Public Health Management Practic* 20 (5): S24–S29.

61 Everly, G.S. Jr., Lating, J.M., Sherman, M.F., and Goncher, I. (2016). The potential efficacy of psychological first aid on self-reported anxiety and mood: a pilot study. *Journal of Nervous and Mental Disease* 204 (3): 233–235.

62 Jorm, A.F. and Kitchener, B.A. (2011). Noting a landmark achievement: mental health first aid training reaches 1% of Australian adults. *Australian and New Zealand Journal of Psychiatry* 45: 808–813.

63 Sorohan, E.G. (1994). When a co-worker dies. *Training & Development* 48 (10): 9.

64 US Department of Health and Human Services (2005). *A Guide to Managing Stress in Crisis Response Professions*. DHHS publication number SMA 4113. Rockville, MD: Center for Mental Health Services, Substance Abuse and Mental Health Services Administration.

8

Safety Officer Duties During an Incident Response

The Incident Commander is responsible for making sure that all those involved in an incident response are safe, and that when the response ends, these workers can go home just as healthy as when the response started. The Incident Commander is liable if workers are injured or killed and is responsible for ensuring that safety standards are followed, including OSHA and state regulations and any relevant safety standards such as NFPA 1500. The Safety Officer must make sure that these responsibilities are met, and an Incident Commander who has a competent and resourceful Safety Officer to rely on can significantly minimize his or her own personal liability [1, 2].

An Incident Action Plan (IAP) is a critical component of any response, and the Safety Officer integrates safety into the incident by ensuring that safety planning and communication are included in the IAP. The IAP may be verbal: In a Type 5 response which can be completed in a few hours or so, the IAP would rarely be written. When the response covers multiple Operational Periods, such as a major response of Type 3, 2, or 1, a written IAP is necessary. A Safety Officer with a good understanding of how IAPs are generated, and the use of standardized forms used in the IAP, can effectively integrate good safety management and practice into the response.

8.1 Initial Response and the Planning "P"

The Planning "P" (Figure 8.1) is a graphical representation of the sequence of meetings, work periods, and briefings comprising the incident action planning cycle.

The initial response of the incident is represented in the leg of the "P." During this phase, personnel and resources are notified of the incident and begin

Health and Safety in Emergency Management and Response, First Edition. Dana L. Stahl.
© 2021 John Wiley & Sons, Inc. Published 2021 by John Wiley & Sons, Inc.

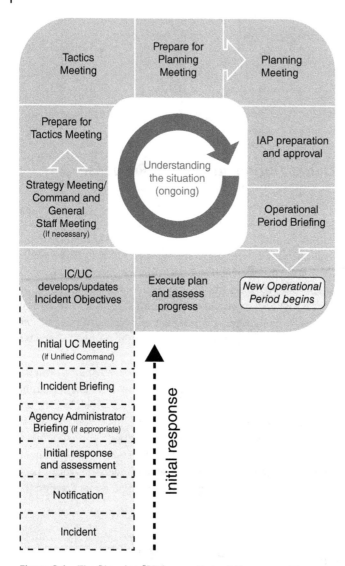

Figure 8.1 The Planning "P". Source: Federal Emergency Management Administration, US Department of Homeland Security [3].

INCIDENT CHECK-IN LIST (ICS 211)

1. Incident Name:	2. Incident Number:	3. Check-In Location (complete all that apply): ☐ Base ☐ Staging Area ☐ ICP ☐ Helibase ☐ Other	4. Start Date/Time: Date: Time:

Check-In Information (use reverse of form for remarks or comments)

5. List single resource personnel (overhead) by agency and name, OR list resources by the following format: State / Agency / Category / Kind / Type / Resource Name or Identifier / ST or TF	6. Order Request #	7. Date/Time Check-In	8. Leader's Name	9. Total Number of Personnel	10. Incident Contact Information	11. Home Unit or Agency	12. Departure Point, Date and Time	13. Method of Travel	14. Incident Assignment	15. Other Qualifications	16. Data Provided to Resources Unit

ICS 211	17. Prepared by: Name: _____ Position/Title: _____ Signature: _____ Date/Time: _____

Figure 8.2 FEMA Form ICS 211: Incident Check-In List. Source: Federal Emergency Management Administration [4].

arriving at the scene. First arriving personnel conduct an initial assessment and take immediate response actions as necessary. As the incident progresses, more information becomes known and can be incorporated into the assessment. The size of the incident, its complexity, and scope of response are clarified. Incident Command is established, and arriving personnel begin to fill in the positions of the ICS organizational structure. Jurisdiction officials may decide to activate the Emergency Operations Center (EOC) if the nature of the incident warrants it.

As resources arrive, they sign in on ICS Form 211 (Figure 8.2). An arriving Safety Officer also signs in on the Form 211, and begins considering an incident safety assessment.

After check in, the Safety Officer, along with other arriving resources, conduct an initial assessment of the scene (Figure 8.3). A review of the Form 211 provides important initial information on who is present at the scene, and is part of this initial safety assessment

An Agency Administrator Briefing may be held as the Incident Commander (or Unified Command) assumes duties. This briefing is intended to ensure a common understanding between the jurisdiction, agency, or organization and the incident personnel regarding environmental, social, political, economic, cultural, or other issues relevant to the incident and its location.

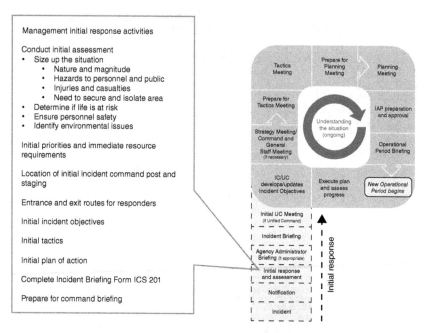

Figure 8.3 Initial assessment.

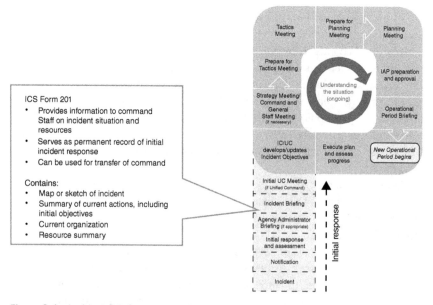

Figure 8.4 Incident Briefing.

An Incident Briefing (Figure 8.4) is provided by Incident/Unified Command to Command and General Staff, including the Safety Officer. An ICS Form 201 (Figure 8.5) may be utilized to facilitate this briefing. Information covered in this briefing includes:

- The situation:
  - Boundaries and scope of the incident;
  - Number of displaced survivors;
  - Sheltering information;
  - Critical infrastructure damage assessment, locations, and types;
  - Status of communications and other utilities;
  - Incident facilities, types, and location;
  - Resources on hand, en-route, and on order;
  - State emergency management organization and facilities;
  - Location of the initial operating facility (IOF)
  - Health-related concerns, including fatalities and injuries;
  - Life-saving operations;
  - Arrangement for use of military resources such as joint forces command.
- The documentation:
  - Stafford Act declaration or interagency memorandum of understanding for non-Stafford Act incidents;
  - Pertinent deliberate plans;
  - Maps of the incident area;
  - Preliminary damage assessment;
  - Geospatial information system (GIS) information and satellite imagery
  - Contact information (telephone numbers and email addresses) for regional response command staff, state officials, state emergency operation centers, and other incident facilities.

Any necessary delegations of authority for the incident are produced during this meeting. By the end of this meeting, Command and General Staff must have gained sufficient information on the incident to begin work, including situational information, and information on constraints and limitations.

If Unified Command is established, an initial Unified Command Meeting takes place (Figure 8.6). During this meeting, members of the Unified Command discuss jurisdictional priorities and objectives, as well as any limitations, concerns, and restrictions. A spokesperson for Unified Command is agreed upon, and initial joint Incident Objectives are developed. The Safety Officer does not attend this meeting, but should be available to answer any questions on safety should Unified Command need information.

INCIDENT BRIEFING (ICS 201)

1. Incident Name:	2. Incident Number:	3. Date/Time Initiated:
		Date: Time:

4. Map/Sketch (include sketch, showing the total area of operations, the incident site/area, impacted and threatened areas, overflight results, trajectories, impacted shorelines, or other graphics depicting situational status and resource assignment):

5. Situation Summary and Health and Safety Briefing (for briefings or transfer of command): Recognize potential incident Health and Safety Hazards and develop necessary measures (remove hazard, provide personal protective equipment, warn people of the hazard) to protect responders from those hazards.

6. Prepared by: Name: _____ Position/Title: _____ Signature: _____

ICS 201, Page 1	Date/Time: _____

Figure 8.5 FEMA Form ICS 201. Source: Federal Emergency Management Administration [4].

INCIDENT BRIEFING (ICS 201)

1. Incident Name:	2. Incident Number:	3. Date/Time Initiated:
		Date: Time:

7. Current and Planned Objectives:

8. Current and Planned Actions, Strategies, and Tactics:

Time:	Actions:

6. **Prepared by:** Name: _____ Position/Title: _____ Signature: _____
ICS 201, Page 2   Date/Time: _____

Figure 8.5 *(Continued)*

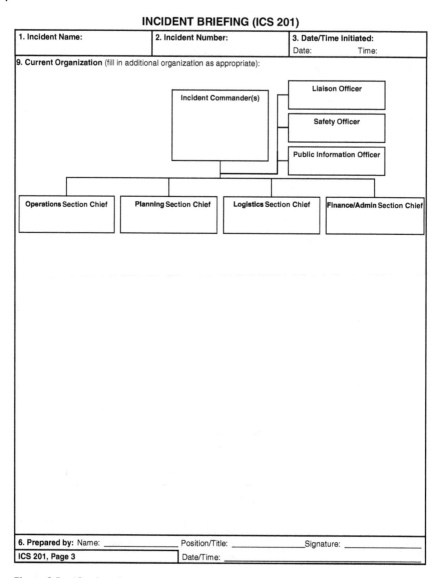

INCIDENT BRIEFING (ICS 201)

1. Incident Name:	2. Incident Number:	3. Date/Time Initiated: Date: Time:

9. Current Organization (fill in additional organization as appropriate):

Incident Commander(s)

Liaison Officer

Safety Officer

Public Information Officer

Operations Section Chief

Planning Section Chief

Logistics Section Chief

Finance/Admin Section Chief

6. Prepared by: Name: _____ Position/Title: _____ Signature: _____
ICS 201, Page 3	Date/Time: _____

Figure 8.5 (*Continued*)

INCIDENT BRIEFING (ICS 201)

1. Incident Name:	2. Incident Number:	3. Date/Time Initiated: Date: Time:

10. Resource Summary:

Resource	Resource Identifier	Date/Time Ordered	ETA	Arrived	Notes (location/assignment/status)
				☐	
				☐	
				☐	
				☐	
				☐	
				☐	
				☐	
				☐	
				☐	
				☐	
				☐	
				☐	
				☐	
				☐	
				☐	
				☐	
				☐	

6. Prepared by: Name: _____ Position/Title: _____ Signature: _____
ICS 201, Page 4   Date/Time: _____

Figure 8.5 *(Continued)*

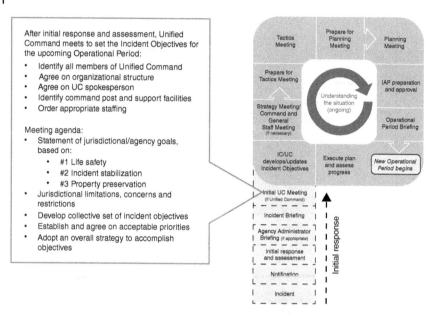

Figure 8.6 Unified Command Meeting.

8.2 The Operations "O"

After the Incident Briefing and the initial Unified Command Meeting, incident response moves into the operations phase. Small incidents, such as a Type 4 or 5 incident, can be completed in a short period of time and do not extend past the first Operational Period. Larger incidents, such as Type 1, 2, or 3 incidents, take more than one Operational Period to complete. After a period of 12 hours or so, crews will need to be replaced with fresh personnel so that they can rest and recover.

Planning for the next Operational Period begins at this time. Planning for the Operational Periods that follow uses a similar process to that followed in the Planning "P" for initial response, although the steps outlined in the leg of the "P" are no longer followed. Instead, the Planning "P" becomes the Operations "O" (Figure 8.7). This cycle continues over additional operating periods until the conclusion of the incident response (Figure 8.8).

8.3 The Incident Action Plan (IAP)

Incident Action Plans (IAPs) contain Incident Objectives established by the Incident Commander or Unified Command, and the strategies and tactics that will be taken to support these objectives over the next Operational Period.

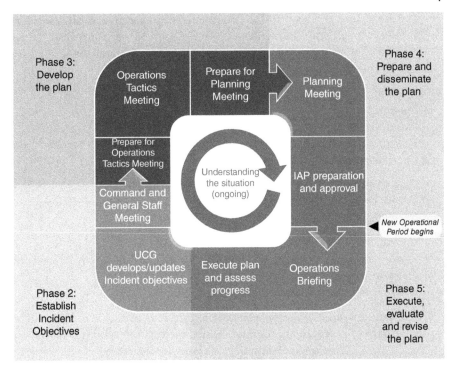

Figure 8.7 The Operations "O". Source: Federal Emergency Management Administration, US Department of Homeland Security [5].

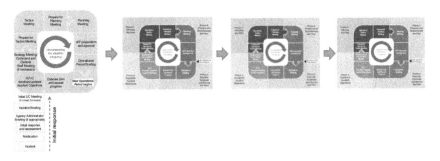

Figure 8.8 The Planning "P" becomes the Operations "O", and then the "POOO."

In any incident, priorities are given in the following order:

1. Life safety;
2. Incident stabilization;
3. Property preservation.

Additional priorities may be decided upon by leadership.

One key characteristic of NIMS is Management By Objectives (MBO). Incident Objectives support priorities. Incident Objectives must be based on realistic expectations given allocated resources, and state "what must be accomplished." Objectives must be SMART:

- Specific;
- Measurable;
- Action Oriented;
- Realistic;
- Time Sensitive.

Objectives should also be flexible. They need to include enough detail to ensure that they are easily understood, but not so rigid that they prevent innovation.

Examples of SMART Objectives include:

- Contain spill by 0400 hours;
- Restore electricity to medical facilities within the jurisdiction by (the second Operational Period);
- Evacuate all personnel from spill containment area by 1200 hours.

Strategies are carefully devised plans of action to achieve one or more objectives, and describe what actions and resources are required. Sample strategies that would support an objective to "Contain spill by 0400 hours" include:

- Shut off flow of oil from tanker;
- Place booms around the perimeter of the spill;
- Dig a trench around spill.

Tactics define how specific outcomes will be performed to support the identified strategy. For example, a tactic that supports the strategy to "place booms around the perimeter of the spill" might be:

- Four-person response crew to place "oil only" booms around perimeter of the spill.

Specific work assignments are then given to work groups to accomplish the identified tactics.

To summarize: Objectives support Priorities, Strategies support Objectives, Tactics are identified to accomplish Strategies, and individual Work Assignments are given to accomplish Tactics (Figure 8.9). IAPs are developed as a work tool to identify, communicate, and document each.

Figure 8.9 Objectives support Priorities, Strategies support Objectives, Tactics accomplish Strategies, and Work Assignments complete Tactics.

8.4 Incident Objectives

Initial Incident Objectives are documented on ICS Form 201 during initial response, and these Objectives guide the initial response. Incident Objectives for the second Operational Period, and those that follow, are documented on ICS Form 202 (Figure 8.10).

The Incident Commander decides upon Incident Objectives. If Unified Command is established, Unified Command must agree upon the Objectives.

Objectives from the initial response or the previous Operational Period are reviewed and evaluated. As the incident evolves, Objectives may need to be modified to account for increased or decreased scope of the response, available resources, learnings from the previous Operational Period, and any safety issues. The Safety Officer does not necessarily participate in defining Objectives, but may be called upon to advise (Figure 8.11).

8.5 Strategies

Once Incident Objectives are agreed to, Strategies are determined by Command and General Staff (Figure 8.12). The Strategy Meeting (Figure 8.13) is facilitated by the Planning Section Chief. The Incident Commander, or Unified Command if established, attends and provides a briefing on direction, objectives, and priorities, and provides enough information that Command and General Staff have a good understanding of the context of these priorities. The Safety Officer attends this meeting.

Objectives may be changed or modified at this time. The Safety Officer should ensure that an appropriate safety objective is included. Once Objectives are agreed to, strategies are discussed, and the Safety Officer should begin thinking about what safety resources will be needed.

INCIDENT OBJECTIVES (ICS 202)

| 1. Incident Name: | 2. Operational Period: Date From: | Date To: |
| | Time From: | Time To: |

3. Objective(s):

4. Operational Period Command Emphasis:

General Situational Awareness

5. Site Safety Plan Required? Yes ☐ No ☐
   Approved Site Safety Plan(s) Located at:

6. Incident Action Plan (the items checked below are included in this Incident Action Plan):

☐ ICS 203   ☐ ICS 207   Other Attachments:
☐ ICS 204   ☐ ICS 208   ☐ _____
☐ ICS 205   ☐ Map/Chart   ☐ _____
☐ ICS 205A   ☐ Weather Forecast/Tides/Currents ☐ _____
☐ ICS 206   ☐ _____

| 7. Prepared by: Name: _____ Position/Title: _____ Signature: _____ |
| 8. Approved by Incident Commander: Name: _____ Signature: _____ |
| ICS 202 | IAP Page _____ | Date/Time: _____ |

Figure 8.10 FEMA Form ICS 202: Incident Objectives. Source: Federal Emergency Management Administration [4].

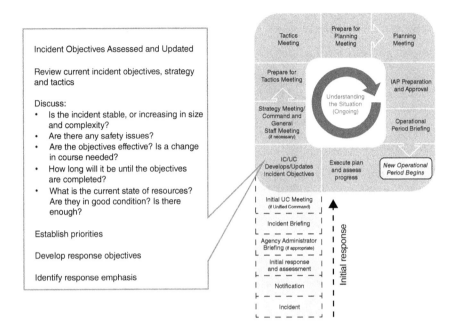

Figure 8.11 IC/UC Develops Incident Objectives.

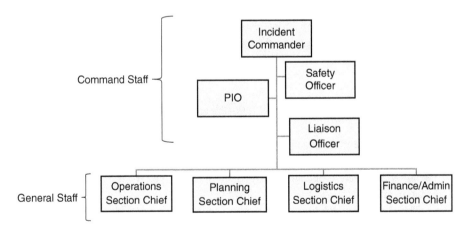

Figure 8.12 Command and General Staff under Incident Command [3].

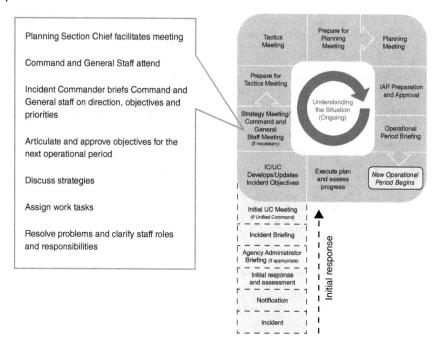

Figure 8.13 Strategy Meeting/Command and General Staff Meeting.

The Operations Section Chief develops Strategies, and works on these following the Command and General Staff Meeting with support from the Logistics Section Chief and the Safety Officer (Figure 8.14).

8.6 Tactics

The Tactics Meeting is led by the Planning Section Chief (Figure 8.15). The Planning Section Chief starts the meeting by reviewing the Incident Objectives and ensures that there is accountability for each Objective. The Safety Officer attends this meeting.

The Operations Section Chief begins identifying work assignments and documenting these on ICS Form 215 (Figure 8.16). The Safety Officer and Planning Section Chief help with this effort.

The Safety Officer also works on the Incident Safety Analysis, Form 215A (Figure 8.17), with the Operations Section Chief.

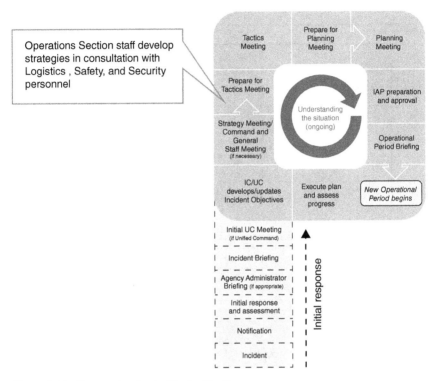

Figure 8.14 Preparation for the Tactics Meeting.

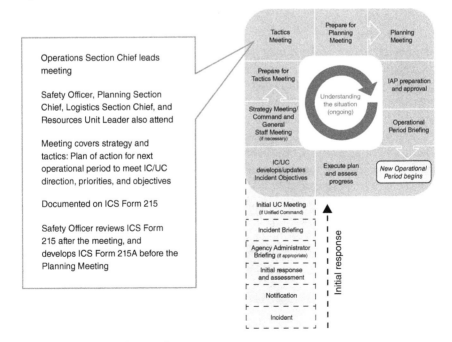

Figure 8.15 The Tactics Meeting.

OPERATIONAL PLANNING WORKSHEET (ICS 215)

| 1. Incident Name: | | | | | | | | | | | 2. Operational Period: Date From:
Time From: | Date To:
Time To: | | | |

3. Branch	4. Division, Group, or Other	5. Work Assignment & Special Instructions	6. Resources								7. Overhead Position(s)	8. Special Equipment & Supplies	9. Reporting Location	10. Requested Arrival Time
			Req.											
			Have											
			Need											
			Req.											
			Have											
			Need											
			Req.											
			Have											
			Need											
			Req.											
			Have											
			Need											
			Req.											
			Have											
			Need											
			Req.											
			Have											
			Need											

	11. Total Resources Required						14. Prepared by: Name: _____
	12. Total Resources Have on Hand						Position/Title: _____
ICS 215	13. Total Resources Need To Order						Signature: _____ Date/Time: _____

Figure 8.16 FEMA Form ICS 215: Operational Planning Worksheet. Source: Federal Emergency Management Administration [4].

8.7 Incident Safety Analysis

A key aspect of safety management is analyzing hazards, including anticipating hazards, recognizing where they may occur, evaluating the hazard, identifying controls, and then confirming that controls work. This concept is conceptualized as ARECC, or Anticipate, Recognize, Evaluate, Control, Confirm.

A Job Hazard Analysis (JHA) is an easy to use tool that many safety professionals utilize to identify safety hazards of a task. Completion of a JHA includes three steps, each of which is recorded in separate columns of the JHA form. The first step of completing a JHA is to break the task down into individual steps, and these are recorded in the first column. Second, hazards are identified for each step identified, and recorded in the second column. Each step of the task must be analyzed for unique hazards. Each step may have multiple hazards associated with it. Lastly, controls or mitigations are identified for each hazard identified, and are written down in the third column. Hazards and protective measures are then communicated to the workers who must complete the task, and if the controls identified are implemented the task can be completed without undue risk (Figure 8.18).

INCIDENT ACTION PLAN SAFETY ANALYSIS (ICS 215A)

1. Incident Name:			2. Incident Number:	
3. Date/Time Prepared: Date: Time:			**4. Operational Period:** Date From: Date To: Time From: Time To:	
5. Incident Area	**6. Hazards/Risks**		**7. Mitigations**	
8. Prepared by (Safety Officer): Name: _____ Signature: _____				
Prepared by (Operations Section Chief): Name: _____ Signature: _____				
ICS 215A		Date/Time: _____		

Figure 8.17 FEMA Form ICS 215A: Incident Action Plan Safety Analysis. Source: Federal Emergency Management Administration [4].

A safety analysis for an incident response is similar to a JHA, with the exception that ICS Forms 215 and 215A are utilized rather than a JHA form.

Work assignments are recorded on Section 5 of the Form 215 (Figure 8.19). Hazards for each work assignment are recorded in Section 6 of the Form 215A, and there should be at least one line of identified hazards and risks for each work

Job Safety Analysis

Clean up a five gallon toluene spill

Prepared by:		Date
Task Description	**Hazards**	**Controls**
1. Barricade location to prevent unauthorized access to area of spill	1.1 Inhalation of toluene vapors while setting up area	1.1.1 Ensure barricades are set up outside of air plume 1.1.2 Wear half mask respirators with organic vapor cartridges while setting up barriers
	1.2 People who normally work in this area may become angry that they can't get to the worksite	1.2.1 Provide communication to all staff that spill area is closed until further notice
2. Place containment around spill and apply absorbent to solidify liquids	2.1. Inhalation of vapors	2.1.1 Wear respiratory protection –half mask respirators with organic vapor cartridges 2.1.2 Stay upwind of spill as much as possible
	2.2 Skin contact with hazardous material	2.2.1 Wear gloves and aprons made of a material that is resistant to toluene (supported butyl rubber) 2.2.2 Wash hands after task is complete
	2.3 Spill material could react with containment material and start a fire	2.3.1 Ensure containment materials are rated for toluene 2.3.2 Have fire extinguisher ready and prepare to use it
	2.4 Slip and fall injuries	2.4.1 Where slip–resistant chemical protective foot wear 2.4.2 Watch footing when walking 2.4.3 Use buddy system to warn when walking in slippery areas
	2.5 Ergonomic injuries	2.5.1 Utilize good body mechanics as covered in training – maintain straight spine, avoid twisting, and use leg muscles when lifting 2.5.2 Don't attempt to lift more than you are able to

Figure 8.18 Example of a completed Job Hazard Analysis (JHA) for cleanup of a small spill.

Task Description	Hazards	Controls
3. Transfer used absorbent materials to waste container	3.1 Inhalation of vapors	3.1.1 Wear respiratory protection – half mask respirators with organic vapor cartridges
		3.1.2 Stay upwind of spill as much as possible
	3.2 Skin contact	3.2.1 Wear supported butyl rubber gloves and aprons
		3.2.2 Wash hands after task is complete.
	3.3 Back injury from lifting material	3.3.1 Use shovel with ergonomic handles
		3.3.2 Don't overload shovel
		4.3.3 Be aware of body mechanics, as covered in training
4. Move waste container to loading dock for pick up by hazardous waste vendor	4.1 Inhalation of vapors	4.1.1 Seal container before moving it
	4.2 Skin contact	4.2.1 Visually inspect container before moving and clean up any drips
		4.2.2 Wear supported butyl rubber gloves and apron
	4.3 Back injury from moving container	4.3 Use a cart to move container to dock
		4.4 Utilize body mechanics as covered in training
5. Clean spill area and return to normal operations	5.1 Inhalation of residual vapors	5.1.1 Wear half mask respirator with organic vapor cartridges
		5.1.2 Continue to stay upwind as much as possible
	5.2 Chemical reaction between toluene and cleaning materials	5.2.1 Check Safety Data sheet and only use cleaning chemicals that don't react with toluene
	5.3 People entering area before fully cleaned	5.3.1 Maintain containment barriers until clearance testing indicates area is safe to re-occupy.

Figure 8.18 *(Continued)*

assignment identified on the Form 215. In a JHA each step of a task is analyzed separately, and similarly, the Form 215A should analyze the hazards of each work assignment separately.

Protective measures or controls are identified for each hazard, and are then recorded in Section 7 of the Form 215A, mitigations (Figures 8.20 and 8.21).

Incident responders are not required to use the FEMA forms, and have the option to utilize equivalent forms instead. Several organizations have developed expanded Forms 215A.

1. Incident Name:
500 Gallon Toluene Spill

3. Branch	4. Division, Group, or Other	5. Work Assignment & Special Instructions	6. Resources		
	Security	Prevent unauthorized access to response area	Req.		
			Have		
			Need		
	Contain ment	Place booms around perimeter of spill	Req.		
			Have		
			Need		
	Packagi ng	Transfer used material to drums	Req.		
			Have		
			Need		
	Transp ort	Haul drums to disposal facility	Req.		
			Have		
			Need		
	Final cleanup	Removal of residual contaminants for return to normal ops	Req.		
			Have		
			Need		
			Req.		
			Have		
			Need		

Figure 8.19 Example of work assignments recorded on a Form 215 for cleanup of a large spill.

Medical facilities utilize the Hospital Incident Command System (HICS). The HICS Form 215A includes a column to document that hazard mitigations identified are completed (Figure 8.22).

The Coast Guard utilizes Form ICS 215A-CG, which includes a column to transfer the work assignments from Form 215 along with the Hazard Analysis and Controls, similar to a JHA (Figure 8.23). This layout intuitively communicates that hazard identification must be associated with work assignments.

The American Industrial Hygiene Association has developed a version of the Form 215A that also intuitively models a Job Hazard Analysis (Figure 8.24). The AIHA Form 215A provides space to transfer work assignments from the Form 215 in Section 4. Section 5, *Hazards*, includes multiple lines to write hazards associated with each work assignment, which serves as a reminder to consider more than

INCIDENT ACTION PLAN SAFETY ANALYSIS (ICS 215A)

1. Incident Name: 500 Gallon Toluene Spill		2. Incident Number: Tol-1	
3. Date/Time Prepared: Date: 7/18/20 Time: 0800		4. Operational Period: Date From: 7/18/20 Time From: 2000	Date To: 7/19/20 Time To: 0800

5. Incident Area	6. Hazards/Risks	7. Mitigations
Security	1. Inhalation of vapors 2. Angry public-could become violent	1. Full face respirators with organic vapor cartridges, stay upwind. 2. Have PIO announce boundary areas and use
Containment	1. Inhalation of vapors 2. Skin contact with toluene 3. Toluene reaction with containment material	1. SCBAs. 2. Fully enclosed encapsulating suits. 3. Ensure containment material resistant to toluene. 4. Establish decontamination
Packaging	1. Inhalation of vapors 2. Skin contact with toluene 3. Back injuries	1. SCBAs. 2. Fully enclosed encapsulating suits. 3. Use ergonomic shovels and body mechanics as covered in training
Transport	1. Inhalation of vapors 2. Skin contact with toluene 3. Back injuries	1. Seal containers before moving. 2. Visually inspect containers for drips and clean. 3. Wear Butyl rubber gloves/apron. 4. Use drum
Final Cleanup	1. Inhalation of residual vapors 2. Chemical reaction toluene/cleaning compounds 3. People entering before clearance testing	1. Half face respirators with OV cartridges, 2. Review technical report analysis before using cleaners. 3. Coordinate with Security group as

Form 215:

1. Incident Name: 500 Gallon Toluene Spill					
3. Branch	4. Division, Group, or Other	5. Work Assignment & Special Instructions	R	H	N
	Security	Prevent unauthorized access to response area			
	Containment	Place booms around perimeter of spill			
	Packaging	Transfer used material to drums			
	Transport	Haul drums to disposal facility			
	Final cleanup	Removal of residual contaminants for return to normal ops			

Figure 8.20 Hazards for each work assignment identified on the Form 215 are analyzed on the Form 215A, in the same manner as is done for a JHA.

INCIDENT ACTION PLAN SAFETY ANALYSIS (ICS 215A)

1. Incident Name: 500 Gallon Toluene Spill		2. Incident Number: Tol-1	
3. Date/Time Prepared: Date: 7/18/20 Time: 0800		**4. Operational Period:** Date From: 7/18/20 Date To: 7/19/20 Time From: 2000 Time To: 0800	
5. Incident Area	**6. Hazards/Risks**		**7. Mitigations**
Security	1. Inhalation of vapors 2. Angry public-could become violent		1. Full face respirators with organic vapor cartridges, stay upwind. 2. Have PIO announce boundary areas and use
Containment	1. Inhalation of vapors 2. Skin contact with toluene 3. Toluene reaction with containment material		1. SCBAs. 2. Fully enclosed encapsulating suits. 3. Ensure containment material resistant to toluene. 4. Establish decontamination
Packaging	1. Inhalation of vapors 2. Skin contact with toluene 3. Back injuries		1. SCBAs. 2. Fully enclosed encapsulating suits. 3. Use ergonomic shovels and body mechanics as covered in training
Transport	1. Inhalation of vapors 2. Skin contact with toluene 3. Back injuries		1. Seal containers before moving. 2. Visually inspect containers for drips and clean. 3. Wear Butyl rubber gloves/apron. 4. Use drum
Final Cleanup	1. Inhalation of residual vapors 2. Chemical reaction toluene/cleaning compounds 3. People entering before clearance testing		1. Half face respirators with OV cartridges, 2. Review technical report analysis before using cleaners. 3. Coordinate with Security group as
8. Prepared by (Safety Officer): Name: _____ Signature: _____			
Prepared by (Operations Section Chief): Name: _____ Signature: _____			
ICS 215A	Date/Time: _____		

Figure 8.21   Completed ICS Form 215A for a toluene spill response.

HICS 215A - INCIDENT ACTION PLAN (IAP) SAFETY ANALYSIS

1. Incident Name	2. Operational Period (#)			
	DATE: FROM: _____ TO: _____			
	TIME: FROM: _____ TO: _____			

3. Hazard Mitigation

3a. Potential/Actual Hazards	3b. Affected Section/Branch/ Unit and Location	3c. Mitigations	3d. Mitigation Completed (Initials/Date/Time)

4. Prepared by Safety Officer	PRINT NAME: _____	SIGNATURE: _____
	DATE/TIME: _____	FACILITY: _____
5. Approved by Incident Commander	PRINT NAME: _____	SIGNATURE: _____
	DATE/TIME: _____	FACILITY: _____

HOSPITAL INCIDENT COMMAND SYSTEM

Purpose: Operational risk assessment to prioritize hazards, safety, and health issues, and to assign mitigation actions
Origination: Safety Officer
Copies to: Planning Section Chief for Incident Action Plan (IAP) and Documentation Unit Leader

HICS 215A Page 1 of 1

Figure 8.22 Form HICS Form 215A: Hospital version of the Form 215A. Source: www.hicscenter.org/sitePages/HICS%20Forms.aspx.

one hazard when reviewing each work assignment. Section 7, *Controls*, includes boxes to write in multiple mitigations for each hazard identified. It also provides a formula for ranking the risk of each hazard in Section 6 so that decisions can be based on priorities for addressing hazards in the event that resources are limited. This format utilizes good safety management practices in an intuitive and easy to use format.

The Operations Section Chief works closely with the Safety Officer in completing the Form 215A, and both sign the form when it is complete.

Resources are required to implement controls, and as the Form 215A is completed, the Safety Officer must identify which resources need to be obtained. The Logistics Section has the responsibility of obtaining resources for the response, and the Safety Officer must communicate these needs to Logistics. ICS Form 213 (Figure 8.25) is used for general communication in the incident, and the Safety Officer can use the Form 213 to request needed safety resources from Logistics.

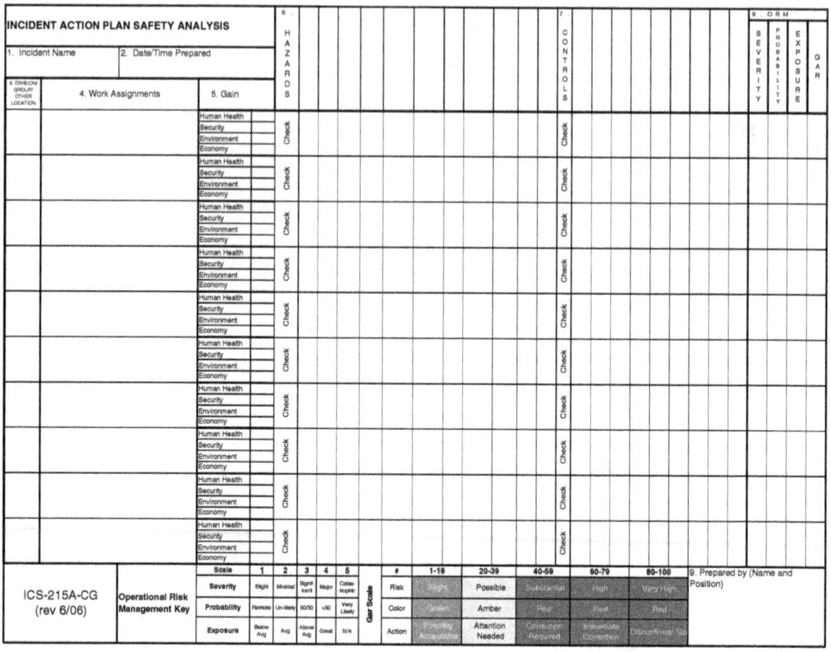

INCIDENT ACTION PLAN SAFETY ANALYSIS

1. Incident Name | 2. Date/Time Prepared

3. DIVISION/GROUP/OTHER LOCATION | 4. Work Assignments | 5. Gain | 6. HAZARDS | 7. CONTROLS | 8. ORM: SEVERITY, PROBABILITY, EXPOSURE, GAR

Human Health / Security / Environment / Economy — Check — Check

Scale	1	2	3	4	5
Severity	Slight	Minimal	Significant	Major	Catastrophic
Probability	Remote	Un-likely	50/50	>50	Very Likely
Exposure	Below Avg	Avg	Above Avg	Great	N/A

Gar Scale

#	1-19	20-39	40-59	60-79	80-100
Risk	Slight	Possible	Substantial	High	Very High
Color	Green	Amber	Red	Red	Red
Action	Possibly Acceptable	Attention Needed	Correction Required	Immediate Correction	Discontinue/ Sto

ICS-215A-CG (rev 6/06) | Operational Risk Management Key | 9. Prepared by (Name and Position)

Figure 8.23 Form ICS-215A-CG: Coast Guard version of the Form 215A. Source: Coast Guard Incident Command System (ICS) [6].

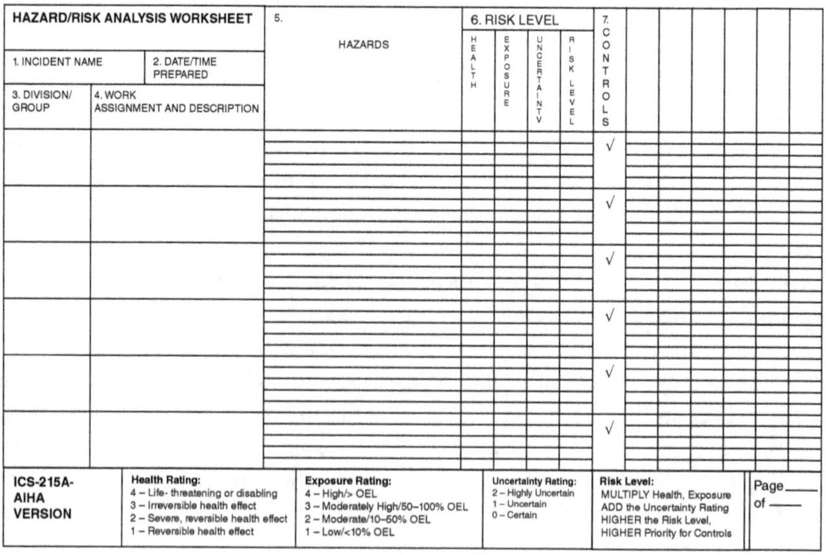

HAZARD/RISK ANALYSIS WORKSHEET

1. INCIDENT NAME | 2. DATE/TIME PREPARED

3. DIVISION/GROUP | 4. WORK ASSIGNMENT AND DESCRIPTION | 5. HAZARDS | 6. RISK LEVEL: HEALTH, EXPOSURE, UNCERTAINTY, RISK LEVEL | 7. CONTROLS

√

ICS-215A-AIHA VERSION

Health Rating:
4 – Life- threatening or disabling
3 – Irreversible health effect
2 – Severe, reversible health effect
1 – Reversible health effect

Exposure Rating:
4 – High/> OEL
3 – Moderately High/50–100% OEL
2 – Moderate/10–50% OEL
1 – Low/<10% OEL

Uncertainty Rating:
2 – Highly Uncertain
1 – Uncertain
0 – Certain

Risk Level:
MULTIPLY Health, Exposure
ADD the Uncertainty Rating
HIGHER the Risk Level,
HIGHER Priority for Controls

Page____ of ____

Figure 8.24 American Industrial Hygiene Association Form 215A. Source: Reproduced with permission of The American Industrial Hygiene Association (AIHA) [7].

GENERAL MESSAGE (ICS 213)

1. Incident Name (Optional):		
2. To (Name and Position):		
3. From (Name and Position):		
4. Subject:	**5. Date:**	**6. Time**
7. Message:		

8. Approved by: Name: _____ Signature: _____ Position/Title: _____

9. Reply:

10. Replied by: Name: _____ Position/Title: _____ Signature: _____

ICS 213   Date/Time: _____

Figure 8.25 FEMA Form ICS 213 Form: General Message. Source: Federal Emergency Management Administration [4].

8.8 The Planning Meeting

The Planning Meeting (Figure 8.26) is led by the Planning Section Chief, who starts the meeting with a situation briefing and an update on resources. The Safety Officer attends.

The Incident Commander starts the meeting with a review of Incident Objectives and any policy issues that must be covered. The Operations Chief follows, and goes over branches and divisions, including boundaries, group work assignments, and strategies. The Planning and Logistic Sections Chief place orders for resources.

Next, the Safety Officer provides an update. This safety update includes a review of any employee accidents, injuries, illnesses, and near misses that have occurred, as well as preventative measures and corrective actions that were taken as a result. The Safety Officer also discusses the top three hazards and safeguards taken for these hazards. Since this is a briefing, and the time allocated to speak is limited, the Safety Officer must be judicious in this discussion to ensure that the most critical information is provided to the Incident Team.

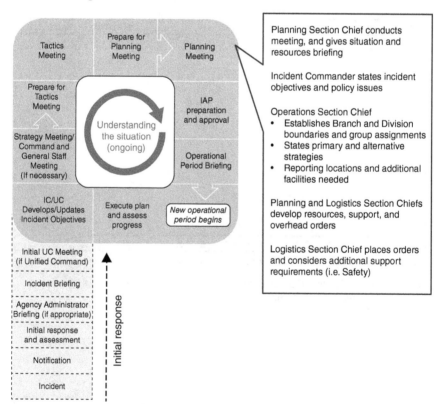

Figure 8.26 The Planning Meeting.

8.9   Development of the Incident Action Plan (IAP)

After the planning meeting, work begins on developing the Incident Action Plan (IAP) for the next Operational Period (Figure 8.27). Sections of the IAP are developed by members of the Incident Management Team, and given to the Planning Section Chief to compile into the final IAP. The Incident Commander decides which forms and documents are included in the IAP. A standard IAP includes:

- An Incident Cover Sheet, with the name of the incident, date and time of the Operational Period that is covered by the IAP, and a photo;
- ICS Form 202, Incident Objectives (Figure 8.10);
- ICS Form 203, Organization Assignment List (Figure 8.28);
- Multiple ICS Form 204s, Division or Group Assignment Lists (Figure 8.29):
  o One form is filled out for each Assignment and included in the IAP;
- ICS Form 205, Incident Communications Plan (Figure 8.30);
- ICS Form 206, Incident Medical Plan (Figure 8.31).

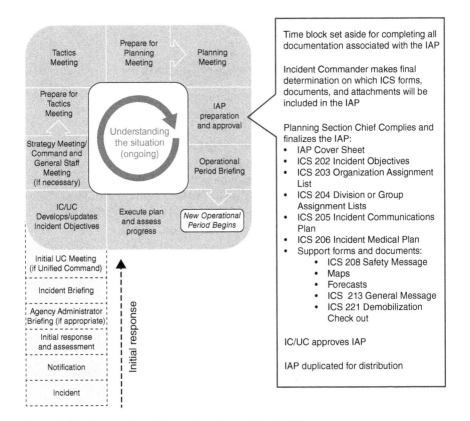

Figure 8.27   Preparation of the Incident Action Plan (IAP).

The Medical Unit Leader, under Logistics, prepares the ICS Form 206, Incident Medical Plan (Figure 8.31). The Safety Officer is responsible for reviewing the ICS Form 206 and signing off on it. The ICS Form 206 focuses on emergency medical procedures to follow in the event that incident personnel are injured or become ill during the response, including location and contact information for medical aid stations, hospitals, and transportation. Attachments can be added to the form. Information on incident stress management, including a description of stress reaction symptoms, how to contact resources for assistance, and stress management techniques, is often added.

The Safety Officer has an opportunity to include additional attachments. Medical monitoring requirements discussed in Chapter 6 should be part of the ICS Form 206, including the process to obtain respirator medical clearances and any other required monitoring. The Form 206 does not include a specific section to add this information, so it should be added as an attachment.

The Incident Commander can decide to include additional forms to the IAP, such as:

- ICS Form 208, Safety Message/Plan (Figure 8.32);
- Maps;
- Weather forecasts;
- ICS Form 213, General Message (Figure 8.25);
- ICS Form 221, Demobilization Check-out (Figure 8.33).

It is notable that the Form 215A is not included in the IAP, nor is the Form 215. However, the Form 215A Safety Analysis contains information that is important for responders to be aware of.

An ICS Form 204 (Figure 8.29) is completed for every Division or Group Assignment identified on the Form 215. This form provides specific instructions for each division or group assigned a work task, and includes resources, contact information, and information on the work assigned. The Safety Officer should make sure that relevant safety information identified in the Form 215A Safety Analysis is transferred to the appropriate 204 forms (there is one 204 form for each "work assignments/Incident Area" line on the Forms 215 and 215A). This information is added to Form 204, Section 7, Special Instructions (Figure 8.34).

Form 204s are kept with each Division or Group assigned a task, and the individual 204 for each Division or Group is reviewed by the Division or Group Supervisor at the beginning of the Operational Period. Inclusion of safety information from the Form 215A Safety Analysis on the Form 204 ensures that this information is reviewed by the Supervisor with all personnel supporting the Work Assignment, and is also available for review by personnel throughout the Operational Period.

ORGANIZATION ASSIGNMENT LIST (ICS 203)

1. Incident Name:		2. Operational Period: Date From: Date To:		
		Time From: Time To:		
3. Incident Commander(s) and Command Staff:		**7. Operations Section:**		
IC/UCs		Chief		
		Deputy		
Deputy		Staging Area		
Safety Officer		**Branch**		
Public Info. Officer		Branch Director		
Liaison Officer		Deputy		
4. Agency/Organization Representatives:		Division/Group		
Agency/Organization	Name	Division/Group		
		Division/Group		
		Division/Group		
		Division/Group		
		Branch		
		Branch Director		
		Deputy		
5. Planning Section:		Division/Group		
Chief		Division/Group		
Deputy		Division/Group		
Resources Unit		Division/Group		
Situation Unit		Division/Group		
Documentation Unit		**Branch**		
Demobilization Unit		Branch Director		
Technical Specialists		Deputy		
		Division/Group		
		Division/Group		
		Division/Group		
6. Logistics Section:		Division/Group		
Chief		Division/Group		
Deputy		**Air Operations Branch**		
Support Branch		Air Ops Branch Dir.		
Director				
Supply Unit				
Facilities Unit		**8. Finance/Administration Section:**		
Ground Support Unit		Chief		
Service Branch		Deputy		
Director		Time Unit		
Communications Unit		Procurement Unit		
Medical Unit		Comp/Claims Unit		
Food Unit		Cost Unit		
9. Prepared by: Name: _____ Position/Title: _____ Signature: _____				
ICS 203	**IAP Page** ____	Date/Time: _____		

Figure 8.28 FEMA Form ICS 203: Organization Assignment List. Source: Federal Emergency Management Administration [4].

ASSIGNMENT LIST (ICS 204)

1. Incident Name:	2. Operational Period: Date From: Date To: Time From: Time To:	3. Branch:

4. Operations Personnel: Name Contact Number(s)	Division:
Operations Section Chief: _____	Group:
Branch Director: _____	Staging Area:
Division/Group Supervisor: _____	

5. Resources Assigned:

Resource Identifier	Leader	# of Persons	Contact (e.g., phone, pager, radio frequency, etc.)	Reporting Location, Special Equipment and Supplies, Remarks, Notes, Information

6. Work Assignments:

7. Special Instructions:

8. Communications (radio and/or phone contact numbers needed for this assignment):

Name/Function	Primary Contact: indicate cell, pager, or radio (frequency/system/channel)
_____ / _____	_____
_____ / _____	_____
_____ / _____	_____
_____ / _____	_____

9. Prepared by: Name: _____ Position/Title: _____ Signature: _____

ICS 204	IAP Page ____	Date/Time: _____

Figure 8.29 FEMA Form ICS 204: Assignment List. Source: Federal Emergency Management Administration [4].

INCIDENT RADIO COMMUNICATIONS PLAN (ICS 205)

1. Incident Name:	2. Date/Time Prepared: Date: Time:	3. Operational Period: Date From: Date To: Time From: Time To:

4. Basic Radio Channel Use:

Zone Grp.	Ch #	Function	Channel Name/Trunked Radio System Talkgroup	Assignment	RX Freq N or W	RX Tone/NAC	TX Freq N or W	TX Tone/NAC	Mode (A, D, or M)	Remarks

5. Special Instructions:

6. Prepared by (Communications Unit Leader): Name: _____	Signature: _____
ICS 205	IAP Page _____	Date/Time: _____

Figure 8.30 FEMA Form ICS 205: Incident Radio Communications Plan. Source: Federal Emergency Management Administration [4].

MEDICAL PLAN (ICS 206)

1. Incident Name:	2. Operational Period: Date From: Date To: Time From: Time To:

3. Medical Aid Stations:

Name	Location	Contact Number(s)/Frequency	Paramedics on Site?
			☐Yes ☐No
			☐Yes ☐No
			☐Yes ☐No
			☐Yes ☐No
			☐Yes ☐No
			☐Yes ☐No

4. Transportation (indicate air or ground):

Ambulance Service	Location	Contact Number(s)/Frequency	Level of Service
			☐ALS ☐BLS
			☐ALS ☐BLS
			☐ALS ☐BLS
			☐ALS ☐BLS

5. Hospitals:

Hospital Name	Address, Latitude & Longitude if Helipad	Contact Number(s)/ Frequency	Travel Time Air	Travel Time Ground	Trauma Center	Burn Center	Helipad
					☐Yes Level:___	☐Yes ☐No	☐Yes ☐No
					☐Yes Level:___	☐Yes ☐No	☐Yes ☐No
					☐Yes Level:___	☐Yes ☐No	☐Yes ☐No
					☐Yes Level:___	☐Yes ☐No	☐Yes ☐No
					☐Yes Level:___	☐Yes ☐No	☐Yes ☐No

6. Special Medical Emergency Procedures:

☐ Check box if aviation assets are utilized for rescue. If assets are used, coordinate with Air Operations.

7. Prepared by (Medical Unit Leader): Name: _____ Signature: _____
8. Approved by (Safety Officer): Name: _____ Signature: _____

ICS 206	IAP Page ____	Date/Time: _____

Figure 8.31 FEMA Form ICS 206: Medical Plan. Source: Federal Emergency Management Administration [4].

SAFETY MESSAGE/PLAN (ICS 208)

1. Incident Name:	2. Operational Period: Date From:	Date To:
	Time From:	Time To:

3. Safety Message/Expanded Safety Message, Safety Plan, Site Safety Plan:

4. Site Safety Plan Required? Yes ☐ No ☐
Approved Site Safety Plan(s) Located At:

5. Prepared by: Name: _____ Position/Title: _____ Signature: _____

| ICS 208 | IAP Page ____ | Date/Time: _____ |

Figure 8.32 FEMA Form ICS 208: Safety Message/Plan. Source: Federal Emergency Management Administration [4].

DEMOBILIZATION CHECK-OUT (ICS 221)

1. Incident Name:		2. Incident Number:	

3. Planned Release Date/Time:	4. Resource or Personnel Released:	5. Order Request Number:
Date: Time:		

6. Resource or Personnel:

You and your resources are in the process of being released. Resources are not released until the checked boxes below have been signed off by the appropriate overhead and the Demobilization Unit Leader (or Planning Section representative).

LOGISTICS SECTION

	Unit/Manager	Remarks	Name	Signature
☐	Supply Unit			
☐	Communications Unit			
☐	Facilities Unit			
☐	Ground Support Unit			
☐	Security Manager			
☐				

FINANCE/ADMINISTRATION SECTION

	Unit/Leader	Remarks	Name	Signature
☐	Time Unit			
☐				
☐				

OTHER SECTION/STAFF

	Unit/Other	Remarks	Name	Signature
☐				
☐				

PLANNING SECTION

	Unit/Leader	Remarks	Name	Signature
☐				
☐	Documentation Leader			
☐	Demobilization Leader			

7. Remarks:

8. Travel Information:

Estimated Time of Departure: _____

Destination: _____

Travel Method: _____

Manifest: ☐ Yes ☐ No
Number: _____

Room Overnight: ☐ Yes ☐ No

Actual Release Date/Time: _____

Estimated Time of Arrival: _____

Contact Information While Traveling: _____

Area/Agency/Region Notified: _____

9. Reassignment Information: ☐ Yes ☐ No

Incident Name: _____

Location: _____

Incident Number: _____

Order Request Number: _____

10. Prepared by: Name: _____   Position/Title: _____   Signature: _____

ICS 221	Date/Time: _____

Figure 8.33 FEMA Form ICS 221: Demobilization Check-Out. Source: Federal Emergency Management Administration [4].

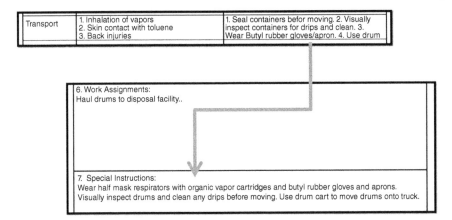

| Transport | 1. Inhalation of vapors
2. Skin contact with toluene
3. Back injuries | 1. Seal containers befor moving. 2. Visually inspect containers for drips and clean. 3. Wear Butyl rubber gloves/apron. 4. Use drum |

6. Work Assignments:
Haul drums to disposal facility..

7. Special Instructions:
Wear half mask respirators with organic vapor cartridges and butyl rubber gloves and aprons. Visually inspect drums and clean any drips before moving. Use drum cart to move drums onto truck.

Figure 8.34 Safety mitigations identified on the ICS Form 215A are transferred to Form 204, Special Instructions, for the work assignment.

8.10 ICS Form 208: Safety Message/Plan

The Safety Officer is responsible for preparing the ICS Form 208, Safety Message/Plan (Figure 8.32) if the Incident Commander decides one needs to be included in the IAP. If the Form 208 is not included, a brief safety message can be inserted into ICS Form 202 (Figure 8.10) under General Situational Awareness. If the nature of the incident is such that more safety information must be communicated than can fit into this box of the Form 202, a Form 208 should be included.

For a short incident, the FEMA Form 208 can serve as the Safety Plan. When an incident is complex, or stretches out over weeks or months, a separate Safety Plan that is more programmatic in nature should be written. Such a plan would go into greater detail about how OSHA requirements are met and how other safety hazards are managed. When a separate, stand-alone Safety Plan has been developed, the Form 208 is used to communicate a daily safety message. A safety message that is included in the IAP is reviewed with all personnel involved in the incident, and so should focus on safety information that is relevant to all personnel. Safety information that is specific to individual work groups should not be included on the Form 208 since work group specific safety information is included on the appropriate Form 204.

If the incident falls within the scope of OSHA's HAZWOPER Standard, 29 CFR 1910.120, a Site Safety and Health Plan must be completed. FEMA has developed an ICS Form 208 HM (Figure 8.35) for use in Hazardous Materials Incidents, and this form can be used to meet this HAZWOPER requirement HAZWOPER.

SITE SAFETY AND CONTROL PLAN ICS 208 HM	1. Incident Name:	2. Date Prepared:	3. Operational Period: Time:

Section I. Site Information			
4. Incident Location:			

Section II. Organization

5. Incident Commander:	6. HM Group Supervisor:	7. Tech. Specialist – HM Reference:
8. Safety Officer:	9. Entry Leader:	10. Site Access Control Leader:
11. Asst. Safety Officer – HM:	12. Decontamination Leader:	13. Safe Refuge Area Mgr:
14. Environmental Health:	15.	16.

17. Entry Team: (Buddy System) Name:	PPE Level	18. Decontamination Element: Name:	PPE Level
Entry 1		Decon 1	
Entry 2		Decon 2	
Entry 3		Decon 3	
Entry 4		Decon 4	

Section III. Hazard/Risk Analysis

19. Material:	Container type	Qty.	Phys. State	pH	IDLH	F.P.	I.T.	V.P.	V.D.	S.G.	LEL	UEL

Comment:

Section IV. Hazard Monitoring

20. LEL Instrument(s):	21. O_2 Instrument(s):
22. Toxicity/PPM Instrument(s):	23. Radiological Instrument(s):

Comment:

Section V. Decontamination Procedures

24. Standard Decontamination Procedures:	YES:	NO:

Comment:

Section VI. Site Communications

25. Command Frequency:	26. Tactical Frequency:	27. Entry Frequency:

Section VII. Medical Assistance

28. Medical Monitoring:	YES:	NO:	29. Medical Treatment and Transport In-place:	YES:	NO:

Comment:

Figure 8.35 FEMA Form ICS 208 HM: Site Safety and Control Plan for work that falls under EPA or OSHA's HAZWOPER requirements. Source: Federal Emergency Management Administration [4].

Section VIII. Site Map

30. Site Map:

Weather ☐   Command Post ☐   Zones ☐   Assembly Areas ☐   Escape Routes ☐   Other ☐

Section IX. Entry Objectives

31. Entry Objectives:

Section X. SOP S and Safe Work Practices

32. Modifications to Documented SOP s or Work Practices: YES: ☐   NO: ☐

Comment:

Section XI. Emergency Procedures

33. Emergency Procedures:

Section XII. Safety Briefing

34. Asst. Safety Officer – HM Signature: Safety Briefing Completed (Time):

35. HM Group Supervisor Signature: 36. Incident Commander Signature:

ICS 208 HM   Page 2   3/98

Figure 8.35   (*Continued*)

The Coast Guard version of the ICS Form 208 (ICS-208-CG) (Figure 8.36) differs from the FEMA ICS 208 in that it functions as a site safety plan only, and is never used simply as a Safety Message. In the Coast Guard system, a Safety Message, if needed, would be written onto an ICS Form 213, General Message, Form.

The ICS-208-CG consists of multiple forms:

- ICS-208-CG-SSP-A: Emergency Safety and Response Plan
- ICS-208-CG-SSP-B: Site Safety Plan
- ICS-208-CG-SSP-C: Site Map
- ICS-208-CG-SSP-D: Emergency Response Plan
- ICS-208-CG-SSP-E: Exposure Monitoring Plan
- ICS-208-CG-SSP-E1: Air Monitoring Log
- ICS-208-CG-SSP-F: Personal Protective Equipment
- ICS-208-CG-SSP-G: Decontamination
- ICS-208-CG-SSP-H: Safety Enforcement Log
- ICS-208-CG-SSP-I: Worker Acknowledgement Form
- ICS-208-CG-SSP-J: Form A Compliance Checklist
- ICS-208-CG-SSP-K: Form B Compliance Checklist
- ICS-208-CG-SSP-L: Drum Compliance Checklist

Form ICS-208-CG-SSP-A (Figure 8.37) includes a checklists of common hazards, PPE for specified tasks, target organs, exposure routes, a site map, and a checklist for decontamination procedures. ICS-208-CG-SSP-B (Figure 8.38) is a hazard analysis, similar to the FEMA Form 215A or a JHA, with a checklist for exposure routes. The ICS-208-CG-SSP-E (Figure 8.39) is an exposure monitoring plan, and includes a place to enter contaminants to be monitored by task, location and time, as well as equipment and sampling materials needed. There is also a section for biological monitoring. ICS-208-CG-SSP-F (Figure 8.40) is for Personal Protective Equipment, and includes the types of PPE to be used, how to inspect PPE, put it on (don) and take it off (doff), and limitations of the PPE including maximum time period of effectiveness. ICS-208-CG-SSP-G (Figure 8.41) is a decontamination plan, and includes a step-by-step procedure to prevent spread of contaminants outside of the response zone. The order of PPE removal is specified, including PPE drop off locations. Boots, hands, faces, or other equipment or body parts may need to be washed at various points between removing and dropping off PPE, and these steps are also included in the specific procedure.

The Coast Guard 208 is tailored toward HAZWOPER compliance and hazards that the Coast Guard typically encounters in their responses. These forms may be useful in certain All-Hazards responses by other agencies or response organizations as well and are available for download from the Coast Guard website.

Site Safety and Health Plan ICS-208-CG (rev 9/06)

Incident Name: _____ **Date/Time Prepared:** _____ **Operational Period:** _____

Purpose. The ICS Compatible Site Safety and Health Plan is designed for safety and health personnel that use the Incident Command System (ICS). It is compatible with ICS and is intended to meet the requirements of the Hazardous Waste Operations and Emergency Response regulation (Title 29, Code of Federal Regulations, Part 1910.120). The plan avoids the duplication found between many other site safety plans and certain ICS forms. It is also in a format familiar to users of ICS. Although primarily designed for oil and chemical spills, the plan can be used for all hazard situations.

Questions on the document should be addressed to the Coast Guard Office of Incident Management and Preparedness (G-RPP).

Table of Forms

FORM NAME	FORM #	USE	REQUIRED	OPTIONAL	ATTACHED
Emergency Safety and Response Plan	A	Emergency response phase (uncontrolled)	X		
Site Safety Plan	B	Post-emergency phase (stabilized, cleanup)	X		
Site Map	C	Post-emergency phase map of site and hazards	X		
Emergency Response Plan	D	Part of Form B, to address emergencies	X		
Exposure Monitoring Plan	E	Exposure monitoring Plan to monitor exposure	X		
Air Monitoring Log	E-1	To log air monitoring data	X*		
Personal Protective Equipment	F	To document PPE equipment and procedures	X*		
Decontamination	G	To document decon equipment and procedures	X*		
Site Safety Enforcement Log	H	To use in enforcing safety on site		X	
Worker Acknowledgement Form	I	To document workers receiving briefings		X	
Form A Compliance Checklist	J	To assist in ensuring HAZWOPER compliance		X	
Form B Compliance Checklist	K	To assist in ensuring HAZWOPER compliance		X	
Drum Compliance Checklist	L	To assistin ensuring HAZWOPER compliance		X	
Other:					

Required only if function or equipment is used during a response

Figure 8.36 Form ICS-208-CG: Coast Guard Site Safety and Health Plan. Source: Coast Guard Incident Command System (ICS) [6].

EMERGENCY SAFETY and RESPONSE PLAN

1. Incident Name	2. Date/Time Prepared	3. Operational Period	4. Attachments: Attach MSDS for each Chemical:

5. Organization IC/UC:
Div/Group Supv:

Safety:	Entry Team:	Backup Team:	Decon Team:

6.a. Physical Hazards and Protection

6.b. ☐ Confined Space ☐ Noise ☐ Heat Stress ☐ Cold Stress ☐ Electrical ☐ Animal/Plant/Insect ☐ Ergonomic ☐ Ionizing Rad
☐ Slips/Trips/Falls ☐ Struck by ☐ Water ☐ Violence ☐ Excavation ☐ Biomedical waste and/or needles ☐ Fatigue ☐ Other (specify)

6.c. Tasks & Controls

6d Entry Permit	6.e. Ventilate	6.f. Hearing Protection	6g. Shoes (type)	6.h. Hard Hats	6.i. Clothing (cold wx)	6.j. Life Jacket	6l. Work/ Rest (hrs)	6.m. Fluids (amt/time)	6.n. Signs & Barricade	6.p. Fall Protect	6.q. Post Guards	6.r. Post Protect	6.s. Work Gloves	6.t. Other

7.a. Agent

7.b. Hazards
☐ Explosive ☐ Flammable ☐ Reactive ☐ Biomedical ☐ Toxic
☐ Radioactive ☐ Carcinogen ☐ Oxidizer ☐ Corrosive ☐ Specify Other:

7.c. Target Organs
☐ Eyes ☐ Nose ☐ Skin ☐ Ears ☐ Central Nervous System
☐ Respiratory ☐ Throat ☐ Lungs ☐ Heart ☐ Liver ☐ Lungs
☐ Kidney ☐ Blood ☐ Circulatory ☐ Gastrointestinal
☐ Bone ☐ Other Specify:

7.d. Exposure Routes
☐ Inhalation ☐ Absorption ☐ Ingestion ☐ Injection ☐ Membrane

7.f. PPE
☐ Face Shield ☐ Eyes ☐ Gloves ☐ Inner Suit ☐ Splash Suit ☐ Level A Suit ☐ SCBA ☐ APR ☐ SAR ☐ Cartridges ☐ Fire Resistance

7.g. Type of PPE

8. Instruments:
☐ O2 ☐ CGI ☐ Radiation ☐ Total HCs ☐ Colorimetric ☐ Thermal ☐ Other

8.a. Action Levels	8.b. Chemical Name(s)	8.c. LEL/UEL %	8.d. Odor Thresh Ppm	8.e. Ceiling/ IDLH	8.f. STEL/TLV	8.g. Flash Pt/ Ignition Pt (F or C)	8.h. Vapor Pressure (mm)	8.i. Vapor Density	8.j. Specific Gravity	8.l. Boiling Pt F or C

ICS-208-CG SSP-A Page 1 (rev 9/06): Page ____ of ____

Figure 8.37 Form ICS-208-CG-SSP-A: Emergency Safety and Response Plan. Source: Coast Guard Incident Command System (ICS) [6].

EMERGENCY SAFETY and RESPONSE PLAN (Cont) | 1. Incident Name | 2. Date/Time Prepared | 3. Operational Period | 4. Attachments: **Attach MSDS for each Chemical**

9. Decontamination:

Instrument Drop Off ☐	Suit Wash ☐
Outer Boots/Glove Removal ☐	Decon Agent: Water ☐
Suit/Gloves/Boot Disposal ☐	Other ☐
	Specify:

Bottle Exchange ☐	SCBA/Mask Rinse ☐
Outer Suit Removal ☐	Inner Glove Removal ☐
Inner Suit Removal ☐	Work Clothes Removal ☐
SCBA/Mask Removal ☐	Body Shower ☐

Intervening Steps ☐ Specify:

10. Site Map. Include: Work Zones, Locations of Hazards, Security Perimeter, Places of Refuge, Decontamination Line, Evacuation Routes, Assembly Point, Direction of North ☐ Attached, ☐ Drawn Below:

11.a. Potential Emergencies:
Fire ☐
Explosion ☐
Other ☐

11.b. Evacuation Alarms:
Horn ☐ # Blasts ☐
Bells ☐ # Rings ☐
Radio Code ☐
Other:

11.c Emergency Prevention and Evacuation Procedures:
Safe Distance:

12. a. Communications
Radio ☐ Phone ☐ Other ☐

12.b. Command #:

12.c. Tactical #:

12.d. Entry #:

13.a. Site Security:
Personnel Assigned

13.b. Procedures:

13.c. Equipment:

14.a. Emergency Medical:
Personnel Assigned

14.b. Procedures:

14.c Equipment:

15. Prepared by:

16. Date/Time Briefed:

**ICS-208-CG SSP-A Page 2.
(rev 9/06):** Page_____ of _____

Figure 8.37 *(Continued)*

CG ICS SITE SAFETY PLAN (SSP) HAZARD ID/EVAL/CONTROL	1. Incident Name	2. Date/Time Prepared	3. Operational Period	4. Safety Officer (include method of contact)
5. Supervisor/Leader	6. Location and Size of Site	7. Site Accessibility Land☐ Water☐ Air ☐ Comments:	8. For Emergencies Contact:	9. Attachments: **Attach MSDS for each Chemical**

10.a. Job Task/Activity	10.b. Hazards*	10.c. Potential Injury & Health Effects	10.d. Exposure Routes	10.e. Controls: Engineering, Administrative, PPE
	⟶		Inhalation ☐ Absorption ☐ Ingestion ☐ Injection ☐ Membrane ☐	
			Inhalation ☐ Absorption ☐ Ingestion ☐ Injection ☐ Membrane ☐	
			Inhalation ☐ Absorption ☐ Ingestion ☐ Injection ☐ Membrane ☐	
			Inhalation ☐ Absorption ☐ Ingestion ☐ Injection ☐ Membrane ☐	
			Inhalation ☐ Absorption ☐ Ingestion ☐ Injection ☐ Membrane ☐	

| 11. Prepared By: | 12. Date/Time Briefed: | *HAZARD LIST: Physical/Safety, Toxic, Explosion/Fire, Oxygen Deficiency, Ionizing Radiation, Biological, Biomedical, Electrical, Heat Stress, Cold Stress, Ergonomic, Noise, Cancer, Dermatitis, Drowning, Fatigue, Vehicle, & Diving | ICS-208-CG SSP-B (rev 9/06): Page ____ of ____ |

Figure 8.38 Form ICS-208-CG-SSP-B: Site Safety Plan Hazard Identification, Evaluation, and Control. Source: Coast Guard Incident Command System (ICS) [6].

CG ICS SSP: Exposure Monitoring Plan	1. Incident Name		2. Date/Time Prepared:	3. Operation al Period:		4. Safety Officer (Method of Contact):			
5. Specific Task/Operation	6. Survey Location	7. Survey Date/Time	8. Monitoring Methodology	9. Direct-Reading Instrument	10. Air Sampling	11. Hazard(s) to Monitor	12. Monitoring Duration	13. Reasons to Monitor	14. Laboratory Support for Analysis
			☐ Personal Breathing Zone ☐ Area Air Monitoring ☐ Dermal Exposure Monitoring ☐ Biological Monitoring: ☐ Blood ☐ Urine ☐ Other ☐ Obtain bulk samples ☐ Other:	Model: Manufacturer: Last Mfr Calibration Date:	Sampling/Analysis Method: Collecting Media: ☐ Charcoal Tube ☐ Silica Gel ☐ 37 mm MCE Filter ☐ 37 mm PVC Filter ☐ Other:________			☐ Regulatory Compliance ☐ Assess current PPE adequacy ☐ Validate engineering controls ☐ Monitor IDLH Conditions ☐ Other________	
			☐ Personal Breathing Zone ☐ Area Air Monitoring ☐ Dermal Exposure Monitoring ☐ Biological Monitoring: ☐ Blood ☐ Urine ☐ Other ☐ Obtain bulk samples ☐ Other:	Model: Manufacturer: Last Mfr Calibration Date:	Sampling/Analysis Method: Collecting Media: ☐ Charcoal Tube ☐ Silica Gel ☐ 37 mmMCE Filter ☐ 37 mmPVC Filter ☐ Other________			☐ Regulatory Compliance ☐ Assess current PPE adequacy ☐ Validate engineering controls ☐ Monitor IDLH Conditions ☐ Other________	
			☐ Personal Breathing Zone ☐ Area Air Monitoring ☐ Dermal Exposure Monitoring ☐ Biological Monitoring: ☐ Blood ☐ Urine ☐ Other ☐ Obtain bulk samples ☐ Other:	Model: Manufacturer: Last Mfr Calibration Date:	Sampling/Analysis Method: Collecting Media: ☐ Charcoal Tube ☐ Silica Gel ☐ 37 mmMCE Filter ☐ 37 mmPVC Filter ☐ Other:________			☐ Regulatory Compliance ☐ Assess current PPE adequacy ☐ Validate engineering controls ☐ Monitor IDLH Conditions ☐ Other________	
			☐ Personal Breathing Zone ☐ Area Air Monitoring ☐ Dermal Exposure Monitoring ☐ Biological Monitoring: ☐ Blood ☐ Urine ☐ Other ☐ Obtain bulk samples ☐ Other:	Model: Manufacturer: Last Mfr Calibration Date:	Sampling/Analysis Method: Collecting Media: ☐ Charcoal Tube ☐ Silica Gel ☐ 37 mmMCE Filter ☐ 37 mmPVC Filter ☐ Other________			☐ Regulatory Compliance ☐ Assess current PPE adequacy ☐ Validate engineering controls ☐ Monitor IDLH Conditions ☐ Other________	
15. Prepared By:			16. Date/Time Briefed:	**HAZARD LIST**: Potential Health Effects: Bruise/Lacerations, Organ Damage, Central Nervous System Effects, Cancer, Reproductive Damage, Low Back Pain, Temporary Hearing Loss, Dermatitis, Respiratory Effects, Bone Breaks, & Eye Burning					
18. Safety Officer Review:			Reporting: Monitoring results shall be logged in the ICS-208-CG SSP-E-1 form (Air Monitoring Log) and attached as partof a current Site Safety Plan and Incident Action Plan. Significant Exposures shall be immediately addressed to the IC and General Staff for immediate correction.					**ICS-208-CG SSP-E (rev 9/06)** Page ____of ____	

Figure 8.39 Form ICS-208-CG-SSP-E: Exposure Monitoring Plan. Source: Coast Guard Incident Command System (ICS) [6].

CG ICS SSP: PERSONAL PROTECTIVE EQUIPMENT	1. Incident Name	2. Date/Time Prepared	3. Operational Period	4. Safety Officer (include method of contact)
5. Supervisor/Leader	6. Location and Size of Site	7. Hazards Addressed:		8. For Emergencies Contact:

9. Equipment:			10. References Consulted:

11. Inspection Procedures:	12. Donning Procedures:	13. Doffing Procedures:	14. Limitations and Precautions (include maximum stay time in PPE):

15. Prepared By:	16. Date/Time Briefed:	Potential Health Effects: Bruise/Lacerations, Organ Damage, Central Nervous System Effects, Cancer, Reproductive Damage, Low Back Pain, Temporary Hearing Loss, Dermatitis, Respiratory Effects, Bone Breaks, Eye Burning	ICS-208-CG SSP-F: (Rev 9/06) Page ____ of ____

Figure 8.40 Form ICS-208-CG-SSP-F: Personal Protective Equipment. Source: Coast Guard Incident Command System (ICS) [6].

Site Safety and Health Plan ICS-208-CG (rev 9/06)

Incident Name: _____   Date/Time Prepared: _____   Operational Period: _____

Purpose. The ICS Compatible Site Safety and Health Plan is designed for safety and health personnel that use the Incident Command System (ICS). It is compatible with ICS and is intended to meet the requirements of the Hazardous Waste Operations and Emergency Response regulation (Title 29, Code of Federal Regulations, Part 1910.120). The plan avoids the duplication found between many other site safety plans and certain ICS forms. It is also in a format familiar to users of ICS. Although primarily designed for oil and chemical spills, the plan can be used for all hazard situations.

Questions on the document should be addressed to the Coast Guard Office of Incident Management and Preparedness (G-RPP).

Table of Forms

FORM NAME	FORM #	USE	REQUIRED	OPTIONAL	ATTACHED
Emergency Safety and Response Plan	A	Emergency response phase (uncontrolled)	X		
Site Safety Plan	B	Post-emergency phase (stabilized, cleanup)	X		
Site Map	C	Post-emergency phase map of site and hazards	X		
Emergency Response Plan	D	Part of Form B, to address emergencies	X		
Exposure Monitoring Plan	E	Exposure monitoring Plan to monitor exposure	X*		
Air Monitoring Log	E-1	To log air monitoring data	X*		
Personal Protective Equipment	F	To document PPE equipment and procedures	X*		
Decontamination	G	To document decon equipment and procedures	X*		
Site Safety Enforcement Log	H	To use in enforcing safety on site		X	
Worker Acknowledgement Form	I	To document workers receiving briefings		X	
Form A Compliance Checklist	J	To assist in ensuring HAZWOPER compliance		X	
Form B Compliance Checklist	K	To assist in ensuring HAZWOPER compliance		X	
Drum Compliance Checklist	L	To assist in ensuring HAZWOPER compliance		X	
Other:					

Required only if function or equipment is used during a response

Figure 8.41   Form ICS-208-CG-SSP-G: Decontamination plan. Source: Coast Guard Incident Command System (ICS) [6].

EMERGENCY SAFETY and RESPONSE PLAN

1. Incident Name	2. Date/Time Prepared	3. Operational Period	4. Attachments: **Attach MSDS for each Chemical:**

5. Organization IC/UC:

Safety:

Div/Group Supv:

Entry Team:

Backup Team:

Decon Team:

6.a. Physical Hazards and Protection

6.b. ☐ Confined Space ☐ Noise ☐ Heat Stress ☐ Cold Stress ☐ Electrical ☐ Animal/Plant/Insect ☐ Ergonomic ☐ Ionizing Rad
☐ Slips/Trips/Falls ☐ Water ☐ Struck by ☐ Violence ☐ Excavation ☐ Biomedical waste and/or needles ☐ Fatigue ☐ Other (specify)

6.c. Tasks & Controls

6d Entry Permit	6.e. Ventilate	6.f. Hearing Protection	6g. Shoes (type)	6.h. Hard Hats	6.i. Clothing (cold wx)	6.j. Life Jacket	6.k. Work/ Rest (hrs)	6.l. Fluids (amt/time)	6.n. Signs & Barricade	6.p. Fall Protect	6.q. Post Guards	6.r. Flash Protect	6.s. Work Gloves	6.t. Other

7.a. Agent

7.b. Hazards
☐ Explosive ☐ Radioactive
☐ Flammable ☐ Carcinogen
☐ Reactive ☐ Oxidizer
☐ Biomedical ☐ Corrosive
☐ Toxic ☐ Specify Other:

7.c. Target Organs
☐ Eyes ☐ Nose ☐ Skin ☐ Ears
☐ Central Nervous System
☐ Respiratory ☐ Throat
☐ Lungs ☐ Heart ☐ Liver
☐ Kidney ☐ Blood ☐ Lungs
☐ Circulatory ☐ Gastrointestinal
☐ Bone ☐ Other Specify:

7.d. Exposure Routes
☐ Inhalation
☐ Absorption
☐ Ingestion
☐ Injection
☐ Membrane

7.f. PPE
☐ Face Shield
☐ Eyes
☐ Gloves
☐ Inner Suit
☐ Splash Suit
☐ Level A Suit
☐ SCBA ☐ APR
☐ SAR
☐ Cartridges
☐ Fire Resistance

7.g. Type of PPE

8. Instruments:
☐ O2
☐ CGI
☐ Radiation
☐ Total HCs
☐ Colorimetric
☐ Thermal
☐ Other

8.a. Action Levels	8.b. Chemical Name(s):	8.c. LEL/UEL %	8.d. Odor Thresh Ppm	8.e. Ceiling/ IDLH	8.f. STEL/TLV	8.g. Flash Pt/ Ignition Pt (F or C)	8.h. Vapor Pressure (mm)	8.i. Vapor Density	8.j. Specific Gravity	8.l. Boiling Pt F or C

ICS-208-CG SSP-A Page 1 (rev 9/06): Page _____ of _____

Figure 8.41 (*Continued*)

EMERGENCY SAFETY and RESPONSE PLAN (Cont)	1. Incident Name	2. Date/Time Prepared	3. Operational Period	4. Attachments: **Attach MSDS for each Chemical**

9. Decontamination:				Intervening Steps ☐Specify:
Instrument Drop Off ☐	Suit Wash ☐	Bottle Exchange ☐	SCBA/Mask Rinse ☐	
Outer Boots/Glove Removal ☐	Decon Agent: Water ☐	Outer Suit Removal ☐	Inner Glove Removal ☐	
Suit/Gloves/Boot Disposal ☐	Other ☐	Inner Suit Removal ☐	Work Clothes Removal ☐	
Specify:		SCBA/Mask Removal ☐	Body Shower ☐	

10. Site Map. Include: Work Zones, Locations of Haza rds, Security Perimeter, Places of Refuge, Decontamination Line, Evacuation Routes, As sembly Point, Direction of North
☐ Attached, ☐ Drawn Below:

11.a. Potential Emergencies:	11.b. Evacuation Alarms:	11.c Emergency Prevention and Evacuation Procedures: Safe Distance:
Fire ☐	Horn ☐ # Blasts ☐	
Explosion ☐	Bells ☐ #Rings ☐	
Other ☐	Radio Code ☐	
	Other:	

12. a. Communications: Radio ☐ Phone ☐ Other ☐	12.b. Command #:	12.c. Tactical #:	12.d. Entry #:
13.a. Site Security: Personnel Assigned	13.b. Procedures:		13.c. Equipment:
14.a. Emergency Medical: Personnel Assigned	14.b. Procedures:		14.c Equipment:
15. Prepared by:	16. Date/Time Briefed:		**ICS-208-CG SSP-A Page 2.** **(rev 9/06):** Page _____ of _____

Figure 8.41   (*Continued*)

EMERGENCY SAFETY AND RESPONSE PLAN (ICS-208-CG SSP-A)

Purpose: The Emergency Safety and Response Plan provides the Safety Officer and ICS personnel a plan for safeguarding personnel during the initial emergency phase of the response. *It is only used during the emergency phase of the response, which is defined as a situation involving an uncontrolled release.* It is also intended to meet the requirements of the Hazardous Waste Operations and Emergency Response (HAZWOPER) regulation, Title 29 Code of Federal Regulations Part 1910.120.

Preparation: The Safety Officer or his/her designated staff starts the Emergency Site Safety and Response Plan. They initially address the hazards common to all operations involved in the response (initial site characterization). Outside support organizations must be contacted to ensure the plan is consistent with other plans (local, state, other federal plans). Form ICS-208-CG SSP-G need not be completed if this form is used. When the operation proceeds into the post-emergency phase (site stabilized and cleanup operations begun) forms ICS-208-CG SSP-B and ICS-208-CG SSP-G should be used. For large incidents, the Emergency Site Safety and Response Plan complements the Incident Action Plan. For smaller incidents, the Emergency Site Safety and Response Plan complements ICS-201.

Distribution: The Emergency Safety and Response Plan completed by the Safety Officer is forwarded to the Planning Section Chief. Copies are made and attached to the Assignment List(s) (ICS Form 204). The Operations Section Chief, Directors, Supervisors or Leaders get a copy of the plan. They must ensure it is available on site for all personnel to review. The Safety Officer is responsible for ensuring that the Emergency Site Safety and Response Plan properly addresses the hazards of the operation. The Safety Officer accomplishes this through on site enforcement and feedback to the operational units.

Instructions:

Item #	Item Title	Instructions
1	Incident Name	Print the name assigned to the incident.
2	Date/Time Prepared	Enter date (month, day, year) prepared.
3	Operational Period	Enter the time interval for which the assignment applies.
4	Attachments	Enter attachments. Material Safety Data Sheets are mandatory under 1910.120. Safe Work Practices maya also be attached.
5	Organization	List the personnel responsible for these positions. IC and Safety Officer are mandatory.
6	Physical Hazards & Protection	Check off the physical hazards at the site. Identify the major tasks involved in the response (skimming, lightering, overpacking, etc.). Check off the controls that would be used to safeguard workers from the physical hazards for each major task.
7	Chemical/Agent	List the chemicals involved in the response. Chemicals may be listed numerically. Check off the hazards, potential health effects, pathway of dispersion, and exposure route of the chemical. Numbers corresponding to the chemical may be entered into the check blocks to differentiate. Check off the PPE to be used. Identify the type of PPE selected (for example: gloves: butyl rubber).
8	Instruments	Indicate the instruments being used for monitoring. List the action levels adjacent to the instruments being used. Identify the chemicals being monitored (2). List the physical parameters of the chemicals. Use a separate form for additional chemicals monitored.

Figure 8.41 (*Continued*)

EMERGENCY SAFETY AND RESPONSE PLAN (FORM ICS-208-CG SSP-A) (Instructions Continued)

9	Decontamination	Check off the decontamination steps to be used. Numbers may be entered to indicate the preferred sequence. Identify any intervening steps necessary on the form or in a separate attachment.
10	Site Map	Draw a rough site map. Ensure all the information listed is identified on the map.
11	Potential Emergencies	Identify any potential emergencies that may occur. If none, so state. Check off the appropriate alarms that may be used. Identify emergency prevention and evacuation procedures in the space provided or on a separate attached sheet.
12	Communications	Indicate type of site communications (phone, radio). Indicate phone numbers or frequencies for the command, tactical and entry functions.
13	Site Security	Identify the personnel assigned. Identify security procedures in the space provided or on a separate attached sheet. Identify the equipment needed to support security operations.
14.	Emergency Medical	Identify the personnel assigned. Identify emergency medical procedures in the space provided or on a separate attached sheet. Identify the equipment needed to support security operations.
15.	Prepared by:	Enter the name and position of the person completing the worksheet.
16.	Date/time briefed:	Enter the date/time the document was briefed to the appropriate workers and by whom.

Figure 8.41 (*Continued*)

CG ICS SITE SAFETY PLAN (SSP) HAZARD ID/EVAL/CONTROL	1. Incident Name	2. Date/Time Prepared	3. Operational Period	4. Safety Officer (include method of contact)
5. Supervisor/Leader	6. Location and Size of Site	7. Site Accessibility Land ☐ Water ☐ Air ☐ Comments:	8. For Emergencies Contact:	9. Attachments: **Attach MSDS for each Chemical**
10.a. Job Task/Activity	10.b. Hazards* ⟹	10.c. Potential Injury & Health Effects	10.d. Exposure Routes	10.e. Controls: Engineering, Administrative, PPE
			☐☐☐☐☐☐☐ Inhalation Absorption Ingestion Injection Membrane	
			☐☐☐☐☐☐☐ Inhalation Absorption Ingestion Injection Membrane	
			☐☐☐☐☐☐☐ Inhalation Absorption Ingestion Injection Membrane	
			☐☐☐☐☐☐☐ Inhalation Absorption Ingestion Injection Membrane	
			☐☐☐☐☐☐☐ Inhalation Absorption Ingestion Injection Membrane	
11. Prepared By:	12. Date/Time Briefed:	***HAZARD LIST**: Physical/Safety, Toxic, Explosion/Fire, Oxygen Deficiency, Ionizing Radiation, Biological, Biomedical, Electrical, Heat Stress, Cold Stress, Ergonomic, Noise, Cancer, Dermatitis, Drowning, Fatigue, Vehicle, & Diving		**ICS-208-CG SSP-B (rev 9/06):** Page_____ of_____

Figure 8.41 (*Continued*)

SITE SAFETY PLAN (FORM ICS-208-CG SSP-B)

Purpose: The Site Safety Plan provides the Safety Officer and ICS personnel a plan for safeguarding personnel during the post-emergencyphase of an incident. The post-emergency phase is when the situation is stabilized and cleanup operations have begun. ICS-208-CG SSP-B is intended to meet the requirements of the Hazardous Waste Operations and Emergency Response (HAZWOPER) regulation, Title 29 Code of Federal Regulations Part 1910.120.

Preparation: The SafetyOfficer or his/her designated staff starts the Site Safety Plan. They initially address the hazards common to all operations involved in the response (initial site characterization). The plan is then reproduced and as a minimum sent to ICS Group/Division Supervisors. They amend it according to unique job oron-scene hazards with support from the Safety Officer and/or his/her staff (detailed site characterization). The plan is continuouslyupdated to address changing conditions. During the first hours of the response, where most response functions are in the emergencyphase, the Safety Officer may chose to use the Emergency Safetyand Response Plan (ICS-208-CG SSP-A) in place of the Site SafetyPlan. For large incidents, ICS-208-CG SSP-B compliments the Incident Action Plan (IAP). For smaller incidents, ICS-208-CG SSP-B compliments ICS Form 201. The Safety Officer is encouraged to use the HAZWOPER Compliance Checklist (Form ICS-208-CG SSP-K) to ensure the IAP and the 201 address the requirements and all other pertinent ICS forms (203, 205, 206, etc.) are completed.

Distribution: The initial Site Safety Plan completed by the SafetyOfficer is forwarded to the Planning Section Chief. Copies are made and attached to the Assignment List(s) (ICS Form 204). The Operations Section Chief, Directors, Supervisors or Leaders get a copy and make on site amendments specific to their operation. They must also ensure it is available on site for all personnel to review. The Safety Officer provides personnel from his/her staff to assist in the detailed site characterization. The Safety Officer is responsible for ensuring that the Site Safety Plan for each assignment properly addresses the hazards of the assignment. The Safety Officer must ensure that the safety plans on site are consistent. The Safety Officer accomplishes this through on site enforcement and feedback to the operational units.

Instructions:

Item #	Item Title	Instructions
1	Incident Name	Print the name assigned to the incident.
2	Date/Time Prepared	Enter date (month, day, year) prepared.
3	Operational Period	Enter the time interval for which the assignment applies.
4	Safety Officer	Enter the name of the Safety Officer and means of contact.
5	Group/DivisionSupv Strike Team/TF Leader	The Supervisor/Leader who receives this form will enter their name here.
6	Location & size of site	Enter the geographical location of the site and the approximate square area.
7	Site Accessibility	Check the block(s) if the site is accessible by land, water, air, etc.
8	For Emergencies Contact	Enter the name and way to contact the individual who handles emergencies.
9	Attachments	Enter attachments. Material Safety Data Sheets are mandatory under 1910.120. Safe Work Practices may also be attached.
10	Job/Task Activity	Enter Job/Task & Activities, list hazards, list potential injury and health effects, check exposure routes and identify controls. If more detail is needed for controls, provided attachments.
11	Prepared by	Enter the name and position of the person completing the worksheet.
12	Date/Time Briefed:	Enter the date/time the document was briefed to the appropriate workers and by whom.

Figure 8.41 (*Continued*)

CG ICS SSP: SITE MAP	1. Incident Name	2. Date/Time Prepared	3. Operational Period	4. Safety Officer (include method of contact)	
5. Supervisor/Leader	6. Location and Size of Site	7. Site Accessibility Land ☐ Water ☐ Air ☐ Comments:	8. For Emergencies Contact:	9. Include - Work Zones - Security Perimeter - Decontamination Line	- Locations of Hazards - Places of Refuge - Evacuation Routes

10. Sketch of Site:
☐ Attached. ☐ Drawn Here

11. Prepared By:	12. Date/Time Briefed:	HAZARD LIST: Physical/Safety, Toxic, Explosion/Fire, Oxygen Deficiency, Ionizing Radiation, Biological, Biomedical, Electrical, Heat Stress, Cold Stress, Ergonomic, Noise, Cancer, Dermatitis, Drowning, Fatigue, Vehicle, & Diving	ICS-208-CG SSP-C (rev 9/06): Page_____ of _____

Figure 8.41 *(Continued)*

SITE MAP FOR SITE SAFETY PLAN (ICS-208-CG SSP-C)

Purpose: The Site Map for the Site Safety Plan is required by Title 29 Code of Federal Regulations Part 1910.120. It provides in 1 place a visual description of the site which can help ICS personnel locate hazards, identify evacuation routes and places of refuge.

Preparation: The Site Map for the Site Safety Plan can be completed by the Safety Officer, his/her staff or by ICS field personnel (Group Supervisors, Task Force/Strike Team Leaders) working at a site with unique and specific hazards. One or several maps may be developed, depending on the size of the incident and the uniqueness of the hazards. The key is to ensure that the workers using the map(s) can clearly identify the work zones, locations of hazards, evacuation routes and places of refuge.

Distribution: This form must be located with the Site Safety Plan (ICS-208-CG SSP-B). It therefore follows the same distribution route.

Instructions:

Item #	Item Title	Instructions
1	Incident Name	Print the name assigned to the incident.
2	Date/Time Prepared	Enter date (month, day, year) prepared.
3	Operational Period	Enter the time interval for which the assignment applies.
4	Safety Officer	Enter the name of the Safety Officer and means of contact.
5	Supervisor/Leader	The Supervisor/Leader who receives this form will enter their name here.
6	Location & size of site	Enter the geographical location of the site and the approximate square area.
7	Site Accessibility	Check the block(s) if the site is accessible by land, water, air, etc.
8	For Emergencies Contact	Enter the name and way to contact the individual who handles emergencies.
9	Include	Ensure the map includes the listed items provided in this block.
10	Sketch of Site	Sketch of site for work. May attach map or chart.
10	Prepared by	Enter the name and position of the person completing the worksheet.
11	Date/Time Briefed:	Enter the date/time the document was briefed to the appropriate workers and by whom.

Figure 8.41 *(Continued)*

CG ICS SSP: EMERGENCY RESPONSE PLAN	1. Incident Name	2. Date/Time Prepared	3. Operational Period	4. Safety Officer (include method of contact)
5. Supervisor/Leader	6. Location and Size of Site	7. For Emergencies Contact:		8. Attachments: **INCLUDE ICS FORM 206 and EMT Medical Response Procedures**

9. Emergency Alarm (sound and location)	10. Backup Alarm (sound and location)	11. Emergency Hand Signals	12. Emergency Personal Protective Equipment Required:

13. Emergency Notification Procedures	14. Places of Refuge (also see site map form 208B)	15. Emergency Decon and Evacuation Steps	16. Site Security Measures

17. Prepared By:	18. Date/Time Briefed:	**HAZARD LIST**: Physical/Safety, Toxic, Explosion/Fire, Oxygen Deficiency, Ionizing Radiation, Biological, Biomedical, Electrical, Heat Stress, Cold Stress, Ergonomic, Noise, Cancer, Dermatitis, Drowning, Fatigue, Vehicle, & Diving	**ICS-208-CG SSP-D (rev 9/06)** Page_____ of _____

Figure 8.41 (*Continued*)

EMERGENCY RESPONSE PLAN (ICS-208-CG SSP-D)

Purpose: The Emergency Response Plan provides information on measures to be taken in the event of an emergency. It is used in conjunction with the Site Safety Plan (Form ICS-208-CGSSP-B). It is also required by Title 29 Code of Federal Regulations Part 1910.120.

Preparation: The Safety Officer, his/her staff member or the Site Supervisor/Leader prepares the Emergency Response Plan. A copy of the Medical Plan (ICS Form 206) must always be attached to this form.

Distribution: This form must be located with Site Safety Plan (ICS-208-CG SSP-B). It therefore follows the same distribution route.

Instructions:

Item #	Item Title	Instructions
1	Incident Name	Print the name assigned to the incident.
2	Date/Time Prepared	Enter date (month, day, year) prepared.
3	Operational Period	Enter the time interval for which the assignment applies.
4	Safety Officer	Enter the name of the Safety Officer and means of contact.
5	Supervisor/Leader	The Supervisor/Leader who receives this form will enter their name here.
6	Location & size of site	Enter the geographical location of the site and the approximate square area.
7	For Emergencies Contact	Enter the name and way to contact the individual who handles emergencies.
8	Attachments	Enter attachments. ICS Form 206 must be included.
9	Emergency Alarm	Enter a description of the sound of the emergency alarm and it's location.
10	Backup Alarm	Enter a description of the sound of the emergency alarm and it's location.
11	Emergency Hand Signals	Enter the emergency hand signals to be used.
12	Emergency Personal Protective Equipment Required	Enter the emergency personal protective equipment that may be needed in the event of an emergency.
13	Emergency Notification Procedures	Enter the procedures for notifying the appropriate personnel and organizations in the event of an emergency.
14	Places of Refuge	Enter by name the place of refuge personnel can go to in the event of an emergency.
15	Emergency Decon & Evacuation Steps	Enter emergency decontamination steps and evacuation procedures.
16	Site Security Measures	Enter site security measures needed for emergencies.
17	Prepared by	Enter the name and position of the person completing the worksheet.
18	Date/Time Briefed:	Enter the date/time the document was briefed to the appropriate workers and by whom.

Figure 8.41 (*Continued*)

CG ICS SSP: Exposure Monitoring Plan

1. Incident Name	2. Date/Time Prepared:	3. Operational Period:	4. Safety Officer (Method of Contact):		

5. Specific Task/Operation	6. Survey Location	7. Survey Date/Time	8. Monitoring Methodology	9. Direct-Reading Instrument	10. Air Sampling	11. Hazard(s) to Monitor	12. Monitoring Duration	13. Reasons to Monitor	14. Laboratory Support for Analysis
			☐ Personal Breathing Zone ☐ Area Air Monitoring ☐ Dermal Exposure Monitoring Biological Monitoring: ☐ Blood ☐ Urine ☐ Other ☐ Obtain bulk samples ☐ Other:	Model: Manufactur er: Last Mfr Calibr ation Dat e:	Sampling/Analysis Method: Collecting Media: ☐ Charcoal Tube ☐ Silica Gel ☐ 37 mm MCE Filter ☐ 37 mm PVC Filter ☐ Other.			☐ Regulatory Compliance ☐ Assess current PPE adequacy ☐ Validate engineering controls ☐ Monitor IDLH Conditions ☐ Other	
			☐ Personal Breathing Zone ☐ Area Air Monitoring ☐ Dermal Exposure Monitoring Biological Monitoring: ☐ Blood ☐ Urine ☐ Other ☐ Obtain bulk samples ☐ Other:	Model: Manufactur er: Last Mfr Calibr ation Date:	Sampling/Analysis Method: Collecting Media: ☐ Charcoal Tube ☐ Silica Gel ☐ 37 mm MCE Filter ☐ 37 mm PVC Filter ☐ Other.			☐ Regulatory Compliance ☐ Assess current PPE adequacy ☐ Validate engineering controls ☐ Monitor IDLH Conditions ☐ Other	
			☐ Personal Breathing Zone ☐ Area Air Monitoring ☐ Dermal Exposure Monitoring Biological Monitoring: ☐ Blood ☐ Urine ☐ Other ☐ Obtain bulk samples ☐ Other:	Model: Manufactur er: Last Mfr Calibration Date :	Sampling/Analysis Method: Collecting Media: ☐ Charcoal Tube ☐ Silica Gel ☐ 37 mm MCE Filter ☐ 37 mm PVC Filter ☐ Other.			☐ Regulatory Compliance ☐ Assess current PPE adequacy ☐ Validate engineering controls ☐ Monitor IDLH Conditions ☐ Other	
			☐ Personal Breathing Zone ☐ Area Air Monitoring ☐ Dermal Exposure Monitoring Biological Monitoring: ☐ Blood ☐ Urine ☐ Other ☐ Obtain bulk samples ☐ Other:	Model: Manufactur er: Last Mfr Calibr ation Dat e:	Sampling/Analysis Method: Collecting Media: ☐ Charcoal Tube ☐ Silica Gel ☐ 37 mm MCE Filter ☐ 37 mm PVC Filter ☐ Other.			☐ Regulatory Compliance ☐ Assess current PPE adequacy ☐ Validate engineering controls ☐ Monitor IDLH Conditions ☐ Other	

15. Prepared By:	16. Date/Time Briefed:	**HAZARD LIST:** Potential Health Effects: Bruise/Lacerations, Organ Damage, Central Nervous System Effects, Cancer, Reproductive Damage, Low Back Pain, Temporary Hearing Loss, Dermatitis, Respiratory Effects, Bone Breaks, & Eye Burning
18. Safety Officer Review:	Reporting: Monitoring results shall be logged in the ICS-208-CG SSP-E-1 form (Air Monitoring Log) and attached as part of a current Site Safety Plan and Incident Action Plan. Significant Exposures shall be immediately addressed to the IC and General Staff for immediate correction.	**ICS-208-CG SSP-E (rev 9/06)** Page ___ of ___

Figure 8.41 (*Continued*)

EXPOSURE MONITORING PLAN (FORM ICS-208-CG SSP-E)

Purpose: The Exposure Monitoring Plan provides plan of monitoring conducted during an incident. The plan is a supplement to the Site Safety Plan (ICS-208-CG SSP-B). It is only required when performing monitoring operations.

Preparation: The Safety Officer, his/her staff member or the Site Supervisor/Leader prepares the Exposure Monitoring Plan. If there is a decision not to monitor during a response, the reasons must be stated clearly in the Site Safety Plan (ICS-208-CG SSP-B).

Distribution: This form must be located with Site Safety Plan (ICS-208-CG SSP-B). It therefore follows the same distribution route.

Instructions:

Item #	Item Title	Instructions
1	Incident Name	Print the name assigned to the incident.
2	Date/Time Prepared	Enter date (month, day, year) prepared.
3	Operational Period	Enter the time interval for which the assignment applies.
4	Safety Officer	Enter the name of the Safety Officer and means of contact.
5	Specific Task / Operation	Enter specific task or operation.
6	Survey Location	Enter the location to be monitored.
7	Survey Date/Time	Enter the date/time for the monitoring teams to survey.
8	Monitoring Methodology	Enter/Check the monitoring method to be used.
9	Direct-Reading Instrument	Enter the instrument model, manufacturer, last calibration date.
10	Air Sampling	Enter Air Sampling analysis method
11	Hazards to Monitor	Enter the hazards to monitor
12	Monitoring Duration	Enter duration of monitoring
13	Reasons to Monitor	Enter Reasons to Monitor
14	Laboratory Support for Analysis	Enter Laboratory Support needed for analysis of samples
15	Prepared by	Enter the name and position of the person completing the worksheet.
16	Date/Time Briefed	Enter the date/time the document was briefed to the appropriate workers and by whom.
17	Safety Officer Review	The Safety Officer must review and sign the form.

Figure 8.41 (*Continued*)

CG ICS SSP: AIR MONITORING LOG

CG ICS SSP: AIR MONITORING LOG	1. Incident Name	2. Date/Time Prepared	3. Operational Period	4. Safety Officer (include method of contact)
5. Site Location	6. Hazards of Concern	7. Action Levels (include references):		8. Weather: Temperature: Wind: Relative Humidity: Cloud Cover: Precipitation:

9.a. Instrument, ID Number Calibrated? Indicate below.	9.b. Monitoring Person Name(s)	9.c. Results (units)	9.d. Location	9.f. Time	9.g. Interferences and Comments

10. Safety Officer Review:	Potential Health Effects: Bruise/Lacerations, Organ Damage, Central Nervous System Effects, Cancer, Reproductive Damage, Low Back Pain, Temporary Hearing Loss, Dermatitis, Respiratory Effects, Bone Breaks, & Eye Burning	ICS-208-CG SSP-E-1 (rev 9/06): Page ____ of ____

Figure 8.41 (*Continued*)

DAILY AIR MONITORING LOG (FORM ICS-208-CG SSP-E-1)

Purpose: The Exposure Monitoring Log provides documentation of air monitoring conducted during a spill. The log is a supplement to the Site Safety Plan (ICS-208-CG SSP-B). It is only required when performing air monitoring operations. The information used from the log can help update the Site Safety Plan.

Preparation: Persons conducting monitoring complete the Daily Air Monitoring Log. Normally these are air monitoring units under the Site Safety Officer. If there is a decision not to monitor during a spill, the reasons must be stated clearly in the Site Safety Plan (ICS-208-CG SSP-B).

Distribution: The Daily Air Monitoring Log when completed is copied and forwarded to the Site Safety Officer who must review and sign the form. The original form must be available on site, readily available and briefed to all impacted ICS personnel.

Instructions:

Item #	Item Title	Instructions
1	Incident Name	Print the name assigned to the incident.
2	Date/Time Prepared	Enter date (month, day, year) prepared.
3	Operational Period	Enter the time interval for which the assignment applies.
4	Safety Officer	Enter the name of the Safety Officer and means of contact.
5	Location & size of site	Enter the geographical location of the site and the approximate square area.
6	Hazards of Concern	Enter the hazards being monitored.
7	Action Levels	Enter the action levels/readings for the monitoring teams.
8	Weather	Enter weather information. Ensure units of measure are listed.
9	Air Monitoring Data	Enter the instrument type and number, persons monitoring, results with appropriate units, location of reading, time of reading and interferences and comments.
10	Safety Officer Review	The Safety Officer must review and sign the form.

Figure 8.41 (*Continued*)

CG ICS SSP: PERSONAL PROTECTIVE EQUIPMENT	1. Incident Name	2. Date/Time Prepared	3. Operational Period	4. Safety Officer (include method of contact)

5. Supervisor/Leader	6. Location and Size of Site	7. Hazards Addressed:	8. For Emergencies Contact:

9. Equipment:			10. References Consulted:

11. Inspection Procedures:	12. Donning Procedures:	13. Doffing Procedures:	14. Limitations and Precautions (include maximum stay time in PPE):

15. Prepared By:	16. Date/Time Briefed:	Potential Health Effects: Bruise/Lacerations, Organ Damage, Central Nervous System Effects, Cancer, Reproductive Damage, Low Back Pain, Temporary Hearing Loss, Dermatitis, Respiratory Effects, Bone Breaks, Eye Burning	**ICS-208-CG SSP-F: (Rev 9/06)** Page ____ of ____

Figure 8.41 (*Continued*)

PERSONAL PROTECTIVE EQUIPMENT (ICS-208-CG SSP-F)

Purpose: The Personal Protective Equipment form is a list of personal protective equipment to be used in operations. The listing of personal protective equipment is required by Title 29 Code of Federal Regulations Part 1910.120.

Preparation: The Personal Protective Equipment form is completed by the Site Safety Officer, or his/her staff. Personal protective equipment common to all ICS Operations personnel is addressed first. Jobs with unique personal protective equipment requirements (fall protection) are addressed next. When the form is delivered on site, the ICS Director, Supervisor, or Leader may amend the list to ensure personnel are adequately protected from job hazards. It must be completed prior to the onset of any operations, unless addressed elsewhere by Standard Operating Procedures.

Distribution: This form must be located with Site Safety Plan (ICS-208-CG SSP-B). It therefore follows the same distribution route.

Instructions:

Item #	Item Title	Instructions
1	Incident Name	Print the name assigned to the incident.
2	Date/Time Prepared	Enter date (month, day, year) prepared.
3	Operational Period	Enter the time interval for which the assignment applies.
4	Safety Officer	Enter the name of the Safety Officer and means of contact.
5	Supervisor/Leader	The Supervisor/Leader who receives this form will enter their name here.
6	Location & size of site	Enter the geographical location of the site and the approximate square area.
7	Hazard(s) Addressed:	Enter the hazards that need to be safeguarded.
8	For Emergencies Contact	Enter the name and way to contact the individual who handles emergencies.
9	Equipment	List the equipment needed to address the hazards. If pre-designed Safe Work Practices are used, indicate here and attach to form.
10	References consulted	List the references used in making the selection for PPE.
11	Inspection Procedures	Enter the procedures for inspecting the Personal Protective Equipment prior to donning. If pre-designed Safe Work Practices are used, indicate here and attach to form.
12	Donning Procedures	Enter the procedures for putting on the PPE. If pre-designed Safe Work Practices are used, indicate here and attach to form.
13	Doffing Procedures	Enter the information for removing the PPE. If pre-designed Safe Work Practices are used, indicate here and attach to form.
14	Limitations and Precautions	List the limitations and precautions when using PPE. Include the maximum time to be inside the PPE, Heat Stress concerns, psychomotor skill detraction and other factors.
15	Prepared by	Enter the name and position of the person completing the worksheet.
16	Date/Time Briefed:	Enter the date/time the document was briefed to the appropriate workers and by whom.

Figure 8.41 *(Continued)*

CG ICS SSP: DECONTAMINATION	1. Incident Name	2. Date/Time Prepared	3. Operational Period	4. Safety Officer (include method of contact)
5. Supervisor/Leader	6. Location and Size of Site	7. For Emergencies Contact:		8. Hazard(s) Addressed:
9. Equipment:				10. References Consulted:
11. Contamination Avoidance Practices:	12. Decon Diagram: ☐ Attached, ☐ Drawn below			13. Decon Steps
14. Prepared By:	15. Date/Time Briefed:		Potential Health Effects: Bruise/Lacerations, Organ Damage, Central Nervous System Effects, Cancer, Reproductive Damage, Low Back Pain, Temporary Hearing Loss, Dermatitis, Respiratory Effects, Bone Breaks, Eye Burning	ICS-208-CG SSP-G (rev 9/06): Page ___ of ___

Figure 8.41 (*Continued*)

DECONTAMINATION (ICS-208-CG SSP-G)

Purpose: The Decontamination form provides information on how workers can avoid contamination and how to get decontaminated. It is a supplemental form to the Site Safety Plan.

Preparation: The Decontamination Form can be completed by the Site Safety Officer, a member of his/her staff or by the Group/Division Supervisor, Task Force/Strike Team Leader on the site

Distribution: This form must be located with Site Safety Plan (ICS-208-CG SSP-B). It therefore follows the same distribution route.

Instructions:

Item #	Item Title	Instructions
1	Incident Name	Print the name assigned to the incident.
2	Date/Time Prepared	Enter date (month, day, year) prepared.
3	Operational Period	Enter the time interval for which the assignment applies.
4	Safety Officer	Enter the name of the Safety Officer and means of contact.
5	Supervisor/Leader	The Supervisor/Leader who receives this form will enter their name here.
6	Location & size of site	Enter the geographical location of the site and the approximate square area.
7	ForEmergencies Contact	Enter the name and way to contact the individual who handles emergencies.
8	Hazard(s) Addressed:	Enter the hazards that need to be safeguarded.
9	Equipment	Enter the decontamination equipment needed for the site. If pre-designed Safe Work Practices are used, indicate here and attach to this form.
10	References consulted	List the references used in making the selection for PPE.
11	Contamination Avoidance Practices	Enter procedures for personnel to avoid contamination. If pre-designed Safe Work Practices are used, indicate here and attach to form.
12	Decon Diagram	Draw a diagram for the decontamination operation. If pre-designed Safe Work Practices are used, indicate here and attach to form.
13	Decon Steps	List the decontamination steps.
14	Prepared by	Enter the name and position of the person completing the worksheet.
15	Date/Time Briefed:	Enter the date/time the document was briefed to the appropriate workers and by whom.

Figure 8.41 (*Continued*)

CG ICS SSP: ENFORCEMENT LOG	1. Incident Name	2. Date/Time Prepared	3. Operational Period	4. Safety Officer (include method of contact)		
5. Supervisor/Leader	6. For Emergencies Contact:			7. Attachments:		
8.a. Job Task/Activity	8.b. Hazards	8.c. Deficiency	8.d. Action Taken	8.e. Safety Plan Amended?	8.f. Signature of Supervisor/Leader
9. Prepared By:	10. Date/Time Briefed:		HAZARD LIST: Physical/Safety, Toxic, Explosion/Fire, Oxygen Deficiency, Ionizing Radiation, Biological, Biomedical, Electrical, Heat Stress, Cold Stress, Ergonomic, Noise, Cancer, Dermatitis, Drowning, Fatigue, Vehicle, & Diving		**ICS-208-CG SSP-H (rev 9/06):** Page____ of____

Figure 8.41 (*Continued*)

SITE SAFETY ENFORCEMENT LOG (ICS-208-CG SSP-H)

Purpose: The Site Safety Plan Enforcement Log is used to help enforce safety during an incident.

Preparation: The Safety Officer and/or his/her staff complete the Site Safety Plan Enforcement Log. The log is completed as Safety personnel are on scene reviewing the site. It should be completed at a minimum once per day. The number of enforcement logs to be completed depends on the size of the incident. Enough should be completed to ensure that site safety is being adequately enforced.

Distribution: The Site Safety Plan enforcement log when completed is delivered to the Safety Officer. The Safety Officer can use the form to amend the Site Safety Plan (ICS-208-CG SSP-A or B).

Instructions:

Item #	Item Title	Instructions
1	Incident Name	Print the name assigned to the incident.
2	Date/Time Prepared	Enter date (month, day, year) prepared.
3	Operational Period	Enter the time interval for which the assignment applies.
4	Safety Officer	Enter the name of the Safety Officer and means of contact
5	Supervisor/Leader	The Supervisor/Leader who receives this form will enter their name here.
6	For Emergencies Contact	Enter the name and way to contact the individual who handles emergencies.
7	Attachments	List any attached supporting documentation.
8 a	Job/Task Activity	Enter only those Job Task/activities for which a deficiency is noted.
8 b	Hazards	Enter the hazard not being sufficiently addressed.
8 c	Deficiency	Enter the deficiency.
8 d	Action Taken	Enter the corrective action taken to address the deficiency.
8 e	Safety Plan Amended?	Enter whether the on site safety plan was amended.
8 f	Signature of Supervisor/Leader	Ensure the Supervisor/Leader signs the form to acknowledge the deficiency.
9	Prepared by	Enter the name and position of the person completing the worksheet.
10	Date/Time Briefed:	Enter the date/time the document was briefed to the appropriate workers and by whom.

Figure 8.41 (*Continued*)

CG ICS SSP WORKER ACKNOWLEDGEMENT FORM

1. Incident Name	2. Site Location:	3. Attachments:

4. Type of Briefing	5. Presented By:	6. Date Presented	7. Time Presented
Safety Plan/Emergency Response Plan ☐ Start Shift ☐ Pre-Entry ☐ Exit ☐ End of Shift ☐ Specify Other:			

8.a. Worker Name (Print)	8.b. Signature*	8.c. Date	8.d. Time

*By signing this document, I am stating that I have read and fully understand the plan and/or information provided to me.

ICS-208-CG SSP-I (rev 9/06): Worker Acknowledgement

Page_____ of _____

Figure 8.41 (Continued)

WORKER ACKNOWLEDGEMENT FORM (ICS-208-CG SSP-I)

Purpose: The Worker Acknowledgement form is used to document workers who have received safety briefings.

Preparation: Those personnel responsible for conducting safety briefings complete this form initially. Once the briefings are completed, workers who were briefed print their name, sign, date and indicate the time of the briefing.

Distribution: This form is returned to the Safety Officer or designated representative at the end of each operational period.

Instructions:

Item #	Item Title	Instructions
1	Incident Name	Print the name assigned to the incident.
2	Site Location	Indicate the location where the briefings are held.
3	Attachments	Indicate any attachments used as part of the briefings.
4	Type of briefing	Check the block next to the type of briefing.
5	Presented by	Enter the name of the person conducting the briefing.
6	Date Presented	Enter the date of the briefing.
7	Time Presented	Enter the time of the briefing.
8	Worker Name, Signature, Date and Time	Workers receiving the briefing print their name, sign, date and enter the time they acknowledge the briefing.

Figure 8.41 (*Continued*)

CG ICS SSP: Emergency Safety & Response Plan 1910.120 Compliance Checklist (Form A)	1. Incident Name	2. Date/Time Prepared	3. Operational Period	4. Site Supervisor/Leader	5. Location of Site
6.a. Cite: 1910.120	6.b. Requirement (sections that duplicate or explain are omitted)	6.c. ICS Form	6.d. Check	6.e. Comments	
(q)(1)	Is the plan in writing?	SSP-A	☐		
(1)	Is the plan available for inspection by employees?	N/A	☐	Performancebased	
(q)(2)(i)	Does the plan address pre-emergency planning and coordination?	SSP-A	☐		
(ii)	Does it address personnel roles?	SSP-A	☐		
(ii)	Does it address lines of authority?	SSP-A	☐		
(ii)	Does it address communications?	SSP-A	☐		
(iii)	Does it address emergency recognition?	SSP-A	☐		
(iii)	Does it address emergency prevention?	SSP-A	☐		
(iv)	Does it identify safe distances?	SSP-A	☐		
(iv)	Does it address places of refuge?	SSP-A	☐		
(v)	Does it address site security and control?	SSP-A	☐		
(vi)	Does it identify evacuation routes?	SSP-A	☐		
(vi)	Does it identify evacuation procedures?	SSP-A	☐		
(vii)	Does it address decontamination?	SSP-A	☐		
(viii)	Does it address medical treatment and first aid?	SSP-A	☐		
(ix)	Does it address emergency alerting procedures?	SSP-A	☐		
(ix)	Does it address emergency response procedures	SSP-A	☐		
(x)	Was the response critiqued?	N/A	☐	Performancebased	
(x)	Does it identify Personal Protection Equipment?	SSP-A	☐		
(x)	Does it identify emergency equipment?	SSP-A	☐		
(q)(3)(ii)	All the hazardous substances identified to the extent possible?	N/A	☐	Performancebased	
(ii)	All the hazardous conditions identified to the extent possible?	N/A	☐	Performancebased	
(ii)	Was site analysis addressed?	N/A	☐	Performancebased	
(ii)	Were engineering controls addressed?	N/A	☐	Performancebased	
(ii)	Were exposure limits addressed?	N/A	☐	Performancebased	
(ii)	Were hazardous substance handling procedures addressed?	N/A	☐	Performancebased	
(iii)	Is the PPE appropriate for the hazards identified?	N/A	☐	Performancebased	
(iv)	Is respiratory protection worn when inhalation hazards present?	N/A	☐	Performancebased	
(v)	Is the buddy system used in the hazard zone?	N/A	☐	Performancebased	
(vi)	Are backup personnel on standby?	N/A	☐	Performancebased	
(vi)	Are advanced first aid support personnel standing by?	N/A	☐	Performancebased	
(vii)	Has the ICS designated safety official been identified?	SSP-A	☐		
(vii)	Has the Safety Official evaluated the hazards?	N/A	☐	Performancebased	
(viii)	Can the Safety Official communicate with IC immediately?	N/A	☐	Performancebased	
(ix)	Are appropriate decontamination procedures implemented?	N/A	☐	Performancebased	

ICS-208-CG SSP-J (rev 9/06) Page _____ of _____

Figure 8.41 (*Continued*)

Emergency Safety & Response Plan Compliance Checklist Form A (ICS-208-CG SSP-J)

Purpose: The Emergency Safety and Response Plan 1910.120 Compliance Checklist is to ensure that incident response operations are in compliance with Title 29, Code of Federal Regulations Part 1910.120, Hazardous Waste Operations and Emergency Response. It also identifies how form ICS-208-CG SSP-J can be used to satisfy the HAZWOPER requirements. This checklist is an optional form.

Preparation: The Emergency Safety and Response Plan 1910.120 Compliance Checklist is completed by the Safety Officer or his/her staff as frequently as necessary whenever the Safety Officer wants to ensure regulatory compliance. It is best used in conjunction with the Site Safety Plan Enforcement Log (ICS-208-CG SSP-H). Many of the requirements are performance based and are best evaluated on scene by the Safety Officer or his/her staff.

Distribution: The Safety Officer should maintain The Emergency Safety and Response Plan (ERP) 1910.120 Compliance Checklist.

Instructions:

Item #	Item Title	Instructions
1	Incident Name	Print the name assigned to the incident.
2	Date/Time Prepared	Enter date (month, day, year) prepared.
3	Operational Period	Enter the time interval for which the assignment applies.
4	Supervisor/Leader	The Supervisor/Leader who receives this form will enter their name here.
5	Location of Site	Enter the site location.
6 a	Cites	These are the regulatory cites within 1910.120. The major headings are highlighted in bold. Informational cites or cites that are duplicative are not included.
6 b	Requirement	This lists the requirement in a question format. Some require documentation or some form of action.
6 c	ICS Form	Lists those requirements covered by ICS-208-CG SSP-A.
6 d	Check Block	Enter the check if the site satisfies the requirement.
6 f	Comments	This provides additional information on the requirement. The user may also enter comments.
7	Prepared by	Enter the name and position of the person completing the worksheet.

Figure 8.41 (*Continued*)

CG ICS SSP: 1910.120 COMPLIANCE CHECKLIST (Form B)	1. Incident Name	2. Date/Time Prepared		4. Site Supervisor/Leader	5. Location of Site
6.a. Cite: 1910.120	6.b. Requirement (sections that duplicate or explain are omitted)	3. Operational Period 6.c. ICS Form	6.d. Check		6.e. Comments
1910.120 (b)(1)(iii)(A)	Organizational structure?	203	☐		
(B)	Comprehensive workplan?	IAP	☐		Incident Action Plan
(C)	Site Safety Plan?	SSP-B	☐		
(D)	Safety and health training program?	N/A	☐		Responsibility of each employer
(E)	Medical surveillance program?	N/A	☐		Responsibility of each employer
(F)	Employer SOPs?	N/A	☐		Responsibility of each employer
(G)	Written program related to site activities?	N/A	☐		
(b)(1)(iii)	Site excavation meets shored or slope requirements in 1926?	N/A	☐		
(b)(2)(i)(D)	Lines of communication?	201 203 205	☐		
(b)3(iv)	Training addressed?	N/A	☐		Responsibility of each employer
(v)–(vi)	Information and medical monitoring addressed?	N/A	☐		Responsibility of each employer
(b)4(i)	Site Safety Plan kept on site?	N/A	☐		
(ii)(A)	Safety and health hazard analysis conducted?	N/A	☐		
(B)	Properly trained employees assigned to right jobs?	N/A	☐		
(C)	Personnel Protective Equipment issues addressed?	SSP-F	☐		
(E)	Frequency and types of air monitoring addressed?	SSP-E	☐		
(F)	Site control measures in place?	SSP-B	☐		
(G)	Decontamination procedures in place?	SSP-G	☐		
(H)	Emergency Response Plan in place?	SSP-D	☐		
(I)	Confined space entry procedures?	SSP-B	☐		
(J)	Spill containment program	SSP-B	☐		
(iii)	Pre-entry briefings conducted?	SSP-I	☐		
(iv)	Site Safety Plan effectiveness evaluated?	SSP-H	☐		
(c)(1)	Site characterization done?	N/A	☐		
(c)(2)	Preliminary evaluation done by qualified person?	N/A	☐		
(c)(3)	Hazard identification performed?	SSP-B	☐		
(c)(4)(i)	Location and size of site identified?	SSP-B	☐		
(ii)	Response activities, job tasks identified?	SSP-B	☐		
(iii)	Duration of tasks identified?	SSP-B	☐		Operational period
(iv)	Site topography and accessibility addressed?	SSP-C	☐		
(v)	Health and safety hazards addressed?	SSP-B	☐		
(vi)	Dispersion pathways addressed?	SSP-B	☐		
(vii)	Status and capabilities of medical emergency response teams?	206	☐		
(c)(5)(i)(iv)	Chemical protective clothing addressed and properly selected?	SSP-F	☐		
(ii)	Respiratory protection addressed?	SSPb and F	☐		
(iii)	Level B used for unknowns?	N/A	☐		

ICS-208-CG SSP-K (rev 9/06): Page 1. Page ____ of ____

Figure 8.41 (Continued)

CG ICS SSP: 1910.120 COMPLIANCE CHECKLIST Form B (cont) 6.a. Cite: 1910.120	1. Incident Name	2. Date/Time Prepared	3. Operational Period		
	6.b. Requirement (sections that duplicate or explain are omitted)	6.c. ICS Form	6.d. Check	6.e. Comments
1910.120 (c)(6)(i)	Monitoring for ionization conducted?	SSP-E	☐	
(ii)	Monitoring conducted for IDLH conditions?	SSP-E	☐	
(iii)	Personnel looking out for dangers of IDLH environments?	N/A	☐	
(iv)	Ongoing air monitoring program in place?	SSP-E	☐	
(c)(7)	Employees informed of potential hazard occurrence?	SSP-B	☐	
(c)(8)	Properties of each chemical made aware to employees?	SSP-B	☐	
(d)(1)	Appropriate site control procedures in place?	IAP, SSP-B	☐	
(d)(2)	Site control program developed during planning stages?	IAP, SSP-B	☐	
(d)(3)	Site map, work zones, alarms, communications addressed?	IAP, SSP-B	☐	
(g)(1)(i)	Engineering, admin controls considered?	SSP-B	☐	
(iii)	Personnel not rotated to reduce exposures?	N/A	☐	
(g)(5)(i)	PPE selection criteria part of employer's program?	N/A	☐	Responsibility of employer
(ii)	PPE use and limitations identified?	SSP-F	☐	
(iii)	Work mission duration identified?	SSP-F	☐	
(iv)	PPE properly maintained and stored?	N/A	☐	Responsibility of employer
(vi)	Are employees properly trained and fitted with PPE?	N/A	☐	Responsibility of employer
(vii)	Are donning and doffing procedures identified?	SSP-F	☐	
(viii)	Are inspection procedures properly identified?	SSP-F	☐	
(ix)	Is a PPE evaluation program in place?	SSP-F	☐	
(h)(3)	Periodic monitoring conducted?	SSP-E	☐	
(k)(2)(i)	Have decontamination procedures been established?	SSP-G	☐	
(ii)	Are procedures in place for contamination avoidance?	SSP-G	☐	
(iii)	Is personal clothing properly deconned prior to leaving the site?	SSP-G	☐	
(iv)	Are decontamination deficiencies identified and corrected?	SSP-H	☐	
(k)(3)	Are decontamination lines in the proper location?	SSP-C	☐	
(k)(4)	Are solutions/equipment used in decon properly disposed of?	N/A	☐	
(k)(6)	Is protective clothing and equipment properly secured?	N/A	☐	
(k)(7)	If cleaning facilities are used, are they aware of the hazards?	N/A	☐	
(k)(8)	Have showers and change rooms provided, if necessary?	N/A	☐	
(l)(1)(iii)	Are provisions for reporting emergencies identified?	SSP-D	☐	
(iv)	Are safe distances and places of refuge identified?	SSPB and C	☐	
(v)	Site security and control addressed in emergencies?	SSP-D	☐	
(vi)	Evacuation routes and procedures identified?	SSP-D	☐	
(vii)	Emergency decontamination procedures developed?	SSP-D	☐	
(ix)	Emergency alerting and response procedures identified?	SSP-D	☐	
(x)	Response teams critiqued and followup performed?	SSP-H	☐	
(xi)	Emergency PPE and equipment available?	SSP-D	☐	

ICS-208-CG SSP-K (rev 9/06): **Page 2. Page** ____ **of** ____

Figure 8.41 (Continued)

CG ICS SSP: 1910.120 COMPLIANCE CHECKLIST Form B (cont)	1. Incident Name	2. Date/Time Prepared	3. Operational Period		
6.a. Cite:	6.b. Requirement(sections that duplicate or explain are omitted)		6.c. ICS Form	6.d. Check	6.e. Comments
1910.120 (l)(3)(i)	Emergency notification procedures identified?		SSP-D	☐	
(ii)	Emergency response plan separate from Site Safety Plan?		SSP-D	☐	
(iii)	Emergency response plan compatible with other plans?		SSP-D	☐	
(iv)	Emergency response plan rehearsed regularly?		SSP-D	☐	
(v)	Emergency response plan maintained and kept current?		SSP-H	☐	
1910.165(b)(2)	Can alarms be seen/heard above ambient light and noise levels?		N/A	☐	
(b)(3)	Are alarms distinct and recognizable?		N/A	☐	
(b)(4)	Are employees aware of the alarms and are they accessible?		SSP-D	☐	
(b)(5)	Are emergency phone numbers, radio frequencies clearly posted?		206	☐	
(b)(6)	Signaling devices in place where there are 10 or more workers?		IAP	☐	
(c)(1)	Are alarms like steam whistles, air horns being used?		IAP	☐	
(d)(3)	Are backup alarms available?		IAP	☐	
(m)	Are areas adequately illuminated?		IAP	☐	
(n)(1)(i)	Is an adequate supply of potable water available?		IAP	☐	
(ii)	Are drinking water containers equipped with a tap?		IAP	☐	
(iii)	Are drinking water containers clearly marked?		IAP	☐	
(iv)	Is a drinking cup receptacle available and clearly marked?		IAP	☐	
(n)(2)(i)	Are non-potable water containers clearly marked?		IAP	☐	
(n)(3)(i)	Are their sufficient toilets available?		IAP	☐	
(n)(4)	Have food handling issues been addressed?		IAP	☐	
(n)(6)	Have adequate wash facilities been provided outside hazard zone?		IAP	☐	
(n)(7)	If response is greater than 6 months, have showers been provided?		IAP	☐	
7. Prepared By:		ICS-208-CG SSP-K (rev 9/06): **Page 3.** Page _____ of _____			

Figure 8.41 (Continued)

HAZWOPER 1910.120 COMPLIANCE CHECKLIST FORM B (ICS-208-CG SSP-K)

Purpose: The HAZWOPER 1910.120 Compliance Checklist is to ensure that incident response operations are in compliance with Title 29, Code of Federal Regulations Part 1910.120, Hazardous Waste Operations and Emergency Response. It also identifies how other ICS forms can be used to satisfy the HAZWOPER requirements. This is an optional form.

Preparation: The HAZWOPER 1910.120 Compliance Checklist is completed by the Safety Officer or his/her staff as frequently as necessary whenever the Safety Officer wants to ensure regulatory compliance. It is best used in conjunction with the Site Safety Plan Enforcement Log (ICS-208-CG SSP-H). The Site Safety Plan Forms (A–G) best meet someof the requirements. The Incident Action Plan is suited to address other requirements, and the Safety Officer should ensure the IAP addresses them. Other requirements are performance based and are best evaluated on scene by the Safety Officer or his/her staff.

Distribution: The HAZWOPER 1910.120 Compliance Checklist should be maintained by the Safety Officer.

Instructions:

Item #	Item Title	Instructions
1	Incident Name	Print the name assigned to the incident.
2	Date/Time Prepared	Enter date (month, day, year) prepared.
3	Operational Period	Enter the time interval for which the assignment applies.
4	Supervisor/Leader	The Supervisor/Leader who receives this form will enter their name here.
5	Location of Site	Enter the site location.
6.a.	Cites	These are the regulatory cites within 1910.120. The major headings are highlighted in bold. Informational cites or cites that are duplicative are not included.
6.b.	Requirement	This lists the requirement in a question format. Some require documentation or some form of action.
6.c.	ICS Form	Lists those ICS Forms that cover the requirement. **IAP designations means it should be covered in IAP, it does not guarantee it is covered. The Safety Officer must ensure this.**
6.d.	Check Block	Enter the check if the site satisfies the requirement.
6.e.	Comments	This provides information on where else the requirement may be met. The user may also enter comments.
7	Prepared by	Enter the name and position of the person completing the worksheet.

Figure 8.41 *(Continued)*

CG ICS SSP: 1910.120 DRUM COMPLIANCE CHECKSHEET	1. Incident Name	2. Date/Time Prepared	3. Operational Period	4. Safety Officer (include method of contact)
5. Supervisor/Leader	6. Location and Size of Site		7. For Emergencies Contact:	8. Note: tanks and vaults should also be treated in the same manner as described below [1910.120(j)(9)]. Many can also pose confined space hazards.

9.a. Cite: 1910.120 (Cites that duplicate or explain requirements are omitted)	9.b. Requirement	9.c. Check	9.d. Comments
(j)(1)(ii)	Drums meet DOT, OSHA, EPA regs for waste they contain, including shipment?	☐	
(iii)	Drums inspected and integrity ensured prior to movement?	☐	
(iv)	Or drums moved to an accessible location (staging area) prior to movement?	☐	
(v)	Unlabelled drums treated as unknown until properly identified and labeled?	☐	
(v)	Site activities organized to minimize drum handling?	☐	
(vi)	Employers properly warned about the hazards of moving and handling drums?	☐	
(vii)	Suitable overpack drums are available for addressing leaking and ruptured drums?	☐	
(viii)	Leaking materials from drums properly contained?	☐	
(ix)	Are drums that cannot be moved, emptied of contents with transfer equipment?	☐	
(x)	Are suspect buried drums surveyed with underground detection system?	☐	
(xi)	Are soil and covering material above buried drums removed with caution?	☐	
(xii)	Is the proper extinguishing equipment on scene to control incipient fires?	☐	
(j)(2)(i)	Are airlines on supplied air systems protected from leaking drums?	☐	
	Are employees at a safe distance, using remote equipment, when handling explosive drums?	☐	
(iii)	Are explosive shields in plane to protect workers opening explosive drums?	☐	
(iv)	Is response equipment positioned behind shields when shields are used?	☐	
(v)	Are non-sparking tools used in flammable or potentially flammable atmospheres?	☐	
(vi)	Are drums under extreme pressure opened slowly & workers protected by shields/distance?	☐	
(vii)	Are workers prohibited from standing and working on drums?	☐	
(j)(3)	Is the drum handling equipment positioned and operated to minimize sources of ignition?	☐	
(j)(5)(i)	For shock sensitive drums, have all non-essential employees been evacuated?	☐	
(ii)	For shock sensitive drums: is handling equipment provided with shields to protect workers?	☐	
(iii)	Are alarms that announce start/finish of explosive drum handling actions in place?	☐	
(iv)	Are continuous communications in place between the drum handling site & command post?	☐	
(v)	Are drums under pressure properly controlled for prior to handling?	☐	
(vi)	Are drums containing packaged laboratory wastes treated as shock sensitive?	☐	
(j)(6)(i)	Are lab packs opened by trained and experienced personnel?	☐	
(ii)	Are lab packs showing crystallization treated as shock sensitive?	☐	
(j)(8)(ii-iii)	Are drum staging areas manageable with marked access and egress?	☐	
(iv)	Is bulking of drums conducted only after drum contents have been properly identified?	☐	

10. Prepared By:

Form SSP-L (rev 9/06) Page _____ of _____

Figure 8.41 (Continued)

HAZWOPER 1910.120 DRUM COMPLIANCE CHECKLIST (ICS-208-CG SSP-L)

Purpose: The HAZWOPER 1910.120 Drum Compliance Checklist is to ensure that incident response operations are in compliance with Title 29, Code of Federal Regulations Part 1910.120, Hazardous Waste Operations and Emergency Response whenever drums are encountered during an incident. This is an optional form.

Preparation: The HAZWOPER 1910.120 Drum Compliance Checklist is completed by the Safety Officer or his/her staff as frequently as necessary whenever the Safety Officer wants to ensure regulatory compliance. It is best used in conjunction with the Site Safety Plan Enforcement Log (ICS-208-CG SSP-H). The Site Safety Plan Forms (A-G) best meet some of the requirements. Other requirements are performance based and are best evaluated on scene by the Safety Officer or his/her staff.

Distribution: The HAZWOPER 1910.120 Drum Compliance Checklist should be maintained by the Safety Officer.

Instructions:

Item #	Item Title	Instructions
1	Incident Name	Print the name assigned to the incident.
2	Date/Time Prepared	Enter date (month, day, year) prepared.
3	Operational Period	Enter the time interval for which the assignment applies.
4	Safety Officer	Enter the name of the Safety Officer and means of contact.
5	Supervisor/Leader	The Supervisor/Leader who receives this form will enter their name here.
6	Location & size of site	Enter the geographical location of the site and the approximate square area.
7	For Emergencies Contact	Enter the name and way to contact the individual who handles emergencies.
8	Note	Tanks and vaults should also be treated in the same manner as described in the checklist (1910.120(j)(9)).
9.a.	Cites	These are the regulatory cites within 1910.120. The major headings are highlighted in bold. Informational cites or cites that are duplicative are not included.
9.b.	Requirement	This lists the requirement in a question format. Some require documentation or some form of action.
9.c.	Check Block	Enter the check if the site satisfies the requirement.
9.d.	Comments	This provides information on where else the requirement may be met. The user may also enter comments.
10	Prepared by	Enter the name and position of the person completing the worksheet.

Figure 8.41 (*Continued*)

However, the checkboxes do not necessarily cover hazards that may be encountered in all types of responses, and the Safety Officer would need to ensure that additional hazards are not neglected in the analysis simply because they do not appear on the Coast Guard checklist. The Coast Guard forms primarily focus on hazardous materials incidents, which may or may not be the primary, or even secondary, incident in an All-Hazards Response.

When hazardous materials present a hazard, such as in an earthquake, landslide, or flood in which the primary incident causes secondary hazmat releases, the hazardous materials are often unknown and not fully characterized. In this case, elements of the Coast Guard forms may be useful, but uncharacterized and unknown hazardous materials need to be treated differently than hazards that are known. For example, a fire in an urban area releases contaminants and carcinogens to which firefighters are exposed and is essentially a "hot hazmat" zone, although the specific contaminants at a given fire are not characterized or identified. Still, a decontamination plan could be modeled on the step by step procedures mandated under HAZWOPER and used by the Coast Guard.

In an All-Hazards response, PPE should be selected based on the fact that many, if not all, hazardous material exposures are uncharacterized, and decontamination procedures should be adhered to. Depending upon the incident, some of the Coast Guard 208 supplement forms could be useful in developing a safety plan, and the Safety Officer should be familiar with any resource that can increase efficiencies.

8.11 Demobilization Planning

As the incident response winds down, resources are released and demobilized. This does not occur all at once, and some resources are released earlier in the response than others. The ICS Form 221, Demobilization Check-Out (Figure 8.33) is completed as resources are released, and must be signed by members of the Logistics, Finance, and Planning Sections, as well as "Other Section Staff." The Safety Officer is not specifically identified on this form, but should work with the Demobilization Leader under Planning to ensure that Safety is included as "Other Section Staff" that must sign off on this form when personnel are released. The Safety Officer should review whether personnel who are demobilizing will require follow up medical monitoring at specified time periods following the response, and that these personnel are aware of how to obtain this medical monitoring. If exposure sampling was conducted, but results were not obtained before personnel demobilized, the Safety Officer needs to ensure that departing personnel will receive their exposure monitoring results. Such information can be included under "remarks" on the Form 221 next to the Safety Officer's signature.

8.12   The Operations Briefing

Once the IAP is completed, and approved by the Incident Commander or Unified Command, it is duplicated and made ready for distribution.

The Operational Period Briefing is conducted as one Operational Period ends and the next begins (Figure 8.42). This meeting is attended by all incident personnel as appropriate. The agenda for this meeting is:

- The Planning Section Chief reviews Incident Objectives and any updates that have been made to the Incident Action Plan;
- The Incident Commander (or Unified Command) provides an incident update;
- The Situation Unit Leader conducts a situation briefing;
- The Operations Section Chief provides an operations briefing;
- The Logistics Section Chief provides updates on transport, communications, and supplies;
- The Finance Section Chief discusses any fiscal issues related to the incident;
- The Safety Officer discusses safety issues. This discussion includes:

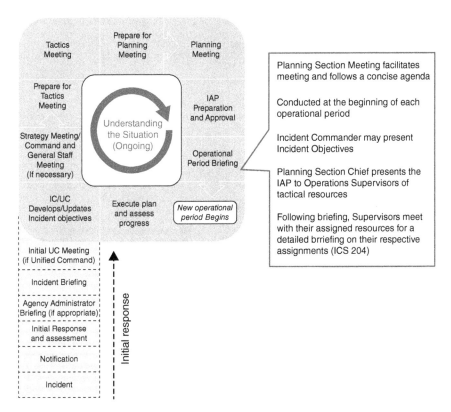

Figure 8.42   The Operations Briefing.

- o Work-related injuries, illnesses, and near misses that have occurred, and corrective actions taken to prevent future occurrences;
- o Highlights Information from the Safety Message (Form 208, or Form 213 for the Coast Guard), and General Safety Information Relevant to all Personnel;
- o The Safety Officer does not discuss detailed information identified on the 215A, since this information has been transferred to individual 204 Forms and will be reviewed by the work group supervisor with individual work teams.
- The Public Information Officer discusses public information issues;
- The Liaison Officer discusses any interagency issues;
- The Planning Section Chief solicits final comments and adjourns the briefing.

8.13   New Operational Period Begins

Following the Operational Period Briefing, personnel from the preceding Operational Period leave the incident and return home or to their designated off-duty areas (Figure 8.43). Incoming personnel transition to their assigned work

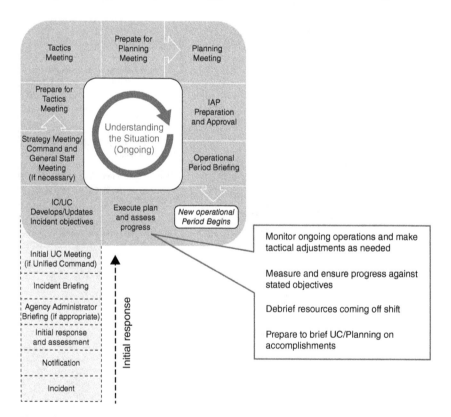

Figure 8.43   The Incident Action Plan is implemented for the new Operational Period.

locations and are briefed by their supervisor on their work assignments. This briefing follows the Form 204, including safety information.

The Safety Officer visits worksites to check in with incident personnel and ensure that work is performed safely during the Operational Period. Each responder records their activities on an ICS Form 214, Activity Log (Figure 8.44).

ACTIVITY LOG (ICS 214)

1. Incident Name:		2. Operational Period:	Date From:	Date To:
			Time From:	Time To:
3. Name:		4. ICS Position:		5. Home Agency **(and Unit)**

6. Resources Assigned:		
Name	**ICS Position**	**Home Agency (and Unit)**

7. Activity Log:	
Date/Time	**Notable Activities**

8. Prepared by: **Name:** _____	**Position/Title:**_____ **Signature:** _____
ICS 214, Page 1	**Date/Time:** _____

Figure 8.44 Form ICS 214: Activity Log.

ACTIVITY LOG (ICS 214)

1. Incident Name:	2. Operational Period:	Date From:	Date To:
		Time From:	Time To:

7. Activity Log **(continuation)**

Date/Time	Notable Activities

8. Prepared by: **Name:** _____	**Position/Title** _____	**Signature:** _____
ICS 214, Page 2	**Date/Time:** _____	

Figure 8.44 *(Continued)*

The Safety Officer must maintain a 214 Activity Log, and may also wish to review the 214 logs of other incident personnel throughout the Operational Period to verify that safety protocols are being followed. The Safety Officer responds to and investigates any work-related injuries, illnesses, or near misses that are reported. If Assistant Safety Officers are assigned, much of the site safety work may be performed by the Assistant Safety Officers, with the Safety Officer checking in periodically.

The Incident Management Team also begins the planning process for the Operational Period that will follow.

8.14 Summary

Managing safety in an incident response is similar to managing safety in any work environment, however, the Safety Officer must be competent in the incident planning process and incident forms.

Work assignments identified on the Form 215 are analyzed for safety hazards using a Form 215A. Safety Information from the Form 215A is transferred to individual Form 204s, and information from the Form 204 is reviewed with each Division or Group at the start of the Operational Period (Figure 8.45).

The Safety Officer is responsible for reviewing the Form 206, Incident Medical Plan, and signing off on it. Before signing the form, the Safety Officer should add attachments outlining behavioral health resources, and any required medical monitoring.

Another form that the Safety Officer is responsible for is the Form 208, Safety Message-Plan. If the response falls under OSHA's HAZWOPER standard, a Site Safety Plan is required. The Coast Guard uses the Form 208 as the Site Safety Plan.

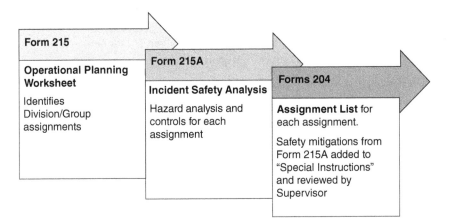

Form 215

Operational Planning Worksheet

Identifies Division/Group assignments

Form 215A

Incident Safety Analysis

Hazard analysis and controls for each assignment

Forms 204

Assignment List for each assignment.

Safety mitigations from Form 215A added to "Special Instructions" and reviewed by Supervisor

Figure 8.45 Work assignments are documented on Form 215, and a safety analysis is performed for each work assignment from the Form 215 and documented on the Form 215A. Safety information from the Form 215A is transferred to the Form 204, and the supervisor reviews this safety information with work group personnel.

In an All-Hazards response, the safety plan may be simple enough that it can fit on the Form 208 in its entirety. If not, a stand-alone safety plan should be written, and then the Form 208 can be included in each Operational Periods IAP as a daily safety message. This daily safety message should include information applicable to all personnel since work group specific safety information goes on the Form 204.

References

1 Federal Emergency Management Administration, Emergency Management Institute (2013). *Independent Study Course IS-00201 Forms Used in the Development of the Incident Action Plan.*

2 Continuing Education Programs, Department of Occupational and Environmental Health Sciences, University of Washington (2017). *Emergency Safety Officer Course.*

3 Federal Emergency Management Administration, US Department of Homeland Security (2017). *National Incident Management System*, 3e.

4 Federal Emergency Management Administration (2010). *National Incident Management System (NIMS), Incident Command System (ICS) Forms Booklet.*

5 Federal Emergency Management Administration, US Department of Homeland Security (2012). *FEMA Incident Action Planning Guide.*

6 Coast Guard Incident Command System (ICS). *Authorized Forms.* https://www .dcms.uscg.mil/Our-Organization/Assistant-Commandant-for-C4IT-CG-6/The-Office-of-Information-Management-CG-61/Forms-Management/ICS-Forms/ smdpage4085/2 (accessed 26 July 2019).

7 Primeau, E. and Weems, L. (2018). *Incident Safety and Health Management Handbook*, 2e. American Industrial Hygiene Association.

9

Assistant Safety Officers, Technical Specialists, and Other Safety Support Roles

The Safety Officer is responsible for the health and well-being of all incident personnel during a response. A successful response depends upon workers who are fully capable of performing all of their assigned tasks. Incident response and recovery workers who are injured or ill cannot fully fulfill their duties. When workers are unable to perform their assigned tasks, the entire response suffers. If the injury or illness is so severe that a worker cannot return to work, they will not be able to participate in future responses. Replacement workers will need to be hired and trained.

More importantly, however, injuries and illnesses can have serious personal costs, both to the injured workers and their families.

The Safety Officer supports the Incident Commander by ensuring that all workers who participate in an incident response can go home to their families at the end of the response in the same state of physical and mental health as when they first report in.

To accomplish these goals, the Safety Officer must proactively manage safety throughout the response. This includes maintaining access and communication between response workers and supervisors, Command and General Staff, and the Incident Commander. Safety cannot be managed from behind a desk, so the Safety Officer must maintain a field presence to observe work as it occurs, identify safety issues, stop work if necessary, and to provide communication access between the safety role and all workers involved. Safety plans must be written, and OSHA or state program requirements must be adhered to. In addition, the Safety Officer must actively participate in the development of the Incident Action Plan for the following Operational Period.

Managing the health and safety of incident response personnel, especially in a large or complex incident, is a big task. Doing so in a manner that is effective at preventing injuries and illnesses, or any adverse health outcome, as well as ensuring that safety codes and standards are adhered to, is a larger job than one person

Health and Safety in Emergency Management and Response, First Edition. Dana L. Stahl.
© 2021 John Wiley & Sons, Inc. Published 2021 by John Wiley & Sons, Inc.

can do alone if it is to be done well. The Safety Officer must rely on Assistant Safety Officers, Technical Specialists, and other support roles in order to meet the responsibilities of this position.

9.1 Assistant Safety Officer

The 2017 National Incident Management System (NIMS) Refresh added and clarified the position of the Assistant Safety Officer. In an ICS structure, an Assistant is a title given for subordinates of principal Command Staff positions. This title indicates a level of technical capability, qualification, and responsibility. While an Assistant Safety Officer is subordinate to the Safety Officer in the reporting structure, an Assistant Safety Officer should have sufficient skills to back up the Safety Officer when needed.

The 2017 NIMS Refresh provides an example of how Assistant Safety Officers can be integrated into the Incident Command System (Figure 9.1). This example places Assistant Safety Officers in support of the more hazardous operations, including a Hazmat Branch and a Fire Suppression Branch under Operations. It also assigns an Assistant Safety Officer to the Food Unit under Logistics. These Assistant Safety Officers have dotted line communication to the groups that they support in the Incident Command Structure, but they each have a solid line reporting relationship to the Safety Officer.

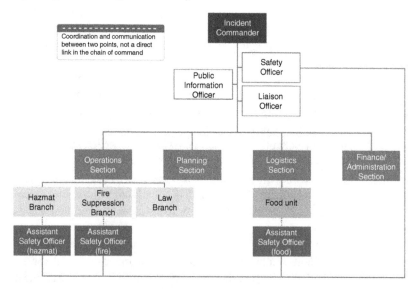

Figure 9.1 Example of how Assistant Safety Officers can be used in an Incident Command System. Source: Federal Emergency Management Administration, US Department of Homeland Security [1].

Assistant Safety Officers provide a field presence that a single Safety Officer cannot achieve on his/her own. The Safety Officer can, and should, continue to make their own field visits to observe field conditions and check in with the Assistant Safety Officers, but the assigned Assistant Safety Officers provide a higher level of presence. The Safety Officer and Assistant Safety Officers must maintain ongoing communications, and this increases the Safety Officer's awareness of what is occurring in the field.

Assistant Safety Officers facilitate safety in the field by providing focused support to branches and groups they are assigned to, and this support can free up the Safety Officer to focus on incident planning and maintaining availability to the Incident Commander.

Assistant Safety Officers can also be utilized in a Unified Command structure. When multiple jurisdictions, agencies, or members of the private sector come together participate in a single response, each entity provides a representative to Unified Command. Each of these entities may have personnel on staff who are qualified to fill the role of a Safety Officer, however, only a single Safety Officer from one agency or jurisdiction is assigned this role. Since the Safety Officer is responsible for all workers involved in the response, this individual needs to have a good working knowledge of the hazards faced by responders from his/her own jurisdiction or agency as well as those in other lines of work who have assigned roles. The Safety Officer may not be as familiar with hazards encountered by workers who perform work other than the type of work that the Safety Officer usually supports. Safety personnel who *are* familiar with this work have valuable knowledge and information that the Safety Officer needs.

For example, if a passenger train is involved in a derailment that results in multiple passenger injuries, or perhaps is involved in a fire, the local fire department would respond and assign a member of the fire department as the Safety Officer. Rail safety staff also show up on scene. The Fire Department Safety Officer will be well versed in hazards related to fighting fires and extricating patients, but this individual generally has less experience working in a rail environment, and because of this the hazards of this environment not foremost in his or her mind. The rail safety representative, however, is well aware of these hazards: The rail safety representative knows to ensure that oncoming rail traffic is stopped, and can point out rail-related hazards to the Fire Department Safety Officer. For example, the rail safety representative could identify locations of rail switches, and remind the Fire Department Safety Officer that these switches are operated remotely with enough force to crush rocks or feet inside steel-toed boots. A diligent Safety Officer would take advantage of this resource by appointing the rail safety specialist as an Assistant Safety Officer, thus ensuring that this safety professional's expertise is utilized to protect all workers.

If a response occurs at a construction site, responders need to be prepared to encounter hazards that are unique to the particular construction site. An on-site construction safety representative can work with the assigned Safety Officer to ensure that these hazards are identified and planned for. Likewise, a Safety Officer at a chemical manufacturing plant incident response, or at any manufacturing plant incident response, should work closely with the plant's safety manager. Incorporating these site safety personnel into the ICS structure as Assistant Safety Officers when they are qualified to fill this position maximizes safety communication across the Incident Command structure and ensures a coordinated safety effort [1, 2].

Site safety personnel who support the response as Assistant Safety Officers must be trained in ICS and have the qualifications to fill this position. When interagency drills and exercises are held, site safety personnel should practice this coordination with the responding agency's Safety Officer so that all learn to work together. Practice and continued interaction builds trust, which is crucial in an actual response.

However, site safety personnel who are not trained in ICS, do not understand the system and language of incident response, nor the duties and responsibilities of the Safety Officer, cannot be effective in this role, and may even interfere with the ability of first responders to perform their jobs. It is highly advisable that any safety personnel who may need to work with first responders in this type of incident complete ICS training, and participate in sufficient planning and exercising to become competent in fulfilling this role before an incident takes place.

9.2 Duties of Assistant Safety Officers

Assistant Safety Officers need to understand the roles and responsibilities of the safety function within an Incident Command Structure. The need to know how to work with the other positions in this system including those under Planning, Logistics, Finance, and Operations, to both incorporate safety into the response and obtain support and resources. Assistant Safety Officers may help the Safety Officer in developing Safety Plans, may contribute initial drafts of these plans, and provide summaries for incorporation into a Safety Message for the IAP on the ICS Form 208.

Assistant Safety Officers may need to back up the Safety Officer if needed. If a Safety Officer needs to respond to an injury or other critical safety issue, an Assistant Safety Officer may need to step in at various stages of the incident planning process or consult with the Incident Commander. To do so, an Assistant Safety Officer must understand this process to the same extent that the Safety Officer does, and also must be on the same page as the Safety Officer as far as how incident safety should be managed. Communication and trust between Safety Officers and Assistant Safety Officers is crucial.

Assistant Safety Officers who are assigned to provide field support must ensure that the safety plan is implemented by the working groups that they support. Assistant Safety Officers may provide a safety orientation to incoming workers, conduct other types of training, conduct air monitoring, evaluate and monitor decontamination protocols, investigate reports of injuries, illnesses, or near misses, identify hazards and follow up on corrective actions, talk to responders about hazards they encounter, and perform other actions supporting field safety. He or she may need to stop work if imminent hazards warrant taking this action. The Assistant Safety Officer must understand the level of risk that is sufficient to issue a stop-work order, the implications of issuing the stop-work order, and how to communicate this action through the chain of command.

Assistant Safety Officers assigned to field support must maintain communication with the Safety Officer throughout the operational period. The Safety Officer must make briefings to other Command and General Staff, and relies on Assistant Safety Officers to communicate appropriate and accurate information. Information from Assistant Safety Officers in the field contributes to the ongoing safety analysis, and includes information that the Safety Officer needs to complete the Form 215A Safety Analysis. The Safety Officer must make sure to include updates from these Assistant Safety Officers in briefings [3].

Assistant Safety Officers representing individual employers participating in the response may be stationed in the field with the workers they support on a day–to-day basis while maintaining communication with the Safety Officer, or may be stationed closer to the Incident Command Post as a resource for the Safety Officer. Assistant Safety Officers assigned as resource support provide expertise on site-specific or industry-specific hazards necessary for decision-making, and assist the Safety Officer in developing Safety Analysis (ICS Form 215A), hazard evaluations, and site safety plans. Their site-specific or industry-specific expertise facilitates situational awareness for all personnel supporting the safety function [2].

9.3 Technical Specialists

Technical Specialists may be appointed by the Incident Commander or Unified Command, and may be assigned anywhere in the organization. Technical Specialists are command advisors, and serve only in an advisory capacity. They do not have the authority to direct incident activities. Technical Specialists normally perform the same duties during an incident that they perform in their day-to-day jobs, and typically, Technical Specialists are well qualified and certified in their fields of expertise. For example, an Incident Commander or Unified Command may appoint legal counsel as a Technical Specialist to advise on legal matters.

The 2017 NIMS Refresh lists examples of Technical Specialists:

- Access and functional needs advisor;
- Agricultural specialist;
- Community representative;
- Decontamination specialist;
- Environmental impact specialist;
- Epidemiologist;
- Flood control specialist;
- Health physicist;
- Industrial hygienist;
- Intelligence specialist;
- Legal advisor;
- Behavioral health specialist;
- Meteorologist;
- Science and technology advisor;
- Pharmacist;
- Veterinarian;
- Toxicologist.

Technical Specialists may be positioned with Command Staff when their expertise is needed to support Command-level decision-making. Alternatively, Technical Specialists may be located within the Planning Section if their expertise is needed to assist in evaluating the situation and forecasting needs, or the Operations or Logistics Sections. An Intelligence Section may be established if warranted. An Intelligence Officer may be appointed as a member of the Command Staff, or an Intelligence Chief can be assigned as General Staff. Intelligence

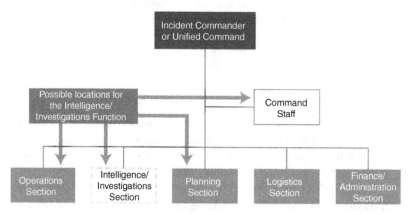

Figure 9.2 Multiple options for placement of an Intelligence Section within the Incident Command System. Technical Specialists may be assigned to Intelligence. Source: Federal Emergency Management Administration, US Department of Homeland Security [1].

may also be placed under Planning or Operations (Figure 9.2). Regardless of placement, individual Technical Specialists can be critical to completion of the Intelligence function [1].

9.4 Industrial Hygienists

Industrial hygienists evaluate environmental health hazards, including chemical, physical, biological, ergonomic, and psychosocial hazards, and identify and implement controls for these hazards to minimize impacts on health.

Industrial hygienists have skill sets that are valuable in incident response, including means and methods for exposure assessment and interpretation of data. In their day-to-day work, industrial hygienists consider and recommend appropriate engineering controls, administrative controls and work practices, and Personal Protective Equipment to mitigate risks to workers. Industrial hygiene skills in evaluating the strengths and weaknesses of controls is invaluable in an emergency situation, in which resources may be scarce, and flexibility and creativity are needed to protect workers. Experience and training are key to this decision-making.

In addition, industrial hygienists bring skill sets that aid in supporting incident safety, including:

- Setting up decontamination protocols;
- Development of site safety plans;
- Evaluate compliance with site safety plans, OSHA rules, or state plan rules during field activities;
- Providing expertise on health and safety issues and regulatory requirements;
- Providing on-site training and "tail-gate" safety briefings;
- Conducting accident investigations, in particular, accidents involving acute chemical, biological, or physical agent exposures;
- Evaluation of ventilation controls;
- Evaluation of Chemical Protective Clothing (CPC);
- Managing use of respiratory protection (respirators);
- Reviewing toxicological effects of common toxic industrial chemicals;
- Interpretation of laboratory data, and data from direct reading instruments used in the field;
- Knowing the capabilities and limitations of direct reading instruments;
- Evaluating biological and dermal (skin) exposures;
- Understanding basic safety requirements, such as permit-required confined space entry and ergonomics;
- Understanding basic environmental health needs, including drinking water quality, waste management, sanitation issues, housing needs, and basic food safety [4].

Industrial hygienists serving as Technical Specialists must be skilled in their field, and be able to serve as technical support for the groups to which they are assigned. The Industrial Hygiene (IH) Technical Specialist must have knowledge of the Incident Command System structure so that they understand which positions they must liaise with on key safety and occupational health issues, how to utilize ICS forms and response-specific forms to document and communicate findings, and to understand how to communicate with the Safety Officer [3].

Industrial hygienists are needed to conduct personal air monitoring of responders in the event that there is potential exposure to airborne contaminants. The results of this personal air monitoring determines whether or not OSHA Permissible Exposure Limits or other applicable occupational exposure limits were exceeded. When exposure monitoring indicates that safe exposure levels are exceeded, steps can be taken to protect workers, such as selecting and providing respirators that protect against the type of exposure and degree of hazard. If the exposure results warrant medical evaluation and follow-up, this evaluation can begin as soon as possible.

A determination that regulatory or recommended exposure limits have not been exceeded is reassuring to workers that were exposed, and reduce anxiety associated with exposure to unknown hazards.

Industrial hygienists who collect personnel air monitoring data must consolidate the data into a report for distribution. This report documents:

- The tasks and work performed;
- How responders are exposed to the contaminant of interest;
- The method(s) used for air monitoring;
- The results of air monitoring;
- An interpretation of the results;
- Recommended actions to be taken as a result of the data that was obtained.

The report should focus on representative sampling rather than individual results, although individuals who participated in sampling should be confidentially notified in writing of the results of their own sample. This report is then submitted to the Safety Officer and the Incident Commander, and to the Planning Section for recordkeeping. It is recommended that the full report list sampling results positions or tasks evaluated in representative sampling rather than names of workers who participated. The final report may be widely distributed, and thus, cannot contain any confidential information.

Personal air monitoring is considered by OSHA to be an exposure record, and OSHA requires that exposure and medical records be maintained for a period of 30 years. Any individual sampling results must be kept with responders' confidential medical records.

Many employers, including cities and counties, local government agencies, and private employers have industrial hygienists on staff to support the employer's day-to-day occupational safety and health programs, and these in-house industrial hygienists can provide support for the response. Industrial hygienists are also employed as consultants, at universities, and with OSHA or state health and safety programs, and the Safety Officer can work with Logistics to pull these resources in when needed. The American Industrial Hygiene Association (AIHA), as well as many AIHA local sections, maintain lists of industrial hygiene consultants.

9.5 Toxicologist

When chemical exposures are unique or unusual, or outside of the industrial hygienist's realm of experience, it may be helpful to bring in a toxicologist. A toxicologist can serve as a Technical Specialist who reviews data related to a chemical release or exposure, or to a chemical that is being proposed for use in the response (such as an oil dispersant), and can evaluate risk to responders, the community, and the environment. The toxicologist should have an advanced degree in toxicology, and experience in evaluating chemical hazards in emergencies.

The toxicologist could serve with the Command Staff in an advisory capacity to the Incident Commander and the Safety Officer. Alternatively, a toxicologist could work with the Planning Section to identify possible future exposures. For example, a toxicologist might analyze the potential health impacts of a chemical release in an area where the released chemical could react with stored chemicals at nearby facilities if it comes into contact with them. A medical toxicologist might work with the Medical Unit in the Logistics Section to evaluate treatment of personnel suffering from chemical exposures.

Toxicologists are often employed at universities, public health departments, environmental agencies, and as consultants, and these employers may be able to provide toxicology resources when needed. Many toxicologists are members of the Society of Toxicology (SOT).

The Agency for Toxic Substances and Disease Registry (ATSDR) supports ATSDR Emergency Response Teams comprised of toxicologists, physicians, and other scientists who can assist in an emergency involving release of hazardous materials to the environment [5].[1]

9.6 Health Physicist

Health physicists specialize in radiation safety, and are often employed by organizations that utilize radiation for beneficial use, such as hospitals and research organizations. They also work for employers that support development of nuclear

---

1 http://atsdr.cdc.gov/emergencyresponse.html (accessed 20 August 2019).

power, weaponry, and manufacture of equipment such as particle accelerators and X-ray machines. If an incident affects such a facility, it is likely that a health physicist is on staff and can be a resource for the response.

Health physicists can support the Safety Officer by providing technical advice and assistance on the health effects of radiation exposure, evaluating exposures, and identifying and implementing appropriate controls. If exposure monitoring of radiological substances is needed, the health physicist can conduct monitoring, interpret results, and write a report.

A health physicist can also serve as an Assistant Safety Officer in the field if an operational response subjects workers to radiation exposure.

If a release occurs that is not associated with a specific facility, or if need for health physicists exceeds available resources, the Incident Management Team may be able to locate health physicists through a state radiation control agency or through local chapters of the Health Physics Society. The American Academy of Health Physics maintains lists of Certified Health Physicists (CHPs).[2]

9.7 Safety Engineer

Responses may involve the use of equipment or complex systems. When new equipment is brought in, or new systems are designed, they should be reviewed by a safety engineer who can do a thorough hazard analysis. This analysis should begin early in the design of the system, and a system safety engineer can utilize analytical tools such as fault-tree analysis to identify where failures can occur, and how these failures can result in hazards that can injure responders or others. Failure points identified in the design phase are then corrected and controlled. Reviews are continued as the system is developed and constructed to ensure that it is implemented as designed and to identify any previously unanticipated hazards. System safety review continues through the life cycle of the machine or system, until the response is complete, and the equipment is dismantled and removed.

Engineers may also need to review installation of fall protection systems, guardrails, scaffolding, material-handling equipment such as cranes, or similar systems before they are used.

Safety engineers must have a bachelor's degree, typically in environmental health or in an engineering discipline.

Some systems may need to be reviewed by a licensed Professional Engineer (PE). PEs can also be assigned as Technical Specialists [5].

---

2 http://aahp-abhp.org/members (accessed August 20, 2019).

9.8 Competent Persons

Several OSHA standards require that competent persons perform specified duties, as discussed in Chapter 4. OSHA rules covering work in trenches, confined spaces, or at heights list specific duties that must be performed by competent persons. Technical Specialists may need to be brought in to fulfill these roles.

9.9 Health and Safety Trainer

Numerous safety training requirements were discussed in Chapter 5. Some responders will have received training through their primary employers, which may or may not be sufficient for the tasks that these workers will perform as part of the response effort. Unless training has been addressed through contracts or mutual aid agreements prior to the incident, this will need to be reviewed and documented. Technical Specialists who review and track training may work under Logistics for resources being requested, under Planning, or directly for the Safety Officer. Tracking the training that is required versus the training that has been completed, and doing it quickly, is a very large job, particularly in responses that incorporate large numbers of workers.

Even if previous training is determined to be acceptable, workers need to receive a safety orientation that covers incident-specific information. A Safety Training Technical Specialist can ensure consistency in the safety orientation information that workers receive, and may need to be a dedicated resource.

Additional trainers may need to be brought in to provide specific types of training, such as fall protection, equipment operation, trenching, confined space, Personal Protective Equipment, respiratory protection, or any other training requirements as discussed in Chapter 5. Different types of expertise are needed for different types of training: For example, a trainer who is qualified to instruct on backhoe operations may not necessarily be qualified to provide training on respirator use.

Safety trainers should report to the Safety Officer, or to an Assistant Safety Officer.

9.10 Respiratory Protection Program Administrator

Response and recovery workers are often exposed to respiratory hazards, such as smoke from fires, dust and debris from volcanoes and storms, chemical, radiological, or biological releases, and other hazards as discussed in Chapter 3. Respirators may be issued to protect workers from these hazards, but if the wrong respirator is selected, if it is not used properly, or if the worker is not medically qualified to wear a respirator, respirators can pose hazards of their own.

As discussed in Chapter 4, employers who issue respirators to employees must:

- Evaluate exposures;
- Select a type of respirator based on the exposure evaluation;
- Ensure employees who wear respirators are medically qualified to do so;
- Fit test respirators to ensure that they do not leak;
- Train workers.

OSHA's Respiratory Protection Standard requires that an employer assign a Respiratory Protection Program Administrator to ensure that this gets done [6].

In the early stages of an incident response, first responders are often firefighters who are equipped with self-contained breathing apparatus (SCBA) and participate in the Respiratory Protection Program managed by their primary employer. As the incident expands, and if nontraditional responders or wildland firefighters who do not have SCBAs are brought in, respirators may need to be procured for these workers. Incident management personnel should work under the assumption that these personnel have little, if any, experience wearing the respirators that they will need. The Respiratory Protection Program Administrator must first ensure that these workers obtain medical clearance before being issued a respirator. Once respirators are issued, workers must be fit tested. A fit test can take between 15 and 30 minutes to complete, so sufficient personnel who are trained and qualified to conduct fit testing must be available to accommodate all intended workers.

Workers must be trained in respirator use. Respirators that are not worn correctly do not protect workers from hazards, and in a worst-case scenario, could create hazards of their own.

Of course, the correct respirators must be selected and procured before they can be issued to workers. The Respiratory Protection Program Administrator must review exposure reports, if available, and may need to consult with the Safety Officer, Assistant Safety Officers, industrial hygienists, or health physicists in order to determine which type of respirator is suitable for the exposure. If Logistics cannot obtain the desired type of respirator, the Respiratory Protection Program Administrator must be able to identify whether alternatives can provide sufficient protection.

Once respirators are issued, they must be maintained. Filters and cartridges must be replaced. If parts fail on the respirator, the Respiratory Protection Program Administrator should be able to make minor repairs, replace parts, or send the respirator system out for repairs.

Respiratory protection programs in General Industry require a dedicated resource to ensure that required program elements are met, and that workers can wear respirators safely. This is just as true in a disaster response as it is in the everyday workplace. Responders in past disasters, including 9/11, suffer today from diseases related to exposures that in all likelihood could have been prevented or at least minimized through effective use of the right respirators.

Without a Respiratory Protection Program Administrator in place to oversee the program, it is all too easy for program requirements to be missed. If workers who are not medically qualified to wear respirators are asked to use one, they may suffer from illness or injury due to the increased cardio pulmonary demand, or may just not wear their respirators because they do not feel good when they do. If tight-fitting respirators are not fit tested, they provide a false sense of security to workers who continue to be exposed to airborne contaminants while they bear the discomfort and risk of wearing the respirator. If respirators are not maintained, or if parts fail and are not replaced, workers are not protected from hazards and work with a false sense of security. If workers are not trained to wear respirators, they are unlikely to use them correctly (if they wear them at all). Noncompliance with respirator use, or wearing respirators in a manner that does not protect workers from respiratory exposures hazards, defeats the purpose of the respiratory protection program.

Since the respiratory protection program is part of the site safety plan, the Respiratory Protection Program Administrator should report through the Safety Officer as either an Assistant Safety Officer or Technical Specialist.

9.11 Decontamination Specialist

A Hazardous Waste Operations and Emergency Response (HAZWOPER)-compliant site safety plan includes plans for decontamination of workers and equipment as they leave the contaminated area (the *Exclusion Zone*) and enter the Clean or *Support Zone*. The Zone in between, or the *Contamination Reduction Zone*, is laid out so that PPE is cleaned and removed in a specified order, with rinse steps taking place at various points between. Decontamination takes place at stations that are set up and monitored in the Contamination Reduction Zone (Figure 9.3).

Development of a decontamination procedure requires knowledge of hazards of contaminants, and experience with effective methods to prevent them from being tracked into clean areas. Some PPE and equipment will need to be disposed of, and drop stations are set up at designated locations per the decontamination plan. The decontaminated specialist must ensure that waste disposal is in accordance with applicable rules and regulations. Other types of PPE can be washed. This may be done at another controlled location after the PPE user drops it off, or it may be cleaned in the Contamination Reduction Zone. Cleaning and rinse liquids

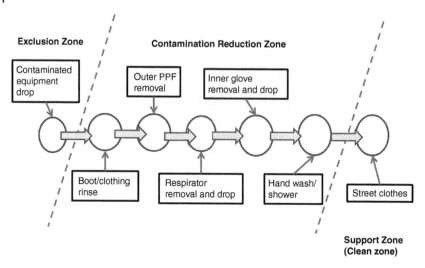

Figure 9.3 Example of a decontamination plan layout. Step-by-step decontamination ensures that contaminants are not tracked into clean areas.

are presumed to be contaminated, and cannot be allowed to run into the ground or to enter any nearby waterways. Instead, rinsate and wastewater must be collected so that it can be disposed of through approved hazardous waste channels.

Personnel are generally staffed within the Contamination Reduction Zone to observe and assist workers moving through the decontamination steps. They can actively assist with PPE removal, or they can monitor workers as they remove PPE and warn them if they inadvertently contact a clean surface with a "dirty" surface. If drop stations become full, they must be changed out. Rinse stations are monitored so that collection containers do not overfill, and to ensure that sufficient clean rinse water and detergent solutions are available. These monitors serve to ensure that contaminants from the Exclusion Zone do not enter the Clean Zone, and that personnel working in the Exclusion Zone are clean before leaving the work area.

An emergency response may not necessarily fall under HAZWOPER, but still carry risk of contamination. Fire departments that adopt "clean cab" procedures to reduce the amount of fire contamination that enters fire apparatus or fire departments can utilize a similar decontamination protocol. Likewise, responders to disasters in which contamination is unknown but probable, such as floods or landslides, can also adopt a similar decontamination layout. Inclusion of monitors inside the Contamination Reduction Zone reduces errors and improves efficiency of decontamination, just as it does in a HAZWOPER-type response.

Contamination Reduction Zone monitors continually evaluate whether or not decontamination procedures ware working as intended. If monitors observe that contaminants are not being removed, or that they penetrate PPE, decontamination methods have to be revised. Similarly, monitors check to make sure there is sufficient space so that personnel performing decontamination steps are not bumping into each other. Monitors evaluate environmental conditions and weather, including wind direction: the Clean Zone should be upwind of the Exclusion Zone.

In an emergency, personnel must be able to evacuate quickly. Emergency decontamination procedures have to be developed and used if there is not sufficient time to fully decontaminate using the standard procedure.

Decontamination procedures are often written by an industrial hygienist or hazardous materials specialist. Decontamination specialists must be able to follow these plans and should have sufficient training and expertise to perform their jobs. Contamination Reduction Zone monitors should be HAZWOPER trained at a minimum, and depending upon the hazard, may need to have some industrial hygiene training as well [5].

9.12   Field Observer for Safety Officer

Assistant Safety Officer can be assigned as field support for particularly hazardous operations. Lower hazard operations also have need for field support. Safety cannot be managed from an office, or a command post, and the Safety Officer must make time for field visits. Still, in a sufficiently large response, planning and Command Staff responsibilities can eat up time that the Safety Officer could otherwise spend in the field. The Safety Officer may assign a Technical Specialist Safety Field Observer who can perform this function for operations that do not carry enough risk to warrant assignment of their own Assistant Safety Officer.

The Safety Field Observer need not be able to fulfill all the functions of the Safety Officer. However, this position should have a strong background in safety practices and protocols, and be sufficiently prepared to advise and correct work practices that could cause injury or illness. The Safety Field Observer must communicate and coordinate with the Safety Officer throughout the response [5].

9.13   Occupational Medicine Specialist

Medical monitoring required under various OSHA regulations was reviewed in Chapter 6. Medical monitoring requirements should be incorporated into ICS Form 206, Medical Plan, which is prepared by the Medical Unit Leader under the Logistics Section and approved by the Safety Officer.

A Technical Specialist with expertise in medical monitoring requirements can assist in ensuring that all necessary medical monitoring requirements are incorporated into the Medical Plan, and oversee that the medical monitoring outlined in the Medical Plan is actually performed.

Medical professionals, such as a physician with a specialty in Occupational Health Medicine or other licensed healthcare professionals, can perform required medical monitoring. This includes assisting workers in completing respirator medical questionnaires and reviewing them to provide medical approvals for respirator use. Unless answers to the medical questionnaire indicate the need for follow up medical testing, many workers can receive their respirator medical clearance in the field.

Other types of medical evaluations must be performed in a clinical setting. A laboratory must be available to run blood and urine screens, and data must be tracked.

Once medical evaluations are completed, the physician or other licensed health-care professional provides a written opinion as to whether or not a worker can perform work that exposes them to the specified hazardous condition. The written opinion may approve work without restrictions, or restrictions may be recommended.

Resources are required to track and manage these written opinions. If medical clearance is required to perform a task, only workers who have received medical clearance can perform that task. Someone must be assigned the responsibility to track which responders and/or recovery workers have and have not received medical clearances, and to communicate this to those who assign work assignments to workers. In addition, these records must be maintained confidentially, and communication about who has and has not received medical approval should be accomplished in as confidential a manner as possible.

Occupational Medicine Technical Specialists who are physicians or licensed health-care professionals can provide medical monitoring. Administrative medical support staff can be assigned to track clearances and work assignments, and to maintain records.

These resources could report up to the Medical Unit Leader in Logistics, or to the Safety Officer, as both sign off on the Medical Plan [5].

9.14 Behavioral Health Specialist

As discussed in Chapter 7, emergency response personnel are subject to numerous psychological stressors. The use of psychological first aid supplemented with professional psychological support when needed can help responders cope with acute stressors that interfere with task performance as well as potentially mitigating long term adverse outcomes. Behavioral health specialists are needed to coordinate and provide support, and should be integrated into the ICS reporting structure.

As behavioral health support is incorporated into the Medical Plan, these resources could report up to the Medical Unit Leader in Logistics, or to the Safety Officer, who both sign off on the Medical Plan.

The number of behavioral health support specialists will be dependent upon the type of response, the degree of trauma to which responders are exposed, and the number of responders involved. Greater levels of support should be provided when the incident is one that impacts a response or recovery worker's own community. Homes may be damaged or destroyed, including the homes of responders, and family members of responders may need assistance. It is possible that community members who are missing, injured, or even killed are people that responders know personally, or may even be related to.

Family members of responders need support as well. If response workers know that their families are being taken care of, they can better focus on the task at hand without worry or distraction. This level of support must be considered in determining how many behavioral support specialists are needed.

9.15 Environmental Monitoring

If contaminants are released into the environment, air monitoring will need to be conducted to evaluate this release. Specialists with expertise in using EPA software to track chemical release plumes (Computer-Aided Management of Emergency Operations or CAMEO) can evaluate travel of a contaminant plume in order to assess impact on nearby communities as well as responders. Results of air monitoring and modeling are then submitted to environmental agencies monitoring the release, or other agencies requiring submitted reports.

The results of air monitoring can be compared with air concentration limits set by local clean air agencies, state environmental agencies, or the EPA. Results that indicate air concentrations exceed these limits can trigger regulatory actions.

Results can also be used to determine whether or not residents of a community can stay in their homes or workplaces, or if they need to be evacuated. Air modeling can be used to determine if and when a plume is expected to reach an occupied area. This information can be used to determine how quickly an evacuation must take place, if evacuation is needed, and to identify a safe location for people to go where they will be free from exposure to the plume.

Industrial hygienists in the response should know the contents of the release plume. If air monitoring and modeling indicate that responders could be exposed to the contaminants in this plume, industrial hygienists can take personal breathing air samples to quantitate worker exposures.

If contaminants are released to soils or waterways, personnel will be required to monitor soil and water samples. Results of this monitoring are also compared with regulatory limits established by the EPA or state environmental agencies, and can be used to assess dermal exposures to workers who come into contact with the soil or water.

9.16   Risk Assessor

Once air, soil, or water samples have been taken, and results are received, the level of risk posed must be analyzed. Environmental risk assessments are completed in order to characterize health risks that contamination poses to humans and animals in this environment, as well as the magnitude of that risk. A risk assessment starts with identifying which chemical contaminants are present in the environment, and at what levels. It also looks at the "receptors" who are likely to be exposed to these chemicals, including humans (residents, workers, visitors, children, the elderly, and sensitive populations) and wildlife (birds, fish, reptiles, mammals, or other wildlife). The risk assessment then evaluates how these receptors are likely to be exposed and the impacts of that exposure. Exposure could occur through ingestion of chemicals directly from the environment or through bioaccumulation (when carnivores consume lower level predators who have ingested the harmful substance), through respiration of air contaminants by air-breathing animals or through respiration of water contaminants in fish, or direct contact with the chemical in air, soil, or water. Additional assessment is based on:

- The degree and type of exposure;
- The biological uptake through each exposure route;
- What is known about the relative toxicity of the contaminants by species;
- Interactions between contaminants that influence the toxicity of each;
- The rate and transport of contaminants in environmental media;

However, even in ideal conditions, much of the information that is needed to conduct a good risk assessment is unknown, and the risk assessor must rely on estimates and good judgment. For this reason, all risk assessments contain a degree of uncertainty, and safety factors are incorporated to account for this inherent uncertainty.[3]

A risk assessor, especially in an incident that is evolving, should be well qualified and experienced. Risk assessors have degrees in scientific fields, generally toxicology, and are experienced and knowledgeable in the risk assessment models used by EPA.

---

3 http://epa.gov/risk/about-risk-assessment (accessed 29 August 2019).

In an incident response, risk assessment specialists must work closely with other technical staff including industrial hygienists, toxicologists, air monitoring specialists, and those who monitor the movement of the plume or release in air, soils, water in navigable waterways including streams, lakes, rivers, or oceans, and in groundwater.

The degree of health hazard to people and the environment is an important consideration in setting incident response priorities, which in turn influence goals and objectives. Findings from the risk assessment should be made available to General and Command Staff for consideration in incident planning. The Safety Officer may be able to obtain additional information on hazards faced by responders by reviewing the risk assessment report.

Risk assessors typically work for environmental regulatory agencies, or as consultants, and these organizations can be contacted for assistance in providing this resource.

9.17 Food Safety Specialist

The Food Unit Leader, in the Logistics Section, is responsible for determining food and water needs for the incident, ordering food, providing cooking facilities, and maintaining food service areas. In addition, the Food Unit Leader is responsible for working with the Safety Officer to ensure food safety and security. This is an important function in any incident: Responders who are not fed and hydrated will not be able to perform their job responsibilities safely, if at all.

The 2017 NIMS Refresh suggests that an Assistant Safety Officer be assigned to support food safety [1]. Food safety, and prevention of food-related illness, is extremely important in any incident. Responders suffering from food poisoning cannot perform assigned duties, and may require medical care. These cases of food poisoning divert medical support resources from the response, which is particularly problematic if medical resources are limited to start with.

Food-related illnesses that cause diarrhea and vomiting are also problematic when plumbing systems are compromised as a result of the incident, and can then escalate into an even larger public health issue.

Cities, counties, and public health agencies employ food environmental health specialists to inspect restaurants and other facilities that serve food. They ensure that local food safety codes are complied with, including food storage, refrigeration temperatures, cooking temperatures, sanitation, and cleanliness. Individuals employed in this line of work are best qualified to support the Safety Officer in ensuring that the food served to responders is safe to eat.

Personnel preparing food should have food handler's permits issued by the county in which they are working. Safety personnel supporting the Food Unit should track food handler's permits, and ensure that all personnel handling food have their required permits and certifications.

9.18 Environmental Health/Sanitation Specialist

The need for portable toilets is very often underestimated in emergency planning. OSHA regulations include requirements for toilet facilities, and the number needed is based on the number of personnel present. If emergency planners identify that there will be a need for portable toilets in emergency plans, and sourcing is identified, it should be a simple matter to procure and locate these portable toilet facilities.

However (I've learned this through personal experience), portable toilets are often not sufficiently planned for, and the need for additional facilities is only identified mid-incident. When this happens, a portable toilet detail needs to be assigned to source toilets, procure them, find a place to put them, and ensure that they are maintained.

It is entirely possible that with sufficient planning this resource could appear seamlessly at the incident site without the need to appoint a portable toilet sanitation specialist. Maintenance of portable toilets would still need to be overseen, but this could be managed as an administrative function in the Logistics Section.

When the quantity of portable toilets has not been sufficiently foreseen prior to the incident, the effort to procure and site them in a time-sensitive manner plays a critical role in the success of the incident response team. The importance of this resource should not be underestimated.

9.19 Safety Support for Temporary Support Facilities

Support centers may be activated to support an incident response, particularly in events requiring significant resources or when needed to support multiple incidents, such as a Multi-Agency Coordination Center (MACC), Emergency Operations Center (EOC), or Joint Field Office (JFO). A JFO is a temporary Multi-Agency Coordination Center, and provides a central location for coordination of federal, state, local, tribal, nongovernmental, and private-sector organizations supporting the incident. A MACC is a place where state, federal, and local agencies can come together to coordinate and support incident response efforts. EOCs may be organized by functional disciplines, such as fire, law enforcement, and medical services, or by jurisdiction such as city, state, county, or tribe, or a combination [7].

These centers are often stood up in designated facilities that have been designed and resourced for this purpose. General office safety support should be provided for these centers when they are operational, including ergonomics support for personnel working at new or unfamiliar workstations, a plan to respond to indoor air quality complaints, evacuation plans, and general building facility safety.

If the designated facility is damaged by the incident or cannot otherwise be occupied, a secondary or temporary facility must be stood up. Safety support for such a temporary facility includes establishing emergency evacuation plans and procedures, fire prevention plans, and other plans necessary to occupy a workspace. Personnel working in the facility also need to be briefed on these safety plans.

9.20   Summary

The Safety Officer has a significant role to play in incident response. If the size and complexity of the incident is such that the Safety Officer cannot single handedly meet his or her responsibilities to maintain the safety of all responders and protect the Incident Commander from liability, additional resources in the form of Assistant Safety Officers and Technical Specialists can and should be brought in. Several types of resources are discussed in this chapter for consideration and the resources needed will vary by incident.

Safety personnel who work in construction, chemical manufacturing, general industry, utilities, transportation, and other sectors that could require an emergency response or state, city, county, or tribal jurisdictions should be trained in ICS and incident response. They should participate in emergency planning and exercises and work with safety personnel who support first responders to build the trust that is needed when an actual incident occurs.

Fire, police, and medical response personnel who are assigned the role of Safety Officer should be aware that sector specific safety staff have knowledge that could be of critical importance in protecting response personnel. If these safety staff have the training and background to integrate into an ICS structure, the Safety Officer should keep these resources close by and maintain open lines of communication.

A number of support positions have been discussed in this chapter, and depending upon the incident, one or more of these positions can be resourced to facilitate safety efforts in the response.

References

1 Federal Emergency Management Administration, US Department of Homeland Security (2017). *National Incident Management System*, 3e.

2 Continuing Education Programs, Department of Environmental and Occupational Health Sciences, University of Washington (2017) *Emergency Safety Officer Course.*

3 Weems, L., Stahl, D., Primeau, E. et al. (2018). *American Industrial Hygiene Association Body of Knowledge Emergency Preparedness and Response for the Industrial Hygienist.* AIHA.

4 Emergency Preparedness and Response Task Force, American Industrial Hygiene Association (2006). *Industrial Hygienists' Role and Responsibilities in Emergency Preparedness and Response White Paper.* AIHA.

5 Primeau, E. and Weems, L. (2018). *Incident Safety and Health Management Handbook*, 2e. American Industrial Hygiene Association.

6 29 CFR 1910.134, Respiratory Protection.

7 Federal Emergency Management Administration, US Department of Homeland Security (2006) *Joint Field Office Activation and Operations Interagency Integrated Standard Operating Procedures*, Version 8.6.

10

Integrating Safety into Emergency Planning

As discussed in the previous chapters, a number of elements need to be incorporated into an incident safety plan. Implementing a comprehensive site safety plan that stands up to regulatory requirements promulgated by OSHA and state health and safety regulatory agencies, and prevents workers from getting injured or sick, or dying, is a noble goal, and one that emergency managers, Incident Commanders, and Safety Officers should strive for.

Given the scope of what needs to be included in such a safety plan, it is unlikely to succeed unless the building blocks for the safety plan have been integrated into the overall emergency plan.

State and local governments are required to develop plans for emergencies. Safety personnel who are employed within these governmental entities can, and, should, participate in planning efforts to advocate for incorporating worker safety considerations into these plans. Stakeholder involvement is an important element of emergency planning, and professional organizations, such as the American Society of Safety Professionals or the American Industrial Hygiene Association are stakeholders that can advocate for including worker safety provisions in emergency planning. Individuals can also participate as stakeholders.

In order to best advocate for worker safety in the emergency planning phase, it is imperative to understand the process and parameters through which emergency plans are developed.

10.1 The Emergency Planning and Community Right-to-Know Act

One of the worst industrial disasters in history occurred in Bhopal, India, on 2 December 1984. An accident at the Union Carbide pesticide plant in Bhopal, India, released a number of toxic gasses, the deadliest of which was methyl isocyanate. At least 30 tons of methyl isocyanate was released, exposing more

Health and Safety in Emergency Management and Response, First Edition. Dana L. Stahl.
© 2021 John Wiley & Sons, Inc. Published 2021 by John Wiley & Sons, Inc.

than 600 000 people. The actual number of people killed is not known, but it is estimated that there were 15 000 fatalities. Survivors suffered respiratory and other health deficits, and children born to survivors suffered high rates of physical and mental disabilities [1].

Governments around the world reacted to this incident. The United States enacted the Emergency Planning and Community Right-to-Know Act (EPCRA), or Title III of the Superfund Amendments and Reauthorization Act (SARA) in 1986 in an effort to prevent a similar incident from occurring. The Comprehensive Environmental Response, Compensation, and Liability Act (CERCLA), or "Superfund," was enacted in 1980 as a means to fund direct responses to releases of hazardous substances, and to fund cleanup of highly contaminated sites identified on EPA's National Priorities List (NPL). The 1986 amendments added requirements for industries to disclose to the community the hazardous chemicals that they used or maintained on site when the quantities of these chemicals meet or exceed established thresholds [2, 3].

EPCRA also requires that state Governors establish State Emergency Response Commissions (SERCs) which in turn appoint Local Emergency Planning Committees (LEPCs) to address emergencies relating to the release of hazardous materials. LEPCs are responsible for developing emergency plans.

10.2 State Emergency Response Commissions (SERC)

State Emergency Response Commissions (SERCs) are responsible for implementing EPCRA provisions within their states. Governors have been responsible for appointing the SERC since 1986: The SERC can be an existing state-sponsored or -appointed emergency response organization, or it can be a stand-alone commission.

The Governor is also responsible for appointing people to serve on the SERC. These personnel must have technical expertise in the emergency response field. For example, the State of Washington SERC includes representatives from:

- The Washington Fire Chiefs Association;
- Department of Agriculture;
- Department of Ecology;
- Department of Labor and Industries (The Washington State Department of Occupational Safety and Health exists within the Department of Labor and Industries);
- Department of Transportation;
- A local emergency manager;
- A local emergency planning committee member;
- The Military Department;

- Private industry;
- Transportation industry;
- Washington State Patrol.[1]

The SERC is responsible for defining Local Emergency Planning Committees (LEPCs) in the state. LEPC districts in different states can look very different. For example, the State of Washington designates that every county establish an LEPC, and some municipalities within the state, such as the City of Seattle and the Joint Base Lewis–McChord, establish their own LEPCs.[2] In California, the SERC has established six LEPCs, one for each mutual aid Emergency Planning District.[3] Some states establish a single LEPC for the entire state.

The SERC supervises and coordinates the activities of the LEPCs, and reviews local emergency response plans developed by the LEPCs.

SERCs also coordinate industry reports of hazardous chemicals exceeding threshold quantities, and develop procedures for distributing this information when members of the public request it [4].

10.3   Tribal Emergency Response Commissions (TERC)

Some tribal nations have established Tribal Emergency Response Commissions (TERCs) that perform the same functions as a SERC. Others opt into agreements with neighboring LEPCs.

EPA consults on a government-to-government basis with federally recognized tribal governments when EPA actions may affect tribal interests. Emergency preparedness and response falls under this scope [5].

10.4   Local Emergency Planning Committees (LEPCs)

The SERC appoints members to Local Emergency Planning Committees (LEPCs). At a minimum, each LEPC must include members from:

- Elected state and local officials;
- Law enforcement;

---

1 https://ecology.wa.gov/Regulations-Permits/Reporting-requirements/Emergency-Planning-Community-Right-to-Know-Act/State-Emergency-Response-Commission (accessed 5 September 2019).
2 https://ecology.wa.gov/Regulations-Permits/Reporting-requirements/Emergency-Planning-Community-Right-to-Know-Act/Local-Emergency-Planning-Committees (accessed 5 September 2019).
3 www.caloes.ca.gov/cal-oes-divisions/fire-rescue/hazardous-materials/state-emergency-response-commission/local-emergency-planning-committee (accessed 5 September 2019).

- Civil defense;
- Firefighting;
- First aid or Emergency Medical Services;
- Public Health;
- Local environmental groups or organizations;
- Hospitals;
- Transportation;
- The media;
- Community groups/general public;
- Owners and operators of facilities with hazardous materials that exceed threshold limits, and are thus subject to SARA and EPCRA provisions.

Each LEPC elects their own chairperson and establishes their own rules for:

- Holding public meetings to discuss the Emergency Management Plan;
- Notification of meetings and other activities undertaken by the LEPC;
- Public commenting rules and response to public comments;
- Distribution of the emergency plan, including submittal to the SERC and other stakeholders;
- Procedures to receive and process requests from the public for information covered under the Community Right-to-Know provisions of EPCRA, including required reports submitted by facilities that have hazardous materials at quantities exceeding thresholds;
- Designation of an official to serve as coordinator for submitted and requested information.

Members of the public can petition the SERC if they believe there should be a modification to the membership of an LEPC [4].

The emergency plan that an LEPC develops must include:

- Identification of facilities that must report quantities of hazardous materials above threshold levels within the emergency planning district;
- Identification of routes likely to be used for the transportation of Extremely Hazardous Substances [2];
- Identification of facilities that contribute risk, or are subject to additional risk, due to their proximity to the facilities that utilize hazardous materials above threshold levels and are subject to the reporting provision;
- How facility owners and operators, local first responders, and medical personnel will respond to releases of these hazardous materials, including procedures each will follow;
- Designation of a community emergency coordinator and a facility emergency coordinator with decision-making authority who can decide to implement the plan;

- Procedures for reliable, effective, and timely notification to persons designated in the emergency plan when a release has occurred;
- Procedures for reliable, effective, and timely notification to the public when a release has occurred;
- Methods for determining that a release has occurred, and the area or population likely to be affected by the release;
- A description of emergency equipment at facilities that are identified in the plan subject to the EPCRA requirements, and identification of personnel responsible for this emergency equipment;
- Evacuation plans, including provisions for precautionary evacuation and alternative traffic routes;
- Training programs, including schedules for training local emergency response and medical personnel;
- How the emergency plan will be exercised, and the schedules for conducting exercises.

Once plans are completed, they are submitted to the SERC. The SERC is responsible for reviewing the plan, and making recommendations to the committee. For example, revisions may be necessary to ensure coordination with response plans submitted by other LEPCs [4, 6].

In practice, LEPCs have varying levels of success in development of emergency plans and effectively implementing them in the community. A 2008 survey of LEPCs found that only 60% of the LEPCs that responded to the survey had reviewed or updated their emergency plans within the previous 12 months, and 42.8% reported that their plan had been reviewed by the SERC in that time. Meeting frequency varied: 9 out of 10 responding LEPCs reported that they had met at least once in the past 12 months, and only 75% reported that they met at least quarterly. Those who had not met reported that this was due to a lack of interest from members, or a lack of funding.

LEPC members are volunteers, and are often busy working at their paid jobs or caring for their families, so achieving high participation can be challenging. Lack of funding is also an obstacle of LEPC success: The majority of LEPCs do not have an operating budget and do not receive direct funding. A little more than half of responding LEPCs receive some form of indirect funding, including space to hold meetings, materials and office supplies, and use of computers or other equipment.

Participation in LEPC activities and success in developing emergency plans is highest in LEPCs that had experienced one or more chemical accidents in their communities within the past five years. The perception that the LEPC had a positive impact on a community also increased with the number of chemical accidents experienced by the community [7].

10.5 Emergency Planning Under the National Response Framework

The Federal Response Plan was first published in 1992, and outlined how the Federal Government responded to states and local government requests for assistance under the Robert T. Stafford Disaster Relief and Emergency Assistance Act. The Department of Homeland Security (DHS) was established in 2002, after the events of 11 September 2001. DHS published the National Response Plan in 2004, building upon the principles outlined in the Federal Response Plan. Lessons learned from Hurricane Katrina, and other incidents lead to the development of the National Response Framework (NRF) in 2008, which superseded the National Response Plan. The NRF is in alignment with the National Incident Management System (NIMS), and establishes a consistent template to be used across the nation to work together to plan and respond to incidents regardless of cause, size, location, or complexity.

The NRF is intended for the *"whole community,"* which includes:

- Individuals;
- Families;
- Households;
- Communities;
- Private sector;
- Nonprofit sector;
- Faith-based organizations;
- Government, including local, state, tribal, territorial, and Federal governments.

The NRF recognizes that the whole community will need to come together after a major disaster, and that government resources will be unable to meet the needs of the community alone. Operational planning is an element of the NRF, and development of Emergency Operations Plans requires the input and participation of this whole community. The National Planning System outlines a six-step process to emergency planning:

- Step 1: Form a collaborative planning team.
- Step 2: Understand the situation.
- Step 3: Determine goals and objectives.
- Step 4: Plan development.
- Step 5: Plan preparation, review, and approval.
- Step 6: Plan implementation and maintenance.

An important aspect of planning is that plans align vertically and horizontally, across levels of government and supporting infrastructure, and along supporting partners. The system of plans developed by the "whole community" must align.

Members of this whole community must understand each other's capabilities and expectations. This approach is reflected in the concept of the planning team: members of the whole community must be represented in this team. While the responsibility for planning lies with the government agency or institution, the plan is developed by the team.

Plans must be flexible: As needs change, the plan must adapt to these needs. The planning team must continue to review and revise the plan as a process of continuous improvement [8, 9].

FEMA has released guidance on developing emergency plans for state, territorial, and local governments, and these planning guidelines are also useful for organizations outside of government, including the private sector. A concept that is central to this guidance is the idea that the process of planning is just as important as the resulting document, thus the importance of involving the whole community and stakeholders in the planning process. Plans must be flexible: No plan can anticipate every scenario, and plans must have the capacity to adapt to an actual situation. However, goals of the plan and the objectives that support the goals are consistent regardless of the incident.

Since disasters impact everyone in a community, plans need to be coordinated and integrated across the community. Plans must integrate vertically from the national level and the National Response Framework through state, territorial and tribal plans, regional jurisdictions, and private and nongovernmental organizations. Incidents start and end locally, but if needs exceed local resources, additional resources from upper levels of government are needed. Plans must be vertically integrated, so that when plans are activated at each successive level of government, a streamlined coordination of response is achieved.

Plans must be horizontally integrated as well, across individual departments or agencies within a jurisdiction to ensure that shared resources are distributed consistently, and that expectations from each organization are aligned within the plan and the organization's capabilities to meet them. A shared understanding of expectations and capabilities is critical, and this shared understanding is developed through working together in developing the plan.

Plans should consider that members of the public will take action to address immediate situations before responders can arrive. If the disaster is sufficiently large, the needs of the community far exceed the number of responders available, so public involvement is in fact needed.

The final plan should be streamlined, easy to read, simple, and flexible. A plan that is too long or overly detailed is unlikely to be read and understood, let alone followed.

Finalized emergency plans can have different formats. An Emergency Operations Plan may use a traditional format which follows FEMA's original guidance from the 1990s. It consists of a Basic Plan, Functional Annexes, and

Hazard-, Threat-, or Incident-Specific Annexes. The Functional Annexes focus on missions such as communication, damage assessment, search and rescue, and how this specific function is managed. These Functional Annexes address general strategies used for any emergency, and which agencies or departments perform these functions.

Hazard- or Threat-Specific Annexes describe actions and procedures that are unique to hazard types, such as tornadoes, earthquakes, hurricanes, or others. It is important that the content of these annexes does not overlap with, or conflict with, the content of the Basic Plan or the Functional Annexes.

Alternatively, an Emergency Operations Plan may follow the Emergency Support Function Format, which is the format used in the National Response Framework. These types of plans consist of a Basic Plan, Emergency Support Functions, and separate Support or Incident Annexes. The Emergency Support Functions may mirror those in the National Response Plan, or they can be defined by the jurisdiction. Support Annexes (such as the Worker Safety and Health Annex) and Hazard-Specific Annexes may or may not mirror those included in the National Response Plan. The jurisdiction has flexibility in designing the plan to best meet specific risks and needs.

A third format suggested in the guidance is an Agency-/Department-Focused Format. This format is best suited for small communities or organizations, including companies and private sector organizations. This plan covers only procedures and actions specific to the organization or the Agency, although other agencies and relationships are referenced. The format consists of the Basic Plan, a section describing Lead Agencies or Departments, a third section addressing Support Agencies or Departments, and a fourth section covering Hazard-Specific Procedures.

Regardless of format, the Basic Plan includes a similar layout:

- Section A: Introductory material, including document signatures and approval, record of changes, record of distribution, and a Table of Contents.
- Section B:
  - Purpose;
  - Scope;
  - Situation Overview;
    - Hazard Analysis Summary;
    - Capability Assessment;
    - Mitigation Overview;
  - Planning Assumptions.
- Section C: Concept of Operations: a description of how the emergency management strategy is used to accomplish a goal or a set of objectives, including coordination structures and any other specialized teams or resources needed;

- Section D: Organization and Assignment of Responsibilities;
- Section E: Direction, Control, and Coordination;
- Section F: Information Collection, Analysis, and Dissemination;
- Section G: Communications;
- Section H: Administration, Finance, and Logistics;
- Section I: Plan Development and Maintenance;
- Section J: Authorities and References [10].

10.6 Community Emergency Response Teams

The Community Emergency Response Teams (CERT) concept was first introduced in 1985 by the Los Angeles City Fire Department. In a large disaster that impacts a large geographical area and a large part of the community, such as an earthquake, the needs of the response will exceed the capabilities of professional emergency responders. Trained volunteers can serve the community to meet immediate needs in such an event. Trained CERT team members may perform basic disaster response functions, such as light search and rescue and disaster medical response. Organization of CERT teams is flexible to support the needs of local and community emergency response organizations. Employers and college or University campuses may support the implementation of a workplace CERT team in the event that a disaster occurs during school or working hours.

In 1993, FEMA began offering training for CERT team members. As a result, CERTs across the United States are now trained in a consistent process.

CERTs can be incorporated into local Emergency Operations Plans for basic emergency response functions, allowing professional responders to focus on more complex tasks.[4]

10.7 Emergency Planning Guidance from the United Nations

The United States enacted the Emergency Planning and Community Right-to-Know Act (EPCRA) in 1986 in response to the Bhopal disaster. At the international level, the United Nations responded to the disaster by creating the Awareness and Preparedness for Emergencies at the Local Level Programme (APELL). This group published the first version of the APELL handbook in 1988. This first version of the handbook, like EPCRA, focused primarily on chemical releases and industrial disasters. The second edition of this handbook, published in 2015,

---

4 http://Ready.gov/cert (accessed 20 September 2019).

recognized that planning for chemical and industrial emergencies should not be separate from the planning process for other hazards, including natural disasters. The second edition of the APELL handbook describes a process that integrates planning for chemical and industrial disasters into All-Hazards planning, and integrates concepts of local community planning, planning within industrial organizations, and government emergency plan development. For example, if LEPCs integrate with jurisdictional emergency planners, the jurisdiction's emergency plan could incorporate EPCRA requirements into an All-Hazards Emergency Operations Plan rather than developing two separate plans that may or may not be consistent with each other.

The APELL planning process starts with an APELL Champion, who may be an industry leader, a nongovernmental community leader, or a government leader. The APELL Champion initiates the planning process by pulling together an initial group of stakeholders. Stakeholders include the local population, local government, and local industry.

Stakeholder representatives come together to form the Coordinating Group. The Champion may or may not be an active participant or even a leader in the Coordinating Group. Regardless, the Champion continues to play a supportive role in ensuring that the Coordinating Group remains active and committed. The Coordinating Group serves as the APELL management team responsible for implementing the APELL process and coordinates with stakeholders to increase communication and cooperation, including cooperation between industry groups and government agencies that regulate these industries who share a common goal regarding emergency preparedness and response.

APELL is a 10-step process that covers 5 phases, including engagement of stakeholders, risk assessment, preparedness, implementation and testing, and maintenance of the plan. Two components that are unique to APELL are the Vision of Success and endorsement from government authorities.

The Vision of Success is an aspirational statement that describes the desired outcome of the plan and all planning members must agree to it. This vision represents a common goal for all members of the planning team, and is supported through the planning process.

A second important aspect of the APELL process is obtaining endorsement from government authorities. The APELL process is similar to that established by EPCRA and the NRF in that stakeholders and community members – referred to as the "whole community" in FEMA guidance documents – are core participants in the planning process. However, it is the government's responsibility to declare an emergency and implement response when needed. A plan created by the community reflects the communities needs and expectations. Subject-matter experts within the community – such as safety professionals – can participate in the planning process to ensure that desired outcomes are included in the plan. If there is a disconnect between the government agencies responsible for activating the plan and those community members who develop it, the planning process is futile. Establishing buy-in from these government agencies, as described in APELL Element 7, is therefore crucial to the planning process [11].

10.8 NFPA 1600

The National Fire Protection Association (NFPA) formed its Disaster Management Committee in 1991, and published the first edition of NFPA 1600 in 1995. Updates to the standard since that time have incorporated contributions from FEMA, the National Emergency Management Association (NEMA), the International Association of Emergency Managers (IAEM), professionals within the private sector, and references to APELL. While the standard initially focused on disaster management, it now covers recovery and business continuity as well.

When adopted by a jurisdiction, NFPA 1600 is a requirement that must be followed. Other jurisdictions may utilize it as a guidance document. Nongovernmental organizations (NGOs) as well as private employers may also adopt NFPA 1600 or utilize it as a guidance in developing internal emergency plans.

NFPA 1600 emphasizes the importance of leadership and commitment: Leadership must demonstrate commitment to the program by supporting the development, implementation, and maintenance of the program, providing necessary resources, and ensuring that the program is routinely reviewed and evaluated. When corrective actions are needed to correct deficiencies, leadership supports implementation of these corrective actions. Leadership also ensures that policies, plans, and procedures are followed.

Leadership appoints a Program Coordinator who has authority and responsibility to develop, administer, evaluate, and maintain the program. Like other emergency management systems, NFPA also utilizes a committee ("Program Committee") that includes the Program Coordinator and others with knowledge and expertise, as well as external representatives, to provide input or assist in coordination of the development of the program. The Program Committee also assists with implementation, evaluation, and maintenance of the program.

The planning process must include key stakeholders, and must start with a risk assessment. The risk assessment must include an analysis of the hazards on a number of operating functions including the health and safety of persons in the affected area and the health and safety of the personnel responding to the incidents. The risk assessment considers a comprehensive list of hazards, including geological hazards, weather events, biological hazards, and human-caused hazards. Hazards identified in the risk assessment need to be addressed, and NFPA 1600 specifies that the traditional hierarchy of controls be utilized:

1. Elimination or substitution;
2. Engineering controls;
3. Administrative controls;
4. Personal Protective Equipment (PPE).

The NFPA 1600 Standard is unique among guidance methodologies in that it acknowledges worker health and safety is of importance in emergency planning and specifies that plans must address the health and safety of personnel. The NFPA standard considers health and safety to be a central component of emergency planning rather than an afterthought.

NFPA 1600 incorporates development of recovery plans into this process. A recovery plan includes components such as damage assessment, rebuilding, and restoration. Communication with stakeholders is essential.

An additional key component of NFPA 1600 is planning for employee assistance and support, including providing shelter for those displaced by the incident and caring for both the mental and physical well-being of employees impacted by the incident [12].

10.9 Regulated Industries

FEMA, APELL, and NFPA provide direction on developing All-Hazards Emergency Plans. This direction may be a requirement, if adopted, or it may simply be a guidance for those entities and organizations that do not fall under a specified requirement to develop and adopt an emergency plan but recognize that doing so is a good operational and business practice.

Additionally, certain industries have specific emergency planning and coordination requirements. Planning requirements vary, especially in regard to involvement of outside stakeholders in the planning process and adoption of NIMS and ICS. Emergency planning requirements for industries that fall under OSHA's Process Safety Management requirements, HAZWOPER, airport operations, and passenger trains are presented here for comparison purposes.

10.10 Process Safety Management–Emergency Response

Processes that utilize highly hazardous chemicals in excess of thresholds listed in 19 CFR 1910.119, Appendix A, and flammable gasses or liquids of 10 000 pounds or more are covered by OSHA's Process Safety Management Standard (PSM). Like EPCRA, PSM was enacted in response to the Union Carbide incident of 1984 in Bhopal, India. Employers covered under 1910.119 must meet a number of requirements, including conducting process safety analysis, pre-startup safety review, development and use of operating procedures, training, management of change, accident reporting, compliance audits, and emergency planning. At a minimum, these employers must develop an Emergency Action Plan per 29 CFR 1910.38.

Responsibility for emergency planning lies with the employer. The employer has an option to rely entirely on in-house personnel to perform emergency response functions, such as internal fire brigades, emergency response teams, and internal medical staff. The employer also has the option of having all employees evacuate from the hazard zone in the event of a hazardous materials release, and relying on local emergency responders to handle the release. Employers can also use a combination of in-house personnel and local responders.

OSHA's PSM Standard Appendix C, nonmandatory guidelines, specifies that when the employer chooses to incorporate local emergency responders into the response plan, the employer must work closely with local emergency preparedness managers. The nonmandatory guidelines also suggest that employers equip an emergency control center and conduct drills and training exercises with local responders who would participate in the response to a hazardous materials release. In addition, the employer should be working with local community emergency planning teams, such as LEPCs.

Nonmandatory Appendix C states that the health and safety of response personnel is the responsibility of their employer and the on-scene Incident Commander.

In-house fire brigades, spill response teams, emergency response teams, and outside emergency responders who are expected to respond to such a release are also covered by OSHA's HAZWOPER Standard, 29 CFR 1910.120 [13].

10.11 HAZWOPER Emergency Planning Requirements

OSHA enacted requirements for Hazardous Waste Operations and Emergency Response (HAZWOPER, 29 CFR 1910.120) in 1990. This was the same year that Process Safety Management was also enacted.

Employers of employees who engage in emergency response to release of highly hazardous materials must develop an emergency response plan. Employers of emergency responders, such as firefighters, do not have to develop unique plans under this standard if state or local emergency response plans are comprehensive and cover elements required under HAZWOPER. Private industries that fall under HAZWOPER's emergency response provisions or OSHA's PSM standard have to develop emergency response plans that include:

- Pre-emergency planning and coordination with outside parties;
- Personnel roles, lines of authority, training, and communication;
- Emergency recognition and prevention;
- Safe distances and places of refuge;
- Site security and control;
- Evacuation routes and procedures;
- Decontamination;
- Emergency medical treatment and first aid;
- Emergency alerting and response procedures;
- Critique of response and follow-up;
- PPE and emergency equipment.

HAZWOPER is the only OSHA standard that requires use of an Incident Command System (ICS). As the HAZWOPER standard was enacted in 1990, the description of ICS in 1910.120 reflects concepts of ICS used at that time rather than those described in the current National Incident Management System (NIMS) refresh. For example, HAZWOPER does not use the term "Incident Commander," and instead states that "the senior emergency response official responding to an emergency shall become the individual in charge of a site specific Incident Command System (ICS)," and further clarifies that as individuals with higher status arrive, this position is passed up the lines of authority. The current refresh of NIMS requires that Incident Commanders be qualified; However, day-to-day status within the organization is not a specific qualification criteria. Additionally, many emergency response organizations find that continuously changing Incident Commanders throughout the course of the incident is disruptive to the response and therefore prioritize qualifications and continuity of leadership over seniority [14–16].

10.12 Airport Emergency Plans

Airports meeting FAA requirements are issued Airport Operating Certificates, and any airport that has been issued an Airport Operating Certificate must implement and maintain an Airport Certification Manual. Airport Certification Manuals must be approved by the FAA, and include a description of operating procedures, facilities and equipment, responsibility assignments, and any other information needed pertaining to operating the airport and meeting FAA requirements. The Airport Certification Manual must also include an Airport Emergency Plan (AEP).

The emergency plan must include plans for rescue and transport of victims, removal of disabled aircraft, emergency notification, and coordination of airport and control tower functions relating to emergency actions. Specific events which the plan must address include:

- Aircraft incidents and accidents;
- Bomb incidents;
- Structural fires;
- Fires at fuel farms or fuel storage areas;
- Natural disasters:
  - Hurricane;
  - Earthquake;
  - Tornado;
  - Volcano;
  - Flood.
- Hazardous materials/dangerous goods incidents;
- Sabotage, hijack incidents, and other unlawful interference with operations;
- Failure of power for movement area lighting;
- Water rescue situations.

In published circulars, FAA specifies that the Airport Emergency Plan must follow NIMS and integrate with state and local emergency plans, as well as emergency plans implemented by airport tenants and other community entities. Since it is expected that a large-scale airport incident would require a greater number of resources than an airport has on hand, mutual aid agreements need to be established with neighboring communities to assist in incidents that occur within airport boundaries. Likewise, an operating airport can be integrated into a community emergency plan. For example, an airport can be identified as an evacuation staging location in a community disaster.

FAA circulars emphasize that development of an AEP should be a team effort, and this team should consist of individuals and organizations that have potential roles in an airport emergency response (Table 10.1).

FAA does not specify that an AEP follow a specific format, but does suggest a format that is consistent with formats recommended in FEMA guidance and NFPA 1600:

- Basic Plan;
  - The legal authority for emergency operations;
  - A summary of the situations addressed by the AEP;
  - General concept of operations;
  - Responsibilities for emergency planning and operations;
  - (If applicable) A statement that the AEP is designed to meet the requirements of 14 CFR Part 139 Certification of Airports.

Table 10.1 Airport Emergency Planning Team Members.

1. Air carriers	14. EPA	27. Police/security
2. Air traffic control	15. EOD (Explosives Ordinance Disposal)	28. Post office
3. Aircraft operations	16. FAA	29. Public information/media
4. Airport authority/management	17. Fire/rescue	30. Public works and engineering
5. Airport employees	18. Government authorities, such as local community emergency planners, TSA, FEMA, etc.	31. Public utilities
6. Airport tenants	19. HAZMAT Response Team	32. Red Cross
7. Animal care/control	20. Health and medical	33. Resource support
8. Clergy	21. Hospitals	34. Search and rescue
9. Coast Guard/Harbor Patrol	22. Mental health agencies	35. State Aviation Authority
10. Communications services	23. Military/National Guard	36. Civil Air Patrol
11. Coroner	24. Mutual aid agencies	37. Morgue
12. Emergency Management Agency	25. National Weather Service	38. Airport Manager, Chair, or appropriate Chief Executive(s)
13. Emergency Medical Services	26. NTSB	

Source: Federal Aviation Administration [17], US Department of Transportation.

- Functional Annexes, which are plans organized around broad tasks:
  o Command and Control;
  o Communications;
  o Alert and Warning;
  o Emergency Public Information;
  o Protective Actions;
  o Law Enforcement;
  o Fire and Rescue;
  o Health and Medical;
  o Resource Management;
  o Operations and Maintenance.
- Hazard-Specific Sections: These should be "stand-alone" sections, with enough detailed information that can be followed without the need to reference the Basic Plan or Functional Annexes during an emergency;

- Standard Operating Procedures (SOPs) and Checklists, providing detailed instructions for individuals or organizations given responsibilities to perform tasks assigned in the AEP. These are generally hazard specific and attached to the Hazard-Specific Sections.

FAA also specifies that incidents must be managed utilizing an Incident Command System, consistent with NIMS [17, 18].

10.13 Passenger Train Emergency Preparedness Plan (PTEPP)

Passenger and Commuter railroads operating on standard gauge track that is part of the general railroad system are regulated by the Federal Railroad Administration (FRA), and are required to develop Passenger Train Emergency Preparedness Plans (PTEPPs). Multiple railroads may operate on the same tracks, including freight railroads. *Joint Operations* refers to these rail operations that are conducted on the same track, and the *Host Railroad* is the railroad that has effective operating control over a segment of track and establishes operational rules. The Host Railroad is responsible for the maintenance of tracks and dispatching of trains. Some of these responsibilities may be performed by other railroads or contractors under contractual arrangements. A *Tenant Railroad* is a railroad, other than the Host Railroad, operating on this section of track.

A single emergency preparedness plan must cover responsibilities of all entities performing joint operations for a single Railroad, such as a Commuter Railroad that operates on shared track on the general railroad system.

PTEPPs must be filed with the FRA. The FRA reviews each plan, and determines whether to conditionally approve the plan. If the plan is not conditionally approved, the railroad must amend the plan to correct deficiencies identified by the FRA. The conditional review assesses whether or not all required elements of the PTEPP have been addressed.

Once the plan has been conditionally approved, the FRA has 180 days to complete a final review that includes ongoing dialogue with the railroad and labor representatives, field analysis, and verification. The FRA then notifies the railroad in writing of the results of the review. If deficiencies are noted, the railroad must correct the plan and address the deficiencies identified by the FRA. Any changes or amendments to the PTEPP must also be reviewed and approved by the FRA.

The FRA is very specific as to the contents of the PTEPP:

- A cover sheet, with name and contact information of the primary contact person, and any Host Railroad's primary contact person;

- A description of the railroad, including operating territory, a description of portions of the territory that are covered by one or more Host Railroads, and a glossary of definitions and abbreviations;
- Required Elements:
  o Communication: This describes the entire communication process, beginning with notification of the train crew to the control center and information given to passengers. The control center then notifies outside emergency responders, adjacent rail modes, and appropriate railroad officials. If one or more host railroads are involved, the control center must also notify the Host Railroads. The plan must identify the employee who is responsible for maintaining these emergency notification contacts;
  o Employee Training and Qualification: All train crew members who have responsibilities under the PTEPP must receive initial training, and periodic training every two years. The PTEPP must include how the railroad will train all of its on-board employees, including formal training plans and information to demonstrate to the FRA how training requirements are met and who conducts the training. Railroads also must describe testing procedures to evaluate employees qualified under the plan:
    - Training for crew members must include:
      - Rail equipment familiarization;
      - Situational awareness;
      - Passenger evacuation;
      - Coordination of functions;
      - "Hands-on" instruction on the location, function, and operation of on-board emergency equipment:
        o How to open emergency windows, doors, and roof exits (if applicable) in adverse conditions, such as when the railcar has overturned;
        o How to use emergency tools and fire extinguishers;
        o How to use portable lighting when the passenger train's main power source is unavailable;
        o How to use public address (PA) systems or alternative mass-communication devices such as megaphones.
    - The plan must cover information about each railroad's control center that provides dispatching. Training for control center personnel must include:
      - Familiarization with the territory that they dispatch;
      - Protocols governing internal communications between appropriate control center personnel whenever and imminent potential emergency situation exists.
  o Joint Operations: When a Passenger or Commuter Railroad operates under Joint Operations, all railroads involved in hosting, providing, and operating

service must jointly adopt a single emergency preparedness plan that clearly addresses responsibilities to each railroad and Host railroad;

o Special Circumstances: The Emergency plan must address circumstances and sections of territory that include tunnels of more than 1000 feet in length, elevated structures including drawbridges, electrified systems, and parallel operations that impact or complicate the emergency response:

▪ A description of passenger safety for emergencies occurring in tunnels more than 1000 feet in length:

• Availability of emergency lighting;

• Access to emergency evacuation exits;

• Benchwall readiness: Benchwalls include walking surfaces that people would walk on to exit the tunnel, and power and communication lines. Deterioration in older tunnel structures can compromise this integrity, and older tunnels may lack emergency lighting or ventilation systems;

• Ladders for detraining;

• Effective radio or other communication between on-board crew members and the control center;

• Options for assistance from other trains.

▪ Elevated structures: The plan must identify whether or not elevated structures have walkways or guardrails. Specific evacuation procedures must be included when the elevated structure crosses over wetlands, lakes, rivers, ravines, or other hazards that would pose evacuation difficulties;

▪ Electrified systems: The plan must include how to de-energize an electrical power system, including responsibilities of the control center and train crew;

▪ Parallel operations: Adjacent rail modes may be impacted by the rail emergency. The plan must identify other operations that could be impacted, and how coordination occurs between these other operations.

o Liaison with Emergency Responders: This section of the plan describes how the railroad maintains a relationship with emergency responders, including developing a training program for emergency responders who may be called on to respond to a train emergency, and a requirement to invite emergency responders to participate in emergency simulations and drills. The railroad must distribute the emergency plan to emergency responders at least once every three years, or earlier if the plan is updated or modified;

o On-Board Emergency Equipment: The plan must describe types and locations of emergency equipment that is required on board operating trains, and how these are maintained. At a minimum this includes:

▪ One fire extinguisher per passenger car;

▪ One pry bar per passenger car;

▪ One flashlight per on-board crew member;

- First aid supplies including gauze pads, bandages, wound cleaners, scissors, tweezers, latex gloves, and a resuscitation mask;
- Emergency lighting.

o Passenger Safety Information: This section must describe how passengers are informed of emergency procedures, including how to recognize and report potential emergencies to crew members; how to operate emergency-related features, such as fire extinguishers or emergency exits; how to recognize hazards; and how to assist fellow passengers. Information should be printed in braille for visually impaired passengers, and evacuation procedures should include information on how to evacuate passengers with disabilities. One or more methods must be used to distribute this information:

- On-board announcements;
- Laminated wallet cards;
- Ticket envelopes;
- Timetables;
- Station signs or video monitors;
- Public service announcements;
- Seat drops.

o Procedures for Passengers with Disabilities. This section includes:

- A statement regarding the importance of identifying passengers with disabilities as soon as possible, and notifying the control center and emergency responders;
- Inclusion of the disabled passenger component in training for on-board train personnel and control center personnel;
- A description of how the railroad engages the disability community in an effort to gain participation from this community in emergency drills and exercises;
- How the handling of passengers with disabilities is evaluated after the emergency or simulation drill, such as debriefing [19, 20].

While the FRA does require Passenger and Commuter Railroads to develop relationships with emergency responders and the disability community, it does not require railroads to engage their participation in developing the PTEPP. Also, the FRA does not require railroads to adopt NIMS or utilize ICS in an emergency, nor does it require railroad personnel to receive training on NIMS or ICS.

Despite the lack of this specific requirement, railroads do have the option to go beyond FRA requirements and incorporate NIMS into their PTEPPs.

Railroad personnel who liaison with emergency responders in an incident are at a disadvantage if they do not understand the management system that they are working in or how to incorporate railroad personnel into this system. This impacts the efficiency of response as well as the safety of responders. A railroad environment contains unique hazards which are most likely unfamiliar to designated emergency responders, and although railroads are responsible for training emergency responders on these hazards, the size of a railroad's territory may be extensive enough that individual emergency responders may work for many years without receiving this training. Incorporating railroad safety personnel into the Incident Command structure would ensure that hazards of the railroad environment are identified, communicated, and incorporated into the incident hazard analysis and incident safety plan. However, railroad safety personnel must have a good understanding of ICS and how they fit into the system in order to be impactful. Emergency responders may be unwilling to work with railroad personnel in high stress situations if they do not understand the ICS organizational structure and appropriate lines of communication. Failure of Command and Operations staff to receive input from rail personnel can compromise the safety of emergency responders in an unfamiliar envorinoment.

10.14 Consolidation of Plans Written to Meet Differing Regulatory Requirements

The responsibility for developing and implementing an emergency plan lies with the jurisdiction. Jurisdictions have responsibility to develop All-Hazards Emergency Plans that integrate horizontally and vertically, and incorporate the whole community. Other entities, including private employers, are obligated to comply with emergency planning requirements set by various regulatory agencies, which may or may not be consistent with NIMS.

Airports and transit agencies are considered Special Purpose Districts under NIMS. Airports, which are regulated by FAA, are required to engage stakeholders and integrate principles of NIMS into their Airport Emergency Plans [17, 18] whereas passenger railroads which are regulated by FRA are not [19, 20]. Industries that process high volumes of hazardous chemicals fall under OSHA's Process Safety Management Standard, which was issued in 1990 and does not reflect the current NIMS doctrine [13].

Regardless of whether or not an emergency plan must adopt the principles of NIMS, there are benefits to doing so. Consistent with the 2017 NIMS refresh, standardization is essential to achieving interoperability among multiple organizations. The use of standardized practices – such as utilizing a standardized Incident Command System in a response or utilizing a standardized planning process – improves integration and connectivity among jurisdictions and operations that need to come together when an emergency occurs. Standardization is essential to interoperability among multiple organizations, and use of common terminology enables effective communication when these organizations must work together.

The use of common terminology has important implications for safety. Multiple examples could be given as to why this is the case, but the most important of these is efficiency of communication. Simply "speaking the same language" is key to both safety and efficiency when in the midst of an otherwise chaotic environment.

A guiding principle of NIMS is *Unity of Effort*, or coordination of activities among various organizations to achieve common objectives. While each organization has specific jurisdictional and regulatory responsibilities, Unity of Effort enables organizations to support each other while meeting each individual organization's mandates [15]. All-Hazards plans adopted by jurisdictions that may be impacted by emergencies at airports, passenger trains, chemical processing plants, or other entities, should integrate with these plans to ensure consistent expectations and protocols. An All-Hazards Emergency Plan can incorporate an Airport Emergency Plan into its aircraft incident Annex, or a nuclear agency's emergency plan into its Radiological Incident Annex, or elements of these plans can be adopted. These plans can also be referenced in the appropriate Annex, and then exercised together to test interoperability between plans. Doing so can ensure that there is a match between capabilities, resources, and expectations. Mismatches between expectations and capabilities can result in excessive risk taking and the need to take shortcuts that compromise safety.

10.15 Integrating Responder Safety Considerations into Emergency Plans

Much work has gone into developing regulatory language and guidance on emergency planning since the mid-1980s. Several consistent concepts have emerged, such as integration of stakeholders and engaging the community in plan development. Lessons learned from disasters such as 9/11, Hurricane Katrina, and others have been incorporated into updated guidance, and there has been a continuous improvement in emergency planning guidance documents that have been issued since then. The United Nations APELL reflects the importance of integration of emergency plans required under specific regulations into All-Hazards Emergency Plans. Such integration of planning efforts is a Best Practice.

NFPA 1600 is unique among emergency planning guidance in that it requires that emergency plans address the safety of emergency response personnel by including worker safety as a common requirement in plan sections or annexes. However, it does not provide specific guidance as to how this should be achieved, and does not require that the emergency plan include a subsection or annex that specifically addresses worker safety.

If the response falls under OSHA's HAZWOPER standard, a detailed site safety plan is required. A site safety plan can reference existing sections of an organization's safety plan, which reduces the size of the site safety plan and effort needed to create it. In responses that do not fall under HAZWOPER, safety plans may be developed on an ICS Form 208 at the discretion of the Incident Commander. These plans are developed at the time of the incident, and as noted during previous chapters, it is a challenge to incorporate all needed safety requirements into such a plan written on a short timeline.

FEMA has developed a Worker Safety and Health Support Annex that supports the National Response Plan and the National Disaster Recovery Framework. This plan describes how Federal agencies, including OSHA, support responder safety. Some, but not all, State emergency plans follow the model of the Federal plan and have written State Worker Safety and Health Support Annexes that describe actions that State agencies will take in an emergency. However, the responsibility for worker safety lies with the primary employer. OSHA and State Health and Safety agencies provide a support, or back-up role, but this does not relieve employers from their responsibilities.

OSHA published a White Paper in 2012 that advocates for workplace Injury and Illness Prevention Plans (IIPPs). Components of IIPPs include management and leadership (including development of written safety programs), worker participation, and integration of health and safety in business planning and continuous improvement. Several states, including California, Hawaii, and Washington require that employers develop IIPPs, and as a result, fatality rates were as much as 31% below the national average [21].

Inclusion of elements of an IIPP in an emergency plan, along with integration of worker safety into planned protocols and procedures in other sections of the plan, would facilitate safety management when an incident response is needed. Relying on an Incident Safety Officer to incorporate OSHA requirements, training, medical management, and behavioral health into a quickly prepared incident safety plan, and implementing these elements, while at the same time conducting a hazard analysis for planned tasks and managing safety in an environment that is rapidly changing is a lot to ask of the Safety Officer. When the Safety Officer cannot do all these things well, or at all, the safety of responders is compromised.

Would we be seeing the same rates of illness in 9/11 responders, firefighters, or other emergency responders if a plan had been in place to ensure that they had been provided with appropriate respirators, fit tested, and trained to use these respirators properly? Would illness rates have been lower if effective decontamination plans had been in place, or if required medical monitoring had been performed? Would PTSD rates be lower among responders if effective behavioral health plans had been planned for? Can we do better in future incidents?

Inclusion of these elements into an All-Hazards Safety Plan that is modeled after an IIPP within the emergency preparedness plan would simplify the job of the Safety Officer during an incident response, and in turn ensure that regulatory requirements are met and that the safety needs of workers are provided for. The All-Hazards Safety Plan could identify resources that would be needed in an incident, such as PPE, respirator fit testing equipment, training materials, medical evaluation providers, and so forth, as well as how these can be sourced and activated during an incident response. Protocols and procedures could be developed for use as written or they could be modified as needed for the specific incident. Like other sections of the emergency plan, the Emergency All-Hazards Safety Plan should be easy to read, simple, and flexible. Planned support can be procured and activated when the incident occurs, allowing the Safety Officer to focus on specific incident safety needs. The incident safety plan would then address site-specific hazards with reference to the All-Hazards Safety Plan, and time would not have to be spent in developing a comprehensive plan.

Many jurisdictions and businesses employ safety professionals to manage day-to-day safety within their work organizations. These same professionals have the skills to support or even lead the development of the safety section of an emergency plan, or even an emergency IIPP, and these personnel should be utilized in the emergency planning process. These same safety professionals can review protocols for specific hazard annexes to ensure that they are consistent with the All-Hazards Safety Plan, and that worker safety protections are incorporated into the protocols and procedures. When jurisdictions do not have safety professionals on staff, or if in-house safety professionals are inadequately staffed to support the emergency planning process, qualified consultants can and should be utilized.

10.16 Participation as a Stakeholder to Incorporate Worker Safety into Emergency Plans

Although many emergency management professionals recognize the importance of worker safety, more needs to be done to improve the safety culture within the field of emergency management.

The majority of emergency planning regulations and guidance documents incorporate the concept of stakeholder and/or whole community input into emergency planning. Professional organizations, such as the American Society of Safety Professionals (ASSP), the American Industrial Hygiene Association (AIHA) and the Fire Department Safety Officers Association (FDSOA) can and do advocate for emergency responder safety. Local sections of these organizations can support emergency planning efforts as stakeholders.

Individuals can also participate as whole community representatives. Safety professionals who participate in this role are also in a position to advocate for the inclusion of worker safety plans in the emergency planning process.

10.17   Summary

Emergency management and emergency planning have evolved since the 1980s, and continuous improvement in emergency planning makes us better prepared for the next disaster that we will face. Consistent elements of emergency planning include development of planning teams, and incorporating stakeholders and members of the community into the planning process. Over time, emergency planning has evolved to accept the concept that aligning expectations and plans into All-Hazards Emergency Plans is a preferred practice, even when plan requirements may originate with different Federal, state, or local agencies.

Still, the concept of continuous improvement tells us that there will always be more that can be done, and that improving our plans and responses is an ongoing effort. One area that can be improved upon is the incorporation of worker safety, including first responders, nontraditional responders, recovery workers, and any others who have a role in emergency response into emergency plans. While NFPA 1600 promotes integration of worker safety into plan elements, a stand-alone safety section or emergency IIPP written in a simple, easy-to-read, and flexible format could provide a roadmap to meeting supporting worker safety during a response.

A key benefit of emergency planning is the emergency planning process itself. The process is at least as important as the final plan, if not more so. During the planning process, ideas are put forth, challenges and obstacles to achieving needed goals are evaluated and addressed, and buy-in is achieved. Subject-matter experts and advocates for worker safety need to be a part of this process.

References

1 Taylor, Alan (2014) Bhopal: The World's Worst Industrial Disaster, 30 Years Later The Atlantic, 2 December 2014.
2 40 CFR Part 355, Emergency Planning and Notification.
3 Public Law 99-499 (1986). Superfund Amendments and Re-Authorization Act of 1986.
4 U.S. Code Title 42, Chapter 116, Subchapter 1, Section 11001, Establishment of State Commissions, Planning Districts, and Local Committees.
5 Environmental Protection Agency (2011). *EPA Policy on Consultations and Coordination with Indian Tribes* (4 May 2011).
6 US Code Title 42, Chapter 116, Subchapter 1, Section 11003, Comprehensive Emergency Response Plans.
7 Environmental Protection Agency (2008). *2008 Nationwide Survey of Local Emergency Planning Committees (LEPCs)*, Final Report.

8 US Department of Homeland Security (2019). *National Response Framework*, 4e.

9 US Department of Homeland Security (2016). *National Planning System.*

10 US Department of Homeland Security (2010). *Developing and Maintaining Emergency Operations Plans.* Comprehensive Preparedness Guide (CPG) 101, Version 2.0.

11 United Nations Environment Programme (2015). *Awareness and Preparedness for Emergencies at Local Level: A Process for Improving Community Awareness and Preparednesses for Technological Hazards and Environmental Emergencies*, 2e.

12 National Fire Protection Association (2019). *NFPA 1600: Standard on Continuity, Emergency, and Crisis Management.*

13 29 CFR 1910.119, Process Safety Management of Highly Hazardous Chemicals.

14 29 CFR 1910.120, Hazardous Waste Operations and Emergency Response.

15 Federal Emergency Management Agency, US Department of Homeland Security (2017). *National Incident Management System*, 3e.

16 Federal Emergency Management Agency, US Department of Homeland Security (2017). *Resource Typing Definition for the National Qualification System Emergency Management Incident Commander.*

17 Federal Aviation Administration, US Department of Transportation (2010). *Advisory Circular AC No: AC 150/5200-31C, Change: 1, Airport Emergency Plan.*

18 14 CFR 139, Airport Certification.

19 49 CFR Part 239, Passenger Train Emergency Preparedness.

20 Federal Railroad Administration, US Department of Transportation (2014). *Guide to Developing a Passenger Train Emergency Preparedness Plan.*

21 Occupational Safety and Health Administration (OSHA) (2012). *Injury and Illness Prevention Programs*, White Paper.

11

Safety in Drills and Exercises

Quality cycles are used in management systems as a process for continuous improvement. This is represented by the Plan-Do-Check-Act (PDCA) cycle that first came into use in Japan in the 1950s. An important concept represented by the PDCA cycle is that the work of the planning team is not done simply upon completion of the plan, because in the real world, things do not always work out according to the plan. Over time, it becomes apparent that certain aspects of the plan do not work as well as they should. Perhaps the plan is not well understood, or the proposed action does not work as intended when put into practice. A corrective action is taken, and incorporated into an update of the plan. Over time, the updated plan is also evaluated and updated as needed.

The Plan-Do-Check-Act cycle is widely attributed to W. Edwards Demings. However, Demings did not like the word "check" and preferred to use the word "study" instead. He felt the word "study" better conveyed that observations should be based on predictions, as is done when following the scientific method [1].

Regardless, both models convey the importance of testing a management plan to identify deficiencies, and then taking corrective action to improve the plan. This is very applicable in emergency planning and management (Figure 11.1).

An Emergency Management Plan is tested when an incident occurs. Ideally, the incident response will play out as described in the plan, victims are rescued before they suffer injury or ill health, and responders are not injured or hurt in the process. It is more likely, however, that responders will encounter something unintended that was not covered by the plan, or that a planned action will not result in the best outcome. Lessons are learned when this happens, and the plan can be improved.

Incidents provide a real-world test of the plan, and have real-world consequences in terms of human life when the plan is inadequate. Emergency plans can also be tested through exercises and drills, before an incident occurs, minimizing these real-world consequences.

Health and Safety in Emergency Management and Response, First Edition. Dana L. Stahl.
© 2021 John Wiley & Sons, Inc. Published 2021 by John Wiley & Sons, Inc.

Figure 11.1 FEMA's emergency management cycle reflects a Plan-Do-Check-Act quality circle.

An exercise should be designed to test specific elements of the plan. People perform physical exercise to make them stronger: Likewise, an emergency plan is exercised in order to make the plan stronger. The exercise should stress the plan, just as physical exercise stresses the body, because the goal is to find weaknesses in the plan that can be improved. While it may feel satisfying to hold a drill in which every element of the exercise is executed perfectly, such an exercise does little to improve preparedness for an actual event.

11.1   Types of Exercises

Exercises may be discussion based and take place in conference rooms, or they may be operations based and take place in the field. A set of exercise objectives is determined for each exercise, and exercises are designed and evaluated to determine whether or not each exercise objective has been met.

Discussion-based exercises focus on strategic, policy-oriented issues, and are led by a facilitator who keeps participants on track to meet exercise objectives.

Discussion-based exercises include:

- *Seminars*: Seminars provide an orientation on authorities, strategies, plans, policies, procedures, protocols, resources, concepts, and ideas. Seminars are discussion based, and can be used when developing plans or procedures, or when making major changes to the existing plans or procedures. They are also used when organizations or jurisdictions plan to work together on a planned response, in order to develop a shared understanding of the capabilities that each organization or jurisdiction brings.
- *Workshops*: Workshops utilize greater participant interaction than seminars. The goal of a workshop is to produce a product such as new Standard Operating

Procedures (SOPs), Emergency Operations Plans, continuity of operation plans, or mutual aid agreements.

- *Tabletop Exercises (TTX)*: In a tabletop exercise, the Facilitator presents a hypothetical, simulated emergency. Players in the TTX discuss issues in depth, identify areas of concern, and solve problems. TTX can range from a basic exercise, in which a scenario is presented and remains constant, to an advanced TTX where players are given pre-scripted messages as the exercise unfolds. These may be in the form of a written message, a simulated telephone call, a video, or other means. Players should discuss issues raised in the scenario in reference to established authorities, plans, and procedures. Participants practice decision-making in a safe environment in which the impacts of these decisions can be played out. Tabletop exercises can reveal gaps in plans that need to be addressed, and areas where differing plans and expectations may come into conflict.

- *Games*: A game is a simulation of operations involving two or more teams. Games can be competitive, and use rules, data, and procedures to depict an actual or hypothetical situation to explore consequences of players' decisions and actions. This type of exercise is useful for validating plans and procedures and evaluating resource requirements. Critical decision-making points must be identified when designing the game.

Operations-based exercises mobilize personnel and resources in response to an emergency scenario. Operations-based exercises include:

- *Drills*: Drills are a coordinated, supervised activity to test a specific function or capability in a single agency or organization, such as an evacuation drill. Drills can also be used to provide training on new equipment, validate procedures, or practice skills.

- *Functional Exercises (FE)*: Functional exercises are conducted in a realistic, real-time environment, although movement of personnel and equipment may be simulated. The exercise follows events developed in an exercise scenario, and event updates or injects may be provided during the course of the exercise. Updates are preplanned, and are included in a Master Scenario Events List (MSEL) provided to exercise controllers. Scenario elements may be injected using a Simulation Cell (SimCell) to simulate real events. Functional Exercises are used to validate and evaluate capabilities, multiple, functions and/or sub-functions, and interdependent groups of functions.

- *Full-Scale Exercises*: These exercises involve multiple agencies, organizations, and jurisdictions working together under cooperative systems such as the Incident Command System or Unified Command. Full-scale exercises are usually conducted in a real-time, stressful environment that is intended to mirror a real incident. Personnel and resources are mobilized and deployed to the scene, where actions are performed as if a real incident had occurred. This type of exercise requires a greater level of support than other types of exercises, and incorporates a greater level of safety risk which must be addressed in the exercise plan [2].

11.2 Exercise Requirements for Airports

The Federal Aviation Administration has adopted FEMA exercise guidance into requirements for airports, and considers exercises as a method to determine if an Airport Emergency Plan (AEP) actually works and is understood by all parties given responsibilities under this plan. Class I airports, or those airports that serve scheduled flights of large air carrier aircraft, are required to conduct a full-scale exercise at least every 36 months [3].

Personnel must be trained and knowledgeable on the AEP before they can participate in the exercise. Training must be provided to airport personnel as well as non-airport personnel who are expected to provide aid and assistance in the event of an emergency. Airport operators are expected to conduct a cycle of training courses, and periodic refreshers. Responders need to be familiar with the AEP, standard operating procedures, and the layout of the airport. Training should include a classroom portion and/or audiovisual training, and on-site familiarization of the airport. Security and access of the airport, communications requirements, and safety issues including aircraft-related hazards must be included in the training.

In a real airport emergency, adjacent airport operations would close to focus on response to the emergency. Airport full-scale exercises are often conducted on or near the airfield, but since airports cannot shut down normal operations without affecting flight schedules across the country, exercises are conducted in the proximity of an operational airfield.

Airport Operations Areas (AOA) pose a number of safety issues to both personnel and aircraft that are not necessarily foremost in the minds of responders who are not familiar with airport operations.

Collision with moving aircraft is one of the more obvious potential hazards. Aircraft move at hundreds of miles per hour when taking off and landing, and cannot avoid objects that are present on runways at these times. Taxiing aircraft are capable of stopping quickly to avoid collisions, but doing so can cause passengers and aircraft crew members to be thrown inside the cabin and injured. Such aircraft incursions are considered serious, and are tracked and investigated by the airport.

Small objects (referred to as Foreign Object Debris or FOD) can be sucked into aircraft engines and cause malfunction, endangering the aircraft. FOD can include items such as plastic or paper bags, tools, parts, hardware, trash, food wrappers, gloves, pens, paper clips, badges, or other similar items, and airport operators go to great efforts to keep such items off the airfield. Any personnel who enter the airfield must be trained on what FOD is and the critical importance of making sure FOD is not introduced into the airport operating area. Still, it is probable that FOD awareness may not be foremost in the minds of non-airport personnel when participating in a realistic or even stressful scenario, and exercise coordinators should have a plan to quickly remove any FOD that may be generated by drill players.

In rare cases, people have even been sucked into aircraft engines.

The back of the aircraft engine also presents a hazard: jet engines exhaust air at speeds of more than 100 miles per hour. This "jet blast" creates enough force to blow vehicles over, and can severely injure any personnel in the vicinity of the jet blast.

The exercise plan must carefully plan movements of exercise players to ensure that they are kept separate from operating aircraft during the course of the exercise. Transport of players to the exercise site must be carefully coordinated, and monitors should be set up along the route to ensure appropriate movement of people and vehicles. All players must be given a safety briefing. Although training provided before the exercise should cover airfield hazards, this information should be reiterated during the safety briefing. In addition, monitors should be stationed at the perimeters of the exercise area during exercise play to prevent inadvertent movement from the designated exercise space and onto the airfield.

Since airport operating areas are restricted sites, security plans must ensure that all drill participants have security clearances and are checked in as they enter the exercise site.

Volunteer "victims" are often recruited to play the part of injured passengers in an aircraft emergency. These volunteers may be airport employees, who are familiar with the hazards of an AOA, or volunteers from organizations such as local theatrical groups who are not. Volunteers must be carefully briefed on the role they will be playing in the exercise. They must also be given a safety briefing, which includes the area boundaries of the exercise area and the critical importance of staying within these limits.

Victims receive moulage to simulate injuries, and are given instructions on how to simulate the behaviors that people with these injuries would exhibit. Volunteer victims may need to sit or lie on the ground for long periods of time as responders assess the situation, develop plans, and prepare to move these "victims" to "safety." These volunteers may get cold or hungry while they wait. People with medical conditions such as diabetes or asthma may experience exacerbations of their condition. In addition, both "victims" and "responders" could be injured during the exercise. Everyone in the incident should be given a code word, such as "Real World" to use in the event that they need to communicate that a real injury or medical emergency needs to be addressed, and that this is not part of exercise play.

Exercise planners should address any liability issues that could be incurred from use of volunteers and non-airport employees from participating in the exercise.

After the exercise, areas for improvement must be addressed and incorporated into an update of the emergency plan. Corrective actions for any deficiencies noted might include procedure revisions, training and retraining, and incorporation of new or different tools and equipment. Subsequent drills and exercises then are conducted to test the efficacy of these updates and improvements [4].

11.3 Exercise Requirements for Passenger Railroads

The Federal Railroad Administration (FRA) requires that Passenger and Commuter Railroads invite emergency responders to participate in full-scale emergency simulations. Railroads that provide commuter or short haul passenger train service, and whose operations include less than 150 route miles and less than 200 million passenger miles annually, must conduct a full-scale emergency simulation every two calendar years. Railroads providing intercity passenger train service, and those that provide commuter or short haul passenger service of 150 route miles or more, or 200 million passenger miles per year or more, must conduct full-scale emergency simulations annually.

The FRA uses the word "simulation" rather than "exercise." Simulation is not a term defined by FEMA, but conveys that the scenario is more of an enactment than a test of the plan. Railroads must invite responders to participate in these simulations, but are not specifically required to include them as participants.

FRA places an emphasis on training of emergency responders in jurisdictions in which they operate. Railroads must develop a training program and make it available to all emergency responders who could reasonably be expected to respond to a passenger train or commuter train emergency. The training must include topics such as access to railroad equipment, location of railroad facilities, and communication. Often, the emergency simulation is conducted after training has been presented, and functions as an extension of the training program.

If a railroad has experienced an actual emergency requiring activation of its emergency plan, they can delay the emergency simulation for 180 days [5, 6].

The responsibility is placed on the railroad to conduct emergency simulation and training every one or two years. However, trains routes cover many jurisdictions, and as a result, many years can pass between trainings conducted by a railroad within any given jurisdiction. Like airports, the railroad environment contains many unique hazards which are not necessarily obvious to those who are not experienced with work in this environment, and as a result first responders can be injured or even killed when responding to train incidents or while crossing train tracks to respond to other incidents. Operation Lifesaver, an organization devoted to educating the public about train safety, has developed training programs and educational materials on railroad safety for emergency responders. This program can supplement training provided by railroads.[1]

Local emergency responders can partner with railroads to fulfill their own exercise requirements, and the conduct of a FEMA full-scale exercise also meets or exceeds FRA's requirements for a full-scale simulation.

These simulations should take place in the jurisdiction of the responders who are participating in the simulation whenever feasible. Depending upon the railroad territory within a particular jurisdiction, the simulation can be conducted in a rail yard, on a rail spur, or on active track that has temporarily rerouted operations. In most cases, the exercise or simulation must be conducted near live tracks, and rail exercise coordinators must incorporate exposure to live tracks into the Exercise Safety Plan. Although the training that a Passenger or Commuter Railroad must provide to emergency responders highlights the dangers of working next to live tracks, the safety plan should assume that some of this may be forgotten in the heat of exercise play. Control measures should be put into place to prevent exercise participants from inadvertently going too close to live tracks. In an actual incident, these adjacent tracks would be shut down, but it is cost prohibitive to close tracks for an exercise when there is no actual emergency.

Additional hazards include railroad switches, which are operated remotely from control centers that may be many states away, rail traffic moving at high speeds, and unstable walking surfaces on tracks and track beds. The safety measures that need to be implemented are similar to those necessary for exercises conducted on an operating airfield, including planning for transportation to and from the exercise site, placing monitors in position to ensure appropriate movements of people and vehicles, and conducting a safety briefing prior to the start of the exercise.

If volunteers are recruited to play the part of "victims" in an exercise, they should also be given a safety briefing. Exercise staff should closely monitor these volunteers to ensure that they do not leave the designated exercise site.

A code word should be given to all exercise players, volunteer "victims," and exercise facilitators to indicate when a "real-world" emergency has occurred, and all responders should be trained to recognize the code word and respond accordingly, temporarily halting exercise play until the real-world incident has resolved.

FRA rules do not require that learnings from the simulation or exercise be incorporated into an update of the Passenger Train Emergency Preparedness Plan (PTEPP). In fact, the lengthy process for obtaining approval from the FRA whenever the plan is changed poses challenges to making changes and updates to the plan. Still, procedures and protocols that support the PTEPP can be updated to improve a future response.

---

1 https://oli.org/training/emergency-responders/emergency-responders-resources (accessed 16 October 2019).

Figure 11.2 Fire responders receive hands-on training on a light rail vehicle while a safety monitor looks on.

The Federal Transit Administration (FTA) and State Safety Oversite Agencies develop state-specific requirements for emergency planning, training, and exercises for rail systems that begin and end on tracks in the same state, do not share track with other railroads, and are otherwise not covered by FRA. These requirements typically include a combination of classroom and hands-on training (Figure 11.2), tabletop exercises, and full-scale exercises.

11.4 Exercising Emergency Plans Under OSHA's Process Safety Management Standard and HAZWOPER

OSHA requires that employers covered by the Process Safety Management Standard develop and implement an Emergency Action Plan that includes response to chemical releases. Guidance provided in nonmandatory Appendix C of the standard suggests that these employers coordinate with local emergency responders in developing response plans. Nonmandatory Appendix C also suggests that conducting drills, training exercises, or simulations is a way to improve preparedness [7]. However, this is not required.

The emergency response section of OSHA's Hazardous Waste Operations and Emergency Response Standard (HAZWOPER) requires use of an Incident Command System that integrates emergency responders into the response. However, there is no requirement to conduct exercises with outside emergency responders in preparation for such an emergency incident [8]. Local emergency responders who are first on scene when a hazardous materials incident occurs face the risk of exposure to chemicals that they may not be familiar with, and any operation that is at risk of such an incident should inform local emergency response departments of site-specific hazards, appropriate response techniques, site emergency procedures, and decontamination techniques [9]. In theory, this information should be transmitted via Community Right-to-Know reporting and incorporated into emergency plans developed by the Local Emergency Planning Committee (LEPC). However, as discussed in Chapter 10, there is variability in participation in the LEPCs across the country, and plans developed by the LEPC may or may not be comprehensive or recently updated. There is also variability in transmission of information included in the plan, and as a result, responders in some jurisdictions will be more prepared than others.

Although not required, planning and conducting exercises is certainly a best practice for the same reasons that such exercises are required in airports and rail systems: Exercises identify areas of the emergency plan that need improvement. LEPCs and manufacturing employers both could use such exercises to test their plans, find out what works and does not work, identify points of confusion that need to be clarified, and work toward continuous improvement.

Exercises are also training opportunities. Employees who work in an operation that falls under Process Safety Management requirements have an opportunity to practice working in an Incident Command System alongside emergency responders who live and breathe ICS in their daily work, and can improve their skills through participation in exercises. This builds trust between individuals that is necessary in an actual response. Emergency responders have an opportunity to learn more about the operation, in particular the hazards of the process and the materials used in this process. Both emergency responders and plant employees can learn from each other, increasing capabilities of each. Knowledge of plant-specific hazards is also critical to keeping emergency responders safe.

As in any exercise, safety of participants is critical. Drills, simulations, functional exercises, and full-scale exercises may need to take place in operational areas, and participants are in turn at risk of exposure to operational hazards. An Exercise Safety Plan should identify these hazards, and controls used to prevent or mitigate exposure to these hazards during the exercise. Safety personnel assigned as exercise "players" should have an opportunity to practice what they would do in an actual response, including assignment of an appropriate Safety Officer and Assistant Safety Officers within the ICS organizational chart. Exercise coordinators should also station safety personnel in positions where they can monitor exercise participants who may inadvertently encounter operational hazards, just as is done for exercises conducted on an operating airfield or near live train tracks.

11.5 Oil Response Plan Training, Drill, and Exercise Requirements

The Oil Spill Prevention Act of 1990 requires that owners and operators of oil facilities prepare a response plan, and implement a training and drill/exercise program. The exercise program may be an extension of the training program: crew members should be trained in their duties and responsibilities. Some organizations also require HAZWOPER training [10, 11].

The National Preparedness for Response Exercise Program (PREP) is a non-mandatory program that meets exercise requirements of the Oil Spill Prevention Act that have been established by multiple federal agencies:

- US Coast Guard (USCG);
- Environmental Protection Agency (EPA);
- Pipeline and Hazardous Materials Administration (PHMSA);
- Bureau of Safety and Environmental Enforcement (BSEE).

Oil response plan holders that follow PREP adopt a triennial exercise cycle that includes:

- Qualified Individual notification exercises: At least once per year, the qualified individual listed in the response plan must be contacted by telephone or radio during nonbusiness hours to ensure that they respond as expected;
- Remote assessment and consultation exercises for vessels: At least annually, each vessel operating in US waters must exercise a scenario in which a substantial threat of discharge could occur, such as grounding, stranding, collision, hull damage, fire, explosion, loss of propulsion, flooding, or equipment failure occurs during nonbusiness hours. A remote assessor must make a determination of an initial course of action and initiate a response plan to prevent a spill;
- Emergency procedure exercises for vessels: Once per quarter, crew personnel must conduct an exercise of initial actions taken to mitigate the effects of a spill;
- Emergency procedure exercises for facilities (optional): An exercise of procedures to mitigate or prevent a spill associated with cargo transfers;
- Incident Management Team exercises: Annually, the Incident Management Team must participate in an exercise of each spill countermeasure described in the spill prevention plan. At least once every three years a worst case discharge scenario must be exercised. Incident Management Team members must demonstrate ability to complete documentation such as required ICS forms, prepare an Incident Action Plan, and a Health and Site Safety plan;
- Shore-based salvage and shore-based marine firefighting management team exercises for vessels: This exercise must be conducted annually to ensure management teams are familiar with response plans and pre-fire plans. This

exercise can be conducted with the annual Incident Management Team exercise, or separately;

- Equipment deployment exercises: Each type of equipment and personnel must be exercised at least once in the three-year cycle to ensure that response equipment is appropriate for the operating environment where it is intended to be used, and that operating personnel know how to deploy and operate it. All personnel who would normally operate or supervise operation of the response equipment should participate, and demonstrate the ability to deploy and operate the equipment while wearing appropriate Personal Protective Equipment;
- Unannounced exercises: Unannounced exercises must take place at least annually. In an unannounced exercise, exercise participants do not have prior knowledge of the exercise, as would be the case in an actual incident. Unannounced exercises may be initiated internally, or by a regulatory agency as a Government-Initiated Unannounced Exercise (GIUE). GIUEs are mandatory, and any covered organization that is directed to participate in one must do so unless specific conditions exist that could compromise safety.

Exercises can include multiple components. For example, if an Incident Management Team exercise or an equipment deployment exercise was not announced ahead of time, the exercise would also meet the requirement to conduct an unannounced exercise.

PREP guidance specifically calls out safety as the first guiding principle of an exercise program, and states that an exercise response plan must consider safety factors. In addition, the guidance specifically states that there is no expectation or justification for placing people at risk during an exercise or response, and that a safety violation is considered a failure to follow response plans [12].

11.6 Other Industries

Emergency plans may be required by Federal Agencies having jurisdiction over the work, or they may be developed voluntarily as a best practice. Any operation that has an emergency plan can benefit from conducting similar exercises regardless of regulatory oversight. Regardless, implementation of an exercise program is the best way to test these plans, test training, and move toward a cycle of continuous improvement.

Exercises provide an opportunity to test the Safety function within an Incident Command System, and to practice safety management within this system. They provide an opportunity for Assistant Safety Officers to learn to work together, even if they work for different employers day-to-day.

Although there is more control over the environment than in an actual emergency incident, exercise players are exposed to safety hazards during exercise play and it is a best practice to include a safety plan within every exercise plan. Consider the "risk a lot, save a lot; risk a little, save a little" mentality that has traditionally prevailed in the world of emergency response: No real people are at risk in an exercise, and therefore there is no reason that responders should ever "risk a lot" for an exercise.

Exercise players may push back on this. They might ask, for example: "Why are you making me wear fall protection? You know I wouldn't wear it in an actual response, so this isn't a good test!" In reality, they should always wear fall protection, whether in an exercise or an actual response. In the heat of a response, when human brains are wired to accept greater risk to achieve a greater reward, these responders may in fact perform a task without putting on their fall protection with both the expectation that they will not fall and that OSHA would understand that the need to save a life outweighed their decision to forgo use of their personal fall protection equipment. Even if both of these preconceptions proved true in an actual incident, where an actual life is at risk, they are certainly not true during an exercise. OSHA or state health and safety agencies that have authority can and will cite safety violations that take place during drills and exercises.

Additionally, use of safety equipment such as fall protection in an exercise builds muscle memory, and increases the chances that it will be worn in an actual incident.

11.7 National Exercise Program

At the national level, exercises result in lessons learned that are then incorporated into the development and update of emergency plans in support of the National Preparedness Goal, as well as updates to risk assessments upon which these plans are based [13, 14]. The National Preparedness Goal identifies 32 Core Capabilities across the five Mission Areas of Prevention, Protection, Mitigation, Response, and Recovery (Figure 11.3) [15], and the primary mechanism for evaluating these core capabilities at the national level is through the National Exercise Program (NEP).

The NEP is conducted as a two-year exercise cycle that involves the whole community. The National Security Council Principals Committee (Figure 11.4) sets Strategic Priorities for each two-year cycle, based on multiple information sources including:

- Stakeholder input;
- Data from the National Preparedness Report;
- Threat and Hazard Identification and Risk Assessment;

Prevention	Protection	Mitigation	Response	Recovery
Planning				
Public information and warning				
Operational coordination				
Intelligence and information sharing		Community resilience	Infrastructure systems	
Interdiction and disruption		Long-term vulnerability reduction	Critical transportation	Economic recovery
Screening, search, and detection			Environmental response/health and safety	Health and social services
Forensics and attribution	Access control and identity verification	Risk and disaster resilience assessment	Fatality management services	Housing
	Cybersecurity	Threats and hazards identification	Fire management and suppression	Natural and cultural resources
	Physical protective measures		Logistics and supply chain management	
	Risk management for protection programs and activities		Mass care services	
			Mass search and rescue operations	
	Supply chain integrity and security		On-scene security, protection, and law enforcement	
			Operational communications	
			Public health, healthcare, and emergency medical services	
			Situational assessment	

Figure 11.3 Core capabilities by Mission Area. Source: US Department of Homeland Security [15].

- Stakeholder Preparedness Review;
- Previous exercises and After Action Reports;
- Real-world incident After Action Reports;
- Intelligence community threat analysis.

Exercises included in each two-year cycle are conducted at all levels of government, by nongovernmental organizations, and in the private sector. Federal agencies are expected to participate in as many NEP exercises that relate to their mission as feasible. State, local, tribal, and territorial partners can receive technical assistance from the National Exercise Division when they participate in the NEP program. Exercise sponsors from state, local, tribal, territories, the private sector, and nongovernmental organizations can submit nominations to include planned exercises in the NEP, and should work with regional FEMA Exercise Officers as

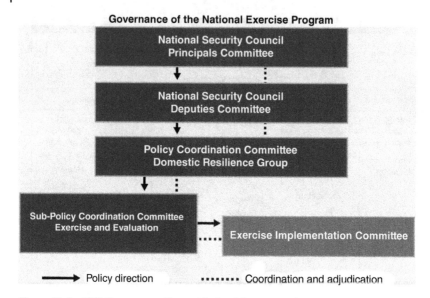

Governance of the National Exercise Program

Figure 11.4 NEP Governance. Source: Federal Emergency Management Administration (FEMA), US Department of Homeland Security [16].

they work through the nomination process. Exercises that support the Principals' Strategic Priorities are selected into the program.

A National Level Exercise is held every two years. Advance planning for this exercise begins four years before it is scheduled to take place to allow for budgeting of the National Level Exercise and for supporting exercises and events that lead up to it. Exercises and events that take place during the NEP cycle lead up to the National Level Exercise, which serves as the capstone exercise for the two-year cycle.

All exercises should be conducted in accordance with the Principal's Strategic Priorities, and should consist of a mix of all exercise types. Exercise objectives reflect the Principal's Strategic Priorities as well as Core Capabilities identified in the National Preparedness Goal. They may also reflect critical tasks identified in the National Frameworks and risk assessments, and any weaknesses identified in previous reviews. Once exercise objectives have been identified and agreed to, an exercise scenario is designed to test the exercise objectives. All aspects of the exercise should reflect a high degree of realism.

Mid-Cycle and End-of-Cycle reports are prepared for senior government leadership, and for identifying issues, trends, and key lessons learned. Issues identified during exercises are remediated. In addition, all exercises conducted within the cycle promote learning and readiness [16].

11.8 Homeland Security Exercise and Evaluation Program (HSEEP)

Exercises conducted as part of the NEP should be conducted in accordance with the Homeland Security Exercise and Evaluation Program (HSEEP). HSEEP is a set of guiding principles and a common approach to exercise program management that includes design and development of exercises, conduct, evaluation, and improvement planning. HSEEP incorporates safety throughout this process. The resources directed toward exercise safety may vary depending upon the hazards of the exercise: Players participating in a tabletop exercise in a conference room, for example, face fewer hazards than those participating in a full-scale field exercise that mobilizes personnel and equipment.

HSEEP offers many best practice for any organization that conducts exercises, even for exercises that are not part of the NEP. Fundamental principles of the HSEEP program include:

- Engagement with elected and appointed officials (or management leaders as is applicable for the organization) who provide guidance and support for the exercise program;
- Exercises driven by capability-based objectives;
- Use of a progressive planning approach, in which various exercises aligned to a common set of exercise priorities and objectives are conducted over time with increasing complexity;
- Engagement of the whole community, as appropriate, in all phases of the exercise program;
- Incorporation of information about known risks into decisions about which priorities, objectives, and core capabilities will be evaluated through exercises;
- Use of a common methodology that provides organizations with a shared understanding of exercise program management, design, development, conduct, evaluation, and improvement planning. Common methodology also promotes exercise interoperability and fosters collaboration.

Exercise planning follows a management cycle that moves across four phases (Figure 11.5):

- Exercise design and development: Exercise planning team members schedule planning meetings, identify and agree to exercise objectives, design a scenario that meets these objectives, plan the exercise and evaluation process, and coordinate logistics;
- Conduct of the exercise: The scenario is played out, and an immediate wrap up takes place at the conclusion of exercise play;

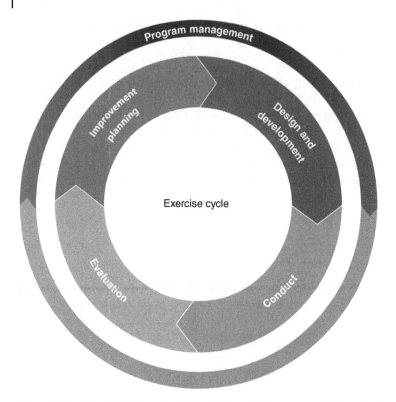

Figure 11.5 The HSEEP Exercise Cycle. Source: US Department of Homeland Security [2].

- Evaluation: Performance is assessed against exercise objectives. Strengths and areas for improvement are documented;
- Improvement planning: Corrective actions identified during exercises are tracked to completion, as part of a system to improve preparedness.

The exercise planning team should include representation from participating organizations and relevant stakeholders. Planning team members are not exercise players, unless resources are so limited that planning team members have to fill player roles in addition to their planning team responsibilities. Exercise planning team members who have to double as players know details about the scenario that are not available to other players, and as a result they have to carefully manage this conflict in roles in order to ensure integrity of the process used to test the objectives that the exercise was designed to test. Ideally, Incident Planning Team members should not be exercise players. For example, the Incident Planning Team Safety Leader should not play the role of the Safety Officer in the exercise: The Safety

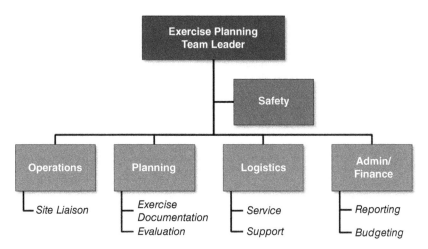

Figure 11.6 The HSEEP Planning Team. Source: US Department of Homeland Security [2].

Officer in exercise play should have the opportunity to make observations and make decisions without the influence that comes from participation in exercise planning.

The HSEEP planning team is organized similarly to an Incident Command Structure (Figure 11.6): Although multiple organizations participate in the planning process, there is a single Exercise Planning Team Leader. There is an Operations section, as well as Planning, Logistics, and Finance sections. An exercise safety function reports directly to the Exercise Planning Team Leader, and is responsible for the safety of exercise players.

HSEEP integrates player safety throughout the exercise management cycle. HSEEP specifies actions that can be taken to ensure a safe working environment during exercise play, including:

- Appointment of a Safety Controller or Controllers;
- Ensuring that advanced life support and basic life support ambulances are available for real-world emergencies that may occur during the exercise. These units must be dedicated to real-world events and do not participate in exercise play;
- Use of a code word or phrase to identify real-world emergencies (for example, "Real World");
- Including safety requirements and policies in the exercise plan. Safety issues such as weather, heat or cold stress, or exposures that are not necessarily included in the scope of the exercise but create an exposure risk for participants, and should be planned for.

The exercise planning team develops an Exercise Plan (ExPlan) that includes specified sections:

- Exercise scope, objectives, and core capabilities;
- Participant roles and responsibilities;
- Rules of conduct;
- Safety:
  - Identified safety issues;
  - Code words or phrases for use in a real-world emergency;
  - Safety Controller responsibilities;
  - Prohibited activities;
  - Weapons policies
- Logistics;
- Security and access to the exercise site;
- Communications, such as radio frequencies or channels;
- Duration, date, and time of the exercise, and the schedule of events;
- Maps and directions.

HSEEP lists responsibilities for Controllers and Evaluators. Controllers and Evaluators perform critical roles during the exercise, but do not participate in exercise play. In essence, these personnel are at the exercise site but are invisible to the players.

Controllers manage exercise play. Controllers direct the pace of the exercise, provide key data to players, and may prompt or initiate certain player actions based upon a predetermined plan outlined in the Master Scenario Events List (MSEL). Controllers may simulate roles of individuals or agencies who are not participating in exercise play, or may provide exercise injects. A Senior or Lead controller is identified who is responsible for the overall organization of the exercise.

Evaluators observe exercise play, and complete exercise evaluation worksheets that assess the degree to which specified criteria is met in support of the exercise objectives. They also capture any unresolved issues and observations, and help analyze exercise results. Evaluators are chosen based on their expertise in specific functional areas. For example, an individual with a safety background could be selected to evaluate the actions of the Incident Safety Officer during exercise play.

Exercise designers develop exercise evaluation forms that can be based on HSEEP templates specific for the core capabilities that the Evaluators are assigned to evaluate, such as the health and safety of workers (Figure 11.7). Evaluators assigned specific functions report to a Lead Evaluator who is responsible for the overall exercise evaluation (Figure 11.8).

Roles and responsibilities are described in a *Controller and Evaluator Handbook*, which is developed as a supplement to the exercise plan or as a stand-alone

EXERCISE EVALUATION GUIDE

Exercise Name: [Insert Exercise Name]
Exercise Date: [Insert Exercise Date]
Organization/Jurisdiction: [Insert Organization or Jurisdiction]
Venue: [Insert Venue Name]

Response
Exercise Objective: [Insert exercise objective]
Core Capability: Environmental Response/Health and Safety Conduct appropriate measures to ensure the protection of the health and safety of the public and workers, as well as the environment, from all hazards in support of responder operations and the affected communities.
Organizational Capability Target 1: [Insert customized target based on plans and assessments] Critical Task: [Insert task from frameworks, plans, or Standard Operating Procedures (SOPs)] Critical Task: [Insert task from frameworks, plans, or SOPs] Critical Task: [Insert task from frameworks, plans, or SOPs] Critical Task: [Insert task from frameworks, plans, or SOPs] Source(s):[Insert name of plan, policy, procedure, or reference]
Organizational Capability Target 2: [Insert customized target based on plans and assessments] Critical Task: [Insert task from frameworks, plans, or SOPs] Critical Task: [Insert task from frameworks, plans, or SOPs] Critical Task: [Insert task from frameworks, plans, or SOPs] Critical Task: [Insert task from frameworks, plans, or SOPs] Source(s): [Insert name of plan, policy, procedure, or reference]
Organizational Capability Target 3: [Insert customized target based on plans and assessments] Critical Task: [Insert task from frameworks, plans, or SOPs] Critical Task: [Insert task from frameworks, plans, or SOPs] Critical Task: [Insert task from frameworks, plans, or SOPs] Critical Task: [Insert task from frameworks, plans, or SOPs] Source(s): [Insert name of plan, policy, procedure, or reference]

Figure 11.7 HSEEP Evaluation Template for evaluation of responder health and safety. Source: US Department of Homeland Security [2].

document. The *Controller and Evaluator Handbook* is provided to all Controllers and Evaluators, and includes an Exercise Safety Plan. Controllers and Evaluators are given additional information immediately prior to the exercise, including key information specific to the functional area that the Controller or Evaluator will be working.

The Exercise Safety Team Leader is responsible for appointing a Safety Controller and, if needed, supporting Safety Controllers. The Safety Controller is

Organizational Capability Target	Associated Critical Tasks	Observation Notes and Explanation of Rating	Target Rating
[Insert Organizational Capability Target 1 from page 1]	• [Insert Organizational Capability Target 1 Critical Tasks from page 1]	[Observation notes and explanation of rating]	[Target rating]
[Insert Organizational Capability Target 2 from page 1]	• [Insert Organizational Capability Target 2 Critical Tasks from page 1]	[Observation notes and explanation of rating]	[Target rating]
[Insert Organizational Capability Target 3 from page 1]	• [Insert Organizational Capability Target 3 Critical Tasks from page]	[Observation notes and explanation of rating]	[Target rating]

Final Core Capability Rating: [Enter Total Rating here]

Evaluator Information
Evaluator Name:
Evaluator Email:
Evaluator Phone:

Ratings Key
P: Performed without challenges
S: Performed with some challenges
M: Performed with major challenges
U: Unable to be performed

Rev. 2017 508 - NPG v2
EEG-Resp-ERH&S

[PROTECTIVE MARKING, AS APPROPRIATE]
Homeland Security Exercise and Evaluation Program (HSEEP)

Figure 11.7 (*Continued*)

responsible for monitoring exercise safety during all phases of the exercise, including setup, conduct of the exercise, and cleanup.

All Exercise Controllers participate in monitoring exercise safety in addition to their other assigned functions, and report any real-world safety concerns to the Safety Controller.

During exercise play, an Incident Command Structure is established, and a Safety Officer is identified. The individual filling the role of Safety Officer during exercise play should identify safety issues related to the scenario and the work done by other exercise players, but is not concerned with real-world safety issues. Real-world safety issues may need to be invisible to the Safety Officer player.

Briefings are held before the start of exercise play. Separate briefings may be provided for elected and appointed officials, Controllers and Evaluators, actors, and players. If Observers are invited, such as agency officials who do not have assigned roles in the exercise but do have a valid reason to participate in this role, they may be given a separate briefing as well. These Observers are often unfamiliar with the safety issues at the site of the exercise. The Exercise Safety Team Leader

Exercise Evaluation Guide (EEG)   [Exercise Name]
                                                          [Exercise Name Continued]

Ratings Definitions

Performed without Challenges (P)	The targets and critical tasks associated with the core capability were completed in a manner that achieved the objective(s) and did not negatively impact the performance of other activities. Performance of this activity did not contribute to additional health and/or safety risks for the public or for emergency workers, and it was conducted in accordance with applicable plans, policies, procedures, regulations, and laws.
Performed with Some Challenges (S)	The targets and critical tasks associated with the core capability were completed in a manner that achieved the objective(s) and did not negatively impact the performance of other activities. Performance of this activity did not contribute to additional health and/or safety risks for the public or for emergency workers, and it was conducted in accordance with applicable plans, policies, procedures, regulations, and laws. However, opportunities to enhance effectiveness and/or efficiency were identified.
Performed with Major Challenges (M)	The targets and critical tasks associated with the core capability were completed in a manner that achieved the objective(s), but some or all of the following were observed: demonstrated performance had a negative impact on the performance of other activities; contributed to additional health and/or safety risks for the public or for emergency workers; and/or was not conducted in accordance with applicable plans, policies, procedures, regulations, and laws.
Unable to be Performed (U)	The targets and critical tasks associated with the core capability were not performed in a manner that achieved the objective(s).

Rev. 2017 508 - NPG v2   [PROTECTIVE MARKING, AS APPROPRIATE]
EEG-Resp-ERH&S   Homeland Security Exercise and Evaluation Program (HSEEP)
                                           3

Figure 11.7 *(Continued)*

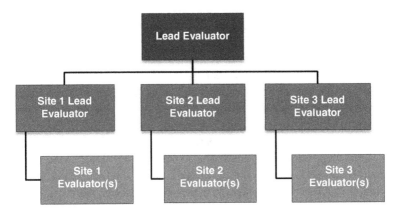

Figure 11.8 Sample organizational structure of an Exercise Evaluation Team. Source: US Department of Homeland Security [2].

should provide a safety briefing for each of these groups, highlighting important and relevant aspects of the Exercise Safety Plan.

An Assembly Area Controller is positioned at the assembly area, where players wait until they are dispatched to the exercise incident scene. The Assembly Area Controller ensures that coordination of pathways in and out of the assembly area are maintained, that traffic flow is managed, and safety is maintained within the exercise assembly area. The Assembly Area Controller takes attendance as units arrive at the assembly area, and also when they return to ensure that all players are accounted for. If weapons are used in the exercise, qualified individuals perform weapons checks and tag each weapon checked to indicate that it is safe for exercise play. The Assembly Area Controller must maintain close communication with other exercise controllers to receive any updates in exercise play that may change the deployment timetable, and in turn, impact traffic flow and staging at the assembly area.

Debriefings with the exercise planning team should be held immediately following the exercise to collect immediate feedback, and to collect any ideas, concerns and proposed improvements while they are fresh in everyone's mind. Players should participate in a Hot Wash led by a facilitator who ensures that the discussion is brief and constructive. Separate Hot Washes may be held for each functional area. Controllers and Evaluators may participate in leading these Hot Washes.

Exercise evaluations are based on documentation collected from Exercise Evaluators as well as information collected during debriefings and Hot Washes. As with other exercise planning phases covered in HSEEP, evaluation is done using a common approach. The Evaluation Team Leader, who is appointed by the Exercise Planning Team and participates as a planning team member throughout the exercise process, oversees the evaluation. Data from the exercise is compiled into an After Action Report (AAR) which provides an overview of performance related to each exercise objective and associated core capabilities. Strengths are highlighted, and areas for improvement are also noted. The AAR is provided to the exercise sponsor, who then distributes it to other participating organizations. Elected and appointed officials in government organizations, or senior management in private organizations, determine which areas of improvement identified in the AAR require further action and appoint responsible individuals to take specified actions to address these areas. Corrective actions are tracked and reported upon until they are completed. Updates to plans, protocols and procedures are made. The exercise cycle is repeated to determine if corrective actions taken have effectively addressed issues, and to identify additional areas where improvement is needed as an ongoing continuous improvement process [2].

Evaluation of the Safety Officer's performance should not be neglected in the AAR. Obstacles and challenges that the Safety Officer faced in the exercise should be noted and addressed. Resolution of these obstacles and challenges can improve safety performance and outcomes in an actual incident.

11.9 Moving Toward a Common Approach to Exercises

NFPA 1600 incorporates an exercise component to their Emergency Planning guidance and includes a reference HSEEP in regards to designing, developing, and evaluating exercises [17]. Thus, jurisdictions and organizations that have adopted NFPA 1600 for emergency planning in turn utilize the HSEEP process when conducting exercises. Use of this common approach is advantageous when conducting interagency exercises: Just as NIMS utilizes a common approach to incident management to provide interoperability and common understanding, HSEEP promotes interoperability and a common understanding in the conduct of exercises.

Federal agencies mandate exercises for airports, railroads, chemical manufacturers, industries at risk of an oil spill, and others. Direction and guidance for exercises in these industries varies, and may or may not be consistent with NIMS and HSEEP. Nonetheless, each of these industries relies on cooperation from local emergency responders. These same emergency responders must prepare to respond to multiple types of emergencies, including oil spills, chemical releases, airfield emergencies, and incidents on railroads. A consistent and interoperable approach allows all to work together regardless of the industry or type of incident.

Industries such as passenger railroads or the oil industry are required to execute emergency response exercises, although the Federal agencies that require these exercises approach this requirement in different ways. Chemical processors must plan for emergencies, but the specific manner in which this is done is not prescribed. Even when not required, it is advantageous for these industries to adopt HSEEP for exercise program management, and there is nothing precluding these industries from doing so.

Adoption of HSEEP has important implications for exercise safety. Integration of a safety representative on the incident planning team who reports to the Exercise Planning Team Leader, incorporation of a Safety section within the written Exercise Plan and also within the *Controller and Evaluator Handbook*, assignment of Exercise Safety Controllers, safety briefings at the start of an exercise, and accountability of personnel are elements that best ensure the safety of all exercise participants. The HSEEP principal of engaging with elected and appointed officials, or senior level management, early and often ensures that they also are on board with, and support, any safety requirements incorporated into the Exercise Plan.

Safety professionals who wish to integrate safety into exercise planning can facilitate this goal through encouraging their employers to adopt HSEEP as an internal process even when it is not specifically required.

11.10 Exercise Safety Plan

The Exercise Safety Plan should address any OSHA or State Plan requirements that are applicable to the exercise, as well as safety requirements for hazards not addressed in the standards. For example:

- Hazard Communication of any chemicals used in the exercise, or any chemicals that exercise participants may be exposed to at the exercise site;
- Personal protective equipment required at the site, including an assessment of hazards that are anticipated to be present and appropriately rated PPE to address the hazards;
- Use of respiratory protection, including requirements that anyone wearing a respirator needs to have completed a medical evaluation and training on the respiratory they will be using. Any personnel wearing a tight-fitting respirator must be fit tested;
- Protocols for any work that requires entry into a confined space, trench, or work at heights;
- Operator training and certification requirements for equipment such as forklifts, backhoes, or other similar equipment;
- Requirements for personnel working around traffic. For example, flaggers may be needed if working in traffic zones, and traffic safety plans may be needed for those working in the staging and assembly areas;
- Ergonomics. For example, removal of escape windows or extrication of "patients" may require awkward postures or forceful exertions;
- Weather-related hazards, including exposure to excessive heat or cold, or sun exposure;
- Site-specific hazards, such as slip, trip and fall hazards and site access hazards;
- Hazards relating to nearby work processes, such as an active airfield, train track, or manufacturing process;
- Inhalation and exposure hazards such as those that might occur from a fire exercise;
- Biological hazards;
- Hazards related to weapons used in the exercise, and how these hazards are controlled;
- Hazards to actors playing the part of "victims" in the exercise scenario, including heat and/or cold stress, fatigue, and injuries when being transported. Whenever

possible, exercise dummies should be used to simulate transport and removal of patients rather than human actors;

- Procedures for "real-world" emergencies, including a code word or phrase, and evacuation routes from the exercise site.

Any person filling the Exercise Safety Leader position should work with the Logistics Exercise Leader to ensure that an appropriate number or restroom facilities are provided for during the exercise, and may utilize OSHA standards as a reference. If food is brought in for exercise participants, the Safety position should work with Logistics to ensure that all appropriate food storage and handling safety protocols are adhered to.

A plan must also be in place to address any real-world medical issues, and to report and investigate any exercise-related injuries or illnesses. Such reports should be submitted to the Exercise Team Leader and senior officials or management.

Psychosocial hazards should also be included. Traumatic events portrayed in an exercise are imaginary, and not real. Adverse psychological reactions among players can be incorporated as injects into exercise play to allow other players to practice their Psychological First Aid skills.

Real-world psychological reactions can occur as well, in exercise players or others supporting the exercise regardless of whether the exercise is a drill, tabletop exercise, or a full-scale exercise. An exercise player may freeze, become overwhelmed, or become unnecessarily confrontational. I've seen this happen on several occasions; even exercises conducted in the relative safety of a conference room can lead to unanticipated reactions. Any such reaction should be treated as a "real-world" incident.

Exercise controllers can practice real world Psychological First Aid techniques in order to move play along, or play may need to be temporarily paused. In addition to other ways in which an emergency plan is tested in an exercise, exercises provide a test of individual resilience, and how individuals may react in an actual incident. Depending upon the degree of reaction, exercise participants can take what they have learned about themselves to improve their individual psychological resilience in the next exercise or actual response, or they may find that they are better suited to roles that do not include exposure to trauma. Regardless, any individual experiencing such a reaction during an exercise needs to be treated compassionately, and in as confidential a manner as possible.

11.11 Summary

Exercises are integral to the emergency planning process, and to the study of how an emergency plan is implemented. Deficiencies that are identified during exercises can be addressed to improve the plan. Exercises are also educational opportunities, both for those with assigned roles in an incident response and for those who support these individuals in a multitude of ways.

There is no excuse for compromising the safety of exercise players, observers, or any other personnel who have assigned roles in the exercise. The HSEEP process integrates safety into exercise planning and conduct. Even if an organization is not required to utilize HSEEP, and does not elect to utilize it voluntarily, safety must be integrated into the exercise planning process. Personnel with assigned safety responsibilities have important roles to play when the exercise is conducted. HSEEP concepts, including assignment of an Exercise Planning Safety Leader, inclusion of a safety section within the Exercise Plan, and assignment of a Safety Controller are components of exercise planning that should always be followed.

References

1 Moen, R.D. and Norman, C.L. (2010). Circling back: clearing up myths about the Deming cycle and seeing how it keeps evolving. *Quality Progress* (November 2010): 22–28.

2 US Department of Homeland Security (2013). *Homeland Security Exercise and Evaluation Program (HSEEP).*

3 14 CFR 139.325, Airport Emergency Plan.

4 Federal Aviation Administration, US Department of Transportation (2010). *Advisory Circular AC No: AC 150/5200-31C, Change: 1, Airport Emergency Plan.*

5 49 CFR Part 239, Passenger Train Emergency Preparedness.

6 Federal Railroad Administration, US Department of Transportation (2014). *Guide to Developing a Passenger Train Emergency Preparedness Plan.*

7 29 CFR 1910.119, Process Safety Management of Highly Hazardous Chemicals.

8 29 CFR 1910.120, Hazardous Waste Operations and Emergency Response.

9 Gallant, B.J. (2006). *Hazardous Waste Operations and Emergency Response Manual.* Wiley.

10 40 CFR Part 112.21, Oil Pollution Prevention-Facility Response Training and Drills/Exercises.

11 33 CFR Appendix D to Part 154, Training Elements for Oil Response Plans.

12 Department of Homeland Security, US Coast Guard; Environmental Protection Agency; Department of Transportation Pipeline and Hazardous Materials Safety Administration; Department of the Interior Bureau of Safety and Environmental Enforcement (2016). *2016 National Preparedness for Response Exercise Program (PREP) Guidelines.*

13 Federal Emergency Management Administration (FEMA), US Department of Homeland Security (2010). *Developing and Maintaining Emergency Operations Plans*. Comprehensive Preparedness Guide (CPG) 101, Version 2.0.

14 US Department of Homeland Security (2018). *Threat and Hazard Identification and Risk Assessment (THIRA) and Stakeholder Preparedness Review (SPR) Guide, Comprehensive Preparedness Guide (CPG) 201*, 3e.

15 US Department of Homeland Security (2015). *National Preparedness Goal*, 2e.

16 Federal Emergency Management Administration (FEMA), US Department of Homeland Security (2018). *National Exercise Program Base Plan*.

17 NFPA 1600 (2019). *Standard on Continuity, Emergency, and Crisis Management*.

12

Safety in Continuity of Operations

During a disaster, emergency response personnel deploy to support the initial response. When resource needs exceed resources, mutual aid resources along with nontraditional responders and volunteers may supplement the response. Emergency Operations Plans are activated. Meanwhile, government must continue to function, hospitals need to continue to provide care to members of the community, banks must remain open in support of our financial institutions, the supply chain must continue to provide needed goods, and the community support must be maintained. These entities rely on continuity plans to maintain operations despite disruptions created by the external disaster and a decrease in personnel who are available to come to work. As discussed in the previous chapters, safety personnel need to support responders who face risks during a response for the greater good. They also need to support the safety of those working to keep society functioning in the face of disruption, many of whom must perform work outside of their normal day-to-day responsibilities, and with fewer resources.

12.1 National Essential Functions

The Federal government has identified National Essential Functions (NEFs) which are the primary focus of government before, during, and after a catastrophic emergency. NEFs include the following:

1. Ensure the continued functioning of our form of government under the United States Constitution, including the functioning of three separate branches of government.
2. Provide leadership visible to the nation and the world and maintain the trust and confidence of the American people.

Health and Safety in Emergency Management and Response, First Edition. Dana L. Stahl.
© 2021 John Wiley & Sons, Inc. Published 2021 by John Wiley & Sons, Inc.

3. Defend the United States against all enemies, foreign, and domestic, and prevent or interdict attacks against the United States or its people, property, or interests.
4. Maintain and foster effective relationships with foreign nations.
5. Protect against threats to the homeland and bring to justice perpetrators of crimes or attacks against the United States of its people, property, or interests.
6. Provide rapid and effective response to and recovery from the domestic consequences of an attack or other incident.
7. Protect and stabilize the nation's economy and ensure public confidence in its financial systems.
8. Provide for Federal government services that address the national health, safety, and welfare needs of the United States.

Continuity of Government at all levels is critical to meeting these NEFs during a catastrophe. This includes government at the Federal level, as well as state, tribal, and local government. However, government cannot function in a vacuum.

Private entities and nongovernmental organizations provide support services and resources that the government depends on. Government relies on an active supply chain to provide resources needed both for disaster response and Continuity of Operations. If the agricultural system fails, people do not eat. If the healthcare system fails, people who become ill or injured cannot be treated, and those with preexisting medical conditions are not supported. If financial systems fail, supplies cannot be purchased and employees cannot be paid for the work that they do. National Essential Functions cannot be maintained if the support they depend on is not there.

Nongovernmental organizations such as faith-based groups and nonprofit organizations support the community. They can assist in providing supplies to the community, provide shelter for those who need it, and provide social support for the community, emergency responders, and those who work to maintain a functioning society. All this is needed to ensure that NEFs are maintained.

A catastrophe disrupts business as usual, but it cannot allow business to stop [1].

12.2 Critical Infrastructure

Maintenance of infrastructure is key to maintaining a functioning society, and the need for maintaining this infrastructure was underscored with the release of Homeland Security Presidential Directive (HSPD) 7 in 2003. HSPD 7 was superseded by Presidential Policy Directive (PPD) 21, issued by President Obama in February 2013. PPD 21 identifies specific critical infrastructure that must continue to function in the event of a catastrophe in order to maintain National Essential

Functions. This critical infrastructure includes both public and private entities in the following areas:

- Chemical;
- Commercial facilities;
- Communications;
- Critical manufacturing;
- Dams;
- Defense industrial base;
- Emergency services;
- Energy;
- Financial services;
- Food and agriculture;
- Government facilities;
- Healthcare and public health;
- Information technology;
- Nuclear reactors, materials, and waste;
- Transportation systems;
- Water and wastewater systems.

PPD-21 recognized the importance of this critical infrastructure to the nation's resilience, and directed that efforts be taken to address the resilience and continuity of this infrastructure when disaster strikes. Some of this infrastructure is managed by government agencies, and others by private entities: Each has a role in supporting the National Essential Functions and our day-to-day communities. Maintenance of critical infrastructure must occur in a manner that reflects this interconnectedness and interdependency [2].

12.3 Importance of Continuity

Maintaining National Essential Functions requires operational continuity among government organizations (Continuity of Government), individual organizations (Continuity of Operations), and Enduring Constitutional Government.

Enduring Constitutional Government (ECG) safeguards the three branches of government: executive, legislative, and judicial. All three branches must support Essential Functions during an emergency, and must have a plan to continue to meet constitutional responsibilities. In the event that leaders are unable to fulfill their assigned responsibilities, there must be orderly succession and appropriate transfer of leadership responsibilities. Continuity of Government (COG) must occur within each branch of government.

Individual organizations that function as critical infrastructure identified in PPD 21 must maintain Continuity of Operations (COO) to support Continuity of Government, Enduring Constitutional Government, and the National Essential Functions. Critical infrastructure depends upon entities such as local government agencies, private suppliers, and support services to maintain their Continuity of Operations, so it is critical that any organization that supports critical infrastructure also must remain operational in a catastrophic event. These dependencies are cascading: Entities that provide primary support for critical infrastructure in turn rely on supporting organizations to succeed in executing their expected functions, and these supporting organizations also have organizations upon whom they depend. In short, a whole community effort is needed to ensure continuity across all levels of society when a disaster occurs.

Therefore, continuity planning takes place at multiple levels. Much critical infrastructure is in the private sector, as are the organizations that this critical infrastructure depends upon to operate. Even businesses that do not directly or indirectly support critical infrastructure should recognize that continuity planning is a good business practice: Businesses that do not have a plan to weather a disaster may not survive the disaster.

Local government has a responsibility to serve and support constituents, and must continue to function despite outside factors. State, tribal, and federal governments rely on local governments to perform their local functions, and in turn maintain Continuity of Government.

Nongovernmental organizations, such as the Red Cross, support disaster operations, and provide support to critical infrastructure such as hospitals. Community groups and faith-based organizations also play a role. These organizations need to plan to continue operations and remain operational when disaster strikes.

Lastly, individuals, families, and households must be prepared to weather disasters. This group comprises the community. Emergency responders on the front lines of a disaster response have households to come home to, as do individuals working for government agencies, nongovernmental organizations, critical infrastructure, and the cascading entities that support critical infrastructure. Families and households provide the support that all response and continuity resources depend on.

An organization that commits to continuity planning should dedicate resources toward developing a continuity plan, testing it, and maintaining it. Often, a continuity manager, or even a department, is given this responsibility. An organization that has not dedicated resources toward continuity planning may give this responsibility to the Emergency Management Department or even the Safety Department.

In organizations with a dedicated Continuity of Operations function, Emergency Management and Safety personnel play a supporting role.

12.4   Essential Functions in Organizations

One of the first steps in continuity planning is to identify the Essential Functions that the organization must perform. Essential Functions are those that support critical tasks that help maintain critical infrastructure, National Essential Functions, or simply ensure that the business survives the disaster.

FEMA guidance provides a process for determining these Essential Functions, and defines both Mission Essential Functions and Primary Mission Essential Functions.

- Mission Essential Functions (MEFs) are those Essential Functions directly related to accomplishing the organization's mission.
- Primary Mission Essential Functions (PMEFs) are those mission Essential Functions that must be continuously performed in support of National Essential Functions.

Essential Supporting Activities (ESAs) support the performance of Mission Essential Functions. For example, a transit agency may identify "operation of busses" as a Mission Essential Function. In order to meet this function, employees with Commercial Driver's Licenses (CDLs) are needed to operate the busses and mechanics are needed to maintain them. None of these employees will do this work if they do not get paid: Payroll employees do not directly contribute to the operation of busses, but meeting payroll is an Essential Supporting Activity that must be performed. If bus drivers do not get paid, the transit agency cannot meet its Mission Essential Function to operating busses.

Likewise, maintaining the safety of bus drivers and those who maintain busses and vehicles is an Essential Supporting Activity.

It is important to distinguish between Important Functions and Essential Functions: All personnel within an organization perform Important Functions. However, when a catastrophe occurs and resources are scarce, it is possible to delay Important Functions. Essential Functions must continue, and resources normally dedicated to Important Functions may have to be temporarily reallocated to the performance of Essential Functions and Essential Supporting Activities.

Once an organization has identified Essential Functions and Essential Supporting Activities, and these have been approved by senior leadership, the next step is to develop a Business Process Analysis (BPA). This analysis is a systematic process that identifies activities and tasks performed within an organization in support of identified Essential Functions. The BPA documents elements including:

- Functional processes;
- Workflows;
- Activities;

- Personnel expertise;
- Systems;
- Resources;
- Controls;
- Data;
- Facilities.

The BPA should answer:

- What products, information, and equipment are required from both internal and external partners to perform the essential activity?
- What products, services, or information result from the performance of this task? What metrics are used to measure performance and standards?
- Is direct leadership needed from within the organization to perform the task? Who in the organization provides this leadership?
- What internal or external staff are needed to directly support or perform this task? What specific skill sets, expertise, and authority are needed to perform this task?
- What communication needs does the task require? Is special software or equipment needed?
- What type of facility is needed to perform this task in?
- What supplies or resources are needed to perform this task? Can they be obtained or purchased during a catastrophic emergency? Can they be relocated from another facility? How will this be funded?
- What internal and external organizations support or ensure task performance? What information, supplies, equipment, or products do these support organizations provide?
- How is the task performed, from start to finish?

Next, a Business Impact Analysis (BIA) is performed to identify and evaluate the threats and hazards that could interfere with actions outlined in the BPA, and in turn, increase the risk that an organization will fail to perform its Essential Functions. The BIA should answer the following questions:

- What is the vulnerability of the essential function to each threat or hazard identified in the risk assessments?
- What would be the impact if the essential function's performance is disrupted?
- What is the timeframe for unacceptable loss of functions and critical assets? [1, 3, 4]

Once risks have been identified, steps can be taken to mitigate these risks [1].

12.5   Risk Mitigation

A risk analysis can reveal risks to buildings and work facilities, personnel, the supply chain, and other industry-specific resources. The plan should then address how each potential point of failure can be addressed.

If work facilities cannot be occupied, alternate locations should be identified where work can be performed. However, moving work to a location that is not specifically intended for the type of work to be performed carries its own risk. Safety personnel should weigh in any proposed alternate locations, and consider potential safety factors:

- Can the work or task be performed safely in the alternate location?
- Does work at the alternate location pose any personal safety risk that differs from that of work performed in the primary location? Such as:
  o Is ventilation sufficient to prevent adverse indoor air quality given the work performed?
  o Do hazards that are primarily addressed through engineering controls at the primary facility need to be mitigated? Will this require use of administrative controls, such as new procedures, or new types of Personal Protective Equipment?
  o Can the facility accommodate the expected number of personnel? Is it likely that occupancy loads will be exceeded, or that the ventilation system is not sufficient to support the numbers of people that will occupy the facility without creating indoor air quality issues?
  o Can workstations be set up to minimize ergonomic hazards?
  o Could overcrowding contribute to safety issues, such as ergonomics, reduced air quality, increased noise levels, or other hazards?
  o Are evacuation plans available, and is there a process to quickly inform new occupants of these plans?
- How will personnel transport themselves and any needed equipment to the new facility? Will the catastrophe pose hazards to transportation? Can personnel commute from their homes, or is the distance too great?

Telework may be an option for some tasks if communication functions that support the intended work are not impacted by the emergency. If the emergency situation creates hazardous commuting conditions, allowing employees the option to telecommute minimizes this personal risk to employees, protecting these employee resources and their ability to continue to perform work. Employees who are injured, or in a worst-case scenario, dead, are not productive workers and cannot support Essential Functions. Employees who are able to telework can also take care of any household impacts caused by the emergency. This eliminates distraction from worry about the employee's household status, including family members, pets, and the home. It also allows employees an option to work when childcares and schools are closed.

OSHA considers that employers continue to have responsibility for the safety of workers who are working from home, although this risk is fairly minimal for office work. OSHA does not conduct inspections of home offices or hold employers liable, and does not expect employers to perform safety inspections of home offices.

Other types of work may carry greater risk. OSHA does conduct inspections of home-based manufacturing work when a complaint or referral is made, and recognizes that certain types of home-based work can be hazardous. Hazards could include unguarded machinery, unsafe use of chemicals, use of lead, or lack of PPE. Safety professionals supporting organizations that consider allowing employees to perform this type of work at home should carefully evaluate how it can be done safely, and what controls need to be implemented to protect employees from hazards.

Injuries that occur as a result of home-based work must be investigated and recorded on the employer's OSHA 300 log if recordability criteria is met. Such injuries and illnesses may be compensable under state Worker's Compensation laws [5].

Another alternative to maintaining Essential Functions is to transfer work assignments to alternate, or back up, personnel. This is referred to as devolution, or the ability to transfer authority and responsibilities from primary operating staff and facilities to other designated staff at alternate facilities. Large organizations that conduct operations in multiple geographic regions can transfer work assignments to operations located outside of the catastrophe zone. Others may need to utilize outside contractors to perform needed work, and government agencies may utilize mutual aid agreements with other government partners.

Plans for devolution should ensure that those entities that take on additional work are capable of performing this work safely. Safety review of devolution plans should look at whether this reassignment of work will instigate the need for additional safety training, medical monitoring, PPE, or the implementation of additional controls at the location taking on the extra work. Safety plans should also take into account the effect of increased workload on ergonomic risk factors, fatigue, and burnout.

An organization must include a plan for personnel accountability, or how to contact all staff and contractors following a disaster event to communicate and coordinate activities. Personnel need to know if and when they should report to work, and if their reporting locations have changed. Organizations also need to find out which employees are able to report to work after the disaster strikes, and which employees face challenges that prevent them from coming in. Work should be assigned accordingly. The continuity plan should specify how accountability and communication takes place.

An order of succession plan is needed to establish who can fill leadership positions in the event that leaders are unavailable. This is not something that can be done on the fly, but must be planned ahead with appropriate legal counsel to ensure compliance with rules and policies. Likewise, the continuity plan should include a process for delegation of authority at multiple levels within the organization to ensure an orderly transfer of responsibilities [1].

12.6 Continuity Plans and the Employees That Carry Them Out

Employers rely on their employees to carry out Essential Functions. In turn, employees who live in a community impacted by the disaster have responsibility to perform Essential Functions for their employer, but they also have many competing personal demands that can impact their ability to meet this responsibility. The disaster may have impacted homes, and essential employees may have to prioritize coordination of repairs to their homes or finding alternative living accommodations while they are also needed at work. Families can be impacted: Schools or childcare centers may close, leaving families without options for taking care of children while they work. Children may be traumatized, and need support from their parents. Family members may be injured, dead, or missing. While employers count on employees to come to work, these distractions may interfere with an employee's ability to do their work well even when they do come in. Such distractions will not impact every employee equally, and it is not possible to predict during planning who will and who will not be impacted. It is impossible to plan which employees will lose family members and which will not have homes to come back to. Individual employees will have different levels of personal resilience as well: Some will be able to effectively balance competing demands, others will not. Again, an employer cannot predict which group any individual employee falls into.

In short, employers need employees who are Ready, Willing, and Able to work during a disaster to perform Essential Functions. The concept of Ready, Willing, and Able includes:

- *Readiness* to respond refers to the ability of an employee to come to work in a timely manner when needed. If the employee's family or household has prepared their own emergency response plan, and the employee has social support to assist in implementing it, the employee is free to focus on performing work contributing to the employer's Essential Functions.

- *Willingness* to respond includes the motivation and likelihood that a worker will actually respond during an emergency. This could be influenced by an individual's perceptions of the hazard: An employee who does not feel appropriately protected from the hazard posed by the emergency may refuse to come to work.
- *Ability* to respond refers to the skill or knowledge needed by the person assigned to perform a task. It includes inner aptitude (i.e. the ability to perform the task under duress) and competencies that can be gained through education, training, and experience [6].

Employers can develop programs to assist in preparing employees to be Ready, Willing, and Able to work in the midst of disaster. This can include providing training for employers who may have to perform Essential Functions and essential support activities that they do not ordinarily do, and the opportunity to gain experience through work assignments that include this type of work prior to a disaster. This type of employer support can increase the probability that employees will be able to perform quality work outside their primary day to day assignments when the time comes.

Safety professionals can help with employee willingness to work by addressing hazards that employees may be fearful of. If a workplace has a strong safety culture, and effectively and visibly responds to worker safety concerns during day-to-day operations, employees will have greater confidence that the employer will do the same when the continuity plan is activated and new hazards present themselves. Safety management is an essential support activity that must be written into a continuity plan.

Employers can improve readiness through support in building employee resilience, such as encouraging employees to build family emergency plans. Employers can offer education programs on the importance of family emergency planning and maintaining emergency provisions and supplies, and can also include resources for strengthening homes in preparedness for a disaster. If such mitigations are taken, homes are more likely to be habitable despite the disaster. Options for childcare can be provided to allow parents to work when schools and daycares close.

Employees who are not assigned Essential Functions, and are told not to report to work, may worry about loss of income and being unable to pay bills. Human resource policies should address how to respond to employees who choose to come to work despite the fact that the organization has determined that it is safest that these employees stay home. Payroll policies should be established to address financial support for these employees. Is there a mechanism to maintain pay for personnel who are told not to report to work? Can they use vacation or sick leave? Once normal operations resume, these employees will be needed to resume the Important Functions that they perform for the organization under normal conditions, and employers who help these employees survive the crisis will not have to replace and retrain these positions once the crisis is over.

12.7 Continuity Safety Plans

Existing organizational safety programs may continue to be applicable during Continuity Operations. However, they may also need to be modified or updated if work changes significantly.

Employees who perform work upon activation of the continuity plan may be required to perform tasks that they are unfamiliar with, or may be assigned to jobs that they do not ordinarily perform. Workers who are new to a job are more likely to be injured at work than they are when performing a job they know well: It has been demonstrated that employees are four times as likely to suffer a lost work time injury in the first month of a new job than employees who have worked for more than a year in the same job [7]. Workplace safety support is necessary to prevent a potential increase in occupational injury rates during Continuity Operations, especially if large numbers of employees are given new work responsibilities or reassignments.

Employees who are assigned to tasks that they do not ordinarily perform may need additional training, and this may or may not be practical to provide during the planning stage. Training on respiratory protection, for example, must be done annually. It is generally not cost-effective to train and conduct fit testing for a cohort of employees who do not normally wear respirators every year and obtain medical clearances on the chance that a continuity plan may be activated in the next 12 months. Therefore, the continuity plan must include procedures to qualify employees for respirator use who are Ready, Willing, and Able to come to work upon activation of the plan if the plan relies on normally unqualified individuals to perform essential work requiring respirators or if work must be performed without engineering controls that would otherwise be operational.

If engineering controls for workplace hazards are impacted by the disaster, employers need to utilize administrative controls such as updated procedures or increase the use of PPE. Administrative controls and PPE are lower on the hierarchy of controls than engineering controls, and are considered less effective. The Continuity Safety Plan should identify when these alternative controls can and should be implemented, and ensure that employees are protected from workplace hazards when utilizing less effective control methods.

Essentially, a Continuity Safety Plan needs to include all the elements that would be required under normal operations, but must be modified to address changing conditions and hazards. In addition, a Continuity Safety Plan should include elements specific to risks that employees face as related to the situation that triggered activation of the continuity plan. These risks are not traditionally addressed in a safety plan prepared for normal operations.

A Continuity Safety Plan should include a section on mental health. Individuals will respond to the stressors posed by the disaster in different ways. While some will cope well, others will need additional support, and it should be expected that employees will be impacted in various ways. Some of those with missing friends or family members, for example, may appreciate the distraction that work brings; others will not be able to focus on work. Those who have friends or family members who have died will experience multiple stages of grief, including denial, anger, and depression. Work can be a respite in the denial stage, but as the grief process evolves, denial gives way to anger, then sadness. An employee who seems to be coping well despite a loss may not continue to cope well as time progresses. Psychological first aid and/or mental health first aid are an important part of a Continuity Safety Plan.

Fatigue is a greater hazard during continuity work than it is when performing work under normal conditions. Employees who fulfill Essential Functions may need to work long hours, in addition to needing to make home repairs, contact insurance companies, attend to family needs, and otherwise deal with the personal impacts of the disaster. Employers should implement a fatigue management plan that includes allowing breaks, providing rest areas, and monitoring for stress.

Transportation disruptions can extend commute times and contribute to fatigue. Commutes that take several hours or more extend into an employee's rest period, and fatigue combined with increased travel times and obstacles creates a risky commute. Employers can reduce this risk by providing local accommodations for employees who have trouble getting into work. This could include renting hotel rooms, or setting up cots on site to allow employees an option to the hazardous commute.

Employers may choose to provide meals for employees. If grocery stores are depleted, if power is out and people cannot cook at home, or if homes are damaged, feeding employees is a tremendous support. However, the employer must ensure that food that is provided has been prepared according to the local food safety guidelines. After all, transportation and healthcare both may be disrupted by the disaster, and it may be harder to get medical care for personnel who develop food-related illness. Disruption in plumbing systems can exacerbate impacts.

Ingredients used in food preparation should be listed, so that individuals with food allergies know which food items are safe for them to eat.

Employees who are assigned responsibilities under the continuity plan must be trained on the continuity plan and the specific tasks they will be expected to perform. This training should integrate safety, including applicable elements of the Continuity Safety Plan and how worker safety will be addressed when the continuity plan is activated. When Continuity Operations are initiated, employers need employees who are Ready, Willing, and Able to work; employees who know that their employer is committed to their safety will be more willing to do their part.

12.8 Reasonable Accommodations During Continuity Operations

The Americans with Disabilities Act (ADA) provides protections for individuals with physical or mental impairment that substantially limits one or more major life activities. This includes employees who have a record of having such an impairment, and those who are regarded as having such an impairment whether or not the impairment limits or is perceived to limit a major life activity. Major life activities are defined as including, but not limited to:

- Caring for oneself;
- Performing manual tasks;
- Seeing;
- Hearing;
- Eating;
- Sleeping;
- Walking;
- Standing;
- Lifting;
- Bending;
- Speaking;
- Breathing;
- Learning;
- Reading;
- Concentrating;
- Thinking;
- Communicating;
- Working;
- Operation of major bodily functions, including but not limited to:
  o Functions of the immune system;
  o Normal cell growth;
  o Digestive functions;
  o Bowel functions;
  o Bladder functions;
  o Neurological functions;

o Brain functions;
o Respiratory functions;
o Circulatory functions;
o Endocrine functions;
o Reproductive functions [8].

Disabilities may not be visible. Individuals with such hidden disabilities may be able to work in their day-to-day jobs without accommodations, and may therefore choose not to disclose that they have a disability. However, if work tasks change during Continuity Operations, such disabilities may present a greater impact to an individual, and will need to be accommodated.

Job positions that require specific physical and mental capabilities should list these in the job description. Likewise, required physical and mental capabilities should be identified for jobs that are listed as Essential Functions or Essential Support Activities in a continuity plan.

Employers must provide means for employees to request reasonable accommodations. This request process should be evaluated to determine if it can be effectively utilized during Continuity Operations, or if it needs to be modified or streamlined. The process of requesting accommodations should be clearly articulated within the continuity plan.

Commonly requested accommodations that should be addressed in the continuity plan include:

- Communications that accommodate those who are deaf or hard of hearing, and those who are blind or have low vision;
- Facilities that are accessible to those with mobility disabilities, including physically accessible entrances, egress routes and exits, and restrooms;
- Quiet spaces or rooms for those with sensory disabilities and those on the autism spectrum [1].

12.9 Medical Support for Employees During Continuity Operations

It should be assumed that the medical system will be impacted by the disaster, and that medical services may become a scarce resource.

Maintaining the health of those who perform Essential Functions is a priority in ensuring that these functions can continue to be performed, and in turn ensuring the continuity of critical infrastructure. Continuity planning should include healthcare access for essential employees, and continuity planners should work with local healthcare providers to identify ways in which essential employees can obtain healthcare when needed without undue disruption to performance of essential tasks.

Personnel may have difficulty obtaining necessary medications and needed health supplies when a disaster disrupts transportation and the supply chain. This can in turn impact the performance of essential employees. Continuity planners should consider this in resource planning, and identify means in which these employees can obtain needed medications and health supplies in the event of long-term community disruption.

12.10 Information Technology Disaster Recovery Plans

Most organizations are highly dependent upon Information Technology (IT) systems, such as telephone systems, internet, software, and industry- and organization-specific programs. When a disaster strikes, it is imperative that systems that support Essential Functions be restored as quickly as possible. An IT Disaster Recovery Plan describes how these systems are to be brought back on line.

FEMA's Continuity Guidance Circular notes that it is a common misconception that IT Disaster Recovery Plans are the same thing as an organization's continuity plan. In reality, these are two separate but interconnected plans. An IT Disaster Recovery Plan should be developed in conjunction with the organization's continuity plan. The essential business processes, Essential Functions and essential records identified in the continuity plan drive priorities in IT in disaster recovery. The IT Disaster Recovery Plan describes how IT systems that support the continuity plan as well as normal operations are brought back on line after they have been disrupted. The ability or inability to bring IT programs back on line in support of Essential Functions is a risk that must be identified in a Business Impact Analysis [1].

Work-arounds may be needed when IT systems are not functional. Such work-arounds may or may not impact employee safety, and a safety review of such work-arounds should at least be considered.

12.11 Safety Program Essential Records

Safety program managers must maintain various records to comply with OSHA or State Program regulations. Many of these records, such as Safety Data Sheets and exposure records must be maintained for the length of an employee's employment, plus 30 years. The continuity plan must address how an organization maintains essential records in the event of a disaster, and safety staff should ensure that these required safety records are included as essential records that must be maintained.

If records are maintained electronically, there must be a mechanism to back up these records and restore them in the event of data loss. Organizational safety personnel need to work closely with IT to ensure that the ability to retrieve these records is part of the IT Disaster Recovery Plan. Some of these records may be covered by HIPAA privacy protections, and safety managers need to ensure that backup systems and data retrieval do not violate HIPAA requirements. It is important that safety personnel are able to confirm training, medical monitoring, and other records when continuity plans are activated and employees are assigned to perform work outside of their primary job assignments.

Additional records may be generated during continuity operations, as employees may need additional training or medical monitoring in order to perform new job assignments. The plan should ensure that any newly generated records are maintained, and can be moved to the recordkeeping system used in normal operations when they resume [1].

12.12 Pandemic Planning

A pandemic event is essentially a worst-case scenario in continuity planning, as it is expected that in a pandemic large numbers of employees will be impacted worldwide for a time period of many months to a year or more. In fact, many organizations first realized the importance of continuity planning in the early 2000s when the threat of the highly pathogenic avian influenza virus (H5N1) was identified.

When a pandemic occurs, the goal is to prevent spread of the virus and minimize illness until a vaccine can be developed. When the 2009 H1N1 pandemic occurred, the virus was first reported in Mexico and California in April, and the World Health Organization declared a pandemic on June 11. A rapid response was initiated to develop a H1N1 vaccine; however, this was not available for distribution until the fall. This time period included the winter flu season in the southern hemisphere, and the beginning of the fall/winter flu season in the northern hemisphere. Fortunately, this virus did not prove to be an exceptionally virulent novel flu strain [9].

Since 2009, the US Department of Health and Human Services has worked to improve efficiencies in the development of the next pandemic flu vaccine, including increasing production capacity. Current plans call for development of the first vaccines to be available for distribution within 4 months of a pandemic declaration, with the expectation that the first doses will become available within 12 weeks [10]. Vaccines targeting non-flu novel viruses cannot be developed as quickly, as similar infrastructure is not in place.

Government, private industry, and other organizations should assume that up to 40% of their staff may be absent for about two weeks at a time during the height of the pandemic [11], and therefore plan to maintain continuity operations for some time.

Unlike many other types of disasters, such as earthquakes, hurricanes, terrorist events, or other similar incidents, a pandemic event does not directly impact physical infrastructure such as buildings, bridges, roads, or information technology. Maintenance of this infrastructure, however, will be delayed if staffing levels are diminished, and if the supply chain is also impacted. For this reason, it is important for organizations identified as critical infrastructure or those that support critical infrastructure identify alternate suppliers in the event that their primary key suppliers are not able to keep up with demands.

Many tools identified in All-Hazards continuity plans will also work in a pandemic, including identifying Essential Functions and ensuring that several layers of personnel are trained and able to perform these Essential Functions. The transfer of responsibilities to unaffected locations, or devolution, may be less of an option in a worldwide pandemic event as it is unlikely that alternate locations are unaffected. However, outbreaks of a pandemic travel in waves, and local outbreaks may occur at different times, have different durations, and vary in severity. If an organization has the flexibility, work can shift between locations as they are impacted and as the pandemic wave travels.

Infection control measures are of utmost importance in a pandemic. Infection control measures could or should also be utilized in an All-Hazards incident if spread of disease is a concern. Since respiratory virus can spread in droplets up to 6 feet away when an infected person coughs or sneezes, social distancing, or maintaining a 6-foot distance between all persons, is an important element of a pandemic plan. This can be accomplished by rearranging work spaces to ensure that personnel are kept 6 feet apart at all times. Work can also be spread across shifts to reduce the number of people on site at any one time. Nonessential meetings should be canceled, and meetings that do need to be held should be conducted by phone or teleconference rather than face-to-face. Work from home options should be utilized whenever possible. Nonessential travel may need to be rescheduled [11].

Protecting employees, and preventing them from becoming sick, is key to maintaining Essential Functions during a pandemic, and the hierarchy of controls should be utilized as appropriate. OSHA identifies risk classifications of employees (Table 12.1), and recommends implementing controls as appropriate for the risk. OSHA identified controls for use in a pandemic include:

- Engineering controls:
  o Installing physical barriers, such as clear plastic sneeze guards;
  o Installing drive through windows for customer service;
  o Use of specialized negative-pressure ventilation for aerosol-generating procedures in healthcare settings where appropriate.

Table 12.1 OSHA employee risk classifications during a pandemic.

Exposure risk	Employee exposure and function

Very high	• Healthcare employees (for example, doctors, nurses, dentists) performing aerosol-generating procedures on known or suspected pandemic patients) such as:
	  o Cough-induction procedures;
	  o Bronchoscopies;
	  o Some dental procedures;
	  o Invasive specimen collection
	• Healthcare or laboratory personnel collecting or handling specimens from known or suspected pandemic patients.

High	• Healthcare delivery and support staff exposed to known or suspected pandemic patients, such as doctors, nurses, and other hospital staff that must enter patients' rooms. • Medical transport of known or suspected pandemic patients, such as Emergency Medical Technicians, in enclosed vehicles. • Performing autopsies on known or suspected patients, for example, morgue, and mortuary employees.
Medium	• Employees with high-frequency contact with the general population, such as schools, high-population-density work environments, and some high-volume retail.
Low (caution)	• Employees who have minimal occupational contact with the general public and other coworkers.

Source: Occupational Safety and Health Administration, United States Department of Labor, and US Department of Health and Human Services [12].

- Work practice controls:
  - o Provision of tissues, no-touch trash cans, hand soap, hand sanitizer, disinfectants, and disposable towels.
  - o Encouraging employees to obtain seasonal influenza vaccine, to prevent influenza from seasonal flu virus that may be circulating at the same time as a novel pandemic flu strain;
  - o Providing employees with up-to-date education and training on influenza risk factors, protective behaviors, cough etiquette, and care of PPE;
  - o Developing policies to minimize contacts between employees, and between employees and clients or customers;
- Administrative controls:
  - o Developing policies that encourage ill employees to stay at home without fear of reprisals;
  - o Discontinuation of unessential travel to locations with high illness transmission rates;

o Practices to minimize face-to-face contact between employees, such as using email or teleconferencing. When possible, flexible work hours and/or telecommuting can reduce the number of employees who must be at work at one time in one specific location;

o Utilize home delivery of goods and services to reduce the number of clients or customers visiting the workplace;

o Maintain communication plans such as internet-based communication to answer employee's concerns.

PPE is the last option on the hierarchy of controls, but it may be one of the only control options for high-risk and very high-risk employees who work with patients. PPE must be selected depending upon the exposure. For example, goggles or goggles plus face shields can be used to protect the eyes, gloves or gloves and surgical protective gear can be used to prevent exposure to hands and skin, and respiratory protective equipment can be used to prevent inhalation exposures. OSHA's PPE standards apply in this situation, including the requirement to conduct a PPE hazard assessment and train employees on use, maintenance, and limitations of the PPE that they use. Respiratory protection standard requirements apply to employees who are given respirators to wear, including training, medical qualification, and fit testing for tight-fitting respirators. Recommendations for specific types of PPE may change depending upon what is known about the virulence and transmission of any new pandemic strain and any new information that becomes available.

Particulate respirators can protect employees from exposure to large and small aerosols and droplets containing infectious material. Ensuring that employees understand the difference between a surgical mask, a dust mask, and a respirator is especially important during a pandemic. NIOSH-approved respirators protect employees in high-risk and very high-risk classifications from exposure to virus, and may possibly be recommended for medium-risk employees as well depending upon availability.

Dust masks and comfort masks that look very similar to N95 respirators can be purchased at retail stores, but do not provide the same protection.

Surgical masks are not respirators and do not protect the wearer from exposure to infectious droplets or small airborne contaminants, but they can be used in other situations:

- Protecting the wearer from splashes of large droplets of blood or body fluids;
- Trapping particles of body fluids containing pathogens expelled by the wearer, and protecting other people against infection spread by the person wearing the surgical mask;
- Placing the surgical mask on sick people to limit spread of infectious respiratory secretions to others;

- Worn by healthcare providers to protect patients from being exposed to any infections carried by the healthcare provider, particularly when performing surgeries or treating open wounds.

Respirators may be in short supply when a pandemic occurs. Many organizations have chosen to stockpile supplies, including N95 respirators, but respirators that have been in storage for a period of years may or may not be suitable for use. In less than ideal storage conditions facepieces can become deformed, reducing the ability of the respirator to provide adequate fit. Rubber parts can become brittle, and elastic bands may dry out and break.

OSHA guidance states that if sufficient supply of respirators is not available during a pandemic, reuse of disposable N95 respirators may be an option. In a non-pandemic situation this would not be acceptable, and reuse should only be considered under the most dire of conditions. When supplies are limited during a declared pandemic, an employer may consider reusing respirators that have not been obviously soiled or damaged. However, any respirator worn in the presence of an infectious patient should be considered contaminated, and the respirator user must take care to avoid touching his or her eyes, nose, or mouth after touching the outside of the respirator.

Employees in the low-risk group may wish to use PPE, including N95 respirators, to protect themselves from exposures. An employer may choose to allow this if N95 respirators are available and not needed for higher risk employees: If there is a shortage of N95 respirators, providing them to high-risk and very high-risk employees is the priority. Medium-risk and low-risk employees have more options to minimize social interactions, and these alternative options should be used to the extent possible [12].

12.13 Training, Testing, and Exercising Continuity of Operations Plans

The importance of conducting drills and exercises for emergency management plans and Emergency Operations Plans was discussed in Chapter 11. Continuity plans, like Emergency Operations Plans, must be tested, evaluated, and improved over time to identify areas that might look good on paper but do not work in a real-life situation, to test clarity and understanding of the plan, and to build muscle memory for participants in the event of a plan activation. Any deficiencies that become apparent through exercising the plan should be addressed and corrected as a means of continuous improvement.

All personnel who are given responsibilities in the plan must receive training on these responsibilities. Through training, employees must come to very clearly understand their responsibilities when the continuity plan is activated. If job responsibilities change under the plan, or if personnel are performing Essential Functions that differ from their day-to-day job responsibilities, they must receive sufficient training to perform competently in their new roles. Training should also include how to relocate work functions to alternate facilities, backup communications and IT systems that may be used in Continuity Operations, mutual aid agreements, telework, orders of succession, and delegations of authority.

Once training is complete, the plan should be exercised. Continuity plan exercises should not be conducted in isolation; rather, aspects of the continuity plan should be exercised along with an organization's overall All-Hazards exercise program. Exercises should be conducted in accordance with the Homeland Security Exercise and Evaluation Program (HSEEP), as discussed in the previous chapter, and incorporate safety in both the exercise plan and exercise play.

Exercises should test at a minimum:

- Continuity plans and procedures;
- Backup communication systems;
- Backup data and records required to support Essential Functions;
- Internal and external dependencies, especially in regard to performance of Essential Functions;
- Recovery from the continuity plan activation and transition back to normal operations [1].

12.14 Reconstitution and the New Normal

As the emergency resolves, incident response transitions to recovery, and Continuity Operations transition back to normal operations, or at least the new normal.

Physical infrastructure may need to be repaired or replaced. Communications systems may need to be restructured. Power grids may need to be replaced.

With reconstitution comes opportunity. Buildings that must be repaired, or even rebuilt entirely, can incorporate green building concepts. New structures can be planned to achieve full LEED (Leadership in Energy and Environmental Design) certification and to maximize energy efficiency once the building is reoccupied. Building materials can be chosen to maximize fire resistance and minimize indoor air quality issues.

Bridges can be rebuilt using designs to maximize seismic resistance using most current knowledge of earthquake-resistant structures. Paints and coatings that are nontoxic to humans and do not create environmental contamination concerns can be chosen.

Communication systems can be rebuilt using most current available technology. If power systems are disrupted, they can be replaced with solar grids and other clean energy sources to minimize carbon emission in the future.

Work processes can be redesigned and rebuilt to eliminate known hazards.

In short, a community can come back after a disaster stronger than it was before. Reconstitution planning should not just have a simple goal of returning to the old normal: Planners should identify the best possible new normal that can be imagined and plan for how it can be achieved. Life may not be exactly as it was before the disaster, but perhaps the new normal can be a better one.

12.15 Summary

Government, critical infrastructure, and our society as a whole must continue to function even when disaster strikes. Continuity planning, including identification of Essential Functions, Business Process Analysis, and Business Impact Analysis, and maintenance of essential records is essential to ensuring Enduring Constitutional Government and Continuity of Government, and to ensuring that businesses survive the disaster. IT Disaster Recovery Plans support Continuity Operations by ensuring that information technology functions are online and support work that needs to be done.

Organizations depend upon employees that are Ready, Willing, and Able to work when the continuity plan is activated. However, employees who work during Continuity Operations may be working in jobs that they are not familiar with while facing hazards that they are also not familiar with. In addition, it is to be expected that these employees, their households, and their families will also be impacted by the disaster.

Safety must be included in continuity planning to address these issues. Safety is an Essential Supporting Activity, and should be identified as such in any continuity plan. Organizational safety personnel should expect to be very busy when Continuity Operations are initiated to ensure that employees performing Essential Functions and Essential Supporting Activities do so without facing undue hazards, or becoming injured or ill, just as safety personnel do during an emergency response.

References

1 Federal Emergency Management Administration (FEMA), US Department of Homeland Security (2018). *Continuity Guidance Circular* (February 2018). FEMA National Continuity Programs.

2 The White House (2013). *Presidential Policy Directive (PPD)-21: Critical Infrastructure Security and Resilience.*

3 Federal Emergency Management Administration (FEMA), US Department of Homeland Security (2017). *Federal Continuity Directive 1: Federal Executive Branch National Continuity Program and Requirements.*

4 Federal Emergency Management Administration (FEMA), US Department of Homeland Security (2017). *Federal Continuity Directive 2: Federal Executive Branch Mission Essential Functions and Candidate Primary Mission Essential Functions Identification and Submission Process.*

5 Occupational Safety and Health Administration (OSHA), US Department of Labor (2000). *OSHA Instruction Directive Number: CPL 2.0.125 – Home Based Worksites.*

6 McCabe, O.L., Barnett, D.J., Taylor, H.G., and Links, J.M. (2010). Ready, willing, and able: a framework for improving the public health emergency preparedness system. *Disaster Medicine and Public Health Preparedness* 4 (2): 161–168.

7 Breslin, F.C. and Smith, P. (2006). Trial by fire: a multivariate examination of the relation between job tenure and work injuries. *Occupational and Environmental Medicine* 63: 27–32.

8 Americans with Disabilities Act of 1990, as Amended by the ADA Amendments Act of 2008.

9 Broadbent, A.J. and Subbarao, K. (2011). Influenza virus vaccines: lessons from the 2009 H1N1 pandemic. *Current Opinion in Virology* October 1 (4): 254–262.

10 US Department of Health and Human Services (2017). *Pandemic Influenza Plan 2017 Update.*

11 Homeland Security Council (2006). *National Strategy for Pandemic Influenza Implementation Plan.*

12 Occupational Safety and Health Administration, US Department of Labor, and US Department of Health and Human Services (2009). *Guidance on Preparing Workplaces for an Influenza Pandemic.* OSHA publication 3327-05R 2009.

Index

Health and Safety in Emergency Management and Response, First Edition. Dana L. Stahl.
© 2021 John Wiley & Sons, Inc. Published 2021 by John Wiley & Sons, Inc.

Printed in the USA
CPSIA information can be obtained
at www.ICGtesting.com
LVHW050856041123
763057LV00005B/49

9 781119 560975